Religious Institutions and Women's Leadership

Studies in Comparative Religion
Frederick M. Denny, General Editor

Religious Institutions and Women's Leadership

New Roles Inside the Mainstream

edited by
Catherine Wessinger

University of South Carolina Press

Copyright © 1996 University of South Carolina

Published in Columbia, South Carolina, by the
University of South Carolina Press

Manufactured in the United States of America

00 99 98 97 96   5 4 3 2 1

Library of Congress Cataloging-in-Publication Data

Religious institutions and women's leadership : new roles inside the
  mainstream / edited by Catherine Wessinger.
      p.   cm. — (Studies in comparative religion)
    Includes bibliographical references and index.
    ISBN 1-57003-073-1
    1. Women clergy—United States.   2. Women in the Catholic
  Church—United States.   3. Women and religion.   4. Women in
  Judaism—United States.   5. Ordination of women—Judaism.
  I. Wessinger, Catherine.   II. Series: Studies in comparative religion
  (Columbia, S.C.)
  BV676.R36   1996
  262'.14'082—dc20   95-40226

Contents

General Editor's Preface

Religion scholarship since the feminist intellectual revolution of the second half of this century has contributed immeasurably to our knowledge and understanding of women's religious lives in many times and places across a range of traditions. Although women have filled important roles and exercised considerable influence in most religions, their leadership activities have not usually been either public or primary. Nor has it always been easy to recover records and accounts of women's religious leadership activities.

Today Protestant, Roman Catholic, and Jewish women are contributing importantly and at times crucially to the leadership of their congregations, communities, and denominations. Catherine Wessinger and her colleagues in this book focus on "new roles inside the mainstream," the mainstream being those patriarchal religious bodies that have dominated in American life. Although women began making breakthroughs in the nineteenth century, with the first ordinations of women, it has been the twentieth century that has witnessed an unprecedented movement toward women's empowerment as religious leaders.

In her introduction Catherine Wessinger argues that only where there is the social expectation of the equality of women can there be women's equal access to leadership roles in a religious institution. Such equality at present occurs only in the West and especially in North America. Whether it will spread to other parts of the world is unknown at this time, but there are signs here and there. Of course, religious institutions in the United States are still strongly patriarchal, even when they allow ordination of women.

The great Muslim theologian and mystic al-Ghazali (d. 1111) was standing by his esteemed teacher al-Juwayni's deathbed when the great scholar remarked that if one wants to know what religion is really all about one should bypass the scholars and preachers and consult the old women. But there is a great difference between acknowledging women's wisdom and insight and according them social equality and access to power in the public arena of religious life. The

essays in this book add much to our growing knowledge and appreciation of the varieties of roles that women are assuming as religious
leaders and the diverse and innovative processes by which mainstream
institutions are evolving under women's influence.

Frederick Mathewson Denny

Acknowledgments

My thanks go first to the contributors to *Religious Institutions and Women's Leadership: New Roles Inside the Mainstream*. Their scholarship and dedication to transforming their respective religious institutions shape this volume; it has been a pleasure and a privilege to work with them. I am particularly indebted to Susie C. Stanley for her meticulous commentary on the manuscript for the "Key Events" chronology which appears at the end of this volume. I also thank Sr. Marie Augusta Neal and Virginia Sullivan Finn for their comments on my introduction.

I am grateful to Denis Janz, my colleague at Loyola University, New Orleans, for encouraging me to pursue this project at a time when I was considering abandoning it. I am also grateful to Rosalee McReynolds, the periodicals librarian at Loyola New Orleans, for acquiring all the issues of *The Woman's Pulpit* published by the International Association of Women Ministers, an invaluable resource for this study. The faculty of the Loyola Institute for Ministry at Loyola University, New Orleans, gave helpful input, especially Marcel Dumestre, Barbara Fleischer, and Reynolds R. Ekstrom, coordinator of the Loyola Pastoral Life Center.

I thank Jill Heine for providing me with information on the Presbyterian reactions to the 1993 Re-Imagining conference. I thank Peggy L. Shriver, former assistant general secretary of the National Council of Churches of Christ in the USA and current head of the NCC's Professional Church Leadership department, for reading drafts of the introduction and chronology and making helpful suggestions.

I am appreciative of the generous summer stipend I received from the Louisville Institute for the Study of Protestantism and American Culture, which enabled me to devote the summer of 1993 to the editing of this book.

I am pleased that this book is being published by the press affiliated with my undergraduate alma mater, the University of South Carolina. My thanks go to Joyce Harrison, acquisitions editor, and Margaret

V. Hill, managing editor, for the professional way in which they saw this manuscript to publication. I especially thank Frederick M. Denny, editor of the University of South Carolina Press Comparative Studies in Religion series, for his helpful comments and for including this book in a superior scholarly series.

Religious Institutions and
Women's Leadership

Introduction

Women's Religious Leadership in the United States

Catherine Wessinger

The United States with its ideal, if not actualized reality, of equality has provided an experimental arena offering opportunities for women to exercise leadership in diverse ways. The nineteenth century in the United States was a time of important beginnings for American women's religious leadership, and the trend of increasing roles of authority for women has continued in the twentieth century. The comparative study of women's leadership in diverse American religious institutions may be useful in indicating the issues pertinent to developing women's leadership in other countries and religious/cultural contexts. All of the historical events that are mentioned in the following discussion are summarized at the end of this book in the section entitled "Key Events for Women's Religious Leadership in the United States—Nineteenth and Twentieth Centuries."

The nineteenth century in the United States, marked by increasing industrialization and urbanization, by immigration, and by increasing access of women to education, was also a time of widespread religious enthusiasm. The Protestant revivalism of the Second Great Awakening, dating from about 1795 to 1830, prompted American women actively to evangelize their families and neighbors. The public revival preaching of Phoebe Palmer (a Methodist) beginning in 1839 stimulated the Holiness movement with its stress on conversion and subsequent sanctification, and this movement in turn gave rise to numerous traveling and preaching women, such as Jarena Lee[1] and Amanda Berry Smith[2] of the African Methodist Episcopal Church. "The Great Disappointment" of 22 October 1844, when the millennial end of the world predicted by Millerite Adventists failed to occur, stimulated the visions of young Ellen G. Harmon (White), who subsequently became the revered prophet of the Seventh-day Adventist Church.[3]

The nineteenth century was also punctuated by the first ordinations of women. Antoinette Brown (Blackwell) was ordained by a
Congregational church in 1853; Olympia Brown and Augusta Chapin
were ordained Universalist ministers in 1863; and Celia Burleigh and
Mary Graves were ordained Unitarian ministers in 1871. Throughout
the nineteenth century, Roman Catholic Sisters worked to establish
educational, medical, and social-service facilities for immigrants in the
cities and for Americans moving westward. Rabbi Isaac Mayer Wise
founded the Hebrew Union College in 1875, and his encouragement of
women students at that time resulted a century later in the ordination
of women as Reform rabbis.[4] The year 1875 was also significant for the
founding of two alternative religions based on the worldviews of
women. Helena P. Blavatsky cofounded the Theosophical Society in
New York City, and Mary Baker Eddy, who subsequently founded the
Church of Christ, Scientist, published her magnum opus, *Science and
Health*. In 1889 Emma Curtis Hopkins, who earlier left Eddy's church
to found her own (New Thought) seminary in Chicago, became the
first woman to exercise the powers of a bishop by ordaining twenty
women and two men.[5]

The twentieth century continued the revivalist fervor of Protestants, which provided preaching women such as Alma White and
Aimee Semple McPherson with opportunities to found their own denominations.[6] The number of Methodist preaching women increased,
and they gradually acquired the official recognition of their Methodist
denominations. The issue of ordaining women to the Reform rabbinate
was first raised by young Martha Neumark in 1921. Although it was
determined that there was no reason not to ordain qualified women as
rabbis, the board of the Hebrew Union College decided that the time
was not yet right.

After World War II additional denominations in the United States
began to ordain women. The African Methodist Episcopal Church
decided to ordain women as ministers in 1948. In 1956 the United Presbyterian Church approved the ordination of women, and the Methodist Episcopal Church gave ordained women ministers membership in
its General Conference. The Lutheran Church in America and the
American Lutheran Church both decided to ordain women in 1970;
Sally Priesand was ordained the first Reform woman rabbi in the
United States in 1972; Sandy Eisenberg (Sasso) became the first Reconstructionist woman rabbi in 1974; and in 1976 the General Convention
of the Episcopal Church decided that women could be ordained as
priests and bishops. An African-American woman, Barbara C. Harris,
became the first woman bishop within the Anglican communion when

she was consecrated suffragan (assistant) bishop in the Episcopal Church in 1989.

The story behind these names and dates is one of women's struggle to find a more central place within the institutional structures of their religious traditions. Some extraordinary women such as Ellen G. White, Helena P. Blavatsky, Mary Baker Eddy, Emma Curtis Hopkins, Alma White, and Aimee Semple McPherson addressed this problem by founding their own religious institutions. The majority of religious women in the United States, however, have served their congregations by providing volunteer labor and financial support. As women are increasingly moving into all fields of endeavor, it is necessary to ask why when women are excluded from the leadership of their religious institutions. Why are women considered incompetent to be religious leaders? What does the lack of women in leadership roles say about how all women are viewed? We need to remember, also, that women who seek access to positions of religious authority are not attempting to gain power over people. Certain women feel called to serve others by the exercise of their talents in religious leadership. The exclusion of women from such roles sends a message to all girls and women that devalues their inherent humanity, worth, and capacities. Conversely, the full inclusion of women in religious leadership sends the message to girls and women that they are as valuable as men in their human nature and talents.

In all cultural settings, including the United States, charisma is typically the first means by which women gain authoritative positions in religion.[7] The importance of charisma, the direct access to the divine, for women's religious leadership can be seen in the nineteenth- and twentieth-century women preachers and church founders within the Pentecostal and Holiness contexts. Charisma also enables women to found religious institutions and inspire movements that are outside the patriarchal mainstream religions. Charisma as a source of authority enables a woman leader to achieve self-empowerment and increased personal autonomy, and she is then able to empower, to a lesser degree, the people to whom she ministers by bringing meaning and healing to their lives. But charisma as the source of women's authority does not usually encourage organized work to reform social structures that oppress women and other groups.[8] Unless additional factors are present, the increased institutionalization of a religious group founded by a charismatic woman results in a shift to male leadership. This shift may take place during the charismatic woman's lifetime and be facilitated by her, or it may occur after her death.[9]

In my first edited book, *Women's Leadership in Marginal Religions: Explorations Outside the Mainstream*, my contributors and I examined a number of alternative religions in America in which women's leadership either predominates or is equal to men's leadership. We studied several religions founded by charismatic women, including Shakerism, Christian Science, and Theosophy, but our main interest was in determining what features support the routine, noncharismatic leadership of women in these religions, even after the death of the charismatic woman founder. We found that certain features advocated by feminist theologians since the 1970s are, indeed, positively correlated with the ongoing religious leadership of women. These characteristics are: a view of God that is not solely masculine but instead sees the divine as either an impersonal principle, an androgynous combination of male and female elements, a great Goddess, or multiple goddesses; a view of human nature that does not blame women for the fallenness or limitations of the human condition; and a view of gender roles that does not insist that marriage and motherhood are the only roles available to women.[10] My contributors and I found that although alternative religions in the United States that do not ordain clergy are more open to women's leadership, women can and do gain access to ordained leadership if these three factors are present along with the social expectation of equality. A society in which women are equal to men is characterized by the following features: girls' and women's access to primary and higher education; women's significant economic earning power and ability to be active and pursue accomplishments outside the domestic sphere; daughters being valued by their parents as much as sons; women's ownership and inheritance of property; women's freedom of self-determination as opposed to being controlled by father, husband, or other male relative; and women's ability to gain status in their own right that is not dependent on the status of fathers, husbands, or sons. As these social and economic conditions become increasingly prevalent in the United States and in other countries, we are witnessing changes in the patriarchal religions that supported male dominance and female subordination.

I wish to stress that the social expectation of the equality of women is crucial for women's equal access to leadership roles in any religious tradition. A patriarchal religious tradition that merely includes goddesses in its cosmology or views God as an impersonal principle remains patriarchal in its subordination and oppression of women. Even in alternative religions that do not see God as solely masculine and possess a view of human nature that does not scapegoat women and have broadened understandings of gender roles, women's leadership will decline if the social expectation of equality wanes.

The key, then, for women's religious leadership is the social expectation of equality. If that is present and enables women to be somewhat (initially) economically independent and have access to education, then women will seek out or create religions that have these three characteristics named above. If such women feel loyalty to a patriarchal religious tradition that lacks or has minimized these elements, then women will begin to introduce these characteristics into their religion, particularly as they gain access to leadership roles (for example, see the chapter in the present volume on Jewish women by Sue Levi Elwell). This is what religious women in the United States have been doing at least since the nineteenth century. I suggest that this is what is happening in other parts of the world as the social expectation of equality increases.

KEY ISSUES

There are significant issues that arise in the process of introducing these characteristics. The first important issue for women's religious leadership is the question of authority.

Authority

There are different sources of authority in religions, and these can and do conflict in the debate over whether women's religious leadership is legitimate. Reference has already been made to the charismatic authority of an unmediated experience of the divine, and women within the Christian tradition have long used this authority to justify themselves against the authority of office in patriarchal institutions. This sort of authority is vividly illustrated in the following story of an encounter between a woman busy nursing soldiers wounded in a Civil War battle and a Union officer:

> Mother Bickerdyke was found, carrying system, order, and relief wherever she went. One of the surgeons went to the rear with a wounded man, and found her wrapped in the gray overcoat of a rebel officer, for she had disposed of her blanket shawl to some poor fellow who needed it. She was wearing a soft slouch hat, having lost her inevitable Shaker bonnet. Her kettles had been set up, the fire kindled underneath, and she was dispensing hot soup, tea, crackers, panado, whiskey and water, and other refreshments, to the shivering, fainting, wounded men.

> "Where did you get these articles?" [the officer] inquired;
> "and under whose authority are you at work?"
>
> She paid no heed to his interrogatories, and indeed, did not
> hear them, so completely absorbed was she in her work of com-
> passion. Watching her with admiration for her skill, administrative
> ability, and intelligence,—for she not only fed the wounded men,
> but temporarily dressed their wounds in some cases,—he ap-
> proached her again:—
>
> "Madam, you seem to combine in yourself a sick-diet kitchen
> and a medical staff. May I inquire under whose authority you are
> working?"
>
> *Without pausing in her work*, she answered him, "I have re-
> ceived my authority from the Lord God Almighty; have you any-
> thing that ranks higher than that?" (my emphasis)[11]

Mrs. Bickerdyke's authority from God parallels the authority of
women preachers and ministers within Protestantism, who assert that
their call from God overrides whatever institutional authority structures men care to set up. (See in this volume the chapters by Rosemary
Skinner Keller and Susie C. Stanley.) The Protestant emphasis on the
"priesthood of the believer" supports the concept that God calls individuals to particular modes of service. However, Roman Catholic Sisters and laywomen also report that they feel called to their respective
ministries.[12] (See the chapters by Marie Augusta Neal, SND de Namur,
and Virginia Sullivan Finn.)[13] Currently in 1994, like Mother Bickerdyke, Roman Catholic women are busy with their ministries, which
they believe are sanctioned by the Holy Spirit, and some even ignore
the increasingly strident demands of Pope John Paul II for them to acknowledge his authority.

Another important source of religious authority is scripture. There
are certain passages in the Bible that either support or prohibit
women's leadership in Christianity. Rosemary Radford Ruether has
categorized these passages into those that support a "theology of
equivalence" and those that support a "theology of subordination."[14]
(The chapter in this volume by Susie C. Stanley on Wesleyan/Holiness
women's elucidation of scripture is an excellent introduction to these
biblical passages.) In Christianity the authority of certain scriptural
passages is used to outweigh the authority of other passages, both by
the proponents and opponents of women's religious leadership. Jewish women also must take account of the authority of scripture in asserting their prerogative of religious leadership. Knowledge gained
through study of holy scripture and the commentary of revered rabbis
has been an important source of authority in Judaism, from which

women were traditionally excluded. (See the chapter by Sue Levi Elwell.) Since the rabbi is an expert in scripture, access to the study of
Torah and Talmud by girls and women in Reform, Reconstructionist,
and Conservative Judaism has resulted in the eventual admission of
women to the rabbinate. In an article in *Lilith* Blu Greenberg reports
that in recent years Orthodox women are becoming learned scholars of
Torah, and she is optimistic that soon the radical step will be taken of
ordaining women as Orthodox rabbis. She notes that currently Orthodox women are serving in leadership roles as presidents and other officers of synagogues.[15]

The type of authority that most often excludes women is that of
office. Authority of office can be derived from the authority of a hierarchy or from the authority of representative bodies. The Roman
Catholic Church is a perfect illustration of the authority of office that
derives from hierarchical authority. In the Roman Catholic Church hierarchical authority is based on the pope's claim to be successor to the
authority that Jesus Christ vested in the apostle Peter (Matthew 16:18).
The pope appoints ordained priests to positions as bishops and cardinals. Only (supposedly) celibate men are ordained priests, and ordination is required to become part of the hierarchy that determines the
theology, ethics, and policies of the Roman Catholic Church. In the
United States there are currently many highly educated lay women
and men who advocate democratic forms of church government and
who have the qualifications to be leaders and theologians in the Roman Catholic Church. So far they have been unable to effect meaningful change in the central institutional structures of the Church because
these structures are not democratic and are restricted to a certain class
of men. Those Catholic priests who speak up for democracy in Roman
Catholicism and equal rights for Catholic women are not likely to be
appointed bishops by John Paul II. Only since 1991 have a few American Roman Catholic bishops begun to call publicly for the ordination
of women and to critique the Roman Catholic Church's teachings on
women.

Protestant and Jewish denominations in the United States are more
democratic, either by vesting authority in individual congregations or
in representative bodies. These denominations have been more amenable to including women's leadership, but change has come about
only after many and prolonged political battles and lobbying efforts.
The authority of office, designated by ordination, election, or appointment, has slowly become available to women in denominations with
more democratic structures able to give the authority of office to qualified women.

Education is a source of authority that is important to anyone seeking to earn the qualifications for the authority of office. American women earned the educational qualifications long before they were granted the authority of ordination to the ministry and the rabbinate. In most cases it finally became obvious that there were no good reasons to continue barring qualified women. This is currently the cause of great tension within the Roman Catholic Church. There are many laywomen, laymen, and Sisters who are highly qualified for church leadership, but in the Roman Catholic Church the decision about admission to institutional policy- and theology-making structures can only be made at the top and passed down. Bishops can include laity in Roman Catholic structures, but ultimately they can do nothing or will do nothing without the sanction of the pope. This dilemma is at the heart of why the American Roman Catholic bishops, after working for nine years, had to give up in 1992 their project of writing a pastoral letter on women in church and society.[16]

Additionally, we must be mindful that there is also the authority of violence that is carried out by individuals or groups. The authority of violence has not been used in recent years to assert the authority of mainstream religious institutions in the United States, but we should not forget that violence is the ultimate means of enforcing subordination by dominant individuals or groups. In this volume Rosemary Skinner Keller's biographical account of Ida B. Wells-Barnett vividly reminds us of this. Religious institutions that do not resort to physical violence still may resort to the spiritual and psychological violence of exclusion or excommunication. In its 1993 excommunication of five Mormon scholars, the male hierarchy of the Church of Jesus Christ of Latter-day Saints made clear that it did not tolerate challenges to its authority. One of the excommunicated Mormon scholars, Lavina Fielding Anderson, stated, "I am an orthodox, believing Mormon and a feminist, and my church has informed me that those are incompatible categories." Anderson expressed her sense of being damaged by her church: "This is the worst thing that has ever happened to me. My people have been Mormons for six generations."[17] Religious institutions may also wage war on and harm scholars by refusing to tenure them and by firing suspect scholars in denominational teaching institutions.

Women's Institutions

Another issue that is important for women's religious leadership is whether or not women (or other subordinated groups) should form separate institutions of their own or if it is better that they be integrated into the dominant institutions. The women's voluntary associations of the nineteenth century, dedicated to temperance, moral reform, abolition of slavery, overseas missions, charitable relief of the poor, and woman suffrage, were important training grounds for women's religious leadership. Protestant women observed that when their separate missionary organizations were absorbed into denominational structures in the early twentieth century, they lost authority and control over their own funds. This situation was the catalyst for Protestant women's demand for equal inclusion within their denominations' institutional structures.[18]

As a result of Jewish women's participation in the 1893 World's Parliament of Religions in Chicago, the National Council of Jewish Women (Reform) was formed with Hannah Solomon as its first president. Bertha Pappenheim founded in 1904 the German Jewish Women's Organization to lobby for Jewish women's full religious rights. Hadassah, the women's Zionist organization founded by Henrietta Szold in 1911, encountered authority challenges from the primary men's Zionist organization.[19]

The question of whether or not to have separate women's institutions also arose during the merger negotiations that produced the Evangelical Lutheran Church in America (ELCA) in 1987. As a result of Lutheran women's lobbying efforts, the ELCA finally decided to have it both ways. An independently incorporated women's organization was created, and the Commission for Women and quotas for proportional representation in decision-making bodies were established within the ELCA to promote women's full inclusion in the church structures. (See the chapter in this volume by Gracia Grindal.)

Another case pertinent to this question is that of the Roman Catholic women currently involved in the Women-Church movement. Women-Church consists of a variety of independent small institutions and of individual women—Sisters and laywomen—who come together to create separate women's spaces in which to celebrate women's liturgies and articulate women's theologies. Presently Women-Church is not separatist in intent, but it seeks to nurture and sustain women, who go back into the patriarchal Roman Catholic Church to work for its transformation.[20] A recent sociological study by Miriam Therese Winter, Adair Lummis, and Allison Stokes reveals that Women-Church–type feminist spirituality groups are also formed by women, including clergywomen, in mainline Protestant denominations, and that these groups often consist of a mix of Catholic, Protestant, post-Christian, and, occasionally, Jewish women who find spiritual nurture in their shared feminist spirituality. Some of the

women in these feminist spirituality groups have left the Christian tradition, but most of the Christian women in feminist spirituality groups
are "defecting in place." They continue to participate in their home denominations, often exercising religious leadership and even ordained
ministry, but their religious worldview is rooted in their feminist spirituality, which they hope gradually to incorporate into the religious life
and institutions of their respective denominations.[21]

These examples suggest that separate women's institutions serve a
valuable purpose while women are seeking equality in mainstream religious institutions. A promising development for Muslim women in
the United States is the North American Council for Muslim Women
(NACMW), which held its first general convention on 13–15 February
1993 in Oakland, California. Its first president is the devout and scholarly Sharifa Alkateeb.[22]

Resistance to Women's Leadership

Another important issue is the resistance to women's leadership
within religious institutions. The resistance may be covert or overt.

Janet R. Marder (writing in this volume on women rabbis in Reform Judaism) calls attention to "hidden resistance" to women's leadership within religious institutions. Whenever ordained leadership is
involved, clergywomen are found to be paid less than their male counterparts, and they more often serve in entry-level positions, either as
assistants or associates, or as solo pastors or rabbis of small congregations with limited funds.[23] There is what Susie C. Stanley calls "a
stained-glass ceiling" that operates to keep clergywomen from moving
beyond entry-level jobs. Whenever there is a shortage of clergymen,
women are utilized to get the work done. In this book examples of this
phenomenon are given by Cynthia Grant Tucker for Unitarian-Universalist women, Jualynne B. Dodson for African Methodist Episcopal
women, Susie C. Stanley for Wesleyan/Holiness women, and Carolyn
DeArmond Blevins for Baptist women. Once the male labor shortage is
over, women leaders are again marginalized and squeezed out of religious institutional structures.

The acute shortage in the United States of Roman Catholic priests
has opened a window of opportunity for the ministries of Sisters and
laywomen as "parish administrators," who are in reality the pastors of
priestless parishes.[24] Catholics' exposure to women pastors in Roman
Catholic parishes generally helps to overcome parishioners' resistance
to women's religious leadership. It may be that this shortage of priests
is so acute that women's officially designated ministries (dare we say

ordained ministries?) will eventually have to be acknowledged by the Roman Catholic hierarchy.[25] But the long and hallowed tradition of using women's talents whenever there is a shortage of men, and then sending women packing when the need is over, is not a basis for much optimism for the eventual equal leadership of women in the Roman Catholic Church. Pope John Paul II has stubbornly refused to let the shortage of Catholic priests in the Western industrialized nations be a factor in his thinking on women's ordination, a topic which he has repeatedly asserted is not open for discussion. John Paul II in his 1994 apostolic letter *"Ordinatio Sacerdotalis"* states: "I declare that the Church has no authority whatsoever to confer ordination on women and that this judgement is to be definitively held by all the Church's faithful."[26]

Balancing Career with Family

An important issue for all professional women is how to balance family life with career. It has often been argued that the admission of women into professional religious leadership will result in the neglect of these women's children and husbands. Women have, indeed, found it difficult to combine career ministry with child rearing and family commitments. Common observation of American life indicates that having children significantly slows women in their careers. Women are less free to relocate in order to take better jobs. Women are more likely to choose part-time work because of child-care considerations, and often so-called part-time work is simply full-time work that is remunerated on a part-time pay scale.[27] The question of how to balance their professional leadership with marriage and child rearing will remain an issue for American women religious leaders. A new development is that male religious leaders may also be becoming concerned about balancing family life and career. (For instance, see the chapter on Reform Judaism by Janet R. Marder.)

ISSUES FOR THE FUTURE

All of these issues concerning women's religious leadership will continue to be debated and explored. I wish now to point to particular issues that will receive increased attention in the future.

Women Transforming Religious Leadership Roles

First, there is the issue of whether women will succeed in transforming religious leadership roles. Most Roman Catholic feminists say that they do not favor women's ordination to the Catholic priesthood as it is currently structured. Roman Catholic feminists state that they want women to be ordained to a renewed priesthood, a ministry that empowers others to share in priestly functions. This transformed Roman Catholic priesthood sounds similar to the ministries of Reform and Reconstructionist women rabbis, who seek to teach other Jews how to do Jewish things at home and in public worship. (See the chapter by Marder on Reform Judaism and the chapter by Rebecca Alpert and Goldie Milgram on Reconstructionism.) Feminist Protestant ministers likewise report that they wish to minister in empowering ways. An important issue for future investigation is whether women are actually transforming religious leadership roles to make them more collaborative and democratic. Women's inclusion in the institutional authority structures of mainstream denominations is perhaps too recent for it to be determined if women will effect any lasting change, but sociological research is beginning to investigate this question.[28]

A qualitative study by Frederick W. Schmidt suggests that there is a variety of ways in which women leaders relate to their mainstream religious institutions. There are the women who feel marginalized by their institutions. They can exercise meaningful religious leadership in their congregations, but they consider themselves to be "outsiders" in relation to their denominations. Other women leaders are less alienated from their religious institutions but nevertheless are "disengaged" from certain of its structures. Since most women religious leaders never make it beyond entry-level positions, some women feel "threatened" by uncertainty about their future within their religious institutions. A number of women take on the role of "reformer" and work to introduce changes. Others become "conformists" in order to survive and continue their ministries within particular institutional settings.[29]

Edward C. Lehman, Jr., has recently produced an exploratory sociological survey of 517 female and male clergy in the American Baptist churches, the Presbyterian Church (U.S.A.), the United Church of Christ, and the United Methodist Church to determine if men and women have different ministerial styles.[30] In exploring this issue, Lehman seeks to determine which perspective, the "maximalist" or the "minimalist," correctly describes the reality. The maximalist view asserts that men and women have two distinct approaches to religious leadership. The masculine style of ministry is described by maximalists as involving the exercise of power over people, a concern for status and personal authority, excessive rationalism, approaching ethical dilemmas in a legalistic manner, and creating a protective distance between the minister and the congregation. The feminine style of ministry is described by maximalists as involving empowerment of the laity, downplaying clerical authority in favor of egalitarianism, a warm and approachable personal style, social activism, reliance on intuition, and the resolution of ethical dilemmas with concern for the well-being of all persons involved. Minimalists assert that differences between women and men are relatively slight and that those that exist are produced by social arrangements and social concepts of gender.

Lehman finds that there is "a complex web of interrelated forces shaping a minister's approach to pastoral work."[31] The factors that influence ministerial style include the type of position, the particular time period in which the minister attended seminary, the occupation of the minister's spouse, and the minister's ethnicity, in addition to the minister's sex. Lehman's sample is predominantly white, although he attempts to include Hispanic Americans, African Americans, Asian Americans, and Native Americans. Due to the small number of non–Euro-Americans in Lehman's sample, he combines these and designates them racial/ethnic clergy. While pointing to the need for more study, Lehman finds that both racial/ethnic clergywomen and clergymen have a masculine leadership style and that high levels of education, high income, and large congregations tend to increase somewhat the masculine style for both.

The rest of Lehman's conclusions focus on white clergy. I will present only a few of the most intriguing of his carefully nuanced conclusions. Lehman finds that white clergymen are particularly inclined to exert power over their congregations only if certain conditions are present, including being positioned as a senior minister with authority over a ministerial staff. He finds that white clergywomen are more likely to seek to empower their congregations only if particular conditions are present, including being positioned as a senior minister with a multiple staff. If a clergyman has a wife whose occupation is high in status, his ministerial style will be more open and feminine. If a clergywoman has an unemployed husband, she will tend to display a more masculine style of ministry. Married couples serving as copastors have the *least* sex-typed leadership styles in their religious leadership. Women and men who are senior pastors are *most* likely to evidence sex-typing; male senior ministers display a more masculine style of ministry, and female senior ministers display a more feminine style. Lehman speculates that women senior ministers perhaps feel more secure in their jobs and thus feel freer to be feminine. I suggest that women senior ministers might display more feminine characteristics to reassure congregants who are uncomfortable with women in positions of authority. Men and women who are solo pastors of relatively small congregations do not evidence significant sex-typing in their leadership styles. Overall Lehman's study reveals that there are "very few conditions under which sex differences predict variations in [the minister] . . . wanting positions of formal authority, interpersonal style, approach to preaching, and criteria of clergy status."[32]

Lehman has produced a careful and significant sociological study of the leadership styles of male and female Protestant clergy. The one point I find unconvincing is his argument that feminists adopt either the maximalist or the minimalist position for polemical purposes. Although the results of his survey provide evidence supportive of both views, the temptation for feminists to take the maximalist position is not merely the result of a wish to affirm "woman's way" of doing things as valid and even superior to "man's way." I suggest that the maximalist view arises out of women's attempts to explain their experiences within women's organizations—consisting of women's more relaxed style of relating to women colleagues and collaborative leadership—and their difficulty in introducing this leadership style into organizations and institutions that include male colleagues. That all feminists don't agree on the maximalist or the minimalist view reflects the ambiguity and complexity of the evidence produced by life experiences as well as by scientific studies.

Lehman's attempt to determine whether women clergy tend to manifest a "feminine" approach to ministry and whether clergymen tend to manifest a "masculine" style of leadership produced results too complex to be summarized completely here, but his study demonstrates the need to rephrase the question. Lehman points out that the task for future study is to determine *under what conditions* female and male clergy manifest different styles of leadership. The complexity of this issue further calls into question whether women will introduce significant changes into traditional religious leadership roles.

Marginalization by Alternative Career Tracks

A second important issue for future investigation is whether women religious leaders are being marginalized by being shunted into alternative career tracks. This question is relevant to the previous discussion of hidden resistance to women's religious authority and also to the difficulty of balancing professional religious leadership with child rearing.

Paula Nesbitt's sociological analysis of the Episcopal Church and the Unitarian-Universalist Association shows that alternative career tracks have developed in these denominations that tend to ghettoize ordained women and keep them out of the prestigious and well-paid ministerial positions.[33] These alternative career tracks were not created for the explicit purpose of diverting women from competing with men for positions, but they nevertheless have that effect. The Episcopal Church established the ordained permanent diaconate so that men could assist Episcopal priests while remaining in secular employment. Women were admitted to the Episcopal diaconate in 1970, and it became an important stepping-stone for women aspiring to the priesthood. In 1981 the Unitarian-Universalist Association created a new ordained status, the minister of religious education. The educational requirements for both these positions are lower than those for the ordained clergy in these denominations and can be acquired without attending seminary. Nesbitt found that male and female Episcopal priests and Unitarian-Universalist ministers enter their denominations' ministries on about the same level but that subsequent jobs for men are more likely to have higher status and pay. Yet again, we see that clergywomen tend to remain in the entry-level positions. Nesbitt suggests that the clustering of clergywomen in lower-status jobs tends to conflate their ordained status with that of the Episcopal deacons and the Unitarian-Universalist ministers of religious education, particularly since women predominate in these positions. The result is that the high-status positions in the two denominations are reserved for ordained men. Nesbitt warns that the increased interest in the Episcopal Church in hiring priests ordained and licensed to minister only in local areas and the UUA's development of a new ordained position of the community minister may result in further utilization of ordained women's services while restricting them to lower-level positions.

History indicates that dual ordination tracks have already functioned to reserve better-paid and prestigious religious leadership positions for men and that in the past this was clergymen's explicit intent. Women were active Methodist preachers since the origins of Methodism in the eighteenth century, but it was not until 1869 that Margaret Newton Van Cott became the first woman preacher licensed by the Methodist Episcopal Church. In 1880 the Methodist Episcopal Church refused to ordain Anna Howard Shaw and Anna Oliver, but Shaw successfully sought ordination in the smaller Methodist Protestant Church.[34] Because of this increasing pressure to ordain women, the Methodist Episcopal Church revoked the preaching license of Van Cott and other Methodist women. During the 1880s Methodist Episcopal women's call to service was channeled into women's missions societies, the deaconess movement, and the Woman's Christian Temperance Union. The Methodist Episcopal Church granted women lay voting rights in 1906. The Methodist Episcopal Church again decided to license women as preachers in 1920 but refused to give them membership in the General Conference, which would have entailed the commitment to place women as pastors in congregations. By 1924 the Methodist Episcopal Church began ordaining women, but only as local preachers and without General Conference membership. Methodist women could be ordained and preach wherever they were invited, but the Methodist Episcopal Church had no obligation to find them salaried employment as pastors of churches. Methodist Episcopal clergywomen finally gained General Conference membership in 1956.

Earlier, in 1868, the African Methodist Episcopal (AME) Church attempted to channel women's leadership into the stewardess position in order to reserve the ministerial positions for men. After repeated requests for over a century, the AME General Conference authorized women's ordained ministry in 1948. (See the chapter in this volume by Jualynne E. Dodson.) It appears that Paula Nesbitt is right to advise the need for more study to determine if dual career tracks remain problematic for women's full inclusion in the leadership of their religious institutions.

Gay and Lesbian Clergy

Another issue that will receive more attention in the future is the question of the ordination of gay men and lesbians. During President Clinton's attempt in 1993 to allow openly gay men and lesbians to serve in the military, he proposed that a person should not be dismissed from military service if that person were seen entering a gay and lesbian bar or church. The news media did not pursue the question of why scandalous behavior should include attending a church that ministers to gay and lesbian people. Mainline religious institutions tend to regard with horror even the presence of gay men and lesbians as believers, and this will be a contentious issue as they continue to assert their right to belong to American institutions. In 1990 two Lutheran congregations in San Francisco ordained and installed as pastors two lesbians and a gay man. This action contradicted the ELCA requirements that bishops ordain ministers and that only celibate gay men and lesbians may be ordained. Subsequently, the two congregations were suspended from the ELCA. Carter Heyward, a lesbian feminist theologian, was one of the eleven women "irregularly" ordained Episcopal priests in 1974. Although the Episcopal Church has not approved the ordination of lesbians and gay men, several bishops have already ordained them. In 1992 a lesbian, the Rev. Dr. Nadean Bishop, a distinguished literary critic and poet, was installed as the senior pastor of an American Baptist congregation in Minneapolis. Slowly certain denominations, including Reform Judaism, Reconstructionism, United Church of Christ, and Unitarian-Universalism, have begun to accept lesbians and gay men as ordained clergy, but this is likely to be a long, long struggle.[35]

Tensions Between Different Kinds of Feminists

Whereas there are tensions between women who do not want to change traditional gender roles and feminist women who do (see the chapter here by Gracia Grindal), yet another difficult issue to address will be the tensions among different types of feminist women. Women of color are increasingly pointing out that the feminist movement in the United States has been dominated by white women. African-American, Asian-American, Native-American, and Latina-American feminists assert that the white feminist perspective falls short of addressing their realities and is blind to its own inherent racism. Euro-American feminists, on the other hand, who are genuinely concerned about the oppression of women in all ethnic communities, are often shocked at being called racists. African-American feminist women identify themselves as "womanists" to indicate their solidarity with the African-American community and to indicate that their analysis and theologizing take into account not only sexism but also racism and classism. Native-American feminist women particularly resent the appropriation of elements of Native-American religions by white feminists for their own spirituality. Native-American women regard this as yet another violation of their traditional culture by white imperialists.

These conflicts and tensions will likely continue as religious feminist women in all these communities engage in the process of getting to know each other better.[36] I suggest that these tensions in the United States are the inevitable result of the process of peoples of color gaining access to economic and educational resources to which, after white men, white women have had the greatest access. As access to economic and educational resources becomes more equally distributed, these tensions, it is hoped, will disappear, and women of all colors can celebrate their commonalities and their distinctiveness.

Backlash

Another issue that will be important to address in the future is the backlash against feminism.[37] The books and lectures by Camille Paglia[38] along with the language of such personalities as Rush Limbaugh with his "Femi-Nazis" are examples of a widespread antipathy against feminism and feminists. Feminists are demonized as being bitter, radical, man-hating, and despotic. When denominations open up rights and positions of authority to women, they usually do so by marginalizing the feminists who worked for such a change. (See the chapters in this volume by Rebecca B. Prichard and Suzanne Radley Hiatt.) Clergywomen who do not have a feminist identity are favored, while clergywomen who are feminists are seen as not *really* "called" to the ministry. An important future issue for religious womanists and feminists is how to address this backlash against women who are committed to working for change in social structures that oppress and exclude women.

An important area in which religious conservatives feel threatened by feminists is that of theology, and a significant episode of backlash continues to play out around the "Re-Imagining" conference that was held in Minneapolis in November 1993. Re-Imagining was a conference to explore feminist theology and liturgy and freely to give expression to the creative feminist theological imagination in reshaping and transforming the Christian tradition. Attendance consisted of 1,743 women and 83 men from 49 states and 27 countries. Typical of ecumenical Women-Church gatherings, the people attending Re-Imagining came from diverse denominations and included 30 American Baptists, 16 Baptists, 266 Roman Catholics, 100 members of the Evangelical Lutheran Church in America, 142 Lutherans, 51 Episcopalians, 386 Methodists, 404 Presbyterians, 145 members of the United Church of Christ, 15 Unitarian-Universalists, 82 members of United Church, Canada, 2 members of the Church of God, 8 Disciples of Christ, 13 Mennonites, 6 Quakers, and others. Two-thirds of those attending Re-Imagining were lay, and one-third were clergy.[39] At Re-Imagining each speaker to the large assembly was first blessed with a chant invoking Sophia, and conference sessions included a discussion of re-imagining Jesus Christ's nature and role in Christianity. The liturgies celebrated at Re-Imagining beautifully and movingly demonstrated that inclusive and feminist hymns, rituals, and artistic expressions have already been produced by Christian women.

There was an immediate backlash from conservative members of the denominations, who sought to punish and exclude women who had participated in the Re-Imagining conference. What Miriam Therese Winter, Adair Lummis, and Allison Stokes have characterized as "women claiming responsibility for their own spiritual lives" (the subtitle of their 1994 book, *Defecting in Place*), critics of the expressions that took place at Re-Imagining labeled as heresy. Denominational financial support for Re-Imagining was questioned, and denominational jobs of Re-Imagining planners were jeopardized. Some women who spoke at the conference began to have their denominational speaking engagements canceled. Some clergywomen who helped organize or who attended Re-Imagining began to receive rejections from consideration for ministerial positions. The reverberations from Re-Imagining are not yet completely played out, but there are signs that religious feminists now exist in sufficient numbers in some Christian Protestant denominations to resist backlash and even to respond firmly and constructively. The fact that these denominations have a democratic polity also helps. The United Church of Christ issued a statement supportive of the Re-Imagining conference; the United Methodist General Commission on Christian Unity and Interreligious Concerns found no reason for disciplinary action; and Rebecca Prichard (in this volume) reports that the General Assembly of the Presbyterian Church (U.S.A.) passed a resolution in June 1994 that included a statement that the exercise of imagination in the theological enterprise is valid. The Minneapolis organizers of the Re-Imagining conference continue to promote the networking of people sympathetic to the re-imagining enterprise through a newsletter and subsequent conferences.[40]

The Case of the Roman Catholic Church

For at least the past two decades, the pope and the hierarchy of the Roman Catholic Church have attempted to contain and rebuff the call of Catholic feminist women and men for theological, ministerial, and institutional change. So many developments occurred relative to women in the Roman Catholic Church in 1994 that the Catholic institutional and historical situation deserves treatment here. There will be a continuing need in the Roman Catholic Church to address women's leadership until certain basic tensions are resolved. The Roman Catholic Church in the United States represents a case in which the highest patriarchal authority is increasingly unable to prohibit the faithful ministries and leadership of numerous women. There is currently a shortage of ordained men in the Roman Catholic Church. Particularly in the United States, Catholic women are being called upon to make important contributions, and they are responding enthusiastically and with dedication. Like the examples of Mother Bickerdyke and the numerous Protestant preaching women cited earlier, Roman Catholic women act on their call to ministry in spite of institutional limitations, and gradually Catholic institutional structures to support them are being developed in the United States at the grassroots level. Increasingly, signals are being sent to Catholic women from the lower levels of the hierarchy, notably the American bishops and the Society of Jesus, that women's religious leadership is valued and encouraged.

During 1994 it appeared that Pope John Paul II was determinedly making an effort to reverse whatever gains feminists have been able to make in church and society. After giving official permission in April 1994 for Roman Catholic girls to be altar servers, John Paul II issued "Ordinato Sacerdotalis" on 22 May 1994, which reaffirmed in strong language the ban on the ordination of women as priests. Throughout the summer of 1994, the pope intensified his campaign to prevent the United Nations International Conference on Population and Development, scheduled to meet in Cairo in September 1994, from advocating the use of artificial contraception as a means to address the world population crisis. Of great concern to John Paul II was that this UN conference would either officially or tacitly approve abortion as a population control measure. From a feminist perspective, a woman's ability to control her own reproductivity and to exercise choice about the number of children she will bear is a key component in the social expectation of women's equality. During the summer of 1994 feminists prepared to argue at the UN International Conference on Population and Development that the primary strategy to limit the currently unchecked world population growth should be the improvement of women's access to education and economic earning power. It is well known that an educated woman working outside the home produces fewer children and that these children have greater chances for survival.

On the issue of women's ordination, the Roman Catholic Church in the twentieth century can be seen as constantly reacting to developments in the Anglican Communion, consisting of the Protestant denominations closest in polity to the Roman Catholic Church. In the early 1970s the ordination of women as priests was greatly debated in the Episcopal Church in the United States, which is the American member of the larger grouping of independent national churches that make up the Anglican Communion. In 1973 the General Convention of the Episcopal Church narrowly defeated a resolution to ordain women as priests and bishops. (For the full Episcopal story, see the chapter in this volume by Suzanne Radley Hiatt.) On 29 July 1974 three retired or resigned Episcopal bishops (men who were still bishops but were not in danger of losing their jobs) ordained eleven qualified women deacons to the Episcopal priesthood. The Episcopal Church quickly declared these ordinations to be "irregular" and invalid. While the debate raged in the Episcopal Church, four more qualified women were "irregularly" ordained by a retired Episcopal bishop. Finally in 1976 the Episcopal Church's General Convention approved the ordination of women to the priesthood, and the ordinations of the first fifteen were eventually recognized as valid.

Concerned by this debate and the prospect of Episcopal women priests, Pope Paul VI directed the Vatican's Congregation for the Doctrine of the Faith to produce a document giving the Roman Catholic Church's position on the ordination of women. Since Thomas Aquinas's thirteenth-century argument that women are defective in their humanity—physically and morally[41]—was no longer credible, the Congregation for the Doctrine of the Faith had to devise another rationale and present it as the "constant teaching of the church." The document known as the "Declaration on the Question of the Admission of Women to the Ministerial Priesthood" ("*Inter Insigniores*," 1976) stated that it was Jesus Christ's intent that only men be ordained to the priesthood, as evidenced by his selection of only male disciples (the twelve); thus the Roman Catholic Church had no authority to go against Christ's intent and begin ordaining women. The declaration further attempted to provide a theological rationale by applying the "nuptial analogy" of Christ's relation to the church, that of a bridegroom to his bride, to the priest's role when celebrating the Mass. In order for the priest to represent Jesus Christ in the Mass, the priest must necessarily be male since Jesus was male. This reasoning was immediately rejected by Roman Catholic feminists, men and women, who argued from New Testament evidence that Jesus had close women disciples as well as men disciples, that there were women apostles (those who were "sent out" by the resurrected Jesus) in the early church, and that Jesus never ordained anyone so the issue could not be one of Christ's intent. Furthermore, an analogy was not meant to be taken literally, and feminist women were insulted by the statement that women could not image Christ. If the logic of both of these arguments was followed out fully, then only *Jewish* men could be ordained priests and ultimately become popes. If the nuptial analogy were applied literally to church membership, only women would be on the congregational side of the altar during the Mass.

On 7 October 1979, on the occasion of Pope John Paul II's first visit to the United States, Sr. Teresa Kane, president of the Leadership Conference of Women Religious, delivered a respectful welcome to the pope in which she challenged him to give women access to all ministries in the Roman Catholic Church.[42] Subsequently, John Paul II reported that he had been literally unable to hear Sr. Teresa Kane's speech. The inability to hear women's voices has continued to affect

Pope John Paul II; Sr. Teresa Kane remains noted for her courageous outspokenness. In response to John Paul II's 1994 apostolic letter reaffirming the ban on the ordination of women, she commented: "The pope has apologized for the way Galileo was treated. I believe that someone, in the future, will apologize for the way he is handling the issue of women in the church."[43]

The Women's Ordination Conference, a national organization led by Ruth Fitzpatrick, resulted from a conference of Roman Catholic women in 1975 in Detroit. In 1983 Roman Catholic women held a conference in Chicago entitled "From Generation to Generation: Woman Church Speaks," marking the beginning of the Women-Church movement. The independent organizations, including the Women's Ordination Conference, that constitute the institutional expressions of the Women-Church movement subsequently sponsored two other conferences, one in Cincinnati in 1987[44] and one in Albuquerque in 1993. Doubtless there will be future Women-Church national conferences.

Pope John Paul II's steadfast refusal to be open to discussion of the key issues pertaining to women and his insistence on from-the-top-down papal authority have resulted in coordinated efforts by dissenting Roman Catholics to purchase in prominent American newspapers full-page ads stating their positions to the pope. These Roman Catholics have not been invited to the Vatican to present their views. In October 1984 Roman Catholic laypeople and twenty-four Sisters signed a statement that appeared in the *New York Times* that "A Diversity of Opinions Regarding Abortion Exists Among Committed Catholics." Subsequently, there was great pressure from the Vatican on the Sisters to retract their statements or face expulsion from their orders. Twenty-two of the Sisters signed compromise statements, a number of which were not retractions but were interpreted as such by the Vatican. In 1988 two Sisters of Notre Dame, Barbara Ferraro and Pat Hussey, voluntarily left their order.[45]

In 1988, as the Episcopal Church elected Barbara C. Harris its first woman bishop and as the first draft was published of the ultimately abortive attempt by American Roman Catholic bishops to write a pastoral letter on women, Pope John Paul II issued his statement on women entitled "On the Dignity and Vocation of Women" ("*Mulieris Dignitatum*"). Although the pope affirmed the equal human dignity of women, he could only conceptualize women's vocations in terms of the sexual condition of the Virgin Mary, as being either virginity (for nuns and Sisters) or motherhood (for married women).

In November 1991 Bishop Kenneth Untener of Saginaw, Michigan, became the first U.S. Roman Catholic bishop to call publicly for the ordination of women. His brave example was followed in 1992 by P. Francis Murphy, auxiliary bishop in Baltimore, and by Michael H. Kenny, bishop in Juneau, Alaska. In an article published in August 1992 in *America*, Bishop Kenny discussed the inadequacy of using the nuptial analogy to prohibit women's ordination.[46]

November 1992 was a busy time for the debate on the validity of women's ordained religious leadership. On 11 November 1992 the General Synod of the Church of England, the "mother church" of the Anglican communion, voted in favor of women's ordination. This began the process of getting parliamentary and monarchical approval of the ordination of women priests in the Church of England. On 18 November 1992, at the annual meeting of the (U.S.) National Conference of Catholic Bishops, the fourth and most conservative (reflecting significant Vatican influence) draft of the pastoral letter on women was not adopted. This defeat of the American bishops' pastoral letter was seen as a victory by Catholic feminists, who saw the letter as internally flawed because the pope would not permit the bishops to follow through logically on the implications for the Roman Catholic Church of their unequivocal statement in the first draft that "sexism is a sin." The final defeat of the American bishops' pastoral letter on women was also seen as a victory by conservative Catholic women, who believed that the U.S. bishops had no business writing a pastoral letter on women when the pope had already done so. A few days after the meeting of the National Conference of Catholic Bishops, Jane Hart Holmes Dixon was consecrated the third woman bishop in the Anglican Communion, the suffragan (assistant) bishop of the diocese of Washington, D.C., in the Episcopal Church. The bishops participating in Dixon's consecration included Bishop Barbara Harris of Boston and Bishop Penelope A. B. Jamieson of Dunedin, New Zealand. A year later on 1 November 1993 Mary Adelia MacLeod was the first woman consecrated diocesan bishop (of Vermont) in the Episcopal Church. Roman Catholic feminist women have been thrilled by these developments in the Episcopal Church.

In 1994, with his health uncertain, Pope John Paul II appeared determined to set the world straight on women before he passed away. In March 1994 thirty-two women were ordained priests in the Church of England, and by that summer there were nearly one thousand women priests in the Church of England. The April 1994 approval of altar girls seemed to be a positive, if small, step in the Roman Catholic Church, but Pope John Paul II quickly dashed hopes of progress with his apostolic letter "*Ordinatio Sacerdotalis.*" Subsequently, it came out that Pope John Paul II had wanted to include in the letter a statement that the prohibition on the ordination of women was an "irreformable" doctrine (implying that it was an infallible teaching), but American bishops dissuaded him from using that word. Instead, John Paul II wrote that this teaching was "to be definitively held by all the church's faithful," leaving some bishops to understand that this was not an irreformable or infallible teaching and that there remained scope for future change.[47] Roman Catholic feminists, women and men, promptly and vocally rejected the logic of *"Ordinatio Sacerdotalis"* on the same grounds as they had refused the 1976 declaration, while Roman Catholic conservatives applauded the pope for closing the debate on women's ordination. In June 1994 the English translation of the new universal *Catechism of the Catholic Church* was published, after a two-year delay during which the formerly gender-inclusive language of the text was changed to exclusive sexist language, with the words *man* and *men* used to refer to all human beings. Statements from John Paul II and the Roman Catholic cardinals during the summer of 1994 indicated that they were preparing to fight vigorously against the pro-contraception position at the September 1994 UN conference on world population and to pressure the UN conference to denounce abortion.

Clearly at issue is papal authority. Despite the encyclical *"Humanae vitae"* issued by Pope Paul VI in 1968 prohibiting the use of artificial contraception, most Roman Catholics in the U.S.—married, single, lay, priests, bishops, Brothers, Sisters—disagree with the teaching that the use of artificial contraception to prevent unwanted pregnancy is sinful. Nevertheless, during the summer of 1994 Pope John Paul II appeared determined to assert this doctrine as applying to the world's population. Dissenting American Roman Catholics signed their names to a full-page ad that appeared in the *New York Times* on 6 September 1994 telling John Paul II: *"we say to you simply: on the issue of contraception, you are wrong."*[48] During the summer of 1994 the Women's Ordination Conference (WOC) encouraged Catholic feminists to write to their bishops expressing their rejection of the papal statement against the ordination of women and enclosing with their letters photos of themselves and their daughters, nieces, and grandchildren.

At the UN International Conference on Population and Development, Vatican representatives backed off on the issue of artificial contraception and focused on abortion. The 182 countries that participated in the conference unanimously approved a twenty-year program of action that endorsed the use of artificial contraception in family planning. The UN document did not endorse abortion as a means of birth control, but it did state that unsafe abortions need to be addressed as a public health problem. Archbishop Renato Martino read a statement to the UN conference that the "Holy See wishes in some way to associate itself with the consensus, even if in an incomplete or partial manner."[49]

After the UN conference, attention in the Vatican shifted to feminism within the church. In October 1994 the Vatican's Congregation for the Doctrine of the Faith took the astonishing step of overturning the 1990 adoption by the U.S. bishops of the New Revised Standard Version of the Bible (NRSV) for use in liturgy and catechetical instruction. This overruling of a decision taken by a national conference of Catholic bishops, which had been approved by the Vatican's Congregation for Divine Worship and the Sacraments, was unprecedented. The Congregation for the Doctrine of the Faith stated that it rejected the NRSV because of its gender-inclusive language.[50] The earlier recasting of the *Catechism* into sexist English and the Vatican rejection of the NRSV confirm beyond a doubt that language has political implications. The rejection of the NRSV may also reflect awareness in the Vatican that it is the first English translation of the Bible that accurately translates Romans 16:7, revealing language that can be understood as naming a woman, Junia, as having been an apostle.

When the American bishops met at the National Conference of Catholic Bishops in November 1994, they discussed and approved a short statement directed to women in light of John Paul II's "*Ordinatio Sacerdotalis*." The bishops' pastoral reflection was titled "Strengthening the Bonds of Peace." The bishops accepted the ban on the ordination of women as definitively stated in "*Ordinatio Sacerdotalis*." The bishops wrote: "We reject sexism and pledge renewed efforts to guard against it in church teaching and practice. We further reject extreme positions on women's issues which impede dialogue and divide the church. We commit ourselves to make sure that our words and actions express our belief in the equality of all women and men." The bishops rejected "authoritarian conduct" and stated with certainty that "discrimination against women contradicts the will of Christ." They pledged to continue the open and honest dialogue that they initiated with Catholic women when they first began their attempt to write a pastoral letter on women in church and society. They expressed gratitude for Catholic women's leadership as it was already being exercised in a variety of parish, diocesan, and educational settings. In light of the prohibition of women's ordination, the American Catholic bishops called for further exploration of "alternative ways in which women can exercise leadership in the church." The bishops affirmed the need for increased use of inclusive language to convey Christian teachings in a manner that is relevant to North Americans. The bishops con-

cluded: "With our Holy Father, we thank God for our sister peacemak-
ers and pray that God will guide us all in the ways of patience, love,
unity, justice and peace."[51]

In 1995 the Thirty-fourth General Congregation of the Society of
Jesus met in Rome and produced a statement entitled "Jesuits and the
Situation of Women in Church and Civil Society." The General Congregation called for individual Jesuits and Jesuit institutions "to align
themselves in solidarity with women," for example, through "genuine
involvement of women in consultation and decisionmaking in our Jesuit ministries."[52] The Jesuits' affirmation of women's leadership was
not a case of Western values being imposed on Jesuits from less-devel-
oped countries because the Thirty-fourth General Congregation was
the first at which Jesuits from Africa, Asia, and Latin America outnum-
bered Jesuits from Europe and North America. "Jesuits and the Situation of Women" additionally affirmed the importance of using
inclusive language.

If an analogy may be permitted, the current conflict in the Roman
Catholic Church is like that between an unyielding, authoritarian father and certain of his educated, self-assertive offspring. He has other
offspring who are happy to accept his authority, as long as he uses that
authority to bolster their own conservative views. (Some conservative
lay Catholics have stated that the Holy Father made a mistake by approving altar girls.) But currently in the Roman Catholic Church in the
United States, the Holy Father has a number of highly educated offspring, many of whom are fully qualified theologians, who are not
willing to accept his pronouncements without question. For a long
time now these upstarts have been rejecting doctrines which the pope
insists they must believe. They claim the Roman Catholic Church as
their home to which they have a birthright, so they disregard and reject
the views that the Holy Father seeks to impose on them. They remain
in their home, but they keep the doors and windows open to let in the
fresh air from outside. Especially during 1994 Pope John Paul II appeared to want to react in a punitive manner; he appeared to prefer to
push out the women and men who were "defecting in place," particularly those who simultaneously participated in the Women-Church
movement and the Roman Catholic Church. These uppity offspring,
who think they know more than father, have acquired the social expectation of equality as a result of the pertinent economic and educational
factors. But the social expectation of equality has not yet entered the
Vatican.

While there are numerous middle-aged and older Catholic women
in the United States who are feminists and choose to remain in the

church, the voices of some of the Roman Catholic mothers in Winter, Lummis, and Stokes's *Defecting in Place* indicate that their daughters see no point in remaining part of a sexist church. Middle-aged and older Catholic women may be willing to work around the strident insistence on official authority and continue their ministries in the manner of Mother Bickerdyke, but will the Roman Catholic Church continue to feel like home to the younger generation of Roman Catholic feminists?[53]

In the meantime, thousands of Catholic women serve in fulfilling ministries at the grassroots levels of the Roman Catholic Church in the United States. American Sisters since Vatican II have creatively shifted the internal governance of their communities to democratic structures, they have aligned their efforts with Catholic laity who seek to bring greater democracy to the church, and they work to empower the world's poor and for social justice. (See the chapter in this volume by Marie Augusta Neal, SND de Namur.) At least fifty graduate programs in ministry and theology have been established in Catholic universities and colleges to educate lay people for parish ministries. The great majority of lay parish ministers are Sisters and laywomen. The Catholic lay ministerial programs are developing institutional structures not only to train lay ministers but also to facilitate ongoing spiritual development and provide them with support. (See the chapter by Virginia Sullivan Finn.)

RELIGIOUS INSTITUTIONS AND WOMEN'S LEADERSHIP:
NEW ROLES INSIDE THE MAINSTREAM

The chapters in *Religious Institutions and Women's Leadership: New Roles Inside the Mainstream* are roughly arranged chronologically, with the accompanying attempt to cluster related religious institutions together. Those institutions that began earlier to address issues of women's religious leadership are placed earlier in this volume, but this organization does not intend to suggest that earlier is better. Rebecca Prichard's chapter on Reformed Protestant women ministers clearly makes this point, as do Cynthia Grant Tucker's chapter on Unitarian-Universalist women ministers and Susie C. Stanley's chapter on Wesleyan/Holiness women. This volume does not discuss women in Eastern Orthodox churches in the United States, because, unfortunately, there is very little scholarship in this area.

The consideration of women's religious leadership in this volume often focuses on ordained Jewish and Christian leadership, but a discussion of American women's religious leadership cannot be confined to only the issue of ordination. Therefore, these chapters also address women's religious leadership as pastors' wives, missionaries, religious educators and writers, Roman Catholic Sisters, pastoral administrators, theologians, independent preachers, social workers, secretaries, heads of women's organizations, and denominational leaders. (The chapter by Carolyn D. Blevins is very strong in presenting Baptist women's nonordained ministries.)

In my first edited volume, *Women's Leadership in Marginal Religions: Explorations Outside the Mainstream*, I stressed that female God-imagery or goddesses do not in themselves promote equality for women in the religions. There are numerous patriarchal world religions that have goddesses and oppress women. What is first necessary for women to attain equality in their religious tradition is the increasing social expectation of equality. The social expectation of equality is based on economic factors that promote women's increased earning power and higher education. Also important is the increased leisure to investigate religious questions. Educated women then can begin to search their own or alternative religions for resources to support women's full participation in a religious tradition. These resources include stories of past heroines and role models, and female God-language. Myths and doctrines that blame women for the fallenness of the human condition and that deny women's full human dignity are either rejected or reinterpreted. Where such resources are lacking, they are invented. Gender-inclusive language becomes an issue and is advocated to replace sexist language that masks women's presence in society and in religious institutions. New myths and doctrines that are supportive of women, or at least not detrimental to women, are imagined and articulated. All of these factors are important supports to women's ongoing leadership in particular religious and cultural environments.[54] Because most of these are innovations in patriarchal religions, conservative believers find them threatening. Therefore, the alternative or marginal religious traditions have been the most amenable to these innovations.

The contributors to *Religious Institutions and Women's Leadership: New Roles Inside the Mainstream* address the key issues for women's religious leadership in various ways. Their chapters clearly show that simply admitting women to religious leadership positions previously closed to women is not enough to counteract the millennia of prejudice. The mainline denominations in the United States that have had the best success in including women in positions of leadership have taken institutional measures to achieve that goal. These range from

Women's Studies programs at seminaries to quotas for proportional representation on governing bodies,[55] to commissions that monitor women's status and lobby for women's causes, to feminist educational materials for congregations. For women to be included fully in leadership in mainstream religious institutions, structures need to be created to advocate for women, to educate people about women's issues, and to nurture women's leadership and self-expression. The inertia of the patriarchal status quo is too much for one woman to effect any significant change singlehandedly. Women's separate institutions certainly benefited American women in the nineteenth century and still do today by providing opportunities for women to gain leadership experience and to network for support. These various institutional measures insure that women's voices begin to be heard and included in the corporate memory of a religious tradition. (See the chapter by Sue Levi Elwell.) Without institutional structures intended specifically to benefit women, women may be included in leadership while remaining marginalized in mainstream religious institutions. Sydell Ruth Schulman, who writes (in this volume) on Conservative women rabbis, indicates that these women are currently carrying on the struggle as individuals. But women were relatively recently, in 1984, admitted to rabbinical training at Conservative Judaism's Jewish Theological Seminary. Support structures and associations could well be developed in the future to benefit Conservative women rabbis.

Barbara Brown Zikmund has correctly observed that women's full inclusion in religious leadership is a *process* and not a one-time event.[56] In all religious institutions, the broad-based social expectation of equality is the key factor promoting women's ordinary, noncharismatic leadership. The date that women are first ordained in a patriarchal denomination does not mark the full inclusion of women in that organization's leadership. Rather, these dates are beginning points for additional struggle by women to be represented fully in their religious tradition. For that struggle to be successful, institutional structures must be created to promote women's religious leadership. These structures will help produce within a religious institution the social expectation of equality that is much more important for women's continuing religious leadership than are particular doctrines, myths, and conceptions of God. Every religious tradition is diverse enough to contain resources that can be used to support or suppress women's religious leadership. The social expectation for the equality or the subordination of women determines how these resources will be used.

NOTES

1. Jarena Lee, "The Life and Religious Experience of Jarena Lee," in *Sisters of the Spirit: Three Black Women's Autobiographies of the Nineteenth Century*, ed. William L. Andrews (Bloomington: Indiana University Press, 1986), 25–48.
2. Amanda Smith, *An Autobiography: The Story of the Lord's Dealings with Mrs. Amanda Smith the Colored Evangelist* (New York: Oxford University Press, 1988).
3. Ronald L. Numbers, *Prophetess of Health: Ellen G. White and the Origins of the Seventh-day Adventist Health Reform*, rev. and enl. ed. (Knoxville: University of Tennessee Press, 1992).
4. Ellen M. Umansky, "Women in Judaism: From the Reform Movement to Contemporary Jewish Religious Feminism," in *Women of Spirit: Female Leadership in the Jewish and Christian Traditions*, ed. Rosemary Ruether and Eleanor McLaughlin (New York: Simon and Schuster, 1979), 339.
5. J. Gordon Melton, "Emma Curtis Hopkins: A Feminist of the 1880s and Mother of New Thought," in *Women's Leadership in Marginal Religions: Explorations Outside the Mainstream*, ed. Catherine Wessinger (Urbana: University of Illinois Press, 1993), 88–101.
6. Susie C. Stanley, *Feminist Pillar of Fire: The Life of Alma White* (Cleveland: Pilgrim Press, 1993); Aimee Semple McPherson, *Aimee: Life Story of Aimee Semple McPherson*, ed. Raymond L. Cox (Los Angeles: Foursquare Publications, 1979).
7. For a full discussion, see Catherine Wessinger, "Going Beyond and Retaining Charisma: Women's Leadership in Marginal Religions," in *Women's Leadership in Marginal Religions*.
8. See, for example, Hans A. Baer, "The Limited Empowerment of Women in Black Spiritual Churches: An Alternative Vehicle to Religious Leadership," *Sociology of Religion* 54 (Spring 1993): 65–82.
9. For examples, see: Kyoko Motomochi Nakamura, "No Woman Liberation: The Heritage of a Woman Prophet in Modern Japan," in *Unspoken Worlds: Women's Religious Lives*, ed. Nancy Auer Falk and Rita M. Gross (Belmont, Cal.: Wadsworth Publishing Company, 1989), 134–44; Rosalind I. J. Hackett, "Sacred Paradoxes: Women and Religious Plurality in Nigeria," in *Women, Religion, and Social Change*, ed. Yvonne Yazbeck Haddad and Ellison Banks Findly (Albany: State University of New York Press, 1985), 247–71; Claude F. Jacobs and Andrew J. Kaslow, *The Spiritual Churches of New Orleans: Origins, Beliefs, and Rituals of an African-American Religion* (Knoxville: University of Tennessee Press, 1991); and Ronald L. Numbers, *Prophetess of Health*.
10. Our beginning point for this investigation was a 1980 article written by Mary Farrell Bednarowski, and these points are a revision of her original four points. See Mary Farrell Bednarowski, "Outside the Mainstream: Women's Religion and Women Religious Leaders in Nineteenth-Century America," *Journal of the American Academy of Religion* 48 (June 1980): 207–31.

11. Excerpt from Mary A. Livermore, *My Story of the War* (Hartford, Conn.: A. D. Worthington, 1890), 488–90, in the documents accompanying Carolyn De Swarte Gifford's article, "Women in Social Reform Movements," in *Women and Religion in America: A Documentary History*, vol. 1 *The Nineteenth Century*, ed. Rosemary Radford Ruether and Rosemary Skinner Keller (San Francisco: Harper & Row, 1981), 318–19.

12. The terminology in this sentence is imprecise, since Roman Catholic Sisters, being unordained, are also laywomen.

13. Women rabbis do not speak in terms of feeling "called" by God to the rabbinate. See Rita J. Simon, Angela J. Scanlon, and Pamela S. Nadell, "Rabbis and Ministers: Women of the Book and the Cloth," *Sociology of Religion* 54 (Spring 1993): 119, 121. See also Martha Long Ice, *Clergy Women and Their Worldviews: Calling for a New Age* (New York: Praeger, 1987), 32–39, 197, for the importance of the call for Christian clergywomen.

14. Rosemary Radford Ruether, "Christianity" in *Women in World Religions*, ed. Arvind Sharma (Albany: State University of New York Press, 1987), 207–33.

15. Blu Greenberg, "Feminism Within Orthodoxy: A Revolution of Small Signs," *Lilith* 17 (Summer 1992): 11–17.

16. The fourth draft of the American bishops' pastoral letter on women in church and society is titled "One in Christ Jesus: Response to Women's Concerns" and is found in *Origins* 22 (10 September 1992): 221ff.

17. Dirk Johnson, "Growing Mormon Church Faces Dissent by Women and Scholars," *New York Times*, 2 October 1993. My thanks go to Keely Harris, a former student at Loyola University, New Orleans, for bringing this article to my attention.

18. Virginia Lieson Brereton and Christa Ressmeyer Klein, "American Women in Ministry: A History of Protestant Beginning Points" in *Women of Spirit: Female Leadership in the Jewish and Christian Traditions*, 302–32.

19. Joan Dash, *Summoned to Jerusalem: The Life of Henrietta Szold* (New York: Harper and Row, 1979), 202–3.

20. Rosemary Radford Ruether, "The Women-Church Movement in Contemporary Christianity," in *Women's Leadership in Marginal Religions*, 196–210.

21. Miriam Therese Winter, Adair Lummis, and Allison Stokes, *Defecting in Place: Women Claiming Responsibility for Their Own Religious Lives* (New York: Crossroad, 1994).

22. *NACMW News* 2 (Summer 1993).

23. Jackson W. Carroll, Barbara Hargrove, and Adair T. Lummis, *Women of the Cloth: A New Opportunity for the Churches* (San Francisco: Harper and Row, 1981), 125–35.

24. Ruth A. Wallace, *They Call Her Pastor: A New Role for Catholic Women* (Albany: State University of New York, 1992).

25. Ruth Wallace cites data from Schoenherr and Young that the ratio of Catholics per priest in the United States was 1,102:1 in 1975, 1,418:1 in 1985, and will be 2,193:1 by 2005. See Ruth Wallace, "The Social Construction of a

New Leadership Role: Catholic Women Pastors," *Sociology of Religion* 54/1 (1993): 34.

26. Text of *"Ordinatio Sacerdotalis"* distributed by mail by Priests for Equality.

27. Carroll, et al., 188–202, 126, 136.

28. Lyn Gesch, graduate student in the Religious Studies Department, University of California at Santa Barbara, is working on this topic for her dissertation. Lyn Gesch, "The Construction of Gender in Ambiguous Work Situations: A Case Study of Women Ministers," paper presented to the Society for the Scientific Study of Religion, November 1992.

29. Frederick W. Schmidt, "Transcending Bureaucratic and Cultural Linkages: Women and the Church," paper presented at the Society for the Scientific Study of Religion, November 1992, in Washington, D.C. Schmidt's study is forthcoming in a book entitled *A Still Small Voice: Women's Ordination and the Church* from Syracuse University Press.

30. Edward C. Lehman, Jr., *Gender and Work: The Case of the Clergy* (Albany: State University of New York Press, 1993).

31. Ibid., 111.

32. Ibid., 187.

33. Paula D. Nesbitt, "Dual Ordination Tracks: Differential Benefits and Costs for Men and Women Clergy," *Sociology of Religion* 54/1 (1993): 13–30.

34. Barbara J. MacHaffie, *HerStory: Women in Christian Tradition* (Philadelphia: Fortress Press, 1986), 84, 112.

35. See *The Woman's Pulpit* (April–June 1990): 4–5; (October-December 1990): 7; (January-March 1992): 4–5; (July-September 1992): 2.

36. These issues receive attention in the issue of *Daughters of Sarah* entitled "Two Heads are Better than One: Reflecting on Womanist Concerns" 19 (Summer 1993).

37. Susan Faludi, *Backlash: The Undeclared War Against American Women* (New York: Doubleday, 1991).

38. Camille Paglia, *Sexual Personae: Art and Decadence from Nefertiti to Emily Dickinson* (New Haven: Yale University Press, 1990); Camille Paglia, *Sex, Art, and American Culture* (New York: Vintage Books, 1992).

39. The Steering Committee, "RE-imagining: Post-Conference Reflections," May 1994; "U.S. Conference 'Re-Imagines' Faith," *The Woman's Pulpit* (April-June 1994): 3.

40. The Steering Committee, "RE-imagining: Post-Conference Reflections," May 1994.

41. Thomas Aquinas, portions of the *Summa Theologica*, in *Women and Religion: A Feminist Sourcebook of Christian Thought*, ed. Elizabeth Clark and Herbert Richardson (New York: Harper and Row, 1977), 78–101.

42. Annie Lally Milhaven, ed., *The Inside Stories: 13 Valiant Women Challenging the Church* (Mystic, Conn.: Twenty-third Publications, 1987), 1–23.

43. "Catholic Women Speak Out," *National Catholic Reporter* 30 (17 June 1994): 3.

44. Ruether, "The Women-Church Movement in Contemporary Christianity,"

198–99; See Rosemary Radford Ruether, *Women-Church: Theory and Practice* (San Francisco: Harper and Row, 1985).

45. Milhaven, ed., 213–41.
46. Michael H. Kenny, "Which Way the Pastoral?" *America* (22 August 1992); P. Francis Murphy, "Let's Start Over: A Bishop Appraises the Pastoral on Women," *Commonweal* (25 September 1992): 11–15.
47. Tom Fox, "Bishops pull pope back from brink," *National Catholic Reporter* 30 (17 June 1994): 3.
48. Flyer distributed by mail by Catholics Speak Out in June/July 1994.
49. Daniel J. Wakin, "Vatican holds its peace as abortion text is OK'd," *Times-Picayune* (10 September 1994): A-13; Vivienne Walt, "Conference may increase status of poor women," *Times-Picayune* (15 September 1994): A-16; Eugene Linden, "More Power to Women, Fewer Mouths to Feed," *Time* (26 September 1994): 64–65; Archbishop Renato Martino, "Holy See: Partial Association with the Consensus," *Origins* 24/15 (22 September 1994): 257, 259.
50. Tom Roberts, "Vatican rescinds inclusive-language approval," *National Catholic Reporter* (4 November 1994): 8–9.
51. U.S. Roman Catholic Bishops, "Strengthening the Bonds of Peace," *Origins* 24/25 (1 December 1994): 417, 419–22.
52. Thirty-fourth General Congregation of the Society of Jesus, "Jesuits and the Situation of Women in Church and Civil Society," *Origins* 24/43 (13 April 1995): 742.
53. Rosemary Radford Ruether writes in "Defecting in Place: Reflections on Women's Spiritual Quest and New Support Groups" in Winter, Lummis, and Stokes, 248–52, that the outcome is uncertain about whether Catholic "defectors in place" will be able to remain in the Roman Catholic Church.
54. Frederick W. Schmidt, cited above, found that clergywomen in the Episcopal Church, the Evangelical Lutheran Church in America, the Southern Baptist Convention, and the United Methodist Church and Roman Catholic women seminary graduates are concerned with these issues and introduce changes along these lines in their own ministries. For the Protestant women, Schmidt suggests that the degree to which their denomination is pursuing more inclusive language is related to their level of comfort or alienation.

An interesting comparison can be made with Empress Wu Tse-t'ien (625-705 c.e.) of T'ang China, who was the only woman to claim the title of "Emperor, Son of Heaven." After becoming the ruler of China, in addition to her successful administration, Wu legitimized her status by the following measures: promoting scholarship that produced biographies of famous women; elevating mothers in traditional ancestor veneration; creating a model of government as mothering; positively reinterpreting *yin-yang* symbolism in the *I Ching* divinations about her reign (previously the dominance of the feminine *yin* was interpreted as indicating disaster); patronizing Mahayana Buddhism with its female Buddhas and *bodhisattvas*; and claiming that she was a *bodhisattva* (individual nearing Buddhahood who compassionately aids all sentient beings). In Mahayana Buddhism, *bodhisattvas* are credited with miraculous powers, including being able to change sex instantly. Therefore, Wu could imply either that she was a female *bodhisattva* or a male *bodhisattva* who had taken female form. Wu also identified herself with the Buddhist *chakravartin*, the virtuous universal emperor. Diana Paul stresses that Wu's patronage of Mahayana Buddhism was not simply out of calculated self-interest, but that Wu probably sincerely believed that she was a *bodhisattva* and a *chakravartin*. Subsequent Chinese Buddhist and Confucian histories of Wu Tse-t'ien were entirely negative, presenting her as a nefarious schemer, who illegitimately seized imperial power rightly wielded by men. See Diana Paul, "Empress Wu and the Historians: A Tyrant and Saint of Classical China," in *Unspoken Worlds*, 145–54.

55. Frederick W. Schmidt's study cited above found that the Evangelical Lutheran Church in America clergywomen he interviewed were relatively secure in their denomination, perhaps because they took comfort in the ELCA's quota system for proportional representation on decision-making bodies.

56. Barbara Brown Zikmund, "Winning Ordination for Women in Mainstream Protestant Churches," in *Women and Religion in America: A Documentary History*, vol. 3 *1900–1968*, ed. Rosemary Radford Ruether and Rosemary Skinner Keller (New York: Harper and Row, 1986), 348.

Protestant Women

Grandes Dames, Femmes Fortes, and Matrones: Reformed Women Ministering

Rebecca B. Prichard

INTRODUCTION

As Prof. Johanna van Wijk-Bos points out in her book *Reformed and Feminist*, there is no such thing as just one "Reformed Tradition."[1] In saying this, she reminds us that even the churches which claim to follow the teachings of John Calvin and the Reformed confessions have sprouted shoots in a variety of cultural and national contexts, and not just Swiss, French, Dutch, and Scottish. This essay will focus on the roles women have played in the Reformed churches; it will begin with a brief history of women's ministry at the time of Calvin but will move quickly to a more narrow focus on the ministry of women in the Presbyterian Church (U.S.A.) and its predecessor denominations. Many of the conclusions drawn will no doubt sound familiar to women in other communions—Protestant, Catholic, and Jewish—but emphasis will be placed on those developments which seem peculiarly Presbyterian.[2] The central thesis of this essay will be the ambiguous but apparent observation that the Protestant Reformation in general and the Calvinist reforms in particular provided both a bane and a boon, a mixed blessing for women who have tried to minister within Reformed churches—from the sixteenth century until now. We will see that women's ministry, then as now, has been tolerated but not promoted; it is counted among the *adiaphora*, or "things indifferent."

REFORMED WOMEN IN THE AGE OF REFORMATION

Jane Dempsey Douglass, in her lucid study *Women, Freedom, and Calvin*, warns against any attempt to try to make Calvin a hero when it comes to women's ministry, although she claims that "his position is remarkably modern for the sixteenth century."[3] Professor Douglass stresses the fact that John Calvin had a striking appreciation for the changing contexts in which the church interprets Scripture. It seems, at first, particularly hopeful that Calvin placed Paul's teachings concerning women's silence among the *adiaphora*, which might be interpreted contextually. As Douglass reminds us, however, Calvin was open to change but was "far too deeply shaped by the prejudices of a patriarchal society to imagine giving up those patriarchal structures in the foreseeable future."[4]

Just what were the reforms that Calvin and his colleagues were promoting and what possible influences might these reforms have had on the roles women were able to play in the Reformed churches? Calvin's reforms were far-reaching, more radical than the Lutheran or the Anglican, in that the break from the Roman Church was more marked in worship, theology, and church order. Calvin was influenced by Luther and Melanchthon, but he was more closely linked to the reformations in Scotland, Strasbourg, France, and Geneva.[5] At least three characteristics of Calvin's reforms provided possibilities for change in the ways women might be involved in ministry. Whether these possibilities have been realized is another question.

Sexuality

The Protestant churches, Lutheran, Reformed, and Anabaptist, encouraged marriage for their clergy. Reformers within and without the Roman Church were critical of the clergy, in large part because monks, priests, and bishops did not seem to be living up to their chaste ideals. Reformed leaders were particularly keen to promote marriage for pastors, many of whom had been monks or priests, and for women who had been nuns. The Protestant Reformers were beginning to question the traditional church teachings regarding sexuality and sin, which included the denigration of women as "carnal" and sexual intercourse as a necessary evil.[6] In order to put into practice these changing views, Protestant pastors actually went into convents seeking converts; many newly "liberated" nuns became the wives of these reformers. Martin Bucer led many Strasbourg pastors to the altar, and he eventually convinced Calvin himself to marry.[7]

While many have noted that the move from the cloister to the kitchen was hardly liberating, the role of pastor's wife within the Reformed communities carried with it some measure of freedom, power, and possibility for ministry.[8] In most Protestant traditions including the Presbyterian, the role of pastor's wife, until recently, has been one of the few visible (albeit limited) positions available to gifted women.[9] It is not surprising that Roman Catholic women have argued that the Protestant Reformation raided perhaps the only domain in which female ministry could flourish—the convent. Protestant women gained a new role, but they lost much in the process.

Although this new wifely role had its limitations, it is clear that many of these women were strong characters, and that they found ways to minister within the new domain they had been given. Wives and mothers were responsible for the Christian education of their children, for the spiritual nurture of the domestic realm. Certain ministerial duties that had often been carried on by women—caring for children, for the sick, for the welfare of the poor, the refugees—continued within the Reformed communities.

Katherine Zell, wife of Strasbourg pastor Matthew Zell, stands out as a great role model for all the Reformed women who married pastors and served the church in this role.[10] She opened her home to refugees and students; she established a ministry to the infirm, including lepers; she had the courage to stand up to the church patriarchs in calling for better conditions for the poor and sick. The ambiguous, limited though real power of the pastor's wife, of the caretaker of the domestic realm, typifies the "indifference" of the Reformed churches to the concerns that have been held by women in religious institutions.

Authority

The Protestant Reformation signified a radical change in authority—away from the sacramental power of the Roman clergy toward the priesthood of all believers; away from the hierarchical power of the papacy toward the teaching and preaching of Scripture. The credibility of the Roman clergy had already been undermined in many circles for moral, financial, and political reasons. Whereas the Roman clergy offered to the faithful the sacraments as a means of salvation, the Protestants wanted the people to understand the word of God. Reformed pastors taught justification by faith through grace. Calvin's emphasis was on the initiating grace of God, which works even through fallible human beings. Liturgy was conducted in the vernacular, and preaching was the center of Reformed worship, so central that French-speaking Protestants were said to *aller au sermon* ("to go to sermon") rather than go to mass.[11] Scripture was translated into German, French, and English for all to read.

The Reformers called for the priesthood of all believers. Calvin proposed a fourfold office of ministry which included pastors, deacons, elders, and doctors or teachers.[12] Pastors still preached and led, but Calvin's proposal opened up the possibility of leadership roles for laypeople, leadership roles within the community of faith that complemented and supplemented pastoral ministry. It is true that male leadership dominated and that preaching was left to the pastors, but women often served diaconal roles.[13] The offices of deacon, elder, and teacher eventually provided entrées for women in the Reformed tradition long before the pastoral office was open to them.

Reformed theology and preaching found followers among women of many walks of life; queens, duchesses, refugees, and widows were among the faithful. Queens and noblewomen played public roles, as *matrones* (women of means), within the Reformed movement; those of lower estate, the *femmelettes* (little women), were restricted to more private forms of ministry.[14] It is difficult to find evidence that female deacons served (at least officially) in Calvin's Geneva, but there are early instances of deaconesses, especially among the widows.[15] The biblical account of Mary and Martha, which gives credence to a kind of ministry of hospitality, together with Paul's teachings about the widows' ministry of service, gave scriptural backing to possible diaconal roles women might play. The flow of refugees to Geneva, Strasbourg, and other Reformed havens demanded a network of caring and compassion. Women were called upon to open their homes and hearts as well as their moneybags.

Eager female students of Reformed teaching and preaching sought the wise counsel of their pastors, as documented by some intriguing correspondence between the Reformers and women faithful.[16] Early Reformed catechisms (as did the Lutheran) became tools for education and literacy, providing additional possibilities for the priesthood of all believers. Many of these *femmelettes* are nameless, never having made it into the history books, but nonetheless, contributing to the growth and nurture of the Reformed churches.

Dissent

Finally, a spirit of dissent which called for an ongoing reformation typified the Protestant movement. The Reformed motto, *ecclesia reformata semper reformanda* (the church reformed and ever reforming), suggests that the Reformed churches were, by nature, engaged in ongoing reformation. Calvin's recognition that the church's authority, Scripture, would be interpreted within changing contexts, provided the basis for a self-critical polity and ethos. Calvin's understanding of God's accommodation to human experience promoted a cooperative, covenantal partnership between God and God's people, a partnership which takes into consideration both human fallibility and human possibility. It is this aspect of Calvin's thought which formed the context for his teachings on the *adiaphora*.

These twin notions, accommodation and *adiaphora*, form the basis of a feminist reading of Calvin. This is to say that Reformed feminists see in these two themes an opening within Calvin's theology and the traditions that sprang from it, a basis for the ministry of both women and men within the church. As Johanna van Wijk-Bos points out: "Accommodation meant the adaptation of a verbal message to an audience, keeping in mind the particular situation, station in life, character, emotional state, and intellectual gifts of those making up the audience. . . . Calvin was the first to expand the concept not only to explain errors and inconsistencies but to explain the relationship between God and human creatures."[17] So we see that although the Bible has been used within Calvinist churches to exclude women from ministry, Calvin himself proposed a contextual hermeneutic which provided a way to apply Scripture to changing times. Those within the Reformed traditions who support the ministry of women give equal weight to scriptural text and historical context when interpreting Scripture.

If Calvin's teachings on accommodation provide a hermeneutical basis for the public ministry of women, his placing of women's ministry among the *adiaphora* has given Reformed women permission to protest against an exclusively male ministry. This *adiaphora* argument is central to Jane Douglass's work on Calvin. "He clearly argues," she says, "in both the *Institutes* and some commentaries that the injunction for women to be silent in church is in the realm of human law and could be adapted to changing cultures and needs of the church," and she goes on to argue: "The certainty that Calvin could have experienced a positive tradition of women's public—though unofficial—ministry in Geneva also helps to support the judgment that Calvin is genuinely open to exceptions to the normal rule of women's subordination."[18]

For Calvin to place women's public ministry among the *adiaphora* was an opening but not an impetus. This weakly permissive approach has prevailed: women's leadership has been tolerated but not promoted. This was true during Calvin's time, during the struggle for women's ordination in America, and it is true now. Little or no effort was made to encourage women's ministry in the sixteenth century, and although some lip service was given then, even by Calvin himself, women were more often chastised when they went too far.

It is clear, however, that certain women were allowed to play certain roles, even in the sixteenth century. The newly "liberated" nuns; the *femmes fortes* (strong women) who took on the role of pastors' wives; the *femmelettes* who came into the Reformed churches as parishioners eager to learn; the *grandes dames* and *matrones* of the Renaissance who supported the reforming movement with their money, their political connections, and their faithful commitment—all these women played their parts in the nurture and growth of Reformed churches and the souls who comprised them.

PRESBYTERIAN WOMEN AND THE STRUGGLE FOR ORDINATION

In 1983 the Presbyterian Church in the United States (PCUS) merged with the United Presbyterian Church in the United States of America (UPCUSA). This reunion began to heal a breach which dated back to the Civil War.[19] In 1992 the reunited body, the Presbyterian Church (U.S.A.), added to its constitution a new "Brief Statement of Faith," which finally gave confessional standing to the ministry of women by affirming that the Holy Spirit "calls women and men to all ministries of the church."[20] This section will summarize the road to ordination traveled by women in these two bodies.[21]

While it is clear that women have served in leadership roles throughout the history of the Presbyterian Church, until recently those leadership roles were not officially sanctioned. While the sixteenth century may have seen a tiny crack in the door for Reformed women's ministry, it has only been in this century that women have been able to be ordained as deacons, elders, and ministers in the Presbyterian Church.[22] It is no surprise to find that female leaders serving in unofficial ways paved the way for the official recognition of women's ministry in the Presbyterian churches. Women were deeply involved in the missionary movement of the nineteenth century, as they were in the Sunday School movement. The nineteenth-century *matrones* were the women of means who funded global mission activity. Pastors' wives were often instrumental in organizing women for service. Many strong women, nineteenth-century *femmes fortes*, traveled overseas as nurses, teachers, and social workers.

Women's missionary societies sprang up in the Presbyterian churches in the nineteenth century, as they did in most Protestant denominations. These circles served a variety of purposes for the women and their churches. The women studied together, prayed together, supported one another spiritually, taught Sunday School, and raised funds for the local and global mission of the Presbyterian Church. In both the

PCUS and the UPC, women were allowed to work together in all these ways; it was only when they sought a more public role that they encountered resistance.

The Nineteenth Century

As early as 1811 the General Assembly of the Presbyterian Church (prior to the schism caused by the Civil War) recognized the important work women were doing through a variety of women's associations: "It has pleased God to excite pious women to combine in association for the purpose of aiding, by their voluntary contribution. . . . Benevolence is always attractive, but when dressed in female form possesses peculiar charms. . . . We hope the spirit which has animated the worthy women of whom we speak will spread and animate other bosoms. . . ."[23] Some twenty-one years later, however, it seems that these same women's organizations had come to be seen as threats to the power structure of the denomination, prompting a biblical injunction: "Meetings of pious women by themselves for conversation and prayer, whenever they can be held, we entirely approve. . . . To teach, exhort, to lead in prayer and in public and promiscuous assemblies, is clearly forbidden in Holy Oracles."[24] Although Presbyterian women were allowed great independence and public ministry on the mission field (in other words, overseas), they were still barred from public ministry, especially preaching in the United States.

It is clear that some women wanted to speak in public and that some men supported this. In the latter half of the nineteenth century there was a flurry of overtures (appeals from the local presbyteries to the national assembly)[25] that indicate controversy surrounding women preaching and speaking in public. The first definitive action of the General Assembly regarding women's ordination was a negative one, concurring with an overture from the Presbytery of Brooklyn, New York, requesting "that the Assembly accept and transmit to the presbyteries for their approval such rules as shall forbid the licensing and ordaining of women to the gospel ministry, and the teaching and preaching of women in our pulpits, or in the public and promiscuous meetings of the Church of Christ."[26]

A remarkable publication, entitled *May Women Speak?*, appeared in 1889. In this pamphlet Dr. George P. Hays, a Presbyterian minister, argued that Paul's injunctions against women speaking in public were specific to their original context. Using the contextual hermeneutics of Calvin, Dr. Hays argued against those who would forbid women to preach, and he further argued for the ordination of women. Dr. Hays pointed out that while presbyteries made exceptions for uneducated men to be licensed and ordained, they would make no exceptions at all for women: "God's blessing and success can make up for every other defect; but if a person's gender is wrong, no endorsement of the Holy Ghost and no favor of Christian people can atone for that in the eyes of the Presbyterian Church."[27]

The Twentieth Century

The UPC allowed for women deacons in 1915, for women elders in 1930, and for women ministers in 1956. The PCUS approved the ordination of women as deacons, elders, and ministers in 1964. The steps toward women's ordination involved political maneuvering paralleled by other Protestant bodies; the key events for Presbyterian women took place in the late 1920s and again in the 1950s and 1960s.[28]

The missionary activities of women during the nineteenth century had given them a certain degree of political power. The Women's Board of Home Missions and the Women's Board of Foreign Missions were autonomous organizations with independent budgets. The General Assembly of 1890 noted the financial success of these women's organizations, pointing out that the Women's Executive Committee raised more money for missionary work than all the churches in the denomination combined.[29] Women had no voice or vote in any of the governing bodies of American Presbyterianism at the turn of the century and basically carried on their work in tandem with the national denominational institutions, but outside the power structure.

When both women's mission boards were eliminated in 1923 in an act of denominational restructuring, many women recognized their exclusion from the decision-making process and their loss of autonomy. The General Council of the UPC appointed two prominent women, Katherine Bennett and Margaret Hodge, to the task of studying "the causes of unrest among women" in the Presbyterian Church. These two women were allowed to sit on the council with voice but no vote. The famous Hodge-Bennett report, published in November 1927, outlined the complaints of women whose money had been welcome by the male-dominated church but whose leadership was not. Hodge and Bennett summed up their argument by asking that women be allowed to "take their place wherever and however their abilities and the needs of the church may call."[30]

This report resulted eventually in three alternatives being put before the General Council: the ordination of women as elders and ministers; the ordination of women as elders; or the licensing of women as "local evangelists" for one year. Although the General Assembly sent all three motions to the presbyteries, only the second overture received enough votes to be ratified. This meant that women could serve in the governing bodies of the church as lay members but not as clergy. It should be noted, however, that the presence of female elders from 1930 until 1956 allowed many women to begin working within the power structures of the church; it is the groundbreaking work of these lay-women which paved the way for women's ordination as ministers.[31]

An overture calling for women's ordination came to the UPC General Assembly in 1953 from the Presbytery of Rochester, asking the assembly "to initiate such actions as may be necessary to permit the ordination of women to the Ministry of Jesus Christ."[32] In 1956 final approval was gained from the presbyteries to add the following sentence to the constitution regarding ordination as ministers: "Both men and women may be called to this office." Although this one sentence appears to be a great victory for Presbyterian women seeking to serve as ordained ministers, the word *may* is consistent with the weakly permissive approach of Presbyterianism to the ministry of women. Boyd and Brackenridge cite the following letter, written anonymously in a church publication, as evidence of the ambiguity of the victory which had been achieved: "As a woman, you will need to remember that such you must remain; you will need to maintain your femininity and learn to be a *woman* minister. You will never be able to do many of the things men ministers do . . . and heaven help you if you expect groups of men, such as a ministerial society, to be able to treat you with equality. There are certain times and places when men simply do not want women along."[33] The letter of the law had been changed but prevailing sexist attitudes had not. It will now be our task to see where these changes have led Presbyterian women since ordination was attained.

STILL IN BUT OUT

Elizabeth Verdesi ends her 1976 book with a series of questions:

> Will Presbyterian clergy and laymen examine the sexual dimensions of relationship to women in the church and accept women as equal partners in practice as well as in theory? Can lay women and men cast aside old prejudices and be open to the contributions of professionally trained women? Is the current consciousness concerning women in the church merely a passing phase, or will it lead to a deeper understanding of the Christian faith in which "there is neither male nor female"? Can *both* men and women in

the Presbyterian Church learn to be open to each other and thus
free to serve their Lord as *persons*?[34]

Some twenty years later it is difficult to answer any of these questions
with a resounding yes.

In 1986 there were 1,524 clergywomen in the Presbyterian Church
(U.S.A.), a 310 percent increase over the ten-year period since Elizabeth Verdesi's book appeared. The most recent statistics available
tell us that there were 2,447 ordained women, or 12.5 percent of the
total clergy, at the end of 1992.[35] The increasing numbers of ordained
women, of female seminarians, and of women in a wide variety of
leadership positions within the Presbyterian Church (U.S.A.) might
suggest a growing acceptance of women's ministry, but in general the
statistical news is mixed at best.[36] The kind of acceptance hoped for by
Verdesi has not been realized.

Edward C. Lehman, Jr., in *Women Clergy: Breaking through Gender
Barriers*, summarizes and evaluates the attitudes of Presbyterians toward women clergy in the mid-1980s.[37] Lehman's research is based on
a survey by a Presbyterian Panel taken in 1980. The survey indicated
that a high percentage of Presbyterians believed a clergywoman could
perform a variety of pastoral functions as well as a man. When given
the choice between a woman minister and a man, however, a minimal
number of people (1 to 4 percent depending on the function) would
actually prefer a woman over a man. This gives credence to our
premise that women's ministry has been permitted but not promoted,
tolerated but not preferred. It would seem that these statistics have not
changed much since 1980.[38]

A case study of clergywomen in one presbytery will serve to illus-
trate the issues facing women ministers in the Presbyterian Church today.[39] The rolls of this presbytery contain sixty active women members
who are ordained clergy. With regard to employment status, twenty-
four are working full-time in ordained ministries, some of them in
more than one part-time position. Sixteen are working part-time in
church-related positions; many of these would rather be working full-
time; some choose to work part-time because of parenting commitments. Eighteen are working outside the church or are unemployed;
some of these have chosen to be at home with their children temporarily; others have left the ministry altogether.

When the type of position held by these women is examined, similar patterns emerge. None of these women is head of staff, that is, pastor of a larger congregation with at least one other ordained associate.
Seven are solo pastors of Presbyterian churches; four full-time, two

temporary. All of these solo pastors are at or near the minimum salary. None pastors a church over 125 members. Four clergywomen are serving non-Presbyterian churches. Seven are full-time associate pastors; one is temporary. Ten ordained women serve in non-parish ministries.[40] Four are working full-time, and one is working part-time in non-church positions. At least three are underemployed, working in jobs for which they are seriously overqualified and under-compensated. Nine are unemployed and three are retired.

This catalogue leads to the following conclusions, which seem to be borne out in conversations with Presbyterian clergywomen from around the country.[41] Clearly women clergy do not have the choices, the mobility, the positions, or the pay of their male counterparts. Women are much more often than men in temporary and part-time (so-called "non-viable") positions within the denomination. There really is something like a glass ceiling which keeps women from moving "up" in the system, because those eight women who are solo pastors are generally more experienced than many men in larger churches with larger pay.[42]

It seems that childcare nearly always falls to the woman, which means that the husband's career usually takes precedence over the wife's. Women's choice to be with their young children limits their career choices; mothers are seen as less committed, less reliable, and not as ambitious as their male counterparts. A double bind is created when some women clergy are willing to take lower-paying positions because of lifestyle choices; in this Presbytery we have often spoken about wanting both kinds of doors to be open—"flexible" positions as well as "prestigious" positions for those who want them. Women of color in this presbytery, who are also clergywomen, are even more limited in their choices and opportunities.[43]

The best-paid and most secure women are usually associates in large, growing, often more conservative churches. Women who are identified as feminists, or who seem critical of hierarchical power structures, are not as likely to be rewarded financially or promoted and vice versa. There also seems to be a growing number of bright and competent women who have served as associate pastors with male supervisors and who have left the ministry because of the subtle oppression and power dynamics of these situations.

Rebecca Tollefson, formerly of the national staff, reports on a research project coordinated by the Women's Ministry Unit, based on the experiences of women associates serving with men who are heads of staff. The study found that "Coercion, intimidation, and a campaign of undermining clergywomen's confidence in her ability to do her tasks seem to be a major means of creating conflict for the associate and provide the impetus for terminating her position with the congregation."[44] Robin Crawford, in his survey of San Francisco Presbytery clergy, notes that "fully half of the women clergy in this presbytery report that they have been sexually harassed on the job."

Evidence shows that full acceptance has clearly not been gained. As in North American culture at large, there seems to be a backlash in the Presbyterian Church (U.S.A.) against women in general, and creative, competent, and critical women in particular in positions of authority. What inroads, if any, have been achieved? I see three areas of hope; these three areas correspond to those reforming trends that gave birth to the Presbyterian tradition.

Theological Inroads

Increasing numbers of women ministers and women seminarians have influenced the fabric of theological education. There are more women on seminary faculties and more feminist scholars, and feminist theology and hermeneutics are filtering into the churches slowly. Senior faculty within the Presbyterian tradition, such as Letty Russell at Yale, Katie Cannon at Temple University, Johanna van Wijk-Bos at Louisville Presbyterian Seminary, and Jane Dempsey Douglass at Princeton Seminary, are having an influence on their students and on the church at large.

Reformed theology is accommodating itself to the changing realities of women's leadership within the church. Theological reflection is more contextual than it once was; that is to say, it takes into consideration the variety of social and cultural contexts of contemporary people of faith. Reformed women theologians are part of the larger search for new theological models. Presbyterian women are particularly interested in remaining faithful to Scripture within changing contexts and so have been actively involved in feminist biblical interpretation.[45] Since Presbyterians see themselves as "pluralistic," "diverse," and "inclusive," it is no surprise that women with a variety of theological perspectives are finding voice within the denomination.

It is not surprising that there has also been a backlash reminiscent of the heresy debates and witch trials of earlier days. The ecumenical conference "Re-Imagining . . . God, the Community, the Church . . . ," held in November 1993 and attended by about sixty Presbyterians—clergy and laity alike—has caused a theological controversy within the Presbyterian Church. Those who attended have been treated with suspicion and even censure. It is heartening, however, to see that a recent General Assembly (June 1994) passed a tolerant resolution, nearly unanimously, which acknowledged "the use of imagination as part of our theological task."[46] Women are having an influence, and it is happening, as ever, in the midst of controversy and struggle.

Worship

This contextualization of theology, the struggle for new images, for the rediscovery of old but less patriarchal images for God, works itself out most clearly in worship. The Presbyterian Church (U.S.A.) has a new hymnal, edited by a woman, that includes new renditions of favorite hymns, new hymns, and hymns from a variety of cultural backgrounds. Congregations can now more easily worship without recourse to exclusively patriarchal images.[47] The New Revised Standard Version of the Bible, which uses inclusive language, is growing in acceptance among Presbyterian churches. A new *Book of Common Worship* is being widely used and is much more free of patriarchal language than the previous *Worshipbook*.

In addition to these new resources, the presence of women, both lay and clergy, leading worship is probably the most visible sign of women's presence within the churches. The transforming power of this visible presence cannot be underestimated for women worshiping in Presbyterian churches. The sheer visibility of women preaching, celebrating, praying in public is perhaps the best argument for the ministry of women.[48]

Critical Mass

Women make up more than half the membership in most Christian denominations, including the Presbyterian. While the percentage of women clergy is still well below that of women laity, the growing numbers are more than mere tokenism today. This means that the presence of women, lay and clergy, on sessions; on presbytery, synod, and General Assembly committees; on governing body staffs; and in seminaries affords the possibility of altering the very power structures that have excluded them from "full acceptance." Women have served in such powerful roles as General Assembly moderator, executive presbyter, and executive director of ministry units in the national church structure.[49] New models of leadership and power are emerging.

One example of the effects of this critical mass is in the area of sexuality. Although the now-famous report "Keeping Body and Soul Together" was widely criticized and ultimately rejected by the General

Assembly, the issues raised are still being debated within the denomination.[50] Sexual misconduct on the part of male clergy has increasingly come to light in the Presbyterian Church (U.S.A.), as elsewhere, largely because of the presence of female leadership in key supervisory positions. Many believe that the incidence of clergy sexual misconduct has not increased but that the ability to hide it is no longer as easy as it once was. Debate about the ordination of gays and lesbians is also debate about the political structure of the denomination. Power structures are being called into question now as they were in the sixteenth century.

This brings us full circle. There is not one story to tell, but many. Good news and bad news go together in most cases and certainly in the case of women seeking to minister in the Presbyterian Church (U.S.A.). We have come a long way; we have lost some ground; there is still much work to be done. It would seem that the possibilities for continuing reformation are still alive at the end of the twentieth century. Presbyterian women are faced with the challenge of all would-be reformers: to be critics, protesters, dissenters within the church, and in that protest to be faithful.

NOTES

1. Johanna W. H. van Wijk-Bos, *Reformed and Feminist: A Challenge to the Church* (Louisville: Westminster/John Knox Press, 1991), 9.
2. Janet R. Marder's chapter in this volume on women in Reform Judaism is particularly striking in its similarity to the Presbyterian situation.
3. Jane Dempsey Douglass, *Women, Freedom, and Calvin* (Philadelphia: Westminster Press, 1985), 10.
4. Not surprising, certain scholars are even less hopeful than Douglass regarding the patriarchal nature of Calvin's views on women. One particularly patriarchal treatment is provided by John H. Bratt, "The Role and Status of Women in the Writings of John Calvin," in *Renaissance, Reformation, Resurgence*, ed. Peter De Klerk (Grand Rapids, Mich.: Calvin Theological Seminary, 1976), 1–18. A rejoinder by Charmarie Jenkins Blaisdell in the same volume (19–32) is much closer to the views of Jane Dempsey Douglass and other Reformed feminists, who see Calvin's views as at least slightly ambiguous on the question of women's roles.
5. See Alexandre Ganoczy, *The Young Calvin* (Philadelphia: Westminster Press, 1987), especially part 3, for early influences on Calvin.
6. This point is made well by Charmarie Blaisdell, who says, "Through attacking vows of celibacy and sanctioning clerical marriage Calvin gave many women an acceptable role within the Christian community" (22).

7. Roland Bainton, in *Women of the Reformation in Germany and Italy* (Minneapolis: Augsburg, 1971), 56–57, describes Bucer's activities with regard to Matthew and Katherine Zell. In *Women of the Reformation in France and England* (Minneapolis: Augsburg, 1973), he notes that Calvin married "while in Strasbourg under pressure from the indefatigable matchmaker, Martin Bucer" (87). Jane Dempsey Douglass (98–101) discusses the difficulties for Catholic women that these activities created in Geneva, noting that "though the Protestants talked of 'freedom' to the nuns they were perceived as bringing a new form of constraint, a constraint to marry and be subject to husbands" (101).

8. The phrase "from cloister to kitchen" comes from Dagmar Lorenz, "Vom Kloster zur Kuche: Die Frau vor und nach der Reformation Dr. Martin Luthers," in *Die Frau von der Reformation zur Romantik: Die Situation der Frau vor dem Hintergrund der Literatur- und Sozialgeschichte*, ed. Barbara Becker-Cantarino, Modern German Studies, 7 (Bonn: Bouvier Verlag Herbert Grundmann, 1980).

9. See Barbara J. MacHaffie, *HerStory: Women in Christian Tradition* (Philadelphia: Fortress Press, 1986), 63–65; and Merry Wiesner, "Nuns, Wives, and Mothers: Women and the Reformation in Germany," in *Women in Reformation and Counter-Reformation Europe: Private and Public Worlds*, ed. Sherrin Marshall (Bloomington & Indianapolis: Indiana University Press, 1989), 20–21.

10. Bainton, *Germany and Italy*, 55–76.

11. Bard Thompson, *Liturgies of the Western Church* (Philadelphia: Fortress Press, 1961), 187.

12. Calvin delineates this fourfold office in Book IV, Chapter III of the *Institutes of the Christian Religion*, ed. John T. McNeill, trans. Ford Lewis Battles (Philadelphia: Westminster Press, 1960). Deacons and elders are lay officers in the Presbyterian tradition, and, like ministers, they are ordained with the laying on of hands, but no formal training or education is required. Elders govern the church with pastors, serving on the local church "session," or board, and in decision-making positions throughout the church. Deacons serve a pastoral function, visiting the sick and caring for the poor and for the general well-being of the faithful. The doctors of the church are the academics and teachers; today these people are both lay and clergy.

13. Douglass (90–92) notes the influence of Bucer and Calvin on Jean Morely, who proposed the possibility of women deacons in his *Treatise on Christian Discipline and Governance*.

14. For a discussion of the *femmelettes*, see Thomas Head, "The Religion of the *Femmelettes*: Ideals and Experience among Women in Fifteenth- and Sixteenth-Century France," in *That Gentle Strength: Historical Perspectives on Women in Christianity*, ed. Lynda L. Coon, Katherine J. Haldane, and Elisabeth W. Sommer (Charlottesville & London: University Press of Virginia, 1990), 149–75.

15. See Jeannine Olson, *Calvin and Social Welfare: Deacons and the Bourse francaise* (Cranbury, N.J.: Associated University Presses, 1989), 81–82, where she describes the activities of women who worked among the poor in sixteenth-century Geneva.

16. Charmarie Jenkins Blaisdell has provided a fascinating summary in "Calvin's Letters to Women: The Courting of Ladies in High Places," *Sixteenth Century Journal* 8/3 (1982): 67–84. The Scottish reformer, John Knox, also seems to have maintained a steady correspondence with a number of women. See Jasper Ridley, *John Knox* (New York and Oxford: Oxford University Press, 1968), especially chapters VIII and XIII, which tell of his relationship with his mother-in-law, Mrs. Elisabeth Bowes, her daughter Marjory, and the mysterious woman from Edinburgh.

17. van Wijk-Bos, 39–40.

18. Douglass, 88, 104–5.

19. These two bodies are often referred to as the "northern" and the "southern" churches, but the UPCUSA had many churches and institutions throughout the South, including black congregations. I will refer to these two bodies as the UPC and the PCUS respectively, even though both denominations went through mergers and reconfigurations during the century that they were divided.

20. Constitution of the Presbyterian Church (U.S.A.), Part II, *The Book of Confessions*, 10.464.

21. The history of women's ordination in the Presbyterian churches is documented in Elizabeth Howell Verdesi, *In But Still Out: Women in the Church* (Philadelphia: Westminster Press, 1973); Lois A. Boyd and R. Douglas Brackenridge, *Presbyterian Women in America: Two Centuries of a Quest for Status* (Westport, Conn.: Greenwood Press, 1983); Elizabeth Howell Verdesi and Lillian McCulloch Taylor, *Our Rightful Place: The Story of Presbyterian Women 1970-1983* (Presbyterian Church, U.S.A., Council on Women and the Church, The General Assembly Mission Board, The Program Agency, 1985); and Karen ("Bear") Ride Scott, "Expanding the Horizons of Ministry: Women of the Cloth in the Presbyterian Church, U.S.A." (D.Min. dissertation, San Francisco Theological Seminary, 1990). It might be noted that these studies are much more thorough regarding the history within the UPC; hence the lopsided emphasis in this overview. Verdesi and Taylor (1985) offer the best update regarding the former PCUS.

22. Note that some other Reformed bodies in North America, such as the Christian Reformed Church, the Cumberland Presbyterian Church, the Presbyterian Church in America, and the Orthodox Presbyterian Church, do not allow for the ordination of women. The Reformed Church in America has begun to ordain women as ministers.

23. *Extract from Minutes of General Assembly*, 1803–1811, 310. Quoted in Verdesi, 37.

24. *Minutes of the General Assembly*, 1832.

25. The Presbyterian Church (U.S.A.) and its predecessors have four levels of government: local church or "session," presbytery, synod, and General Assembly. The system is representative in that each local church is represented by elders and ministers in the presbytery, each presbytery sends delegates to the synod, and each presbytery has commissioners, both elders and ministers, to the General Assembly, which is a national body meeting once a year. Much of the business in the General Assembly is based on "overtures" which come from the "lower" governing bodies.

26. *The Presbyterian Constitution and Digest*, vol. I, chap. XIV, sec. 1, p. 847. Note that in nineteenth-century parlance "promiscuous" meant something like "public," no place for women who were relegated to the private sphere.

27. Rev. George P. Hays, *May Women Speak?* (Women's Temperance Publication Association, 1889), 47. A summary of Dr. Hays's essay is provided in Verdesi, 43ff.

28. Lois A. Boyd and R. Douglas Brackenridge, "Presbyterian Women Ministers: A Historical Overview and Study of the Current Status of Women Pastors," in *The Pluralistic Vision: Presbyterians and Mainstream Protestant Education and Leadership*, ed. Milton J. Coalter, John M. Mulder, and Louis B. Weeks (Louisville: Westminster/John Knox Press, 1992), 289–307, recount some of this history.

29. Verdesi, 61.

30. Selections from this report are reprinted in Barbara J. MacHaffie, ed., *Readings in HerStory: Women in Christian Tradition* (Minneapolis: Fortress Press, 1992), 192–98.

31. Elisabeth Lunz, in the introduction to *Voices of Experience: Lifestories of Clergywomen in the Presbyterian Church (U.S.A.)*, ed. Alice Brasfield and Elisabeth Lunz (Louisville: Women's Ministry Unit, 1991), 1, notes that "without the power of persuasion and action of unordained women, ordination to the offices of elder and minister would not have been opened to women in either of the former denominations that now form the Presbyterian Church (U.S.A.)."

32. *Minutes of the General Assembly* (Journal) 1953, 24.

33. "A Letter to Miss Candidate," *Monday Morning*, 1962, quoted in Boyd and Brackenridge, *Two Hundred Years*, 155.

34. Verdesi, 182.

35. The most current available statistics are summarized in an article by Deborah A. Bruce in *Monday Morning*, 20 December 1993. These numbers are based on a survey conducted by the Women's Ministry Unit during 1993. The results of this survey support the general conclusions in this essay; it contains good news and bad news. While numbers of women clergy are growing, so are their experiences of sexism; fully four out of five respondents report experiencing sexism in their careers.

36. The National Council of Churches, "Ministry in the 21st Century," 15, reports that between 1972 and 1987 the number of women seminarians preparing for ordination increased fivefold. Edgar W. Mills, in "An Analysis of

Clergy Supply and Demand Factors in the Presbyterian Church (U.S.A.)," prepared in June 1992 for the General Assembly Special Committee to Study Theological Institutions, offers evidence that women clergy among seminary M.Div. graduates constitute an increasing percentage (he estimates over 50 percent by 1996), and while the number of women in both installed and temporary positions has grown substantially between 1983 and 1990 (91 percent growth for all positions and 132 percent for solo pastorates), so have the numbers of women in "limbo" or "non-viable positions." "One consequence," says Mills, "of a declining supply of viable positions is the increase of temporary and part-time work for women clergy" (20). Women in the "ecclesiastical limbo" of unclassified status (not currently serving in a ministry deemed "valid" by the presbytery) increased 179 percent during this period, while unclassified men decreased 12 percent (21).

37. Edward C. Lehman, Jr., *Women Clergy: Breaking through Gender Barriers* (New Brunswick & Oxford: Transaction Books, 1985).

38. A Presbyterian Panel report conducted in 1989 found that less than 2 percent of members and elders indicated that they would prefer a female as their minister, while over 50 percent of the members said they preferred a male minister.

39. I am basing this case study on observations made in my role as associate presbyter in San Francisco Presbytery from 1990 to 1992. Statistical analysis was accurate as of September 1992.

40. San Francisco Presbytery has a woman executive and as of this research had a woman associate. When a woman was elected stated clerk (parliamentarian), one female elder spoke on the floor of presbytery against so much female leadership in one presbytery.

41. The irony of this case study is that the sixty clergywomen in San Francisco Presbytery represent a trend that is actually ahead of the national statistics; in other words, if clergywomen in San Francisco think it is bad, it is much worse elsewhere.

42. The Rev. Robin Crawford conducted another clergy survey in this presbytery on behalf of the Committee on Ministry. He found that women were much more troubled by salary inequities and job discrimination than were men.

43. There are nine women of color among the sixty; only one of them is in a full-time permanent position. Others are part-time, temporary, or have left the ministry altogether.

44. This quote is from an unpublished report on women associates compiled by Rebecca Tollefson and Johanna van Wijk-Bos.

45. See, for instance, Letty M. Russell, ed., *Feminist Interpretation of the Bible* (Philadelphia: Westminster Press, 1985).

46. The text of the resolution, which was adopted by a margin of 516 to 4, reaffirms the contextual nature of reformed theology when it says, "Reformed Christians, preeminently among all Christians, have remembered

that their particular expressions of the truth in Jesus Christ are neither infallible nor absolute. . . . We affirm that our task as a church is to confront and converse with our culture from the perspective of our theological tradition. This task requires the use of imagination."

47. The new hymnal contains many new hymns written by the likes of Brian Wren, Jane Parker Huber, and others who resist monarchical and patriarchal images in favor of those affirming nurture and partnership. One of Brian Wren's hymns describes God as "endless dance of love and light." Favorite hymns have been recast, poetically altering patriarchal and militaristic imagery. For instance, an alternative version of "Praise My Soul the King of Heaven" is included alongside the original, sans the kingly and fatherly metaphors.

48. Bear Scott, in her D.Min. dissertation, recounts the work of the Women in Ministry Project in the early 1980s, in which placing women in visible positions was a key strategy for increasing their employment opportunities. See especially pages 131–34.

49. The moderator of General Assembly, which is the highest office in the Presbyterian Church (U.S.A.), is elected annually. Executives are administrative positions within the various governing bodies of the church, from presbytery to synod to General Assembly.

50. This report examined a wide variety of sexuality issues, but most controversial was its support of the ordination of self-affirming gay and lesbian persons.

Women's Ministries Within the United Church of Christ

Barbara Brown Zikmund

THE UNITED CHURCH OF CHRIST

In 1957 four distinct and unique American Protestant denominational traditions merged to form the United Church of Christ (UCC). Its founders represented several important developments in American Protestantism. They came together with keen appreciation for their traditions, but they also felt a special calling to witness to Christian unity in the modern world.

First of all, the UCC was a major ecumenical step for the Congregationalists, rooted in colonial New England but more recently merged with a small denomination known as the Christians. Congregationalism was the established religious tradition of New England with historic roots in English Puritanism and religious separatism. The Christians came from an independent movement on the American scene which rejected all party labels and developed simple church structures especially suitable to American frontier life. In the 1930s the Congregationalists and the Christians joined together to establish the National Council of the Congregational Christian Churches, thereby preserving important Puritan and separatist legacies in one denomination. These Congregational Christians had a strong history of women's ministries.

The other partner in the formation of the United Church of Christ was the Evangelical and Reformed Church, itself another ecclesiastical merger of the 1930s. The origins of the Evangelical and Reformed Church lay deep within the Protestant Reformation of central Europe. First there was the German Reformed Church established by colonial immigrants in Pennsylvania and North Carolina well before the Revolutionary War. Theologically they looked to the Swiss Reformation and its Heidelberg Catechism, keeping alive a confessional appreciation for liturgy and early Christian theology. Second, in the mid-nineteenth century a new wave of German immigrants spread across the mid-western frontier, some of whom founded "Evangelical" churches. They drew upon both Lutheran and Reformed practice to nourish a practical piety with special sensitivity to the health and welfare needs of society. In the 1930s this German Evangelical Synod of North America joined with the German Reformed Church in the United States to form the Evangelical and Reformed Church. They were committed to an ecumenical vision which transcended their German ethnicity. Women played key roles in many of their outreach ministries.

These four legacies, however, tell only part of the UCC story. Congregational Christian outreach and hospitality toward African Americans led to a distinct black church heritage within the UCC. Evangelical and Reformed assistance to Hungarian immigrants produced a separate Hungarian synod within the UCC. Over and over the churches and organizations which eventually became part of the present-day United Church of Christ engaged in mission and outreach to a broad mix of ethnic, racial, and theological traditions in American life. The United Church of Christ continues this legacy with its strong advocacy for persons on the edges of mainstream culture and its aggressive support for the ministries of women.

The current theology of ministry in the United Church of Christ can be captured in two paragraphs from its Constitution:

> The United Church of Christ recognizes that God calls the whole church and every member to participate in and extend the ministry of Jesus Christ by witnessing to the Gospel in church and society. The United Church of Christ seeks to undergird the ministry of its members by nurturing faith, calling forth gifts, and equipping members for Christian service.
>
> (paragraph 17)

> The United Church of Christ recognizes that God calls certain of its members to various forms of ministry in and on behalf of the church for which ecclesiastical authorization is required. . . .
>
> (paragraph 18)

The UCC constitution goes on to assert that the church commissions, licenses, and ordains in order to regularize this "authorizing" process. Such authorizing, however, according to the UCC *Manual on Ministry*, always builds upon "the theological conviction that every member of the Church is a 'minister' of Jesus Christ by virtue of the member's baptism and participation in the Body of Christ." The *Manual* notes that "baptism" is the basic act which "authorizes" all members of the church as ministers of Jesus Christ. Ordination, commissioning, and licensing recognize that certain persons are called to service requiring "ecclesiastical authorization," but the church always does such "setting apart" in the context of the "ministry of the whole people of God."[1]

The ministries of women in the United Church of Christ is grounded in this inclusive theology. Unfortunately, the historical and contemporary reality of women's experience in the United Church of Christ, and its predecessor denominations, has not always been true to this theology.

COLONIAL WOMEN IN MINISTRY

When the Congregationalists and the German Reformed colonists came to the American colonies in the seventeenth and eighteenth centuries, they came as families. Unlike the Spanish, Dutch, and Portuguese, who sent the men to "bring" New World treasures back to Europe, the early American colonies were populated by men, women, and children. Grounded in the Protestant Reformation, Congregational and German Reformed women were expected to be persons of faith—diligent in the care of their own souls and careful cultivators of authentic household religiosity. Although female piety may not have been very visible, it was a cornerstone of family religious life and the foundation of all ministry (male and female) in colonial America.[2]

Women quietly nurtured a significant private ministry during the colonial period. Because women necessarily confronted the specter of death with every pregnancy, they were regularly challenged to think through questions of grace and salvation. Some clergy encouraged women to hold "private meetings" for "prayer and mutual confession of spiritual needs and feelings." Literacy for women was promoted to enable Bible reading and spiritual growth. The imagery and principles of a hierarchical, affectionate marriage maintained social stability and actually increased gender equality.[3]

The story of Anne Hutchinson in the Massachusetts Bay Colony is a case in point. Her religious concerns were never questioned. Her leadership became a problem, however, when she became too public in her quest for religious meaning, and especially when her popularity began to challenge male authority.[4] So, too, women who were accused of witchcraft in the early colonies highlight the fact that early Congregationalism sometimes had difficulty honoring the spiritual gifts of women.[5] Throughout the early colonial period Congregational women accepted Reformation understandings of salvation which primarily blamed, even as they honored, women.

Eventually the popular theological assumptions about the connection between human sin and women began to soften. By 1725 the famous congregational pastor Cotton Mather had called women "People who make no Noise at all in the World: People hardly Known to be in the world"—people who were nevertheless the salvation of the church. He noted that "as there were three Maries to one John standing under the Cross of our dying Lord, so still there are far more *godly Women*, than there are *godly Men....*"[6] In time the Congregationalists, with their establishment mentality, and the leaders of the German Reformed Church, with their ethnic habits, became more appreciative of women's ministries.

It was still the case, however, that for many colonial women the primary way in which a Congregational woman could exercise a more public ministry was by marrying a clergyman. Many did, becoming theologically knowledgeable and working with their husbands in long and productive pastorates. Many Congregational clergymen leaned on their wives for intellectual, practical, and spiritual support. Jonathan Edwards, probably the greatest theologian of early Congregationalism, looked to his wife Sarah for more than domestic services. On his deathbed he whispered, "Give my kindest love to my dear wife, and tell her that the uncommon union which has so long subsisted between us has been of such a nature as I trust is spiritual, and therefore will continue."[7]

EMERGING FORMS OF INDEPENDENT MINISTRIES FOR WOMEN

As colonial experience adjusted to the needs of the emerging United States of America, women's faith and contributions to church life became more public. A good example of recognized but unauthorized female ministry is found in the life of Sarah Osborn. From the 1760s until her death in 1796 Sarah led many revivals near her home in Newport, Rhode Island. As a schoolteacher, mother, and religious leader she was highly respected and lauded by the well-known Congregational clergyman Samuel Hopkins. Although she was never ordained, he considered her an exemplary Christian and saw to it that her memoirs were published.[8]

The Christians, like the Baptists and the Quakers, supported more public visibility for women as preachers in their frontier revivals. Women not only provided hospitality and financial support for the

fledgling Christian movement, they also functioned as itinerant evangelists, moving around the countryside "witnessing" and "sharing"
their faith. In 1814 a woman named Abigail Roberts was converted by
a woman preacher named Nancy Cram. The life and ministry of Nancy
Cram remains a mystery, but Abigail Roberts became an important
unordained "female laborer" among the Christians, founding many
churches until her death in 1841.[9]

By the early nineteenth century there was a "feminization" of
Congregationalism, if not all of American Protestantism. Women became more visible and active in church and society—functioning in the
church, and for the culture, as guardians of morality. Whereas in the
colonial period definitions of domesticity and the private world of
women were self-contained, as Congregationalism moved west the social significance of household, family, and women steadily increased.
Ideals of female piety in Congregationalism, and to a lesser extent in
the growing immigrant population, shifted from cultivating individual
charity and devotion to active engagement through voluntary female
organizations.[10]

Ironically, as Congregational women became more involved in
church and society, clergy also expanded their understandings of ministry. Pastorates became shorter, and more church work was done by
laity, especially women. Seminaries were founded to provide graduate
professional education for male pastors. All clergy developed more
mobile careers and identified themselves with emerging denominational structures.

This affected women in two ways. First, there was more specialized work for women to do in local congregations and in wider
mission—in Christian education, music, medicine, social outreach, and
evangelism. These were not ordained ministries, but by the twentieth
century all of the denominations which are presently in the United
Church of Christ had developed special tracks to educate, credential,
and support women in various forms of specialized ministries. Second,
the creation of national and regional denominational structures within
Congregationalism and among the various Christian groups led to
greater awareness of the need to regularize authorization for ministry.
Although Congregationalism was at the center of early New England
history, Congregationalists did not actually organize themselves as a
national denomination until after the great Yankee migrations west
and the trauma of the Civil War (250 years later). Prior to that time,
regional structures and national organizations for abolition, mission,
education, peace, and temperance enabled cooperation among Congregationalists without any national denominational bureaucracy.[11]

Principles of local congregational autonomy, religious liberty, and an educated clergy had long informed Congregational and Christian practice regarding ordination. Even with the pressures for more centralized denominational life, Congregationalists remained true to these principles, becoming the first major ecclesiastical community to ordain a woman in 1853.[12] During the same period the Christians enjoyed the evangelical gifts of women as itinerant preachers, formally ordaining a woman in 1867.[13] In the ethnic enclaves of the German Reformed Church and the German Evangelical Synod the issue of women's ordination was never raised. There might be a contradiction between the image of woman as delicate, retiring, and gentle and her increasingly important role in church and society, but this contradiction actually aided a process by which the churches came to sanction new forms of public behavior for women—new ministries.[14]

SPECIALIZED MINISTRIES IN MISSION, MEDICINE, EDUCATION AND SOCIAL SERVICE

Early in the nineteenth century Congregationalists (along with many other American Protestants) felt a strong call to take the gospel of Jesus Christ to other parts of the world. Beginning with the so-called "Haystack meeting" in 1810, the American Board of Commissioners for Foreign Missions (ABCFM) mobilized thousands of mainstream American Protestants to support mission work in Asia and Africa. Women organized into auxiliary ladies' associations to raise money for this worthy effort. But women also felt the call to serve as missionaries themselves.[15]

Initially, the male-dominated mission boards argued that single women should not be sent out as missionaries. It was too dangerous, and it was not seemly for a Christian woman to be unaccompanied. Not to be stopped, many committed women found husbands with shared enthusiasm for the mission field and enjoyed years of service in foreign-mission settings.

Some mission work, however, was difficult for married women, who were limited by their obligations to their own families. Gradually, with the encouragement of missionary wives, public opinion shifted and single women were invited to consider mission appointments. Furthermore, recognizing that single women needed extra support, women throughout the Congregational churches organized independent women's boards of missions—establishing four separate "Woman's Boards" to support the ministries of single women missionaries in their work with women and children.[16]

The ministries of single women were also recognized and affirmed in the German Evangelical tradition. Building upon the biblical legacy of the "deaconess" and drawing upon a nineteenth-century revival of deaconess sisterhoods in several denominations, German Evangelicals in St. Louis, Missouri, founded the Evangelical Deaconess Society in 1889. Over the next thirty years thirteen additional deaconess institutions were established and over five hundred deaconess sisters trained.

A deaconess was a single woman who lived in a community and dedicated herself to a ministry of mercy. All deaconesses were trained as nurses, and most worked in hospitals and homes for children and the aged. Some went on to specialized teaching or service in local parishes. Deaconesses were consecrated to their ministry in a formal liturgical ceremony similar to the ordination of a pastor. The order of service included the laying on of hands and an ordination prayer that dated back to the fourth century.[17]

In her consecration a deaconess promised obedience to God and to the rules of the motherhouse, willingness to do any work required, and faithfulness in all things. Her promise was not considered a vow for life, but it was a pledge related to her vocation. Unless she left to get married or to be with her family if they needed her at home, she was a deaconess until her death. After consecration she was called "Sister," a title of respect and appreciation for her ministry.

Although the deaconess movement was most successful within the German Evangelical churches, there were several deaconess institutions established by the German Reformed Church. Also, Congregationalists in Illinois organized the American Congregational Deaconess Association in 1901. For various reasons, however, this form of ministry for women failed to attract Congregational women.[18]

Congregational women, however, developed other modes of ministry in the nineteenth century. With and without formal relationships to churches many Congregational women organized maternal societies to help mothers with infant care, moral reform societies to rescue young girls from prostitution, Sunday schools to educate unchurched urban children, abolition societies to support the underground railroad and work for the end of slavery, and temperance unions to protect homes and families from the destructive consequences of alcoholism. The involvement of Congregational women in these benevolent volunteer societies was phenomenal.[19]

By the end of the nineteenth century the foreign mission movement was at its peak and more than half of all American Protestant missionaries overseas were women. To prepare women for these ministries and other forms of service, many denominations saw the rising need to organize schools and colleges for women.[20] Furthermore, by the end of the century progressive church leaders, inspired by the social gospel, saw a growing need for male and female Christian workers to meet the social-service needs of rapidly growing cities.

In 1886 the Schauffler College of Religious and Social Work was established in Cleveland to prepare Slavic immigrant women to do religious work with their own people.[21] In 1889 the trustees of Hartford Theological Seminary (Hartford, Connecticut), a seminary for Congregational pastors (men), became the first seminary to vote to admit women to all courses of study. Initially there were not many women students, but those who came were expected to prepare for "religious work other than the pastorate." In 1902 the nearby Springfield, Massachusetts, Bible Normal School (formerly the School for Christian Workers) worked out a cooperative arrangement with Hartford Theological Seminary and moved to Hartford. After it changed its name to the Hartford School for Religious Pedagogy, and still later when it was known as the Hartford School for Religious Education, it became a center for preparing women to serve in emerging professional roles as directors of Christian education (DCE) or directors of religious education (DRE).[22]

One of the most interesting chapters in the education of women for ministries in Congregationalism is the story of the Congregational Training School for Women, established in Chicago in 1909. In 1900 Florence Amanda Fensham, a missionary on furlough from her mission school in Turkey, challenged the Chicago Theological Seminary (CTS) to admit her to the regular seminary program leading to the bachelor of divinity degree (even though she had no desire to be ordained). Fensham was awarded the degree in 1902 and returned to the mission field. A few years later she came back to Chicago. When a special undergraduate program (the Christian Institute) closed in 1909, Florence Fensham took the lead in establishing a new institution dedicated to graduate theological education for women.

The Congregational Training School for Women was incorporated as a separate institution in close relationship to the Chicago Theological Seminary. Twenty young women lived together, did practical work in the city, and took courses from their own instructors as well as faculty at CTS. After graduation they worked in urban social work, became foreign missionaries, and most frequently became church or pastor's assistants in local congregations. In 1910 Fensham founded the Congregational Woman's League of Church Assistants to promote the "interests of the Congregational churches, especially in matters relating to the service rendered by salaried women workers." By 1915 there were 125 such workers, and in 1919 the number had risen to 300.

Local churches, however, did not treat these women well. Many times laity considered a church assistant to be little more than the church secretary or office girl. Male ministers could be supportive, but many times they were threatened by a competent woman. There was little opportunity for promotion and advancement.

By 1922 a growing concern for professional standards in religious education led the Congregational Training School for Women to develop a bachelor of religious education degree. (This was a master's-level program—in the 1960s the graduate level B.D. degree became the M.Div. degree, and the B.R.E. became the M.R.E.) In the 1920s many seminaries, stimulated by the pioneering educational work of John Dewey and George A. Coe, instituted graduate programs in religious education. Within a few years (1926) agreements were made with the Chicago Theological Seminary to absorb the religious education program, and the Congregational Training School for Women went out of existence. "Christian education" had become a primary channel for women's ministries in Congregationalism (and in the other denominations which eventually merged to form the United Church of Christ). Seminaries enrolled more and more women in special master's programs, and larger churches looked for these professionally trained women to run their educational programs.[23]

LAYWOMEN'S ORGANIZATIONS

Women who did not prepare for special ministries of mission, social service, or education found ongoing support for their ministries in local Congregational women's organizations.[24] Following the Civil War Congregational women established four independent Congregational women's mission boards (based in Boston, Chicago, California, and the Hawaiian islands). German Reformed women were slower to organize, with the first local women's missionary society emerging in 1877. Women in the Christian denomination organized their national Woman's Board for Home Missions in 1890. Finally, the National Union of [German] Evangelical women was established in 1921.[25]

By the 1920s, after women had won the right to vote, some people began to doubt the legitimacy of separate women's organizations in the churches. Congregational leaders argued that the Woman's Boards should end their separate existence and create a more efficient denominational bureaucracy by merging into the American Board of Commissioners for Foreign Missions (ABCFM). Eventually, in 1927, three of the women's boards did join the ABCFM. (Women in the Hawaiian islands kept their independence.) Although the women lost control of their money and their direct connection to many women missionaries, they were guaranteed one third of the votes on the governing board of the ABCFM. At a time when women had minimal representation on national structures in any denomination this was a major breakthrough.[26]

Local and regional women's organizations of various types, however, continued to flourish at the local and regional levels in Congregational, Christian, Evangelical, and Reformed churches. By the time that the United Church of Christ came into being in 1957 there were two national women's associations: the Women's Fellowship of the Congregational Christian Churches; and the Women's Guild of the Evangelical and Reformed Church. In the early years of the UCC, however, their existence remained ambiguous.

As the UCC ordered its national life in the early 1960s, creating innovative structures for its work, the UCC introduced a new arrangement to serve the needs of laity—the Council for Lay Life and Work. Top denominational leaders argued that "separate women's denominational structures were out-of-date."[27] At its inception a woman, Helen Huntington Smith, was called to serve as its national executive. Unfortunately, this arrangement meant that there was no national UCC office with primary responsibility for women's concerns.

ORDAINED MINISTRY

The first woman formally ordained to the Christian ministry in a major denomination in America was Antoinette L. Brown. Raised in upstate New York, a hotbed of antislavery and women's rights thinking, "Nettie" Brown, as she was called, went to Oberlin College in the 1840s. Founded by Congregationalists, it was the only college in the country where women could enroll in the same collegiate courses with men (coeducation). Brown became fast friends with Lucy Stone, a feminist radical. She also became convinced that she was called to preach the gospel. She graduated from the collegiate program and persuaded the Oberlin faculty to admit her to the advanced theological courses. In the end, the faculty refused to award her a theological degree and insisted that a male student read her final essay at graduation.

Antoinette L. Brown was ready. Without a great deal of fanfare, in 1853 she received a call to serve as pastor of a small Congregational church in South Butler, New York. Following the practice of Congregationalism, the churches in the area gathered for her ordination service on 15 September. Luther Lee, a fiery Wesleyan Methodist preacher, preached the sermon, insisting that the Holy Spirit had called Antoinette to her ministry. He reasoned, "We are not here to make a minister. It is not to confer on this our sister, a right to preach the gospel. If she has not that right already, we have no power to communicate it to her."[28] He simply acknowledged that God had called her and that the churches rightly gathered to celebrate that fact. She was twenty-eight years old and had already made a reputation for herself as a lecturer on temperance, slavery, and literary topics.

Brown's ordination took place without a lot of controversy because of the free church polity which allows individual congregations to ordain their own pastors. Her ministry in South Butler was short, however, and after a few years she resigned due to ill health and doctrinal doubts. In 1856 she married Samuel C. Blackwell, brother of Elizabeth and Emily Blackwell, early women physicians. Much later, after her children were grown, she authored numerous books on philosophy and science, supported the suffrage campaign, and returned to active ministry within the Unitarian fellowship.[29]

As the role of women became more public, Congregational and Christian leaders affirmed the "ordination of women" but continued to view the few women they ordained exceptions to the rule. For example, Christian "female laborer" Melissa Timmons (later Terrill) was ordained at the Ebenezer [Christian] Church in Clark County, Ohio, on 7 March 1867. In September of that same year the local Deer Creek [Christian] conference met and resolved, "while we do not approve of the ordination of women to the Eldership of the church, as a general rule, yet as Sister Melissa Timmons has been set forward to that position at the request of the church of which she is now a member . . . we send her credential letters of an ordained minister of good standing in this Conference."[30]

Today Antoinette Brown (Blackwell) is remembered by the United Church of Christ when it honors the history of ordained women in the denomination, yet Brown's ordination was not a portent of things to come. In 1889, over thirty-five years later, there were only 4 ordained Congregational women ministers listed in the national Congregational yearbook. By 1899 the number had risen to 49, with 89 in 1910, and 109 in 1920.[31]

In the 1920s the National Council of Congregational Churches appointed a commission to investigate the number, standing, and need for women ministers in Congregational churches. This commission reported that in 1919 there were 67 women ministers among the 5,695 clergy in the denomination. Eighteen women were pastors of "very small" churches, 14 were copastors with their husbands, 14 were religious educators or church assistants, and 21 were employed outside the churches. The commission reported that the women presented no serious problem to the denomination—"being too few in number and too modest or at least inconspicuous in their form of service."[32] Women could serve successfully in small churches, but the commission suggested that women would be of greater use in the field of religious education or as church assistants.

In 1930 there were 131 ordained clergywomen out of 5,609 Congregational ministers, or 2.2 percent. As the Congregationalists approached their 1931 merger with the Christians, the 1930 yearbook also reported that there were 45 women among the 917 Christian clergy—fewer in number but a better percentage. In 1940 the number of Congregational Christian clergywomen increased to 184, or 3.1 percent of clergy in the new denomination—numbers which might have been higher had more of the clergy and churches joined the merged denomination. World War II provided more opportunities for women, yet the 1950 statistics show only a modest increase in clergywomen to fewer than 207 out of close to 6,000 clergy.

The Congregationalists and the Christians were pioneers in their support of women's ministries. Yet for one hundred years ordained clergywomen exercised only a small percentage of the ministries carried out by women in these denominations. Furthermore, women were never more than about 3 percent of Congregational Christian clergy. Women regularly responded to their call to ministry by marrying a pastor or a missionary, training and going out on the mission field themselves or serving in special ministries of education and social service.

Thus far the story of ordained ministry within the United Church of Christ is an exclusive Congregational Christian legacy. Whereas Evangelical and Reformed laywomen did extraordinary ministries of service and mission, and no formal rule prevented the authorization of clergywomen, it was not until 1948 that the Evangelical and Reformed Church ordained a woman to the ministry of word and sacrament (clergy status). Within the polity of the church, in some local congregations rooted in the German Reformed tradition, there is provision for the ordination of lay elders. Presumably female lay elders had been ordained earlier, although there is no national recognition of that development.

The first ordained Evangelical and Reformed clergywoman was Beatrice M. Weaver (McConnell). She was a graduate of Ursinus College, attending Lancaster Theological Seminary in the late 1940s, when she learned about a special scholarship for Ursinus graduates awarded by Saint Paul's Evangelical and Reformed Church in Lancaster. As part of the scholarship arrangement she agreed to teach a Bible study class for older women, do hospital visitation, and meet weekly with Saint Paul's pastor, Titus Alspach. After she preached a sermon at the church in January 1948, he asked her if she wanted to be ordained. She replied that she did. Eventually she was called as assistant pastor by Saint Paul's, serving six and a half years. Not only was she the first woman to be ordained pastor by her denomination, she was the first woman to graduate from Lancaster Theological Seminary with a B.D. degree.[33]

There was only one public protest to her ordination. A letter to the editor appeared in the denominational magazine *The Messenger* lamenting the fact that just as female schoolteachers did not maintain the educational standards of male schoolteachers (like the ones the writer remembered from when he was in school sixty-five years earlier), female Sunday school teachers and (by implication) the ordaining of women to the ministry were having a negative impact: "Now the [Sunday school] teachers are girls and women. What is the result? Said a minister of his confirmands: They are getting worse every year, actually the children in darkest Africa cannot be more ignorant than these. God says, 'Let your women keep silence in the churches.' "[34]

Generally speaking, however, this milestone passed virtually unnoticed. Several months later well-known theologian Reinhold Niebuhr, himself a member of the Evangelical and Reformed Church, wrote a small article on the place of women in the church in relation to the World Council of Churches Assembly in Amsterdam. He noted that concern about the ordination of women in America was not as high as in Europe, probably because American women "do not feel nearly as frustrated as the women of the Continent." This did not mean, continued Niebuhr, that the problem of ordination for women ought not to be considered seriously in America. The position of women in churches was an inferior one, but apparently it was "not so inferior as to arouse the resentment which it did in Europe."[35]

The next year a second Evangelical and Reformed woman, Ruth Ann Blasberg, was ordained as a chaplain to students at the University of Wisconsin. In 1950 Mary Edith "Tinker" Williams was ordained and commissioned to go as a missionary with her husband, Philip, to Japan. And the following year, 1951, Johanna W. Stroetker graduated from Eden Theological Seminary with a B.D. degree and became the fourth clergywoman in the Evangelical and Reformed Church.[36]

Concern for clergywomen within the Congregational Christian churches and in the Evangelical and Reformed Church in the early 1950s focused on the individual ministries of particular women and the general need for more clergy in the churches. Articles reported that women ministers were keeping little churches from dying out, uniting small congregations, and serving on tiny salaries. Few people objected to women serving as clergy in Congregational Christian and Evangelical and Reformed churches, but it was assumed that their numbers would remain small.[37]

THE MODERN WOMEN'S MOVEMENT AND WOMEN'S MINISTRIES IN THE UCC

As the modern feminist movement gained momentum in the early 1970s, things began to change. The UCC became aware of sexism in past and present structures of its life, and in 1971 the General Synod declared that discrimination against women was an issue. As a consequence, a Task Force on Women in Church and Society was appointed by the Executive Council of the denomination, with a staff person reporting directly to the president. The Task Force worked for the next four years to inquire into and implement the concerns expressed in the General Synod's Pronouncement on the Status of Women. In 1972 it launched a publication for women, *Common Lot*. In 1973 it established the Antoinette Brown Award, to be given to two outstanding ordained women at each General Synod.

At the end of its mandate, in 1975 the Task Force presented a fifty-page report documenting the existence of women's structures in the church (women's fellowships, guilds, and task forces), the situation of women employed in the church (clergywomen and laywomen), the circumstances of women in seminaries, and the dilemmas of the modern family. It made concrete recommendations to eliminate "the institutional and cultural sexism which permeates both the institutional church and the society."

The report contained the results of a survey of clergywomen in the UCC. It noted that over 50 percent of the women who responded to the survey (211 out of 350 mailed questionnaires) were ordained since 1960; about half were married and half were serving in local churches. Of the women who responded, 46 percent were over the age of fifty. The salaries of these women were far below the average salaries of men in the denomination.

The report also contained information about UCC women in seminaries. In 1971–72 women constituted 8.5 percent of UCC students enrolled in seminaries. Four years later, in 1974–75, women made up 21 percent of UCC seminarians. At several UCC seminaries in 1974–75 women were approaching 40 percent of the total student body.

The Task Force offered program recommendations to guide the work of instrumentalities and agencies in their efforts to improve the situation of women. It also proposed a new structure for continuing the commitment of the denomination to women—the Advisory Commission on Women, staffed through the executive office. Finally, it presented an affirmative action plan aggressively to increase opportunities for women and minorities throughout the UCC.[38]

By the end of the 1970s the percentage of women clergy in the UCC, which had hovered around 3 percent for several decades, began to change. In 1955 women accounted for 3.5 percent of UCC clergy, most of whom were Congregational Christian.[39] By 1980 women were 9 percent of all UCC clergy, and by 1990 they were 18 percent.[40]

After four years the Advisory Commission on Women came to an end, and in 1979 the denomination established the Coordinating Center for Women in Church and Society, administratively attached to the office of the president. In that same year the First National Meeting of UCC Women was held in Cincinnati, Ohio; and within several years (1982) the Coordinating Center initiated United Church of Christ Women in Mission (UCCWM). Although UCCWM was not a national organization, individuals and local associations or women's fellowships could join and receive resources and information. In 1995, of the 1,209 memberships in UCCWM, 324 are group memberships.[41] A new sense of women's ministries, local and national, lay and ordained, began to spread across the church.

One expression of these changes was the 1983 election of an ordained woman, Carol Joyce Brun, as secretary of the church—the second-highest staff position in the denomination. During the mid-1980s women and men throughout the UCC debated the future of women's structures in the denomination. Through task force, advisory commission, and coordinating center, for fifteen years the UCC had tried various ad hoc ways to support the ministries of women. A consensus began to emerge that it was time for a permanent denominational office dedicated to support the ministries of women. In 1987, thirty years after the formation of the UCC, the Coordinating Center for Women in Church and Society was formally approved as a permanent constitutionally authorized instrumentality of the church.[42]

In the midst of this structural and constitutional debate, a core of clergywomen in the United Church of Christ decided to band together and create a support network for ordained women in the denomination. In July 1984 ninety UCC clergywomen gathered in Milwaukee, before the Second National Meeting of UCC Women, to create the national Network for United Church of Christ Clergywomen. They composed the following statement, distributed by flyer.

> Surrounded by a great cloud of witnesses,
>   women in ministry in the United Church of Christ
>   seek to respond to our call from God.
>   While affirming the partnership of ministry through baptism,
>   we claim and support the gifts women clergy bring
>   to the leadership of the church in these days.
>   We celebrate our life together in the Body of Christ,
>   our freedom in the Spirit,
> and our wholeness born in the creative action of God.
>   We bear witness to the Biblical understandings
>   VISION   of vulnerability and power.
>   We confess our failure
>   to be who God intends us to be.
>   We embrace both
>   the pain and the joy of that journey we share in faith.
>   Therefore, we covenant to be together in a supportive community
>   in which we will:
>   As a network,
>   be connected by our own affirmation
>   and exist by our own action for mutual support
>   of women clergy
>   as well as for active help and encouragement
>   in the process of placement.
>   As a network united by personal decision,
>   be agents of change who enable women to live out
>   ordained ministry in the United Church of Christ
>   while we strive
>   for justice and peace for all persons.
>   As a network, live out our vision
>   through the offering of our stories, our gifts
>   and our resources as a means to empower all.
>   As a network celebrating the continual working of
>   the Holy Spirit,
>   seek to be open to the leading of God
>   to new commitments and visions.

For about six years the network effectively nurtured the growing numbers of UCC clergywomen. By 1990, however, its capacity to continue as a self-supporting organization was waning. The Coordinating Center for Women (CCW) and the Office for Church Life and Leadership (OCLL) worked with the network leadership to devise a questionnaire to go to all clergywomen in the UCC to "assess the present needs of clergywomen and possible ways of facilitating the supportive structures needed within the church as a whole." The survey was distributed in late 1990 to 1,549 clergywomen—with a 22 percent response (353).

Three concerns surfaced in the answers given by those who responded: their need for assistance in balancing ministry, family, personal, and professional time; their interest in working the placement system in the denomination to get the most satisfying position; and their desire to correct the great differential between the salaries of male clergy and female clergy. Although the women lamented the fact that the national Network for UCC Clergywomen had to disband, they were appreciative of its work and asked that CCW and OCLL continue to find ways to support clergywomen.[43]

In 1993 a new newsletter for United Church of Christ clergywomen, entitled *Called, Blessed & Sent*, was launched by the two instrumentalities to serve the needs of UCC clergywomen. The first issue stated that the newsletter was committed to rekindling "our own sense of the One who has and does call to us." It sought to nurture "our sense of the ways in which we are and have been blessed." And it affirmed the fact that "as women, called and blessed, we are also sent . . . to a wide variety of settings for ministry."[44]

In order to learn more about the placement situation of clergywomen, in February of 1990 a consultation was held with placement officers, local church pastors, network representatives, persons from the Office for Church Life and Leadership (OCLL), and research staff from the United Church Board for Homeland Ministries (UCBHM). The following information was uncovered:

> 18% of all clergy in the United Church of Christ in 1990 were clergywomen. This represents a 100% increase in the past ten years (9% of clergy in 1980 were clergywomen).

> While 18% of clergy are clergywomen, only 13% of senior or solo pastors are women.

> Women represent 52% of associate pastors or ordained Christian education staff, 25% of clergy serving non-UCC churches, 38% of clergy in counseling or health care ministries, 29% of chaplains or missionaries, 16% of those in conference or denominational work, 25% of those who are unclassified or are on leave of absence, and 4% of retired clergy.

When surveys were distributed to conference placement personnel to gather their perceptions of the placement difficulties experienced by women, preliminary results from fifty placement officers showed that the unreadiness of churches to accept women clergy, and geographic and family limitations of the women presented greater difficulties than any lack of skills or other personal characteristics of the women themselves. "For example, 85% of placement officers cited geographic limitations and 57% said that being part of a clergy couple or other family circumstance had been substantial barriers to the placement of women."[45]

The numbers of UCC clergywomen continue to increase. In 1994–95, 64.7 percent of UCC seminarians who were pursuing a master of divinity degree (the basic preparation for ordination) were women. This is the highest percentage ever.[46] *UCC Yearbook* statistics for 1993 list 1,796 ordained women, out of 10,142 UCC clergy (17.7 percent).[47]

The United Church of Christ has many women in its membership and a growing number in its leadership. It has been and is being indelibly blessed by the ministries of laywomen and ordained women who are repeatedly called, blessed, and sent into the church and the world to serve.

NOTES

1. *United Church of Christ Manual on Ministry: Perspectives and Procedures for Ecclesiastical Authorization of Ministry* (Cleveland: Office for Church Life and Leadership, 1986), 6.
2. Laura Thatcher Ulrich, *Good Wives: Image and Reality in the Lives of Women in Northern New England 1780-1835* (New Haven: Yale University Press, 1977); Charles Hambrick-Stowe, *The Practice of Piety: Puritan Devotional Disciplines in Seventeenth Century New England* (Chapel Hill: University of North Carolina Press, 1982).
3. Amanda Porterfield, *Feminine Spirituality in America: From Sarah Edwards to Martha Graham* (Philadelphia: Temple University Press, 1980); Porterfield, "Women's Attraction to Puritanism," *Church History* 60 (June 1991): 196–209.
4. Selmar R. Williams, *Divine Rebel: The Life of Anna Marbury Hutchinson* (New York: Holt, Rinehart and Winston, 1981).
5. The classic work about this phenomenon is Marion L. Starkey, *The Devil in Massachusetts: A Modern Enquiry into the Salem Witch Trials* (Garden City, N.Y.: Doubleday, 1949).

6. Cotton Mather, *El-Shaddi. A Brief Essay . . . Produced by the Death of . . . Mrs. Katharine Willard* (Boston, 1725), 21; quoted in Gerald F. Moran, " 'The Hidden Ones': Women and Religion in Puritan New England," in *Triumph Over Silence: Women in Protestant History*, ed. Richard L. Greaves (Westport, Conn.: Greenwood Press, 1985), 127.

7. Elizabeth D. Dodds, *Marriage to a Difficult Man: The "Uncommon Union" of Jonathan and Sarah Edwards* (Philadelphia: Westminister Press, 1971), 201.

8. [Sarah Osborn], *Memoirs of the Life of Mrs. Sarah Osborn*, ed. Samuel Hopkins (Worcester, Mass.: Leonard Worcester, 1799).

9. Barbara Brown Zikmund, "Abigail Roberts: 'Female Laborer' in Christian Churches," *Historical Intelligencer* 2 (1982): 3–10.

10. Richard D. Shiels, "The Feminization of American Congregationalism, 1730-1835," *American Quarterly* 33 (1981): 46–62; Ann Douglas, *The Feminization of American Culture* (New York: Knopf, 1977).

11. John von Rohr, *The Shaping of American Congregationalism: 1620–1957* (Cleveland: Pilgrim Press, 1993), 275–78.

12. Antoinette Brown was ordained in South Butler, New York, on 15 September 1853.

13. Melissa Timmons (later Terrill) was ordained at the Ebenezer Church in Clark County, Ohio, on 7 March 1867.

14. Page Putnam Miller, *A Claim to New Roles*, ATLA Series 2 (Metuchen, N.J.: Scarecrow Press, 1985), 203–11.

15. R. Pierce Beaver, *American Protestant Women in World Mission: A History of the First Feminist Movement in North America* (Grand Rapids, Mich.: Eerdmans, 1968).

16. Barbara Brown Zikmund and Sally A. Dries, "Women's Work and Woman's Boards," in *Hidden Histories in the United Church of Christ*, vol. 1, ed. Zikmund (New York: Pilgrim Press, 1984), 140–53.

17. A copy of this prayer from the Evangelical Book of Worship is reprinted in note 45 in Zikmund, *Hidden Histories*, vol. 1, 184–85.

18. Ruth W. Rasche, "The Deaconess Sisters: Pioneer Professional Women," in Zikmund, *Hidden Histories*, vol. 1, 95–109. For several pages about the deaconess movement in Congregationalism see Dorothy C. Bass, "The Congregational Training School for Women," in *Hidden Histories in the United Church of Christ*, vol. 2, ed. Zikmund (New York: Pilgrim Press, 1987), 151–53.

19. See Anne Firor Scott, *Natural Allies: Women's Associations in American History* (Urbana and Chicago: University of Illinois Press, 1993).

20. Elizabeth Alden Green, *Mary Lyon and Mount Holyoke: Opening the Gates* (Hanover, N.H.: University Press of New England, 1979).

21. Grace L. Schauffler, *Fields of the Lord: The Story of Schauffler College* (Oberlin, Ohio: Oberlin College, 1957).

22. Elwood Street, "A Living Vision: A Brief Story of The Hartford Seminary Foundation," *The Bulletin of the Hartford Seminary Foundation* 25 (October 1958): 1–61.

23. Bass, 151–53.
24. Barbara Brown Zikmund, "Women's Organizations: Centers of Denominational Loyalty and Expressions of Christian Unity," in *Beyond Establishment: Protestant Identity in a Post-Protestant Age*, ed. Jackson Carroll and Wade Clark Roof (Louisville, KY.: Westminster/John Knox Press, 1993), 116–38.
25. Zikmund and Dries, 143–51.
26. Priscilla Stuckey-Kauffman, "Women's Mission Structures and the American Board," in Zikmund, *Hidden Histories* vol. 2, 80–100.
27. From a typescript chronology prepared by the UCC Coordinating Center for Women in 1989.
28. An excerpt from the sermon is reprinted in Zikmund, "The Struggle for the Right to Preach," in *Women and Religion in America: A Documentary History*, vol. 1, *The Nineteenth Century*, ed. Rosemary Radford Ruether and Rosemary Skinner Keller (San Francisco: Harper and Row, 1981), 214–17.
29. Elizabeth Cadzen, *Antoinette Brown Blackwell: A Biography* (Old Westbury, N.Y.: Feminist Press, 1983).
30. John Franklin Burnett, *Early Women of the Christian Church: Heroines All*, booklet 6 (Dayton, Ohio: Christian Publishing Association, n.d.), 26.
31. I am indebted to Marilyn Hedges-Hiller for much of the statistical information which follows. It is taken from an unpublished paper she did as a student in the UCC history and polity class at Pacific School of Religion, "A Trickle of Ordained Women," November 1992.
32. National Council of the Congregational Churches of the United States, *Minutes of the Nineteenth Regular Meeting* (New York: Office of the National Council, 1921), 39–41.
33. This information comes from two telephone interviews with Mrs. Beatrice Weaver McConnell conducted by Marilyn Hedges-Hiller in November 1992 and summarized in her unpublished paper cited above.
34. J. Konosky, "To Be Seen, Not Heard," *The Messenger* 13 (20 July 1948): 35.
35. Reinhold Niebuhr, "Women in the Church," *The Messenger* 13 (9 November 1948): 6.
36. *The Messenger* 14 (8 November 1949): 32; 15 (12 September 1950): 29; and 16 (19 June 1951): 19.
37. Margaret M. Morton, "The New Vocation for Women," *Advance* 147 (7 September 1955): 12.
38. [UCC], *Report of the Task Force on Women in Church and Society*, March 1975, 49 pages.
39. Jackson W. Carroll, Barbara Hargrove, and Adair T. Lummis, *Women of the Cloth* (San Francisco: Harper and Row, 1981), 6.
40. [Marge Royale], "Placement of Clergywomen: A Report to General Synod Eighteen," prepared by the Office for Church Life and Leadership and the Research Office of the United Church of Christ Board for Homeland Ministries, [1991] (typescript), 1.
41. Statistics quoted by staff at CCW in a telephone conversation.

42. From a typescript chronology prepared by the UCC Coordinating Center for Women in 1989.

43. Leslie Carole Taylor, "The Responses to the Questionnaire to All United Church of Christ Clergywomen," 27 November 1990 (typescript).

44. *Called, Blessed & Sent*, no. 1 (Summer 1993).

45. [Royale], 4.

46. Statistics for 1994–95 are from a report by Charlotte Still, "Statistics of UCC Seminarian Enrollment 1994–95," 10 March 1995, UCC Office of Church Life and Leadership, 8.

47. Statistics provided by the UCC secretary's office through the UCBHM Office for Research.

Women and the Unitarian-Universalist Ministry

Cynthia Grant Tucker

INTRODUCTION

Unitarian Universalists (UUs) will boast that almost 100 years before they became one religious body in 1961, their churches of origin led the way in accepting women as clergy with full denominational endorsement. Such broad-based approval had not been forthcoming when a local Congregational church—a kindred group whose system of governance UUs retained even after they severed their trinitarian ties—agreed among themselves to have Antoinette Brown serve as their pastor and then petitioned their conference to ordain her. A precedent therefore remained to be set ten years later when, in Malone, New York, the Saint Lawrence Association of Universalists met and agreed to extend ministerial fellowship to Olympia Brown. Later the same year a second Universalist woman, Augusta Chapin, received ordination; and three years later a third, Phebe Ann Hanaford, entered the ranks. The Unitarians followed suit in 1871, credentialing Celia Burleigh in Connecticut and Mary Graves in Massachusetts.[1] Today, 130 years later, and three decades after the two groups were merged, this small denomination of just under 200,000 members has one of the highest percentages of women's names on its ministers' rolls.

This distinction would not surprise those who first saw these iconoclasts break rank with orthodox creeds and heard them defend their revolt as the means toward a more democratic, inclusive faith. Their distinctive formation as separate religious groups during the later eighteenth and early nineteenth centuries had involved a rejection of Calvinist doctrine that emphasized human depravity and restricted salvation to only those few who had been "elected to grace." Even beyond this initial dissention, both Universalists and Unitarians showed a continuing willingness to break with orthodoxies, though the ideas and institutions they challenged were characteristically different. Universalists retained a Christian biblicism that held fast to Scripture as revelation and emphasized God's intercession through Jesus' atonement, but when it came to the secular systems that fostered caste and oppressed certain groups, these mavericks were no great respecters of authority. They agitated against tax support of "established" state churches and stood at the front lines in opposition to slavery. Unitarians, more cerebral and affluent, were slower to protest the social order but were more radical theologically. By taking the Bible as fallible, insisting it stand up to reason and the facts of cultural history, they pulled away from the Christian belief in a supernatural Jesus and the miraculous demonstration of his divinity. The eruption of the Transcendentalists' mystic thought on the movement's fringe, while itself an internal rebellion against the empiricist element, provided further nourishment for Unitarian individualism. Universalists and Unitarians shared an aversion to dogmatic rule and ecclesiastical hierarchies; this led them to build their societies on simple covenants that made all members equal and congregations self-governing.

Yet if anything tested the limits of how far these groups were willing to go in dismantling orthodox thought that impeded the claims of conscience and freedom in worship, it was women's aspirations to preach and to serve in the parish ministry. In fact, despite their indictment of undemocratic, exclusive theology, and despite their professed belief in universal human worth and freedom, most of these rebels, though first among Protestant groups to accede to the women's demand for ordination, did so with little enthusiasm. While their own theologians had been bold enough to amend the terms of salvation and even to change Jesus' status from that of God to exemplary mortal, they were squeamish about any tampering with the sexes' traditional roles and especially any encroachment by females upon the church's male sanctum. Seminaries were slow to let women enroll, and women who did enter programs soon learned this was no guarantee that churches would call them or pay them a living wage, or that their denominations would extend their institutional networks to bring them in and help them survive. Through devotion and skill in ministry, these clergy were able to silence the doubts many congregants had about women trying to do "a man's job." But even at the grass roots, ambivalence tended to linger and feelings got tangled, while at the denominational levels, resistance was institutionalized. When demographic changes at the turn of the century reenforced a nationwide cry for manlier culture and virile religion, the female clergy's early gains were wiped out. Further significant progress was blocked for some seventy years; the doors to the ministry did not swing freely again until the 1980s. Anxieties triggered by freeing the church from oppressive notions of separate spheres for the sexes may never be put to rest altogether, but women today are finding more opportunities in parish and other ministries. And as Unitarian Universalists look ahead to the twenty-first century, watching the burgeoning ministerial sisterhood take a place in their movement, most seem at least cautiously optimistic about how this influx is changing their liberal faith, and indeed, how it may even transform the concepts of ordination and ministry.

1863–1900: THE ENTERING WEDGE

Universalist and Unitarian women were slow to seek high-profile roles in their churches, but there were a few who complained early on about their second-class treatment. Judith Sargent Murray, whose husband had founded America's first Universalist church in 1779, was often provoked to remind the "haughty sex" that their own theological argument had God creating all people as equals, and women were therefore entitled to use their abilities as God meant them to, not as men dictated.[2] Universalist Mary A. Livermore also had seen enough as a minister's wife—and during the Civil War as one of the Sanitary Commission's relief volunteers—to conclude that too much of the nation's business "was badly done, or not done at all" because women's talents were not being utilized.[3] On the Unitarian side, there were women like Julia Ward Howe to lecture the men about the hypocrisy of claiming to be a free and democratic church when they would not open the pulpits to all who were qualified to preach.

By the end of the war, it was not only access to pulpits that women like Howe were demanding. Like evangelicals, liberal churchwomen had already, for some twenty years, been appearing on platforms as part-time or licensed preachers. While still frowned upon, these daring displays were becoming familiar enough to embolden others to make themselves more visible. Some women now started to realize that they were as much as running their churches and doing a parish ministry, not only managing social events and raising the funds for new buildings, but writing the prayers and hymns and providing the music for the services, tending church schools, and making most of the parish calls. As Mary H. Graves explained of her own early decision to seek ordination, once a self-respecting, devoted churchwoman discovered that she had already been doing the minister's job, and doing it well without the help of a minister's wife, it was only a matter of time before she would want her work to be recognized by having it called by its proper name and being rewarded monetarily.[4]

The chance for Graves's generation to gain this professional status presented itself when denominational leaders began to push harder for westward and rural expansion. When it became clear that few of the men were about to give up the comforts of organized churches or work for frontier wages that could not support growing families, calls began to go out for sisters and daughters to carry the good news and build congregations. Almost at once both denominations saw women come forward to take up the challenge, though hardly a large enough number to crowd out the ministry's men. In fact, in 1875, a woman who signed on complained that in a field of almost seven hundred Universalist preachers, there were only ten women, including herself, who had not been deterred by the prejudices.[5] The Unitarian sisters, slower to start, were an even smaller minority. Yet few as they were, they were soon a conspicuous presence that stirred up enormous debate over whether females, however accomplished they were, and whatever the need for more clergy, could or should serve in the church's most sacred office.

In orthodox trinitarian pulpits, opponents of women as ministers readily cited Saint Paul, who considered the female unworthy of speaking or teaching in public places; Eve's role in Adam's temptation and fall had proved that she was a weaker vessel who lacked the wit to discern higher truths and interpret God's word for mankind. Religious liberals who wished to protect the ministry as a male bastion, however, were no longer well positioned to draw on Original Sin for ammunition and instead had to fall back on arguments allegedly based on sound reason. "While we do not think it is 'wicked,'" explained the Boston-based *Universalist*, "we believe it is unwise for a woman to devote herself to the ministry." When they utilized Scripture, it was to suggest that in biblical history there was no precedent for women being ordained. Jesus had chosen no woman to be his apostle, and that seemed sufficient grounds for not redrawing the boundaries of women's employment now.[6]

Liberals who fought such redistricting to achieve egalitarianism also enlisted the widely held wisdom that God—whether One-in-One or One-in-Three—had created the sexes differently and given them separate domains for their work. The woman who took it upon herself to preach and lead worship was "out of the sphere" that her nature—abounding in feeling, intuitive powers, and unencumbered by intellect—had appropriately "prescribed for her." Her heroism might overcome bias, but it could not stand up against nature's plan.[7] More concretely, the critics predicted that woman's frail constitution would never weather the rigors of preaching and church politics. "Can the greater delicacy and sensitiveness of woman bear the buffets and the frowns, the criticisms often harsh and unfeeling?" they asked doubtfully. "Can she preserve her good nature, her self-possession, her cheerfulness, despite the crosses incident to all public positions, and which are most bitter in the pastoral career?" Nature would settle the question.[8]

Those who rebutted these arguments in support of the new women's ministry sometimes exploited the same premises to assert that women's unique attributes would enhance, not diminish, a vocation that needed more balance. So long as they trusted their "own simple sling," the "slender woman's arm" would serve them well, would "reach its target," without any need for "man's armour" or heavy equipment.[9] Yet others who rushed to defend women's ministry tried to demolish the notions about separate natures and spheres. The picture of women as vines that needed to wrap themselves around strong, manly oaks might "be all very well in poetry," but it could not stand up against the plain facts. Citing their long list of credits in building and rescuing churches, this group pointed out that whenever most needed, "the ever womanly" rolled up her sleeves and tackled a "man's work" and more.[10]

After watching a string of men fail in the work because they lacked physical stamina, the sister clergy who came in to help fill the vacuum or pick up the pieces had good cause to scoff at the claim that members of their sex were too frail for the rigors of parish duties. Ida B. Hultin, who often had driven her horse and cart forty or more miles a day over rough terrain to tend to a passel of fledgling churches in Michigan, had her response ready whenever she heard this objection from a male colleague. "I wonder," she asked, "if he stops to consider how much of his work his wife does," and where "he would find himself were there only men in his congregation."[11] Nor had they patience with all of the talk about women's especially sensitive feelings compensating for weaker intellects. They blamed this "mistaken psychology" for filling society with dysfunctional "hard-hearted men and hysterical women."[12]

Between these two camps was a third, whose approach in defending the women as clergy was not just to free the debate from the context of separate spheres, but to move it away from the prism of gender entirely. All that was called for, these advocates pleaded, was a "human ministry." The pedants, said one sympathetic brother, could sift for as long as they liked through the dusty rubble of Eden to justify banning Eve's daughters from pulpits, but women need only show what they could do, and the matter of sex would dissolve.[13] Clearly, the women themselves would have liked nothing more. For however compelling the feminist consciousness had been that led them to leave their traditional sphere, they had ventured into this new field, they said, not because it was "man's work" or "woman's," but because it was "human work" and they had been called to it by a higher authority.[14] Unfortunately, as resistance mounted, the question of gender was forced on them and became an unyielding focus.

The difficulty of escaping the grip of gender was nowhere more evident than in the constant discussion and real importance of marriage for women who wanted to make the church their lifework. As early as 1870 the *Universalist* made the prediction that "a Woman Ministry" would be impracticable and never get off the ground because its ranks would be largely young females whose domestic yearnings would quickly take over and sidetrack everything else. Within five years, half or two-thirds would surely be married, the editors warned, and then "they would undoubtedly 'retire' from the ministry"; "in any case, they should."[15] Unfortunately, this gloomy prediction was not altogether unjustified. Roughly half of the Universalist and Unitarian women ordained in the nineteenth century married, and most who had gained their credentials before they got married did not use them afterward. Indeed, the first woman to be ordained, Antoinette Brown, had married quickly to Samuel Blackwell and soon had a baby. Once a mother as well as a wife, she found she had underestimated what marriage would cost her career in the church, even though she had tried to brace herself for some necessary adjustments. As she told her friend Susan B. Anthony in the spring of 1860, it was hard to preach on a regular basis when one had a three-year-old needing new clothes, a house that was "very dirty," the winter's coal to take in, a garden to cover, and bulbs to dig up and store.[16]

This litany of frustrations was often recited in private by nineteenth-century women who tried to mix marriage and full-time ministry. Liberal women who married before they received ordination may well have had fewer illusions about their vocational prospects, especially if, as frequently happened, they married men who were clergy; but their subsequent pastorates were just as prone to frustrations of being eclipsed by their husbands' ministries and being pulled thin by competing demands of family and church. It is not surprising that half of the women who wanted to enter the field decided that wedlock and motherhood were not compatible with a parish ministry and avoided conventional marriage entirely, opting instead to live and work independently or in long partnerships with other women.[17] Yet even so, as a capsule for much of the sexist resistance to women who wished to be ministers, the factor of marriage was used to impede even those who resolved to stay clear of the wedded life.

Marriage was raised as a specter when women aiming at ordination began to go after the same sort of schooling as their male counterparts. Though, in general, Universalists and Unitarians were pioneers in establishing coeducational institutions of higher learning, they were not as receptive when women wanted to enter the theological schools; and they rationalized their discomfort by claiming that all but a fraction of females, however sincere, would yield to some suitor and give up their pulpit ambitions. Any expenditure made to prepare them for ministry would be a wasted investment and far too costly.[18] Canton, the Universalist Theological School at Saint Lawrence University, only grudgingly opened its doors to Olympia Brown in 1860 after the Unitarians' seminary in Meadville, Pennsylvania, refused to risk the "experiment" of accepting her.[19] While Meadville's trustees found the courage to take their first woman in 1868, others took longer. The Universalist divinity school at Tufts, just outside of Boston, dug in its heels for most of the century, and the Unitarians at Harvard held out for another fifty years. The women, for their part, were unrelenting in taking Harvard to task and consistently generous in their reports of the schools that let them enroll. Meadville, said one loyal graduate, was setting the liberal example by giving her sisters a chance to retire the stereotypes and show that the question of ministry was one not of gender but fitness.[20] Unfortunately, once away from the campus, there was not much chance to prove the point.

As a rule, for a Universalist or Unitarian woman to find a congregation, she had to marry into it, or organize one herself. Or else, as most did, she could go to a poor or faltering church where the trustees were willing to take her only because she was better than nothing and thought it only fitting to pay her accordingly. From most accounts, once given the chance to meet the people and prove herself, the capable minister found that the issue of gender became less insistent. To be sure, there were times when a young bride-to-be who belonged to her church would explain sheepishly that her fiancé insisted on having a "real minister," not a woman, officiate and they would have to go elsewhere for the wedding. Or visitors strange to the church might come up to her after the service to complain that they could not join in the prayers because a woman was leading them.[21] But the membership figures, treasurers' ledgers, and personal tributes in archives attest to abundant support at the grassroots for women who stood in the pulpits and sat with the sick.

One reason for people's attachment to women parish ministers was that, despite the alarmists' assertions, few seemed to be abandoning their womanly sphere or violating their nature to fit themselves into a "manly" vocation. Actually, far from repudiating their sex's traditional roles, most allied their new offices with them by building their ministries on the domestic model of churchly homemaking for a worshipful clan. These women used sermons and liturgy, much more than male colleagues tended to do, to speak of the values that strengthened the family and home. Some modified old hymns and readings to foster more balanced domestic relations, removing obstructive elements like the word *obey* from the wedding vows, and more or less cautiously making the language more gender-inclusive and less patriarchal. Yet Sunday worship and preaching were not the whole of their work. Committed to a ministry that went beyond once-a-week pulpit appearances, they devoted themselves to tending the needs of their church families all through the week. By building up Sunday schools, leading adult study groups, and packing the church social calendar, they gave the popular phrase "the church home" more literal meaning than ever before. Unitarian lay preacher Caroline Dall spoke for most of the ordained sisterhood when indicting the academic and bureaucratic approach to the ministry for being "nowhere so narrow as in its human sympathies." The clergywomen, she urged, must try to reorder their brothers' priorities, not get caught up in the "pulpit graces," but seek to uplift the "religious household" by leading a "Committee of Comfort" that reached out to the parish's poor, friendless, and emotionally broken.[22]

This domestic conception of ministry gave the historically male role of pastor a new shape the women wore to advantage. It relaxed the laypeople's anxieties about putting women in charge of the church and met the distinctive demands of those who broke with orthodox thought. In their rural outposts away from the New England centers where Universalists and Unitarians had been the established religious groups and still had some safety in numbers, liberal parishioners often were scorned and ostracized by neighbors who treated them as blights on the Christian community. Made the objects of purges at public revivals and anxious about children taunted at school or having their businesses boycotted, unorthodox families were grateful to have sympathetic and practical pastors who put aside pulpit abstractions and sought to enfold them in warm, loving faith communities.

Women ministers in these dissenting traditions were well situated to understand their congregants' isolation and need for support, for they also felt like outsiders in most public precincts. Even where their ordination's legitimacy was questioned, its aura of mystery tended to set them apart from the lay community. Their choice of vocation, if not quite dislodging them from woman's sphere, placed them on its edge. Yet at the same time their gender prevented them from being accepted fully into ministry's male preserve. Marginalized and scattered, women in pastorates knew the importance, as well as the difficulty, of finding firm allies and pooling their strength. When they went to the annual gatherings of liberal clergy to make such connections, they often were greeted by cold or incredulous stares from colleagues who seemed to regard them as aberrations and wished they would leave.[23] A friendlier atmosphere could be expected at district and regional meetings where women, who made up the parishes' voting majorities, took part as delegates, though not all of them were enthusiastic about having women as ministers. In this pioneer era as now, clergywomen reported as much if not more opposition coming from other women who depended for their self-esteem on attentive associations with male authorities. It is not surprising that women ministers found their staunchest allies in the all-female organizations that served as magnets for the denominations' most progressive women.

To be sure, some of those who were trying hard to break down the gender distinctions preferred to stay at a distance from any exclusively female associations, but most who were trying to integrate came to value the women's alliances as natural allies who understood the opposition they faced. The women in these alliances had themselves been chastised for banding together and independently carving out unordained ministries as missionaries, teachers, social workers, and fundraisers. Universalists who first established the Women's Centenary Association (later the Women's National Missionary Association) had so threatened the "zealous defenders of man's prerogative" that the brethren searched desperately for a way to discredit their constitution and scolded them for being too independent and weak in their loyalties.[24] When a few of the sisters decided to challenge the male prerogative further by stating their wishes to be ordained, the women's alliances raised scholarships to help them attend theological schools. And as proud families will, when one of their own did at last receive ordination, the organizations embraced her achievement as few of her male colleagues would, having her offer the prayers at their meetings, asking that she speak at yearly conventions, enlisting her to serve as an officer, and even helping to subsidize her salary.

The sympathy that created a haven for clergywomen in these women's groups by recognizing the kinship of lay and ordained members' ministries was an impulse that also reached out as a bridge across doctrinal differences. The Unitarian women's leadership, putting aside their discomfort with strong trinitarian accents, envisioned a national women's alliance becoming a conduit for close conversation with Universalists and other sisters of liberal religious persuasions. It was "too much," they realized, "to claim all the mental clearness and courage" for themselves. The men, who were "more theological," had made far too much of such "stumbling blocks" and ended up "sore with bruises," they cautioned. Women, whose natures knew "no separation," should try to forget the theology and be united by bonds of a "living faith and burning love."[25] This ecumenical vision was not as compelling to laywomen at local levels, where attacks on their faith were felt most directly and liberals were most protective of their distinctive religious identity. Women clergy, however, with needs that were not being met by their own denominations, were ready to minimize theological differences to find more support and opportunity for active service. Many Universalist and Unitarian clergywomen became so accustomed to serving in either tradition and being embraced by their congregations that they were unprepared and hurt when bureaucratic officials refused to accept them and what they were preaching as legitimate.[26]

These clergy were also ready to join when their longtime advocate Julia Ward Howe created a nonsectarian Woman's Ministerial Conference for lay and ordained sisters who were engaged in "the work of the Christian ministry." With a membership overwhelmingly Universalist and Unitarian with just an occasional sprinkling of Methodists and Baptists, this largely letterhead organization gave clergywomen a chance once a year to meet in Boston and tell their stories, exchange information, and update their mailing lists. Members had different conceptions of the force that empowered their ministries, some invoking an immanent and androgynous deity, and others addressing their prayers to a loftier, heavenly father; but they shared the conviction that God, however conceived, had ordained their work. To build up their small membership by emboldening others who felt called to ministry, the conference's members took every occasion to magnify their numbers. When traveling, they carried the pictures of sister ministers with them to show there were others like them at home; and again to suggest a significant presence, they helped Howe assemble an album, containing the photographs of women preachers and ministers, for public display at the Columbian Exposition in 1893.[27]

Nor was this publicity's representation of an emerging female clergy mere wishful thinking without any basis in fact. There was certainly reason to be optimistic when their numbers, though still small, had been rising rapidly since the early 1880s. Indeed, in the 1890s the Universalist conferences granted credentials to forty-six sisters, more than in all of the previous decades combined. Unitarians brought in a smaller but highly productive number who virtually took command of frontier expansion in the Western Conference and set a record for building and financing churches. Yet ironically, just when it started to seem as if women's ministry had the momentum to enter the twentieth century and flourish there, the movement suddenly came to a halt and went into a rapid decline from which it would take more than seventy years to recover.

1900–1974: YEARS IN ECLIPSE

Evangelical overchurching in the small towns was one of the factors involved in a sudden reduction of new women being ordained and the deep erosion of ground that those who were already out in the field had worked so hard to cultivate. The steady migration of small-town people to cities also took heavy tolls in the parishes where the sisters most often had found their work. Then, too, as the Social Gospel started to penetrate mainline Protestantism in the 1890s, Universalist and Unitarian clergy began to see many young families defecting to "more respectable" churches where they could hear "liberal" preaching without being marked as nonconformists.[28] But these trends, which hurt almost all liberal pastors, as well as many conservatives, were only a part of the undertow that wiped out the sisterhood's base. Since the 1880s the women had also been laboring under a rising concern that the country was in a "crisis of effeminacy." Triggered in large part by years of peace which gave young males no chance to prove their manhood by marching off to battle, and by dislocations brought on by a changing marketplace, the anxiety over the loss of America's muscle had gradually escalated into a full-scale crusade to restore the toughness and vigor that people imagined had once made their young nation great. Americans started to beef up their sports by making them more combative and violent; school boards took steps to contain the preponderance of female teachers in grade schools; novelists and entertainers fed a growing public appetite for brute instinct and force. Voters chose Teddy Roosevelt—Rough Rider, boxer, and cowboy—to take a strong hand in the world arena and lift their ideal to presidential proportions.

The fears about lost muscularity were apparent also in efforts to make the church less sissified and more manly, to instill a more businesslike attitude and to cleanse it of such feminine taints as sermon sentimentality and the presence of clergy in skirts. Administrators who wanted to strengthen the liberal movement had cause enough to plead for a more conscious entrepreneurial attitude when they had to contend with the individualistic member societies that did not take the trouble to balance their books or pay back their loans from national headquarters. But liberal churchmen had deeper reasons for tagging more businesslike conduct as specifically "masculine." Liberal clergy had for a long time been specially vulnerable to the common perception of male ministers as something less than whole men. Having excised the fierce admonitions and fiery doctrines of orthodoxy, both liberal traditions were preaching a gentler Scripture that seemed pale without the "exacting masculine pages" of flaming evangelical Bibles. The loss of status as the established state churches, on top of these softer revisions, had opened them up to charges that they were doctrinally spineless and effete.[29] Then, too, as one Unitarian pastor complained in 1907, this pantywaist reputation was in itself an appeal for a delicate breed who had little executive fortitude and was turning to the ministry as an escape from strenuous, manly society. The more robust types, like himself, had begun to fear for their own masculinity and were now either fleeing the pulpits or demanding an overhaul.[30]

In 1903 the desire for manly renewal through closer fraternal bonding prompted a group of deeply committed Universalist ministers to organize under the name Fraters and start a tradition of yearly retreats at the Wayside Inn in Sudbury, outside of Boston. At the institutional level, liberal reformers used several strategies to reinvigorate languishing churches. On one front, though marching separately, they kept step with the orthodox Protestant troops whose campaign for virility peaked with the Men and Religion Forward Movement's revivals of 1911 and 1912. Here the strategy was to draw men into churches by shifting the center of church life away from a domestic agenda and making it more like the masculine world of fraternal societies and business. Locally churches went after a muscular market by setting up men's clubs and athletic teams and adopting the corporate techniques of bureaucracies.[31] To beef up the liberal community through a broader evangelism, national leaders created such groups as the Unitarian Laymen's League.

Displaced sister clergy had different ideas about why the church had gone into decline and what it would take to reverse the trend. Marie Jenney Howe, who as much as gave up on the Unitarian parish ministry when she departed in 1904 for the secular platforms of social reform, was convinced that the churches were making a bad situation even worse by trying to pump up the men with muscular sermons. The brothers already knew all too well how to swagger and actually needed to learn the gentle virtues of self-sacrifice and tenderness. It was the women who ought to be given the lessons in self-reliance, assertiveness, and business sense; and unless the pulpits could get the right messages through to the right constituencies, she saw little hope for the church's revival and usefulness in society.[32] The church had evicted its best female talent, said Caroline Bartlett Crane—after losing her place in the pulpit and creating an alternate ministry in public health and urban ecology—because men were too insecure to acknowledge the need for the "mothering" work that would give their religion real strength.[33]

Ignoring the women's critiques, virility forces were also installing new locks to protect institutional bastions against any further female encroachment. Though Harvard alone still had all the doors barred, and none of the coeducational schools officially narrowed their policies, there were other ways of reestablishing male exclusivity. In 1906 the trustees of Beuchtel College, in Akron, Ohio, closed off its one opening for a female on the faculty by putting a man in the Chloe Pierce Chair, despite the outrage of Universalist women throughout the country. Never mind that the women's own national body had raised the funds to create the chair in the early 1870s to insure that the students at Beuchtel would always be taught by at least one woman, as well as by faculty men. Meanwhile, the schools were discouraging women who wished to enroll by letting them know at the start that when parishes wrote to them asking for ministers, they "very seldom" if ever asked for a woman.[34] Samuel Eliot, the American Unitarian Association's chief officer, devised as a more productive tactic a plan for opening training schools for parish assistants where women's ambitions would be directed away from theological schools and into a field where they could serve churches without doing harm to the ordained ministry. Ironically, just as the unemployed remnant of female clergy predicted, this plan did nothing to fill the need for capable parish ministers, but merely hastened the exodus of talented laywomen out of the church and into social work, which they found to be much more rewarding and genuinely ministerial.[35]

Social work was but one of the alternate ministries to which women now turned. Another, just as inevitable, was the steady crusade for the franchise. The right of both sexes to vote had always been seen by the women in pulpits as part of the universal suffrage assured by liberal religion's gospel, and for many the movement perpetuated their sense of still working as liberal ministers.[36] During wartime still other alternatives to parish ministry opened up. When hostilities broke out in 1914, some used their unemployed pulpit abilities on behalf of the women's peace movement and later the League of Nations. Other women, both lay and ordained, reemerged as a preaching reserve that was activated to fill the pulpits their husbands, brothers, or pastors left empty when they signed up as chaplains or soldiers; and these sisters fell in line with the rest of America's clergy and preached the same message supporting preparedness and the righteous war. Though often rewarded for these tours of service by being ordained, when the men returned home, most reservists complied with the expectation that they leave the pulpits and put their credentials in storage.

A more permanent place for the women to do ministerial work in the church was education, a field that had always been closely allied with the liberal religious movements and one that had long been accepted as being within women's natural sphere. As early as 1870, when Amy Bradley went south and organized two schools for more than three hundred young scholars, Ellen Emerson heard her father's Unitarian associates "uphold" Bradley expansively, speaking of her as "a minister with a parish." Since nobody seemed to think that women who took up such service deserved ordination, religious education came to be seen as a safe place for them to use their abilities in the church.[37] It also seemed the best place for women who somehow had been ordained, so when the denominations created departments of education, women were recruited for administrative posts, though invariably under male supervision. For those such as the Unitarians' Rev. Florence Buck, and later the Universalists' Rev. Edna Bruner, such employment offered a steady income and the professional recognition that women found hard to get, even with ordination, through parish ministry.

Elizabeth Padgham, whose long and fulfilling settlement with a small Unitarian church in New Jersey made any departure from parish work seem second-best, declined when offered the chance to become Buck's successor in 1925. Most women who wanted the challenges of administration, however, did not have the options that Padgham had outside of the Sunday school wing. Inevitably, this became the arena where churchwomen began to establish themselves professionally as directors of religious education, and to make the case that they were engaged in a ministry of the highest order deserving the full recognition of ordination.[38] Predictably, too, this official stamp was eventually approved, and by the 1980s women were being received into fellowship as ministers of religious education. There is much to be said for the argument that teaching has served women well as a preparation and bridge to the parish ministry. Yet many still grumble, in public and private, that even with such useful training and the stamp of ordination, some women still find themselves stuck in history, passed over for senior pulpit positions but readily called to take charge of the Sunday school. Indeed, the results of a study—focusing on the Episcopal Church and the UUA and published in 1993 by an outside scholar, Paula D. Nesbitt—support the in-house complaints that the dual ordination tracks, with their separate provision for those in church education, frequently ghettoize women and may well be more detrimental than helpful to their careers.[39]

When a fuller reconstruction of this history has been written, it will become even clearer that these so-called "decades of silence" that stretched from the turn of the century to the early 1970s were not silent at all. More accurately described as an era of whispered and masked parish ministries, this period of male hegemony saw a continuing female devotion to lay ministerial service through counseling, social work, mission schools, health centers, camps, and the tending to broad congregational needs for which churches could not hire men who would do more than preach.[40] At the same time, however, for women unable to quiet their sense of having been called to a fully recognized parish ministry, these years were marked also by muted suffering and irrepressible protests that nobody outside their group and beyond their few supporters took seriously. The depressed economy during the 1930s made matters worse, and by 1935 the general superintendent of the Universalist Church acknowledged that "a tremendous prejudice against women ministers" made it almost "impossible" to get a female candidate "a hearing at any salary whatsoever." Even so, Universalist and Unitarian leaders came under fire for having abandoned the women for a warped vision of vigorous ministry.[41]

A typical handling of the complaints after World War II was to trot out the names of the nine ordained women who were still alive and then close the case by declaring that if there were no others out there, it was as much a reflection of personal choice as of any real prejudice.[42] Yet however unconscious or strong the denials, the institutional powers continued to think of the ordained community as a brotherhood in the narrowest sense, and to speak of its weakness and strength in the gendered terms that depreciated the female and kept women outside the frame of reference. The specifically male, fraternal concept of personal and professional growth that the clergy embraced in 1903 would prove to be an enduring model. In 1945, when young ministers fresh out of Tufts felt the need to increase their religious and intellectual powers, they started a new men's society under the name of Humiliati and patterned their organization after the Fraters.[43]

1974–1992: YEARS OF RENEWAL

When UU women's determination to serve in the recognized ministry started to show signs of new life soon after their two denominations were merged in 1961, the stirrings had little to do with the institutional cross-pollination. Rather, the stimulus came from the 1963 publication of Betty Friedan's *The Feminine Mystique*, which gave the word *liberation* a radical meaning for numerous women who felt that something was wrong with their church lives but had no name for the problem. This book, say those whom it spurred to revive the lost dreams of Olympia Brown, produced an enormous epiphany: despite all the fine liberal claims, their religious traditions had not set them free. Their churches held on to the old patriarchal beliefs and theological relics that gave men as much as they wanted but yet prohibited females from using their minds and personal skills in the challenging work the church most needed. By 1964, with consciousness rising, reformers succeeded in placing a resolution before the Unitarian Universalist Association's General Assembly of member societies calling for the recruitment of all able candidates for the ministry irrespective of sex; the development of a salary structure commensurate with professional standards applied equally to women and men; and adequate support of the theological schools for financial assistance to female as well as male students preparing for ministry. Subsequent resolutions in 1970 and 1973 targeted equal employment opportunity in the UUA. With a follow-up resolution in 1977, calling for the elimination of sexist assumptions and language by the UUA administrative officers and staff, the denomination also created the Women and Religion Committee to assist in the implementation of these objectives.

The passage of resolutions, however, was one thing, and substantive change quite another. In May 1974 the UU Women's Federation, roused by the same broad concerns that had bridged women's lay and ordained work a century earlier, published an overview of the problems that still blocked women's progress. Of the more than 750 clergy whom the UUA recognized as part of its ministerial "fellowship," fewer than forty were women. Only five of these women had pulpits, and these few were working for *very* low salaries, some of them earning their substandard incomes by serving in more than one church.[44] Women who came back from theological schools and job interviews also could testify to an unyielding and devastating prejudice. By bringing the hushed anxieties and muttered complaints out into the open and making their contexts a matter of record, this exposé helped to crystallize needs that led to the founding in 1974 of the Ministerial Sisterhood Unitarian Universalist (MSUU). Established for women engaged in or preparing for "professional religious leadership," this organization was quickly cemented by *Gleanings,* a seasonal newsletter, which two decades later is serving as a hub for communication among more than 400 readers as well as a valuable archives for scholars.

From the vantage point of the UUA, the denomination has come a long way toward inclusiveness since "the great watershed achievement" of the 1977 Women and Religion Resolution. Judith Meyer, the association's vice president for program and the highest ranking female minister on the staff in 1992, cites as evidence the development and use of affirmative action workshops to move congregations "beyond categorical thinking" when searching for new leadership; a "sexism audit" initiated to root out inhibiting practices and attitudes within the association's own operations; the development of adult education curricula to introduce Unitarian Universalists to feminist thought and women's forgotten culture; and a burgeoning enrollment of women in theological schools that has made them a once unimaginable, clear majority at Harvard. In 1976 the UUs were represented in its three affiliated and other accredited seminaries by a total of 57 women and 93 men; by 1979 the women had pulled up and outstripped the men by a hair's breadth, 97 to 92; and by 1989 the women had claimed a commanding majority of 233 to 136, a ratio that was about the same in 1992.[45] Also cited as evidence of a raised consciousness is the growing number of women who now have a hand, by dint of employment as faculty and administrators, in shaping these students' programs at UU schools. At Harvard in Cambridge and at Meadville-Lombard in Chicago, women hold associate deanships; at Starr King in Berkeley, a woman serves as the president and two others serve as deans.

Other insiders have cheered the good work but have been more reserved in their estimates of how much the 1977 resolution has really achieved. From their point of view as UUA staff members at the headquarters based in Boston, the association's corporate behavior is not empowering women, despite the presence of females at all levels and their numerical advantage as a majority. One ordained minister, who joined the staff of the UUA in 1986 and subsequently returned to the parish ministry, found that the organizational structure, a hierarchy, only kept growing taller and more stratified with no sign of being reshaped by the feminist concepts of "spirals" and more inclusive dialogue, much less by any organized women's caucuses. As far as this woman could see, there was neither the apparatus nor personal "impulse" to change the structure. "Well socialized, well mannered," she and her sisters learned "to work within it."[46]

From another perspective, the UUA director of ministerial settlement, Daniel D. Hotchkiss, sees women in the 1990s making "slow but unimpeded progress into the higher reaches of the UU ministry" without encountering the kinds of prejudice and fear that work against candidates who are gay, lesbian, people of color, middle-aged or beyond, or disabled. At the same time, he not only grants that women, like men, may fall into these other groups but notes that they are more likely to be the targets of age discrimination. "Some search committees seem to perceive women as quite young, until suddenly they are too old," and this, he tells congregations, is in itself "one way sexism operates" in the settlement process. Nor does Hotchkiss let pass the grim irony that older women, most frequently passed over now, are also most likely to be the best tested and most experienced, having begun to serve an "unrecognized ministry" during the years that an unawakened denomination delayed their ordinations "artificially."[47]

Nevertheless, statistical studies, including some made by the subjects themselves, support Hotchkiss's view that UU women have made significant strides in getting ordained and settled in churches. By the 1980s women were outstripping men every year in the numbers ordained, in some instances by as much as three to one, and this pattern continues. In the 1990s one out of four of the twelve hundred ordained clergy are women. And though they still tend to be serving most often in smaller congregations—for example, those of one hundred members or fewer—which typically offer the lowest salaries, when counting only the clergy credentialed since 1980, women seem to be getting some larger churches about as fast as their male counterparts. On the other hand, men are still more often listed as serving in senior and solo pastorates, and women as having associate, part-time "extension," interim, and nonparish settlements. In 1990 this younger vintage had thirty-five men (22 percent) and thirty-four women (19 percent) listed as being "not settled at all."[48] If statistics like these speak ambiguously about their prospects for fair and equal opportunity in parish ministry, many women within the denomination have seen as a clearer sign of progress the UUA's appointment in 1993 of Rev. Diane Miller to succeed the retiring Rev. David Pohl as director of ministry.

Also conveying what numbers alone cannot, a prodigious output of sermons and essays—including two volumes distributed under the title *Transforming Thought* by the UU Women's Federation—shows plainly that Unitarian Universalist women's formation of ministry tends to be diverse and dialogic. As the twentieth century wanes, the sisterhood's words and understanding of clerical service reflect the expansive tendencies of a denomination enriched not just by the merger of separate religious traditions but also by the absorption of feminist thought that has its own range of inflections. While some are upholding the Christian witness within the UUA by retaining such liturgy as the Lord's Prayer or the Communion service, a far greater number, wary of Christianity's patriarchal warp, are either trying to stay and fix it or to replace it with a new liberal message that puts an end to the sanctification of male domination and exploitation of women.[49] Some women clergy are seeking a greater religious pluralism by developing educational and liturgical materials that support the new pagan and nature-centered spirituality. Like the pioneer pastors whom Julia Ward Howe brought together one hundred years ago, UU women are learning that their common ground as clergy will have to be solid and broad enough to support some weighty differences.

Meanwhile, as some women take on these issues to find a comfortable place for their work within the inherited structure, others, both lay and ordained, have been trying to broaden the framework and rethink the meanings of *ordination, clergy,* and *ministry.* Chaplains, teachers, health workers, scholars, artists, and other service professionals, conscious of doing "the transforming work of their liberal religious community," are pressing for recognition as a society for the larger ministry.[50] Not only are these conscious efforts to liberate old definitions of ministry changing the institutional system by bringing women into the field, but they are helping to quicken a consciousness of the liberals' informing belief that the ministry is the work of all Unitarian Universalists.

NOTES

1. In the Universalist tradition, the rite of ordination was administered by associations and conferences, while among the Unitarians, clergy were usually ordained by churches and only occasionally by the broader conferences. For an overview of these movements, see David Robinson, *The Unitarians and the Universalists* (Westport, Conn.: Greenwood Press, 1985). Catherine F. Hitchings's bibliographical dictionary—*Unitarian and Universalist Women Ministers,* 2nd ed. (Boston: Unitarian Universalist Historical Society, 1985)—is at present the most comprehensive historical

source on the UU's ordained sisterhood. In addition to individuals whose works are cited, I wish to acknowledge with gratitude assistance provided by Gordon Gibson, David A. Johnson, Marjorie Leaming, Lucile Longview, and Alan Seaburg.

2. Constantia [Judith Sargent Murray], "On the Equality of the Sexes" (1790), in *Up From the Pedestal*, ed. Aileen S. Kraditor (Chicago: Quadrangle Books, 1968), 34.

3. See Livermore's *The Story of My Life* (Hartford, Conn.: A. D. Worthington, 1897).

4. "Amongst Ministers," *Unitarian* 2 (March 1907): 99.

5. Rev. Elizabeth M. Bruce, quoted in *Universalist* 46 (5 June 1875): 2.

6. "Women as Preachers," *Universalist* 41 (23 July 1870): 1.

7. Ibid.

8. "Altogether Wrong," *Universalist* 44 (26 July 1873): 2; *Universalist* 41 (23 July 1870): 1.

9. Mrs. C. T. Cole, "Charge Given at Mary Safford's Ordination," *Unity* 5 (1880): 160–61.

10. Rev. Eleanor E. Gordon, "Just Like a Woman," *Woman's Standard* 17 (December 1904): 1–2; (January 1905): 1–2.

11. Rev. Ida. B. Hultin, "Women in the Ministry," *Woman's Standard* 3 (January 1889): 3.

12. Gordon, "Just Like a Woman" (December 1904): 1–2.

13. John Tunis, "Women in the Ministry: An Appeal to Fact," *Unity* 15 (1885): 92–94.

14. Rev. Eleanor E. Gordon, "Amongst Ministers," *Unitarian* 2 (March 1907): 98.

15. *Universalist* 41 (23 July 1870): 1.

16. Elizabeth Casden, *Antoinette Brown Blackwell* (Old Westbury, N.Y.: Feminist Press, 1983), 127.

17. This pattern emerges from Hitchings's biographical data. See also Cynthia Grant Tucker, *Prophetic Sisterhood: Liberal Women Ministers of the Frontier, 1880–1930* (Bloomington: Indiana University Press, 1994), 152 and *passim*.

18. *Universalist* 41 (23 July 1870): 1.

19. Olympia Brown, *An Autobiography*, ed. Gwendolyn B. Willis, *Journal of the Universalist Historical Society* 4 (1963): 26.

20. Rev. Marion Murdock, "Women at Meadville." Handwritten paper delivered at the Semi-Centennial of the Meadville Theological School, June 1894. Meadville-Lombard Theological School archives, Chicago.

21. Mary E. Collson reported such an incident in her unpublished memoir, "My Search for an All Right World," p. 35. Mississippi Valley Collection, Memphis State University. For Collson's story, see Cynthia Grant Tucker, *Healer in Harm's Way: Mary Collson, a Clergywoman in Christian Science* (Knoxville: University of Tennessee Press, 1994).

22. Caroline Dall, *College, Market and Court*, mem. ed. (Boston: Rumford, 1914), 233–36.

23. Rev. Eleanor E. Gordon, "The Story of a Long Life, Part 3," pp. 4, 6. Typescript, courtesy of Donald Gordon.

24. Ida. M. Folsom, ed., *A Brief History of the Work of Universalist Women, 1869–1955* (Boston: Association of Universalist Women, 1955), 6.

25. Letter from Rev. Celia Parker Wooley to Rev. Jenkin Lloyd Jones, 15 September 1894, Meadville-Lombard Theological School archives; letter from an eastern organizer [Mrs. Richardson] to a western sister, 1 January 1889, Meadville-Lombard Theological School archives.

26. In a letter to American Unitarian Association Secretary George Batchelor, 2 March 1897, Rev. Eliza Tupper Wilkes complained of his having demeaned her work by dismissing it as not really "Unitarian."

27. The records of the Woman's Ministerial Conference are housed at Harvard Divinity School, and the scrapbook of photographs at the Schlesinger Library, Cambridge, Massachusetts.

28. James H. Madison, "Reformers and the Rural Church, 1900–1950," *Journal of American History* 73 (1986): 649–50.

29. *Messages of the Men and Religion Forward Movement*, 7 vols. (New York, 1912), III: 45–46.

30. See for example D. Roy Freeman, responding to a survey in *Unitarian* 2 (July 1907): 248–49.

31. Gail Bederman, " 'The Women Have Had Charge of the Church Work Long Enough': The Men and Religion Forward Movement of 1911–1912 and the Masculinization of Middle-Class Protestantism," *American Quarterly* 41 (September 1989): 412–65.

32. Letter from Rev. Marie Hoffendahl Jenney to Charlotte Perkins Stetson, 12 August 1899, reprinted in Zona Gale, *The Living of Charlotte Perkins Gilman* (New York, 1935; rpt. New York: Arno Press, 1972), xx–xxii; "The Young Woman and the Church," *Old and New* 13 (September 1905): 35.

33. "The Church and the Women," 14. Typescript. Caroline Bartlett Crane Papers, Western Michigan University archives, Kalamazoo, Michigan.

34. Louis Beales Fisher, *A Brief History of the Universalist Church for Young People* (Boston: Young People's Christian Union, 1913), 167.

35. See Tucker, *Prophetic Sisterhood*, 147–56, on the Tuckerman School and Eliot's role in promoting a manlier ministry.

36. Casden, 124–125. See also Tucker, 171–88, on the ministry of social work.

37. Letter from Ellen Tucker Emerson to Father [Ralph Waldo Emerson], 20 January 1870. *The Letters of Ellen Tucker Emerson*, vol. 1, ed. Edith E. W. Gregg (Kent, Ohio: Kent State University Press, 1982), 539.

38. See Elizabeth H. Baker, *Struggle for a Profession: A History of the First 25 Years of the Liberal Religious Education Director's Association* (Boston: LREDA, 1974).

39. Paula D. Nesbitt, "Dual Ordination Tracks," *Sociology of Religion* 54 (1993): 13–30; Rev. Marjorie Newlin Leaming, "Women in the Unitarian Universalist Ministry," paper presented to the UU Ministers Association Executive Committee, 6 May 1974, page 8.

40. Describing a situation familiar to many churches at the time, Mabel Hussey, president of the New York League of Unitarian Women and a member of the Rutherford, New Jersey, church, told AUA officer G. G. Davis—in a letter dated 26 June 1939—that none of the men who succeeded Elizabeth Padgham had either her skills or commitment. The current minister was "no doubt a man of excellent character," but he was "hesitant and . . . no leader." His teaching appointment elsewhere came first and the church took "second place," and attendance had dropped to no more than thirty. AUA Records, Harvard Divinity School archives, Cambridge, Massachusetts.

41. Roger F. Etz to Rev. Ward Brigham, 23 May 1935; Rev. Eleanor E. Gordon to Frederick May Eliot, 2 February and 29 November 1939. Both letters in the collection of the Harvard Divinity School.

42. *Christian Leader* 128 (16 March 1946): 144.

43. Patricia McClellan Bowen, "The Humiliati of Tufts: A Model of Renewal in Religion," D.Min dissertation, Meadville-Lombard Theological School, Chicago, 1978, p. 57.

44. Mary Lou Thompson, "Where Are Women in the UU Ministry?" *Speak Out* [Supplement to *UU World*] (1 May 1974): 1–2.

45. Rev. Judith Meyer, "The Faith of a Feminist" (Boston: Unitarian Universalist Association, 1991); *Cleansing Our Temple* sensitizes congregations to sexist behavior; Rev. Shirley A. Ranck's curriculum, *Cakes for the Queen of Heaven*, promotes the reclamation and celebration of women's sacred history and culture, while its sequel, Elizabeth Fisher's *Rise Up and Call Her Name*, encourages a multicultural appreciation of women's spirituality and worship experiences. These curricula materials are available from the UUA Department of Religious Education, which also provided seminary enrollment figures to the author.

46. Rev. Lucy V. Hitchcock, "Women, Power and Structure Within the UUA," *Gleanings* 16 (Fall 1989): 7–11. Reprinted from *Critical Mass* (Primavera,1989). During the 1980s grassroots dissatisfaction with the 1977 Resolution found a needed forum for further dialogue in Sara Best's newsletter, *Reaching Sideways*, which Best came to regard as a "ministry" in its own right.

47. Letter from Daniel D. Hotchkiss to Cynthia Grant Tucker, 23 March 1992; phone interview, 12 March 1992.

48. These statistical counts were made independently by Rev. Shirley A. Ranck and provided to the author.

49. Edited by Betty. B. Hoskins (Boston, 1988, 1989). Third in this series is Mary Moore's *Finding Our Way: Responding to Clergy Sexual Misconduct* (Boston: Unitarian Universalist Women's Association, 1992).

50. Rev. Jody Shipley, "Please Call Us Clergy," 25 July 1990 (typescript). Rev. Jody Shipley is minister of UU Fellowship of Stanislaus County, Modesto, California.

Conversions and Their Consequences: Women's Ministry and Leadership in the United Methodist Tradition

Rosemary Skinner Keller

INTRODUCTION

> When the spirit of God has been generated in a human being, it must not be shut up in the prayer-meeting or the church building, but turned on the saloons, the gambling houses, the haunts of shame.

Frances Willard challenged her sisters in the Woman's Christian Temperance Union (WCTU) with these words in her Presidential Address of 1897.[1] Willard's own activist persuasion to build a better world was undergirded by her commitment to the Christian faith which was born and nurtured in "my own Methodist hive," the communities of home and church in which she grew up.[2] Her spirited words focus the goal of "conversions and their consequences," the unity of spirituality and social responsibility, in the lives of evangelical women in the United Methodist tradition.[3]

This study of lay and clergy ministerial leadership centers on the relationship between the process of conversion and the fruits of the sanctified life in selected women's experiences. A case-study approach is employed to analyze and compare the formative experience of five female pioneers from the origins of the denominational tradition in North America in the late eighteenth century through the nineteenth and early twentieth centuries. The essay considers both the personal and social motivations which led, first, to changes in these women which were inward and personal and, second, to commitments by the women to change social structures of the home, church, and society in ways that were radical for their times.

Their experiences demonstrate an evolving and expanding tradition of conversions and their consequences in the lives of women in the United Methodist tradition. The women include: Catherine Livingston Garrettson, who stretched the boundaries of her household to make it a center of public domesticity during the American Revolution; Amanda Berry Smith, one of the first African-American women in the preaching tradition; Jennie Fowler Willing, lay volunteer women's society worker who was a primary organizer both of the Woman's Foreign and Home Missionary Societies in the Methodist Episcopal Church; Frances Willard, social reformer, whose name was virtually synonymous with the largest and most powerful women's organization of the nineteenth century, the WCTU; and Ida B. Wells-Barnett, African-American journalist, who pioneered the antilynching crusade and organized early black women's clubs.

Before turning directly to the women's stories, the terminology of the study needs to be defined. The United Methodist Church was created in 1968 by a union of the Methodist Church and the Evangelical United Brethren, both denominations formed by earlier mergers. It is today one of the two largest Protestant denominations in the United States. Its roots were laid in England and continental Europe in the early eighteenth century and grounded in the American colonies prior to the American War for Independence. United Methodism is usually equated with Wesleyanism, identified with the founder of the Methodist movement, John Wesley. But in addition to its Methodist heritage, United Methodism's branches of the United Brethren Church and the Evangelical Association, which originated in North America close to the time of the first Methodist societies, should be recognized.

The theological terms *conversion, sanctification,* and *calling* are little used today in mainstream Christianity, and particularly in United Methodism. However, they are central to the historic denominational tradition in the nineteenth century, and their understanding and significance are essential for interpreting the lives of the women studied.

Conversion points to a new beginning, often marked by a particular event but always part of an ongoing process, in which the direction of a person's life—one's goals, motivations, and purposes—is turned from individualistic, secular aims and values to the will of God for one's life. Conversion attests to something as radical as new birth. The recognition that sin is social as well as personal has run through the United Methodist tradition, issuing in the need for transformation of institutions as well as individuals.

Sanctification points to the new life of the Christian, which is begun in conversion and continues throughout one's life as it is nurtured in spiritual growth. It does not refer to idealized life of sainthood but to the experience of growing in heart and mind to reflect the love of God and neighbor in one's thoughts and actions. John Wesley's commission to early pastors to "reform the continent and spread gospel holiness across the land" provides a central historic emphasis of the denomination to work for the transformation of institutions as well as individuals, that they would reflect a sanctified social vision of wholeness, inclusivity, and equality of humanity.

Finally, calling from God may issue immediately from the conversion process or be experienced at any point or points on the ongoing journey of the sanctified life. As true of the Puritans, United Methodists historically have understood both a general calling to a way of life and a particular calling to one's work. United Methodists affirm the general calling of the ministry of all Christians to be lived out in secular society and work, as well as in the church. While a person may be called to a representative ministry in a church institution, no one is called to a "religious life or vocation" that sets an individual apart for a sacred life outside the mainstream of society.

CATHERINE LIVINGSTON GARRETTSON (1752–1849)

Catherine Garrettson was one of the earliest American-born converts to the Methodist movement. She has been identified primarily as the wife of Freeborn Garrettson, one of American Methodism's earliest circuit riders in the late eighteenth century. Catherine grew up in a family in which conversion was neither anticipated nor welcomed. Diane Lobody sums up the family's long-held belief that "Wealthy people simply did not have evangelical conversion experiences; having been born once into the dynasty of the Livingstons, a concomitant birth into the kingdom of God was assumed."[4]

Judge Robert Livingston, Catherine's father, was an American revolutionary patriot who served the people as a provincial judge and colonial legislator. This inheritance specifically was passed on to his oldest son, Robert, a delegate to the Continental Congress and member of the committee to draft the Declaration of Independence. The judge and his wife, Margaret Beckman Livingston, accommodated each other's religious traditions: family members worshiped together during winters in Catherine's father's Anglican church in New York City and in summers in the Dutch Reform Congregation of her mother in the Rhinebeck area of upstate New York.

Personal and social events colluded during and following the War for Independence, creating the dire need within Catherine for a conversion experience. After three male family members died within three weeks and were survived by three widows, Catherine recalled that she "wildly ran out of the House impiously exclaiming 'what have we done, to merit such afflictions!' "[5]

With the family estate laying in ruins at the hands of British troops, the Livingston women soon returned to begin reconstructing their property and genteel life. The family, Catherine included, once again threw itself into its customary schedule of parties and balls, leading Catherine to struggle inwardly with the shallow quality and lack of purpose of her family's and social circle's grand style of living amidst destruction and a world of need.

Catherine's desire for conversion arose from her recognition of the meaninglessness and impermanence of an entire social system: her upper-class life and its economic affluence, social prestige, and religiously comfortable environment. Through a process of conversion, extending at least from 1776 until 1789, "Catherine's entire sense of self had changed, and she plunged herself into a devotional piety and radical asceticism that stood in obstinate opposition to the values, the principles, and the life-style of the Livingstons and their social circle." A dream in 1789 vividly conveyed her new birth:

> I was wandering with one of my brothers in a large building; after passing through many strange scenes, he took me to a trunk where he said he had a nest of birds' eggs. I took one of the eggs, and while in my hand, the most beautiful bird came out I had ever seen. Its size was that of a blue bird, the plumage like the peacock, but the colors rich and more bright. After looking at it some time, I went to the door and gave it liberty, which it unwillingly received. I returned to the nest, and found a wren just bursting its shell; here all my interest was at once fixed. I watched and as soon as it was disengaged I put it in my bosom. There were more birds, but I felt no interest in any.[6]

As Catherine interpreted her dream, the flamboyant peacock symbolized her old, now discarded self, while the wren was her newly converted evangelical being.

The Livingston family strenuously opposed Catherine's marriage to Freeborn Garrettson, the itinerant preacher whose values were in direct opposition to its own. After his conversion, Freeborn had freed his slaves, become a pacifist during the Revolutionary War, and preached a gospel of God's freely given grace in Jesus Christ, leading persons to respond by radically committing their whole beings to God's purposes. Catherine sought a calling from God which would make her "a profitable servant. . . . Set me upon some work. I long to be doing something." However, she vigorously decried the idea of having "any desire to become a public speaker."[7]

In a day before public ministries of women were sanctioned, Catherine's marriage in 1793 opened the door to "a socially acceptable and personally fruitful setting" of public domesticity in which to carry out her calling to profitable servanthood. Conversion had led to sanctification in Catherine's experience, the process of living out her calling for the rest of her life.

The Garrettsons built a large home in the Rhinebeck area which Bishop Frances Asbury named Traveler's Rest, a retreat "center of Catherine's ministry of hospitality and the headquarters for her evangelistic endeavors." Though Catherine identified it as her private household and herself a wife and mother, Lobody interprets it as very much a public household:

> Within this home that was both public and private, Catherine constructed a ministry that was entirely acceptable as a feminine enterprise and yet as vibrantly pastoral as any man's ministry. She organized and presided over regular services of worship (barring only the celebration of the sacraments); she taught Bible and theology to children, young people, and adults; she mobilized and conducted prayer groups; she expounded the scriptures within the setting of home worship, she solicited testimonies of salvation and encouraged unbelievers to repent; and she functioned, both in person and in correspondence, as a pastoral counselor and spiritual director for a great variety of persons. She was in practice a preacher, teacher, evangelist, and pastor.[8]

Catherine Garrettson's ministry was unique for her day in the American colonies. Due to the upheaval of the War for Independence and the necessity to lay foundations for the new nation, most women in the United Methodist tradition continued to maintain conventional roles in the home. By 1849, the year of Catherine Garrettson's death, white women were entering a variety of public ministries as lay preachers and traveling evangelists, and as organizers of women's organizations in church and social reform movements. In the United Methodist tradition, women described these consequences of conversion and call as expressions of the life of holiness. African-American women emerged as preachers in the broader Methodist tradition before their white sisters did, evidenced by autobiographical accounts of

Jarena Lee, between 1809 and 1816, and Zilpha Elaw and Julia Foote, also in the early nineteenth century.[9]

AMANDA BERRY SMITH (1837–1915)

Amanda Smith was the most well known among African-American female evangelists in the nineteenth century, a pioneer preacher both to white and black audiences in the United States and in Africa, India, and England. With a background both in the African Methodist Episcopal Church and the Methodist Episcopal Church, Smith was described by Methodist Episcopal Bishop James Thoburn, after working with her in India, as the person from whom "I had learned more that had been of actual value to me as a preacher of Christian faith . . . than from any other one person I had ever met."[10]

Born in slavery on a Maryland farm, Amanda Berry was the daughter of Samuel and Marian (Matthews) Berry. She gained her freedom as a small child when her father bought the family out of slavery and moved its members to Pennsylvania. She was educated entirely at home by her parents and made her way in the world as a washerwoman and domestic servant until becoming a full-time revivalist and evangelist.

Amanda Berry's first marriage, to Calvin Devine, resulted in the birth of a daughter, Mazie, whom she raised to adulthood. Devine enlisted in the Union Army but never returned home after the Civil War. Amanda's conversion occurred after his departure and before her second marriage to James Smith. The death of her second husband came the same month in which she received her direct commission from God: Amanda understood herself released from marriage, her socially defined purpose, for her own vocation in ministry.

The process of conversion, sanctification, commission, and call can be traced through Amanda Berry Smith's own account in her autobiography and Nancy Hardesty and Adrienne Israel's interpretation.[11] While dreams and visions are normative to evangelical conversions of white as well as black persons, they are characteristically more dramatic in African-American experiences, as can be seen in comparing Amanda Smith's account to Catherine Garrettson's. In Smith's conversion narrative God and the Devil are cast as contending authorities of divine liberation and social subjection in a society characterized by white male patriarchal authority and racial and sexual oppression.

Smith's conviction of her personal sin of pride is characteristic of eighteenth- and nineteenth-century conversion accounts and contrasts with the collective nature of sin that Garrettson saw in her affluent family lifestyle. Smith wrote, "I cannot remember the time from my earliest childhood that I did not want to be a Christian, and would often pray alone." But she constantly confronted her own strong will and pride in her effort to relate to God on her own terms. She prayed and struggled week after week. God continually showed her "I was a dreadful sinner, but still I wanted to have my own way about it." As Garrettson's family believed their upper-class status and conventional piety set them beyond the need for conversion, Smith also appealed to some class difference within the African-American community in her defense. In her mind she told God, "I am not so bad as Bob Loney, Meil Snively, and a lot of others. I am not like them, I have always lived in first-class families and have always kept company with first-class servant girls, and I don't need to go there [to the altar] and pray like those people do."[12]

The disobedience and willfulness that kept her from giving herself fully to God came to a head when Smith was nineteen. "I prayed incessantly, night and day, for light and peace." But at the same time, "I began to plan my spring suit; I meant to be converted, though I had not given it all up . . . I had it all picked out in my mind, my nice spring and summer suit. I can see the little box now where I had put my money, saving up for this special purpose. . . . The Devil told me I was such a sinner God would not convert me. When I would kneel down to pray at night, he would say, 'You had better give it up; God won't hear you, you are such a sinner.' "[13]

Smith's "idea of great sin was disobedience," springing from her love of worldly goods. In the sun, moon, stars, and wind Amanda saw entities that always obeyed God's purpose, so she sought their intervention on her behalf. "O, Moon and Stars, you have never sinned like me, you have always obeyed God, and kept your place in the heavens; tell Jesus I am a poor sinner." Amanda saw her craving for the new suit as preventing her conversion. "I wanted relief from the burden and then all at once there came a quiet peace in my heart and that suit never came before me again."[14]

But Amanda Berry Smith still felt the need to make a positive commitment of her will to God, and the conversion process continued. Standing at her ironing board one day, she experienced the Devil continually telling her that there was no hope for her conversion. Placing the will of God before the command of her white employers, she determined to do no work in setting their meal on the table for supper. She went down to the cellar to die, "and O, Hallelujah, what a dying that was!" Smith pleaded to God three times to convert her soul. "Then somehow I seemed to get to the end of everything. I did not know what else to say or do. Then in my desperation I looked up and said, 'O, Lord, if Thou wilt help me I will believe Thee,' and in the act of telling God I would, I did. O, the peace and joy that flooded my soul!"[15] She realized that only as she consciously responded to God's action on her life could the conversion be real. God was not the only actor in the drama.

Smith graphically described her new life in physical terms: "I looked at my hands, they looked new; I took hold of myself and said, 'Why I am new, I am new all over. . . .' There seemed to be a halo of light all over me; the change was so real." She went into her dining room and looked at herself in a tall mirror "to see if anything had transpired in my color, because there was something wonderful had taken place inside of me, and it really seemed to me it was outside too, and as I looked in the glass I cried out, 'Hallelujah, I have got religion; glory to God, I have got religion.' "[16]

The subsequent experience of entire sanctification brought to Amanda Berry Smith a radical acceptance of her blackness. It came on a Sunday morning in 1868 when she felt compelled to attend an all-white church, the Green Street Methodist Episcopal Church, in New York City to hear the Holiness preacher John Inskip:

> Somehow I always had a fear of white people—that is, I was not afraid of them in the sense of doing me harm, or anything of that kind—but a kind of fear because they were white, and were there, and I was black and was here! But that morning on Green street, as I stood on my feet trembling, I heard these words distinctly. They seemed to come from the northeast corner of the church, slowly, but clearly: "There is neither Jew nor Greek, there is neither bond nor free, there is neither male nor female, for ye are all one in Christ Jesus." (Galatians 3:28) I never understood that text before. But now the Holy Ghost made it clear to me. And as I looked at white people that I had always seemed to be afraid of, now they looked so small. The great mountain had become a mole-hill.[17]

The primary expression of sanctification gained after the death of her second husband lay in Smith's preaching mission. Amanda Berry Smith's preaching eventually took her to three continents. She spent several months both in England and India, eight years in Liberia, and many more in the United States, evangelizing primarily in Holiness camp meetings.

Smith's call to preach, which came as vividly in a vision as had her experiences of conversion and sanctification, was a confirmation of the sure path on which God had set her. It happened again in a church service two years later, an event which Smith described as "My Last Call." This time she was led to the Fleet Street African Methodist Episcopal Church in Brooklyn. The old Devil Tempter kept prodding: "Now if you are wholly sanctified, why is it that you have these dull feelings?" Smith then described "My Last Call":

> I was sitting with my eyes closed in silent prayer to God, and after he had been preaching about ten minutes, as I opened my eyes, just over his head I seemed to see a beautiful star, and as I looked at it, it seemed to form into the shape of a large white tulip; and I said, "Lord, is that what you want me to see? If so, what else?" And then I leaned back and closed my eyes. Just then I saw a large letter "G," and I said: "Lord, do you want me to read in Genesis, or in Galatians? Lord what does this mean?"
>
> Just then I saw the letter "O." I said, "Why, that means go." And I said "What else?" And a voice distinctly said to me "Go preach."
>
> The voice was so audible that it frightened me for a moment, and I said, "Oh, Lord, is that what you wanted me to come here for? Why did you not tell me when I was at home, or when I was on my knees praying?" But His paths are known in the mighty deep, and His ways are past finding out. On Monday morning, about four o'clock, I think, I was awakened by the presentation of a beautiful, white cross—white as the driven snow. . . . It was as cold as marble. It was laid just on my forehead and on my breast. It seemed very heavy; to press me down. The weight and the coldness of it were what woke me; and as I woke I said: "Lord, I know what it is. It is a cross."
>
> I arose and got on my knees, and while I was praying these words came to me: "If any man will come after Me let him deny himself and take up his cross and follow Me." And I said, "Lord, help me and I will."[18]

For women in the United Methodist tradition, conversion was primarily a matter of the will: giving up selfish desires and taking on the purposes that God had for their lives. "Surrender of the will" was their language commonly used to signify the process of new birth and the new life of calling and sanctification that issued from it.

JENNIE FOWLER WILLING (1934–1916)

The conversion of Jennie Fowler Willing led her to pioneer in initiating early organizations for female causes both in the church and in society. The daughter of Horatio and Harriet (Ryan) Willing, she mar-

ried William C. Willing, a Methodist Episcopal pastor, in 1853. They
began their life together in New York state but spent most of their marriage and ministry in Illinois. Jennie and William were childless but
prided themselves on a marriage which they termed a "partnership of
equals." William encouraged his wife, who saw herself as timid and
shy before she entered into a full-fledged public ministry in church and
social reform work throughout most of their marriage.[19]

When Willing looked back on her own conversion experience later
in life, the theme of release from a woman's traditional middle-class
lifestyle within the home to a broader field of service in the world is
dominant:

> I shall never forget that hour when I made that surrender. One af-
> ternoon when the Holy Spirit sent His light into the depths of my
> soul, I discovered, hidden away, like the wedge of gold in my soul,
> a determination to work, and study, and make something of my-
> self. Not that I might win the wealth and honors of the world, but
> I would make for myself a dainty, little snuggery into which I
> would bring a few fine books and pictures, some good music, and
> a coterie of choice friends. The loud, rough, coarse old world might
> wag its way, and not a whit would I care for its tinsel and show,
> nor its troubles either—do you see? The Lord in kindness threw a
> picture upon the canvas that day, that gave me to see how wick-
> edly selfish was my little scheme. I saw myself in a hospital with
> scores of people who were dying, and there was no one to give
> them their medicine, or even a cup of cold water. I had been sent
> there under orders to help all whom I could possibly reach; and
> there I was, planning to fit up my exquisite little room, in one cor-
> ner, its walls padded to shut out the groans, and to shut in the deli-
> cacy and beauty that I hoped to gather about me. I saw that
> selfishness like that could never get into heaven. . . . When I saw
> that, I was enabled to say "I give it all up. Henceforth for me, only
> thy will, and thy work." The pain of the surrender was so severe
> that a knife seemed to pierce my heart, and the tears leaped from
> my eyes. Let me add that all these years, just in proportion as I
> have held myself loyal to that surrender, has God given me richly
> to enjoy the things that I put aside to accept His will.[20]

Her "surrender" to God marked a conversion in Willing's life
from the values at the heart of middle-class culture, just as Garrettson
and Smith had understood themselves released from personal material
goals. With conversion came a calling from God to fulfill God's purpose for their lives. And that calling issued in an expanded life for each

woman, bringing release from particular constrictions which society put upon women of their class, race, and time: for Garrettson from private to public domesticity, for Smith from washerwoman to world evangelist, and for Willing from "professional" manager of the middle-class home to lay "professional" volunteer in church and society.

Willing's life expressed the "Do Everything Policy" that Frances Willard conceived for white middle-class female reformers of her day. In organizing and coordinating the work of the newly formed Woman's Foreign Missionary Society and Woman's Home Missionary Society of the Methodist Episcopal Church, Willing's work lay at the heart of her sanctified life. But at different times in her life, out of her calling to "accept His will," she also taught English at Illinois Wesleyan University, where she helped organize the Woman's Education Association, worked in the WCTU crusades, had a local preacher's license, and pastored a church in Chicago. When she was sixty-one years old, after her husband's death, Willing opened the New York Training School and Settlement House in Hell's Kitchen in New York City. She was president emerita of the Eighteenth Street Methodist Episcopal Church Woman's Foreign Missionary Society, president of the Frances Willard WCTU of New York City, and organizer of the New York State WCTU at the time of her death at age eighty-two.

Jennie Fowler Willing went further than most professional female volunteers of her day in her understanding of the shortcomings of philanthropy and the relationship of middle-class reformers to underprivileged persons in need. As noted by Joanne Brown, her words anticipate those of liberation theologians of the late twentieth century:

> The subject race must be made to comprehend its own dignity. The principle violated in human servitude is the inherent greatness of humanity, and they who are under can be trusted to rise to equality or superiority only as they apprehend this principle. Without that apprehension, a change of position would be only a change of tyrannies. To lift up a man, or a race, one need not trouble himself to make the oppressor understand the worth of the slave. Let him teach the slave his own dignity and trust him to make his master comprehend that lesson. The liberator must also see so plainly the tremendous import of human life, that he will go down among the oppressed and share the obloquy of their wrongs, sustained by his belief in the intrinsic human royalty.[21]

FRANCES WILLARD (1839–1898)

Frances Willard once introduced Jennie Fowler Willing by stating that her life personified this goal: "The life of aimless reverie must be replaced by the life of resolute aim."[22] This transformation of will lay at the heart of conversion and its consequences in the lives of both Willing and Willard. Willard's leadership of the WCTU, the largest women's organization of its time in the world, from 1879 until 1898 was the product of the consequences of the converted life.

The daughter of Mary Thompson (Hill) Willard and Josiah Flint Willard, Frances spent most of her growing-up years living with her family on a farm in southeastern Wisconsin "reveling in a carefree, country existence." She received much of her three and a half years of formal education at home during this period. Her parents, who had been Congregationalists, joined the Methodist Church while in Wisconsin. In 1858, when Willard was nineteen, the family moved to the newly founded village of Evanston, just north of Chicago, "a calculated relocation in order to live in a center of Methodist education and acquire for their children 'enlightened intellects' capable of directing 'regenerate hearts.' " To this end their son, Oliver, entered Garrett Biblical Institute, on the North Western University campus, to become a candidate for the Methodist ministry, and Frances and her sister, Mary, matriculated at the North Western Female College.[23]

The Christian nurture, so intently bred into Willard, led her by her late teens to commit herself to a life of moral earnestness. Her quest was graphically focused when she was nineteen years old and her life was threatened by typhoid fever. As Willard struggled between the two voices of faith within her, those of reason and the heart, the "crisis was resolved, at least momentarily, when her soul responded to what she perceived as the warm, comforting call of God rather than to the cold, dismal voice of reasoning skepticism. . . . At the urging of the voice of God within her, Willard called to her mother, watching in the room next door to her as she lay ill. 'Mother,' she announced weakly, 'I wish to tell you that if God lets me get well I'll try to be a Christian girl.' "[24]

Carolyn Gifford sums up Willard's quest of conversion and its consequences: "For Willard, as for the evangelical world in which she lived, a moral life was synonymous with a holy life, one lived in conformity with God's will and with God's aid. Acquiring character was a Christian aim sought by the converted."[25]

For Frances Willard at age nineteen, her striving to gain character was an effort to prepare herself for conversion, which meant to her: to become a Christian, or to be relieved of the tension "between her in-

tellectual knowledge of Christ and her continuing inability to transform that knowledge into the trusting certainty of his presence. . . . She
was convinced that she must feel Christ in her heart as well as comprehend his Person and meaning with her mind."[26] Willard sought, in
John Wesley's words, that her heart would be "strangely warmed."

Preaching during a December 1859 revival in Evanston, Methodist
Episcopal Bishop Matthew Simpson told Willard and other congregants that they should not be troubled waiting for the right *feeling* in
their hearts prior to conversion. Rather, they should simply seek to live
a good life, and in time the right feeling would follow. This no-non-
sense advice provided the impetus for a conversion experience in
Frances Willard's life that was significantly different from the experiences of her Methodist sisters presented in this chapter.

By a willful act, not by a warmed heart, Willard made the decision
at age nineteen and went forward to the altar of the Methodist church
in Evanston to affirm her faith publicly. After joining the church on
probation one year later, she was subsequently baptized and received
into membership.

The spiritual journey during the year-and-a-half period, from hearing Bishop Simpson's sermon until becoming a member of the church,
amounted to a conversion process in Willard's life. If a date of conversion had to be named, it would be 5 May 1861, the day on which
she was taken into full church membership and, in her words, "Mary
[Willard's young sister] and I publicly declared our determination to
endeavor—with God's help—to live as *Christians*".[27] For Willard, this
decision marked the change in values, motivation, and direction that
defines conversion.

Brief excerpts from her journal during this period, that have been
edited by Gifford, document the conversion process in Willard's life:

> *December 22, 1859.*
> Though I have yet no evidences of that change of purpose—that
> reconciliation to God—that active Peace—which I believe accom-
> panies conversion, I am not discouraged. I see many reasons to
> hope that gradually I shall come to be "in the light as He is in the
> light." I enjoy reading the Bible, and I used to dislike it; I am will-
> ing & glad to talk with my friends about the Interest of all our
> lives, and I used never to mention it; I find it today comparatively
> easy to be silent when angry . . . if I read the Bible thoughtfully,
> and reflect upon what the Past has done, the Present is Doing &
> the Future will do for me, I shall "through the forbearance of
> God" come to be a child of His.

May 5, 1861.
An eventful day to me.

    Mary & I publicly declared our determination to endeavor—
with God's help—to live as *Christians*; we were baptized, received
into the Church & Communed. . . .

    . . . Life looks rich & beautiful to me—full of joy and blessed-
ness. I think only too much about it, & with all this, I feel that no
purpose is so deep & all pervading with me, as the purpose to live
for God in the world, & no desire is so strong as the desire to have
Him smile upon me here & take me to Himself *at last.*[28]

    To live as a Christian, to follow the path of the sanctified life, meant
that Frances Willard would focus her vision of social reform upon the
cause of women for the rest of her life. She believed that in Christianity
lay the greatest promise of women's emancipation, a resolve that she
shared with Jennie Fowler Willing. Seeking to reform Christianity itself, Willard, as a delegate from her Rock River Conference in the
1890s, became one of the first female delegates who tried, unsuccess-
fully, to be seated at the General Conference of the Methodist Episcopal
Church.[29] Willard stated that if she had been born at a different time
she would have been a minister; she even wrote a book defending the
right of women to preach that was entitled *Woman in the Pulpit.*[30]

    Willard's commitment to advance the cause of women through her
faith was grounded in her vocation, first as a public school teacher,
then as president of the Northwestern Ladies College from 1870 until
1874, and finally as president of the WCTU from 1879 until her death in
1898. Believing herself called by God, she also called upon the WCTU
to make the same commitment.

    Realizing that most of the women who united in the WCTU shared
her allegiance to the institutional church, Willard used conservative
language to enlist them in enlarging, indeed in breaking down, spheres
of women's activity in society. She redefined womanhood in terms of
"calling," using that language to prod women to speak and protest in
churches, city and state governmental chambers, saloons, and gam-
bling halls. In similar language, she urged them and their daughters to
vote, seek college educations, and enter professions. Temperance work
was an expression of "home protection," and Willard sought to spread
the moral influence of the home and womanhood throughout society.
Language such as "the ballot for home protection" and to "make the
world more home-like" effectively released thousands of women to
their callings from God. "Perhaps they could indeed 'Do Everything,'
since God expected this of them. At least they could try."[31]

IDA B. WELLS-BARNETT (1862–1931)

Ida B. Wells-Barnett was an African-American woman who agreed with Frances Willard on the sanctity of the home and the "Do Everything Policy" for women, while arguing bitterly with Willard regarding the relationship of black and white women in the antilynching crusade. She is distinguished today as an African-American woman who pioneered as a journalist and speaker in the antilynching movement and as the organizer of the first black woman's club in Illinois. Her life presents a fifth and final model of conversion and its consequences in the lives of women in the United Methodist tradition.[32]

In common with the other women previously discussed, the consequence of her conversion was a radical social commitment. But distinctive from the women studied earlier, Ida B. Wells-Barnett's conversion resulted from an agonizing personal experience of oppression.

Like her predecessor Amanda Berry Smith, Wells-Barnett was born in slavery in the South, at Holly Springs, Mississippi, and her father bought the family's freedom when she was only three years old. Unlike Smith and her vibrant description of conversion, Wells-Barnett did not report a specific conversion experience, and so what conversion meant in her life must be reconstructed.

Wells-Barnett's childhood and young adult religious life can be compared in significant ways to that of Frances Willard. From her earliest years, Ida and her family attended the local Methodist Episcopal Church. Her parents were devoutly religious, permitting only the Bible to be read in the home. Consequently, as a child, she read the Bible over and over.[33]

Wells's mother, Lizzie Bell, the child of a slave mother and an Indian father, had come from Virginia. James Wells, Ida's father, was active in Reconstruction politics and expanded Ida's and her siblings' world by introducing them to leading African-American politicians. He also enabled Ida to attend Rust College. However, her education was tragically interrupted when her parents and one sister died in a yellow fever epidemic. To support her remaining five sisters and brothers, Ida B. Wells adopted the same initial occupation as did Willard: she became a public school teacher.

Wells soon questioned her commitment to the vocation of teacher. During these early years she began to write for black newspapers, and from the first she protested the social conditions to which the African-American community was subjected, particularly the degradation of inferior education and the horror of lynching.

Emilie Townes describes Ida's life-turning experience when she was twenty-two years old:

> Wells boarded a train for the ten-mile trip from Memphis to Wood-stock to join her family. As was her custom, she seated herself in the women's car. The conductor refused her ticket and ordered her into the smoking car with other blacks. Wells refused to move, and it took three men to pry her from her seat and throw her off the train when it stopped at the next station. As she tumbled down the stairs to the platform, white passengers stood up and applauded.[34]

Ida B. Wells sued and was awarded five hundred dollars in damages. However, the Chesapeake and Ohio Railroad appealed, and the decision was reversed in its favor three years later by the Tennessee Supreme Court. Wells agonized over the higher court's reversal. She struggled with her personal sense of duty in light of her shattered belief in the legal system of justice: "I have firmly believed all along that the law was on our side and would, when we appealed to it, give us justice. I feel shorn of that belief and utterly discouraged, and just now, if it were possible, would gather my race in my arms and fly away with them."[35]

Conversion and call were central to her personal response, as she appealed to God to direct her life so that she could address this social outrage: "O God, is there no redress, no peace, no justice in this land for us? Thou hast always fought the battles of the weak and oppressed. Come to my aid at this moment and teach me what to do, for I am sorely, bitterly disappointed. Show us the way, even as Thou led the children of Israel out of bondage into the promised land."[36] Though human justice was denied, Ida B. Wells was uplifted and empowered by God to assume a role of social leadership on behalf of her people.

Wells did not speak directly of a conversion experience. Rather, she assumed her conversion and the responsibility that it laid upon her. As she wrote in her diary on 3 January 1887, "God help me to be a Christian! To so conduct myself in my intercourse with the unconverted."[37] Her immediate call, she decided at age twenty-five, was to teach a Sunday school class for young African-American men. She was convinced that their moral and vocational development was essential to enable the black community to rise in its standard of living.

In 1895 Wells married Ferdinand Barnett, a Chicago lawyer, and took the hyphenated last name of Wells-Barnett. The couple had five children, and Ida remained a strong advocate of the cult of True Womanhood, the conviction that her sex was invested with the primary responsibility of purveyor of moral integrity and virtue in both home and society.[38] For a time during her marriage and motherhood, Wells-Barnett retired into the home. However, she had already established herself as a prophetic crusader to fight the horror of lynching. Public outcry, particularly among African Americans, brought her back into public life. Wells-Barnett carried her campaign throughout the North and England to mobilize support. Her calling to her "intercourse with the unconverted" was primarily directed to larger social arenas, although she remained active in the church. She never wavered in interpreting the responsibility of her sanctified life as rooted in her calling from God.

Further, Wells-Barnett interpreted that faith to others, even her African-American brothers whom she believed falsely accused under the United States legal system, as the great hope of their lives. In her autobiography she told of visiting twelve black men who were sentenced to death on charges of murder and leadership of a riot in Arkansas. She wrote:

> Finally I got up and walked close to the bars and said to them in a low tone, "I have been listening to you for nearly two hours. You have talked and sung and prayed about dying, and forgiving your enemies, and of feeling sure that you are going to be received in the New Jerusalem because your God knows that you are innocent of the offense for which you expect to be electrocuted. But why don't you pray to live and ask to be freed? The God you serve is the God of Paul and Silas who opened their prison gates, and if you have all the faith you say you have, you ought to believe that he will open your prison doors too.
>
> If you do believe that, let all of your songs and prayers hereafter be songs of faith and hope that God will set you free; that the judges who have to pass on your cases will be given the wisdom and courage to decide in your behalf. That is all I've got to say. Quit talking about dying; if you believe your God is all powerful, believe he is powerful enough to open these prison doors, and say so. Dying is the last thing you ought to even think about, much less talk about. Pray to live and believe you are going to get out.[39]

In fact, the men were not set free but were put to death. But Ida never faltered in her trust in the all-loving and powerful God who finally would bring justice. This grave miscarriage of justice confirmed her prophetic calling to expose the "terrible indictment of white civilization and Christianity. It shows that the white people did just what they accused the Negroes of doing; murdered them and stole their crops, their stock, and their household goods. And even then they were invoking the law to put the seal of approval on their deeds by legally executing those twelve men who were found guilty after six minutes' deliberation."[40]

CONCLUSION

Ida B. Wells-Barnett, prophet to African Americans and Euro-Americans, to the Christian Church and the United States, follows in the train of Catherine Livingston Garrettson, Amanda Berry Smith, Jennie Fowler Willing, and Frances Willard in expanding the vision and contribution of women to ministerial leadership. Their experiences of conversions and their consequences need to be analyzed in light of the United Methodist background.

In the United Methodist tradition, John Wesley's conversion experience on Aldersgate Street in London has become "a virtual paradigm of conversion within the tradition."[41] That paradigm has been assumed as normative from the perspective of male experience, and only within the last decade and a half have the stories of women been recovered to provide a broader dimension. Wesley's understanding of sin and the process of conversion was highly individualistic and personal. In his account Wesley testified that his heart was "strangely warmed" and then "an assurance was given me that He had taken away *my* sins, even *mine*, and saved *me* from the law of sin and death."[42] This paradigm of conversion is taken for granted far beyond the United Methodist tradition.

Beyond their personal experiences, the motivations of these five women's conversions were rooted in corporate causes of class and race. Catherine Garrettson's conversion resulted from her confrontation with the meaninglessness and impermanence of her upper-class life, including its economic affluence, social prestige, and religiously accommodationist environment. Amanda Berry Smith recognized her willfulness in elevating herself within the class structure of her African-American society, believing herself more worthy in God's eyes, as well as her community's, than lower-class black persons. Similarly, Jennie Fowler Willing's conversion account provides a radical rejection of the values of her middle-class lifestyle and the isolation from the world's needs inherent in individualistic values.

For Ida B. Wells-Barnett, her personal confrontation with the sin of corporate racist structures lay at the heart of her conversion experience. The social outrage inflicted upon her by the legal system in upholding the injustice of her ouster from the Chesapeake and Ohio train caused Wells-Barnett to turn to God to relieve social injustice. She made herself ready for conversion by trusting in God to destroy social sin and utilizing her personal efforts to help do so.

In the United Methodist tradition, the commission to "reform the continent and spread gospel holiness across the land" constitutes the vision of sanctification in personal terms and the reign of God on earth in social terms. The balance has been erroneously tilted to emphasize either social responsibility or personal spirituality, at the expense of the other, by various groups within the denomination and mainstream Protestantism over the centuries. The case studies present documented examples of women who integrated and balanced the personal dimensions of faith with the public expressions of action.

Beyond their obvious contributions to human betterment through social reform movements, these women's experiences of calling meant expansion of long-held female roles through God-given sanction. Personal fulfillment in terms of more purposeful lifestyles was not antithetical but rather the natural outgrowth of their responses to the calling of God.

This study presents notable differences in the experiences of evangelical women in the United Methodist tradition from those studied by Virginia Brereton in her book *From Sin to Salvation: Stories of Women's Conversions, 1800 to the Present*.[43] Brereton terms evangelicalism as "coterminous with mainline Protestantism" in the nineteenth century and claims that the experiences she describes were the norm among nineteenth-century women who were Methodists, Congregationalists, Presbyterians, Baptists, and members of Reformed groups. However, the stories of women whom she studies fit more into the traditional male model of an individualistic understanding of sin, with no reference to a critique of sinful social structures. Further, while Brereton notes that many of the women in her study entered wider fields of church activity after their conversions, no mention is made of evangelical women being drawn into wider and more radical realms of social reform.

Evidence of the natural affinity of United Methodism to the liberation traditions of feminist and womanist theology and ethics emerges through the experiences of women studied in this essay.[44] The emphasis of feminism has been upon rights, equality, and opportunities for white women, while black womanism places the similar causes of African-American women at the center of its agenda. Both traditions cross denominational lines, but in the United Methodist heritage they each affirm conversion as a radical change in allegiance and loyalty to Christ, leading to personal appropriation of grace and institutional responsibility for the human and created order. Calling and sanctification offer the potential for the genuinely radical experience, both personally and socially, at the heart of the meaning of transformation. Describing women's experiences helps to expand the United Methodist tradition by spelling out experiences which may also apply to men's spiritual journeys.

This study provides a corrective to the view of notable secular feminist scholars, such as Carolyn Heilbrun, who contend that response to calling from God means a submergence of a woman's personal will.[45] These scholars also hold that women in religious communities have fallen back on the call of God for sanction of liberation, rather than claiming authority for their own actions and lives. Such an analysis fails to recognize the significance of the divine dictum in calling persons to their full personhood as the highest authorization of human liberation, of greater ultimate and immediate value than that provided by any social institution.

The women studied in this essay represent an evangelical tradition—a belief that God brings good news of new life to individuals and social structures—that holds together spirituality and social responsibility in the mainstream United Methodist heritage. This tradition has provided a sanction for women's ministries based upon the belief that commission and ordination for ministry, whether for women or men, laity or clergy, comes primarily from God—not from human sanction. Working out of their God-given authority, women began to open doors for institutional participation and leadership in the United Methodist tradition from the founding of the American nation.

Today the Women's Division of the Board of Global Ministries of the United Methodist Church is one of the strongest, largest, and most activist agencies of the denomination. It provides the national organizational structure for United Methodist Women, the grassroots laywomen's society that works for causes of women and children from the local church and community level to national and international mission fields. Similarly, the General Commission on the Status and Role of Women has provided strong advocacy in opening church leadership opportunities for women, particularly clergy rights and professional lay positions.

Women gained full ordination rights and conference membership in the Methodist Church in 1956, before its merger with the Evangelical United Brethren in 1968. Women in the United Methodist Church began to enter seminaries to prepare for ordination in significant numbers by the late 1960s. The numbers have steadily increased to the point that most United Methodist seminaries today have either equal counts of men and women preparing for ordination or more female than male students. The denominational process, whereby bishops appoint clergy to local congregations rather than churches calling their own pastors, has enabled congregations in United Methodism to adjust more easily to female leadership than in some denominations. Eight women have been elected bishops of the United Methodist Church since 1980. There are now female district superintendents, administrative officers serving under bishops, in every geographical jurisdiction of the denomination. The experience of women in the nineteenth-century United Methodist tradition provides much for women and men to appropriate today in developing models of ministry, leadership, and life that are expansive for the late twentieth century.

NOTES

1. Frances Willard, Presidential Address to the Woman's Christian Temperance Union, 1897, in Ida Tetreault Miller, "Frances Elizabeth Willard: Religious Leader and Social Reformer," Ph.D. dissertation, Boston University, 1978, 185.

2. *Report of the International Council of Women, Assembled by the National Woman Suffrage Association (25 March–1 April 1888)* (Washington, D.C.: Rufus Darby, printer, 1888), 423–24. Quoted in Carolyn Gifford, " 'My Own Methodist Hive': Frances Willard's Faith as Disclosed in Her Journal, 1855–1870," in *Spirituality and Social Responsibility: Vocational Vision of Women in the United Methodist Tradition*, ed. Rosemary Skinner Keller (Nashville: Abingdon Press, 1993), 81.

3. This essay primarily grows out of my editorship of the above volume, a collection of fourteen biographical studies and primary source documents on the pioneer ministries of United Methodist women from the eighteenth through the twentieth centuries. My thanks to six of the authors of that volume, Carolyn Gifford, Diane Lobody, Nancy Hardesty, Adrienne Israel, Joanne Brown, and Emilie Townes, whose essays are drawn upon in this study.

4. Diane Lobody, " 'A Wren Just Bursting Its Shell': Catherine Livingston Garrettson's Ministry of Public Domesticity," in *Spirituality and Social Responsibility*, 21; see also Lobody, "Lost in the Ocean of Love: The Mystical Writings of Catherine Livingston Garrettson," Ph.D. dissertation, Drew University, 1990.

5. Garrettson, "Autobiography," 2, 3, in Lobody, " 'A Wren Just Bursting Its Shell,' " 22.

6. Ibid., 24.

7. Letter from Garrettson to Catherine Rutsen, 17 March 1791, Ibid., 28.

8. Ibid., 29; see also documents 5 and 6, 56–59.
9. Willard L. Andrews, *Sisters of the Spirit: Three Black Women's Autobiographies of the Nineteenth Century* (Bloomington: Indiana University Press, 1989).
10. James Thoborn, "Introduction," in Amanda Smith, *An Autobiography: The Story of the Lord's Dealings with Mrs. Amanda Smith, the Colored Evangelist* (Chicago: Meyer & Brothers, Publishers, 1893; rep., Noblesville, Ind.: Newby Book Room, 1972), ix.
11. Ibid., 43–49; see also Nancy Hardesty and Adrienne Israel, "Amanda Berry Smith: A 'Downright, Outright Christian,' " in *Spirituality and Social Responsibility*, 61–79.
12. Smith, 43.
13. Ibid., 44.
14. Ibid., 45.
15. Ibid.
16. Ibid., 47.
17. Ibid., 80; quoted in document 1, Hardesty and Israel, 72.
18. Smith, 147, 148; quoted in document 2, Hardesty and Israel, 73.
19. Joanne Brown, "Shared Fire: The Flame Ignited by Jennie Fowler Willing," in *Spirituality and Social Responsibility*, 99–115; see also Brown, "Jennie Fowler Willing (1834–1916): Methodist Churchwoman and Reformer," Ph.D. dissertation, Boston University, 1983.
20. Brown, "Shared Fire," document 45.
21. Jennie Fowler Willing, *Diamond Dust* (Cincinnati: Walden & Stowe, 1880), 159; quoted in Brown, "Shared Fire," 104.
22. Frances Willard, *Woman and Temperance* (Chicago: Woman's Temperance Publication Assn., 1883), 147; quoted in Brown, "Shared Fire," 99.
23. Gifford, " 'My Own Methodist Hive,' " 81, 86.
24. Frances Willard, *Glimpses of Fifty Years: The Autobiography of an American Woman* (Boston: Woman's Temperance Publication Assn., 1889), 623; quoted in Gifford, " 'My Own Methodist Hive,' " 83, 84.
25. Gifford, " 'My Own Methodist Hive,' " 83.
26. Ibid., 84.
27. Journal of Frances Willard, 5 December 1859, quoted in Gifford, " 'My Own Methodist Hive,' " 93. The forty-nine-volume journal kept by Frances Willard from 1855 to 1870, and 1893 and 1896 (along with three brief volumes from the 1880s) is deposited at the Frances E. Willard Memorial Library in the national headquarters of the Woman's Christian Temperance Union, Evanston, Illinois. The volumes have been microfilmed as an addendum (series 5) to the *Temperance and Prohibition Papers*, ed. Randall C. Jimerson, Frances X. Blouin, and Charles A. Isetts.
28. Ibid., 92–94.
29. Carolyn Gifford, "For God and Home and Native Land," in *Women in New Worlds*, 3 vols., ed. Hilah F. Thomas and Rosemary Skinner Keller (Nashville: Abingdon, 1981), I: 310–27.

30. Frances Willard, *Woman in the Pulpit* (Chicago: Woman's Christian Temperance Publishing Association, 1888).
31. Gifford, "For God and Home and Native Land," 321.
32. Emilie Townes, "Because God Gave Her Vision: The Religious Impulse of Ida B. Wells-Barnett," in *Spirituality and Social Responsibility*, 139–93; see also Dorothy Sterling, *Black Foremothers: Three Lives* (Old Westbury, N.Y.: Feminist Press, 1979) and Townes, *Womanist Justice, Womanist Hope* (Atlanta: Scholars Press, 1993).
33. "Introduction," in Ida B. Wells-Barnett, *Crusade for Justice: The Autobiography of Ida B. Wells*, ed. Alfreda Duster (Chicago: University of Chicago Press, 1970), xv.
34. Townes, "Because God Gave Her Vision," 143.
35. "Introduction," in Wells-Barnett, *Crusade for Justice*, xvii.
36. Ibid.
37. See Wells's diary for 3 January 1887, in Townes, "Because God Gave Her Vision," document 1, 155.
38. The phrase and theme of the cult of True Womanhood was much used by writers on the subject of women in the nineteenth century and was analyzed by Barbara Welter in her classic article, "The Cult of True Womanhood: 1800–1860," in *Dimity Convictions* (Athens: Ohio University Press, 1976), 21–41.
39. Wells-Barnett, *Crusade for Justice*, 401–3; see also Townes, "Because God Gave Her Vision," document 8, 163.
40. Townes, "Because God Gave Her Vision," 163.
41. Charles Wallace, "Wesleyan Heritage," in *Encyclopedia of the American Religious Experience*, 3 vols. (New York: Scribners, 1988), 527.
42. Elisabeth Jay, ed., *The Journal of John Wesley: A Selection* (New York: Oxford University Press, 1987), 35.
43. Virginia Brereton, *From Sin to Salvation: Stories of Women's Conversions, 1800 to the Present* (Bloomington: Indiana University Press, 1991); see also Barbara Epstein, *The Politics of Domesticity: Women, Evangelism, and Temperance in 19th Century America* (Middletown, Conn.: Wesleyan University Press, 1981).
44. See Rosemary Radford Ruether and Rosemary Skinner Keller, eds., *Women and Religion in America: A Documentary History*, 3 vols. (New York: Harper & Row, 1981, 1983, 1986); see also Katie Cannon, *Black Womanist Ethics* (Atlanta: Scholars Press, 1988).
45. Carolyn Heilbrun, *Writing a Woman's Life* (New York: Norton, 1988).

Women's Ministries and the African Methodist Episcopal Tradition

Jualynne E. Dodson

INTRODUCTION

At the 1948 meeting of the General Conference of the African Methodist Episcopal (AME) Church, the governing body of the world's largest centrally organized Christian denomination of African Americans authorized the ordination of women into the Church ministry. When the General Conference met in 1994, two women were formal candidates for the highest position in the ecclesiastic structure, the position of bishop. This twentieth-century reality of AME women in the ordained ministry has been achieved through 174 years of women's struggles with and against institutional barriers. The struggle began in the second decade of the nineteenth century when AME women quietly supported activities to enhance the life of an embryonic religious association of African Americans. In 1844 the contention became visible through the defeat of a petition to authorize women to preach and exhort under the authority of the denomination. However, it would take 104 years for AME women to achieve ministerial authorization and another 46 years for their candidacy for the order of bishop to be considered.

The issue of women's participation in religious associations has confronted churches in the United States throughout the nineteenth and twentieth centuries. The central question of their right to ordination has been taken up by every Protestant denomination in the country. However, unlike other bodies, including African-American associations, the AME Church has had to respond to official requests to authorize women's participation in the ordained ministry since the 1840s. This chapter considers the story of women's struggles to attain formal and authorized ordination into the ministry of the African Methodist Episcopal Church.

The story begins with the denomination's official organization in Philadelphia in 1816. There were no formal positions for women then, and without their insistence and persistence no changes to include them would have occurred. This study will examine the impact of women's participation on nineteenth-century organizational structure and practice of the AME Church with an intent to clarify and highlight women's activities as the force that produced changes in denominational structure. The emphasis will be on previously unarticulated facts which support the idea that women's collective work, as well as their individual activities, were focused toward creating structural arrangements that included women.

WOMEN IN THE EARLY GROWTH OF THE AME CHURCH

The Preaching Women

There is little doubt that Jarena Lee, born in 1783, was the earliest African-American woman to request a license to preach under the authority of African Methodism. Some would even propose that she was the earliest black woman preacher in the United States. Mrs. Lee approached Rev. Richard Allen of the Philadelphia Bethel Church for license to preach under the authority of his congregation. The year was 1809, and a connectional association of African Methodists had yet to be organized; even independent Bethel Church had not yet been legally incorporated.

Mrs. Lee was denied a license, but she returned to Rev. Allen in 1817. This second request to license a woman occurred in a different social context. Legal status of the Philadelphia church had been established, and a connectional association of congregations called the African Methodist Episcopal Church had been officially organized.[1] Allen was now bishop of the nascent body and was all too familiar with its scarce resources. Among the many needs of the religious association was the need for effective preachers whose skill and commitment would attract new members. Requiring that only men could be preachers might be a luxury white Methodists could afford, but among the impoverished African-American community, the overriding consideration was to attract all individuals who could preach and who were devoted to African Methodism.

Allen did not officially defy Methodist tradition by issuing a license to Jarena Lee. To do so would delegitimize the young Church among the larger, more powerful white community of Methodists, not to mention within the Protestant community in general. But Richard

Allen could see that within situations of scarcity, all available and successful resources should be used. Allen knew that Jarena Lee was available and had been effective in preaching the Word since her 1809 contact with him, so he directed her "to hold prayer meetings in her own hired house and to exhort as she found liberty."[2] This response of not condemning but also not condoning women's functioning in ministerial capacities became a characteristic pattern for the first fifty years of African Methodism. This response was also supported by social facts which circumscribed the denomination: women were the majority of members in every AME congregation; women were regularly responsible for membership increases; and women consistently organized new local AME churches.[3] As such, few male leaders were prepared to stifle Church growth by broaching the question of official authority for women's preaching ministry. White Methodists might have the social wherewithal to insure that only men preached, but African Americans were a long way from such stability.

Allen avoided violating social norms requiring men preachers by only giving tacit acceptance of Mrs. Lee's request. By approving her, and thereby other women, as an exhorter and prayer leader in her own hired house, there was no discord with Methodist tradition or practice. Prayer leaders and exhorters were restricted to encouraging others to convert to Christianity through compelling testimonies. Exhorters and prayer leaders were to use personal experiences and conviction of their faith as the mechanisms in such persuasive activities. At no time were they to take a biblical text and proceed to explicate it. Within these commonly held understandings about distinctions between church preachers and others, and because their exhorting did not take place in church buildings but in homes or hired houses, leaders of African Methodism could truly say that women were not authorized African Methodist preachers. This side-stepping of Methodist doctrine and tradition allowed the AME hierarchy conveniently to capitalize on women as a resource without sharing authority with them.

By 1844, however, change was detectable. Women had taken the informal approval of their work and functioned in the preaching ministry as seriously and forthrightly as if it were authorized. Jarena Lee, for example, held many prayer meetings and found considerable liberty to exhort men and women to accept Jesus. When Bishop Allen identified to her places and situations where the African Methodist message was needed, Mrs. Lee understood this to be an official preacher's "speaking appointment." She also understood her presence at AME Conference meetings, with the Bishop and other clergy, as their authorization of her gospel work.[4]

Other women also understood the approval of their work by denominational clergy as affirmation, and they embarked upon a ministry of preaching. For example, local history of Bethel Church in Philadelphia recorded Sophie Murray as the "first evangelist" and one whose work was revered throughout the community. The same history recounted Elizabeth Cole as a woman who "held many glorious prayer meetings, and many souls were brought to the saving knowledge" by her preaching. In Washington, D.C., Harriet Felson Taylor performed the unauthorized but approved functions of a preaching minister. She "distinguished herself as the 'First Female Exhorter and Local Preacher' " of her home congregation.[5] Without formal position as clergy and without official authorization for their preaching, antebellum AME women were, nevertheless, an active component of the young denomination's growth and expansion. They also would be responsible for structural changes which would soon occur on behalf of all AME women.

Women's Collective Ministry

Individual women preachers were not the only force propelling antebellum African Methodism toward change. There were collectivities of AME women's groups whose work and success combined with that of preaching women to predict structural transformation. When ministry is understood as transmitting and nurturing Christians in their faith, guiding members in the particulars of their African Methodist tradition, and exhorting and inspiring conversion of non-Christians, the nineteenth-century work of women's groups must also be counted within the scope of ministry. Women's collective ministerial activities were a visible part of the AME landscape during the first thirty years of the denomination.

The locally based associations named Daughters of Conference began functioning as early as the 1816 organization of the connectional body of African Methodism. These women's groups existed in almost every congregation and assumed responsibility for attending to and improving material conditions of the clergy. They often supplied local pastors with food, repaired their clothing, provided covering for beds, and generally assured that a pastor's household materials were in good condition. This nurturing work of the women gave visible notice to the larger black community as well as the denomination that women's presence made for a successful local ministry. In 1827 the AME Church officially recognized Daughters of Conference but did not provide an authorized, structural position for their work.

In a similar vein, the collective activities of African-American women in New York City were so visible during the 1820s that they were acknowledged by the local press. These women held spiritually inspiring meetings and took responsibility for distribution of literature for Christian education and evangelization. It is possible that women of this New York group moved into the conversion work of preaching and/or participated in a network of female preachers. Historical facts about such an 1820s–1830s organization have yet to be verified, but official AME Church records refer to such a network of women.[7] The network may have been just a product of a male clergy's vivid imagination, given their sense of threat from women's preaching success. Nevertheless, the facts that women preached, that women traveled in their preaching, and that official records chronicled an organization suggest the visibility and effectiveness of AME women such as those in New York City.

By 1844 the stage was set and the denomination could not continue to ignore or marginalize the preaching and collective work of women. The city was Pittsburgh, Pennsylvania, and the occasion was the seventh meeting of the General Conference of the AME Church. It was Tuesday, 14 May 1844. Nathan Ward, spokesperson for a small group of delegates to the legislative body, requested that the Conference "make provisions for females to preach and exhort." Ward understood the situation and knew that, unlike petitions from AME women, the Conference had to respond to a request from official male delegates. The petition was defeated, and the 1844 vote against including women into the ordained ministry was the first of several.[8]

At the next meeting of the General Conference in 1848, a more strongly worded petition was presented. Daniel A. Payne, soon to be elected bishop, took the lead in preparing a written document which articulated the hierarchy's opposition to "the licensing of females to travel in the connection."[9] Payne's written response was necessary because the 1848 petition specifically requested approval to license women to preach in the connection with "ministerial privileges, akin to those of men."[10] A petition so clearly worded demanded a written negative response. But men's opposition did not silence women. Those who felt they had been divinely called to ministry pressed forward.

In 1852 the question of admitting women into the formal structure of AME ministry again confronted the General Conference. Again the focus of the confrontation was women who preached. This time it was the senior bishop who recommended that the body consider the question and take distinct action. Again the petition was defeated, and again negative votes of male authorities would have little real consequence for preaching women. On the contrary, women's varied ministerial activities were having an impact on the Church.

General Conference meetings were designed to conduct the denomination's business in sequential, regulated fashion as prescribed by the *Book of Discipline*. During the nineteenth century, though women were powerful and influential within local congregations, nowhere in the *Book of Discipline* were they authorized to participate in official business of the AME connectional body. However, on the three occasions cited, the "regular" business of the General Conference was interrupted to consider the "irregular" question of women's right to preach. In 1864 it was interrupted a fourth time, and again the vote was negative. Not only were women forbidden to preach under the authority of African Methodism, but they continued to have no right to hold any position within the organizational structure of the connection.

The consideration of women's rights at each of four General Conference meetings was not only irregular but significant. The Conference was a legislative body that only met every four years with a responsibility to attend to decisions which facilitated the Church's smooth functioning until the next gathering. Women could not be ordained into the clergy and therefore could not be delegates to the General Conference. Although laymen were eligible for participation as early as 1844, women were still prohibited from voting in the General Conference until they were eligible to be elected delegates to that body. Therefore, on those four occasions prior to 1868, when the body was forced to consider questions of women's participation, AME men were forced to relinquish precious time to hearing, discussing, and voting to continue their all-male clergy. Clearly, the question of women in the governing structure of the Church was a contested topic.

Newspaper editorials and official AME Church position papers were written on the subject. Men and women preached about women's ordination, and numerous local and regional groups debated the issue.[11] All the while, without representation in the governing body of their denomination, women continued to sustain membership and organize and demonstratively enhance the quality of life of the local as well as connectional AME Church. And women preachers, the heart of the contestation, went about their work with extraordinary benefit to the expansion of African Methodism.[12] It was the Church that was being affected by women's activities, rather than the other way around.

The exclusion of women from taking part in the governance of denominational affairs, not merely their exclusion from clergy positions, became a glaring contradiction by the 1860s. Women's membership in the AME Church had far exceeded men's from the beginning of the connection. Women functioning in ministerial activities were often as successful as men, and the myriad of women's associations were renowned for contributing to the social and economic stability of the denomination. There was no rational justification to continue excluding AME women from all positions of institutional structure.

By 1868 delegates attending the General Conference began to discern the contradiction between their all-male hierarchy and the significant contributions made by women to African Methodism. The representatives devised a plan of structural accommodation that would address the absence of women but not relinquish men's exclusive access to ministerial authority. They voted a new position into Church polity for women.

The new position was termed "stewardess." Stewardesses were officially charged to "look after the females of the church," and even this gender-specific task was subordinated to the supervision of churchmen. Indeed, a local pastor could choose, should a congregation not have the requisite "three to nine most influential women," to nominate qualified men as stewardesses. No such substitution option existed for the position of steward when there was, as was normally the case, a numerical absence of influential men within a given congregation.[13]

In spite of restrictions, stipulations, and impotence, however, the office of stewardess was a major accomplishment for AME women. This was a formal position within the official structure of the denomination. Never before had the AME Church included any official place for women's service, not even their nurturing role so broadly upheld by United States patriarchy. There was no official license for women to preach, but at last women were an authorized component of denominational polity.

The 1868 accommodation for stewardesses in no way modified the gender-based allocation of Church authority, but it was a significant reflection of women's power and impact on the denomination. No changes would have been made had not women's support for African Methodism been visible through their membership numbers, their collective actions, their financial contributions, and the diversified successes of all their activities on behalf of the AME Church.

THE AME CHURCH AFTER THE CIVIL WAR

Events during and after the Civil War dramatically altered the social and political context of African Methodism. On 1 January 1863, as the Emancipation Proclamation was issued, legal prohibition against independent black denominations operating in southern states was nullified. The 1863 declaration, coupled with successes of the northern Union Army, meant that the recently freed slave population was now a vast missionary field for African Methodism. Relying on its working relationship with national governmental offices, the AME Church, as did other black as well as white denominations, affiliated its clergy to military units of the Union Army. This association brought entire congregations of ex-slaves into the denomination as African Methodist ministers accompanied successful campaigns of the Union Army. Three years after the 1863 AME re-entry into the South, denominational membership increased to 73,000. This was more than three and a half times the number of congregants just one decade earlier. More significantly, women were the majority of the new members, a fact not unnoticed in 1868 and greatly influential in the decision in favor of the stewardess office.

Southern women were as actively involved with their local congregations as their northern sisters. They had aid societies, benevolent associations, Daughters of Conference, as well as stewardesses. There were also ex-slave women who were preachers, and, as elsewhere, their activities were successful but unauthorized. Charlotte S. Riley of the South Carolina Annual Conference, for example, expressed her call to gospel ministry and preaching. By the closing decades of the century, her effectiveness was eventually chronicled in the official record of conference activities, the *Journal of Proceedings of the Thirty-Third Session of the South Carolina Annual Conference*. The work of Lillian Thurman of the Alabama Annual Conference was also influential. This dynamic African Methodist woman caused an AME official to admit publicly the error of his position against women preaching. He said, "Heretofore I have not wanted to hear a woman preacher, but now I am convinced that the Lord sends out various instruments to carry his work."[14]

Unlike the former situation of the Church in the North, however, it was not southern women's preaching activities that caused structural changes. Rather, it was their missionary endeavors. Though not a direct or overt challenge to male clergy, women's activities in this arena proved to be the force that caused the hierarchy to take action it had not planned and which it did not desire.

Social Class Stratification

The mass influx of southern members to the post-Emancipation AME Church brought qualitative as well as quantitative new challenges. Most new congregants to the denomination were ex-slaves or their children. They had little if any experience with social and cultural behaviors expected by the third- and fourth-generation free-black descendants who led the denomination. Social standards regarding conduct, dress, worship practices, songs and singing, election procedures, and disciplinary action were no longer taken for granted but were regularly challenged by southerners who knew that not to challenge meant they would have no voice in AME decision-making.[15]

A glaring example of the growing, geographically grounded but obvious social-class tension was the inability of members of the General Conferences to elect new bishops from 1868 through 1880. Southern delegates persistently challenged northern candidates as not representing congregants from the South, while northern AME delegates bemoaned the common and unrefined style of their southern brothers. Northern African Methodists' resistance to the challenges were intense, but southerners quickly learned to accomplish goals by using their numerical strength in the voting process. Southerners learned to vote as a block and delay, if not stop, certain decision-making. They succeeded in preventing the election of bishops for twelve years—three successive quadrennial sessions. A visible social-class differential had seized the post–Civil War AME Church.[16]

In many ways the class tensions were grounded in paternalistic attitudes held by northern African Methodists, descendants of free blacks. Their expectations were that new, ex-slave members needed to be socialized to appropriate civil attitudes and demeanor. Little, if any, thought was given to the possibility that ex-slaves might already have "civil" demeanor, as well as experience-based attitudes about appropriate church behavior for Christians. After all, although they had been slaves, a great many had converted to Christianity and for many years had been active members of congregations—even though the congregations were plantation missions. Ex-slaves were well aware of what was needed to be good Christians and intended to transfer that consciousness to African Methodism. What they were *not* prepared to do was again be prohibited from determining the affairs of *their* own local churches or *their* new denomination. Nowhere was this more actively expressed than among southern AME missionary women.

Women and Structural Change

African Methodist missionary activities reached beyond the southern states of the United States and had begun to do so as early as 1827. In that year, and again in 1830, clergymen had been sent by the denomination to establish congregations in Haiti and Santo Domingo.

These international efforts were supplemented in the 1840s by the Church's successful missionary work west of the Allegheny Mountains. With the western expansion, the Parent Home and Foreign Missionary (PHFM) Society was established as the organizational home for African Methodist missionary enterprises. Organized endeavors were not successful, however, and to salvage the Church's reputation, not to mention rescue the lagging missionary work, an open letter to the wives of bishops was published in the *Christian Recorder*, the official newspaper of the AME Church.

The year was 1874, and the letter entreated that as "representative" AME women, bishops' wives "ought to organize a Women's Missionary Society." Women had already demonstrated their reliability, as well as their success, in supporting Church activities and in fund-raising. The male leadership wanted women's successful attributes used on behalf of organized mission work, inasmuch as men had failed in this area for the last forty years or more. The problem to surface eventually, however, was that the men had not considered that the expanded southern AME membership was not equitably represented among the council of bishops. No southern ex-slave had become bishop, which meant southern women were not among those wives of bishops who supposedly "represented" AME women.

Nevertheless, the open letter for women to organize was answered positively, and in August of 1874 in Philadelphia, AME women held the first meeting of the Women's Parent Mite Missionary (WPMM) Society. The society immediately took over support for missionary efforts in Haiti and by 1876 had raised $600. Between 1878 and 1880 the society had increased their funds and raised $1,810.10 while expending $1,583.33. Although the WPMM Society functioned throughout the denomination, most contributions came from the Northeast and the South.[17]

The South was not only contributing to the financial wherewithal of the Women's Parent Mite Missionary Society, but by 1880 AME membership had greatly increased due to converts from the South. In that year, also, southern delegates to the General Conference demonstrated the strength of their regional consciousness by electing three bishops from their area of the country. None of these events went unnoticed by southern women. They also observed that no position of leadership in the Women's Parent Mite Missionary Society was held by a southerner. True, they now had three wives of bishops to represent the region, but most of the society's leaders, including the three southerners, were of light skin color, reflecting mulatto and/or free-black heritage. The socioeconomic status differences were clear; there were no ex-slave women among those who led the WPMM. The denomination would have to respond to the presence of these ex-slave women.

Women of the South "became restless and dissatisfied" with discriminatory practices in the Women's Parent Mite Missionary Society, but their sense of a collective ministry in service to African Methodism prohibited retreating from the denomination. Instead, in September 1893 a delegation of southern women petitioned support from the bishop in charge of missionary work for the AME Church. Their entreaty was to establish a second women's organization, one which would involve the "thousands of women in the south and west who desired to work for missions." Significantly, the petitioned bishop was one of the first southerners elected to the office and astute enough to hear validity within the women's insistence. If nothing more, he felt his own agenda to initiate African Methodist missionary activities in South Africa would be helped by efforts of a second women's society. Bishop Henry McNeal Turner supported the petition.[18]

At the 1896 meeting of the Church's legislative body, the Woman's Home and Foreign Missionary Society (WHFMS) was officially incorporated as the second, specifically southern, women's missionary organization of the AME Church. This was yet another instance where the presence and activity of women were causing the entire structure of African Methodism to change.

Tension between the two women's missionary groups lingered. In a speech to the 1900 General Conference, Sara J. Duncan, general superintendent of the southern WHFM Society, made reference to the strains in polite supportive language, saying that "the Woman's [Parent] Mite Missionary Society (WPMMS) with her broad mother heart, *warmed* toward the Women's Home and Foreign [Missionary] Society."[19] The politeness of language would not cool the tension, however, as most in the Church's male-dominated hierarchy felt a single society for women's missionary work was more than sufficient. A campaign, composed mostly of male leaders, was waged for some time against the second organization.

Throughout 1903 and 1904 Sara Duncan continued to speak for southern women and their right to organizational expression. She wrote a highly charged and lengthy article, "In Vindication of 'Vital Questions'—Our Missionary Department," in response to a male-authored column, that appeared in the *Christian Recorder* on 3 December 1903. Her belief in southern women was so strong that in 1903 she closed her report to the bishops with a listing of their missionary achievements and with a challenge to the older northern women's missionary society. She said: "The [northern] Parent Mite Missionary is stronger financially and they operate systematically, ... and yet have not reached perfection. ... When we are near forty years old you will see that [financial] number in thousands instead of hundreds."[20]

For the quadrennial period 1907–1911, the WHFM Society's financial contributions were achieving Mrs. Duncan's prediction. The northern society contributed $13,960.55 to the AME Church's Missionary Department. The younger southern organization contributed $30,945.32 for the same period.[21] Rivalry between the two women's groups had expanded to another level, financial competition. In 1915, after the southern society had increased its contributions yet again, an article in a second denominational newspaper reflected the continuing internal discord. This time the difficulty centered on the women's right to receive funds they had collected. Specifically, the southern women wanted credit for their fundraising activities. Such recognition was not possible at that time, because funds collected under women's work were received by males—pastors, bishops, stewards—and forwarded to the male-controlled Missionary Department of the Church.[22]

Women were petitioning to have a direct relationship to the governing domain of male authority. It was an unheard of request, and the male leadership tried to ignore it. To respond, or even to acknowledge that women had made such a petition could prove threatening to men's authority within the Church. Even the patriarchal structures of Christian Protestantism could be threatened. African Methodist men stood at a crucial battlefront and quickly deflected the potential threat of the southern women's request for greater control over money they raised by returning the topic to its bishop's committee. The men suppressed the challenge even further by requiring an additional administrative procedure for financial missionary matters.

At the close of the nineteenth century, southern AME women in the Women's Parent Mite Missionary Society found discrimination based on socioeconomic status intolerable. They had come to the independent denomination prepared and experienced with active church participation. They had come expecting to be dynamic self-governing agents in their own religious association. Southern women adopted the issue of class discrimination and, in a manner that must be considered radical for the period, changed the structure of the denomination on behalf of those who were left out of its organizational arrangement—southern women. They insisted on an additional women's missionary society under their direction.

Although the success of a second women's missionary society demonstrated women's ability to influence and alter organizational structure, in many ways it also served to divert their focus from the earlier goal of ordination. The issue of preaching women and formal ordination had come before the General Conference as late as 1884 when Bishop Turner was reprimanded for violating Church law in ordaining Sarah Hughes of North Carolina. In 1888 the governing body rigidified its prohibition against women's ordination, and the topic did not enter legislative discussion again until the two women's missionary societies were merged in 1944.[23]

The process of merger had begun as early as November 1907 when, under deep tensions of competition, the northern WPMM Society authorized participation in a joint committee which would design articles of agreement for a single women's missionary society.[24] However, it was not until 1944 that the two societies were able to present the General Conference with an agreed-upon resolution for merger. At that same General Conference meeting, one hundred years after Nathan Ward introduced his 1844 petition, the resolution to ordain women was defeated yet again by a "small vote."[25] The women's missionary work had been merged into a single organizational arrangement, but it would take another four years—another quadrennial—before African Methodism would officially authorize the ordination of women.

Ordination does not automatically mean ministerial appointments, success, or advancement within the clergy. Twentieth-century AME women had to battle a denominational consciousness deeply wedded to men as clergy. More important, they had to fight sexist attitudes and behavior that pervaded U.S. society, including the African-American community. In spite of structural changes that had brought women into the Church's formal arrangements, there was no widespread acceptance of their ministerial leadership. Rather than regular assignment to pastor congregations based upon need and qualifications, women were overlooked, denied, or given the most difficult appointments.[26]

Such a situation began to be altered in the 1970s as women throughout the United States began to challenge their denominations on their right to ordination. African Methodist women's century-long struggles were bolstered as their Church began to respond. By the 1980s AME women were visibly located in almost every level of denominational structure, except the order of bishop. Clearly, during the next quadrennial, 1994–1998, women should continue to pursue another aspect of their goal of full participation in the Church's formal polity.

NOTES

1. A distinguishing characteristic of Methodist denominations is the linking of their congregations through a governing system of conferences led by the elected episcopacy. This system is called a "connection." Each congregation is required to belong and participate in a local, regional, and national (including international) conference. All conferences but the national/international, or General Conference, meet annually and ensure that congregations adhere to denominational doctrine as described in the *Book of Discipline*. Every four years elected representatives from each of the governing divisions meet at a General Conference to set Church policy and elect bishops. An elected bishop presides over each meeting of the several conference bodies within his district.

2. Jarena Lee, *Religious Experiences and Journal of Mrs. Jarena Lee: Giving an Account of Her Call to Preach the Gospel* (Philadelphia, 1849), 7–15.

3. Jualynne Dodson, "Women's Collective Power in the A.M.E. Church," Ph.D. dissertation, University of California, Berkeley, 1984.

4. Lee, 15–17; see also Daniel A. Payne, *History of the African Methodist Episcopal Church* (Nashville, Tenn.: Publishing House of the A.M.E. Sunday School Union, 1891 [rpt., Johnson Rpt. Corp., 1968]), 41.

5. Joseph Thompson, *Bethel Gleanings* (Philadelphia: Robert L. Holland, 1881), 34–37; see also John Francis Cook, "Outstanding Members of the First Church—September 1, 1840," manuscript, box 1 (circa 1841), Cook Family Papers, Moorland Spingarn Research Center, Howard University, Washington, D.C., p. 2.

6. *African Repository*, 1826, 290–1.

7. See Payne, 237.

8. Charles Spencer Smith, *A History of the African Methodist Episcopal Church* (Philadelphia: Book Concern of the A.M.E. Church, 1922), 422.

9. Benjamin W. Arnett, ed., *The Budget* (N.p., circa 1888), 170; see also Benjamin Tucker Tanner, *An Outline of Our History and Government for African Methodist Churchmen* (Philadelphia, 1884), 185–86.

10. Payne, 301.

11. See *A.M.E. Church Review*, 1884 to 1907 for a series of articles on the question; see also Sara Hatcher Duncan, *Progressive Missions in the South and Addresses* (Atlanta, Ga.: Franklin Printing and Publishing Co., 1906).

12. See *Christian Recorder*, new series no. 103, 91509 (18 March 1871).

13. Henry McNeal Turner, *The Genius and Theory of Methodist Polity, or the Machinery of Methodism* (Philadelphia: Publication Department, A.M.E. Church, 1885), 165–66.

14. *AME Journal of Proceedings of the Thirty-third Session of the South Carolina Annual Conference* (Philadelphia: A.M.E. Publishing House, 1897), 4, 22; see also Winfield Henri Mixon, *History of the African Methodist Episcopal Church in Alabama* (Nashville: A.M.E. Church Sunday School Union, 1902), 109–11.

15. Smith, 125–27.
16. Bishop R. R. Wright, Jr., *The Bishops of the A.M.E. Church* (Nashville: A.M.E. Church Sunday School Union, 1963), 336–38; see also Smith, 95–136.
17. Dodson, 134–35.
18. Bishop R. R. Wright, *Centennial Encyclopaedia of the African Methodist Episcopal Church* (Philadelphia: Book Concern of the A.M.E. Church, 1916), 320; see also Reverdy Cassius Ransom, *Preface to History of A.M.E. Church* (Nashville: A.M.E. Sunday School Union, 1950).
19. AME Church, *Journal of the Twenty-first Quadrennial Session of the General Conference of the African M.E. Church* (Philadelphia: A.M.E. Book Concern, 1900), 23 (my emphasis).
20. Duncan, *Progressive*, 143.
21. AME Church, *The Twenty-first Quadrennial Report of the Home and Foreign Missionary Department of the African Methodist Episcopal Church* (New York: Bible House, 1900), 20; see also Wright, *Centennial Encyclopaedia*, 320.
22. Bishop R. R. Wright, *The Encyclopaedia of the African Methodist Episcopal Church* (Philadelphia: Book Concern of the A.M.E. Church, 1947), 425; see also *Voice of Missions*, 23 February 1915.
23. For a full discussion of this story, see Stephen Ward Angell, *Bishop Henry McNeal Turner and African American Religion in the South* (Knoxville: University of Tennessee Press, 1992), 181–84.
24. Wright, *Encyclopaedia* (1947), 424–25.
25. Wright, *Encyclopaedia* (1947), 551.
26. Detailed examples of such treatment were revealed during group interviews conducted by the author with clergywomen attending meetings of "Black Women in Church and Society," Atlanta, Georgia, 1978.

The Promise Fulfilled: Women's Ministries in the Wesleyan/Holiness Movement

Susie C. Stanley

INTRODUCTION

While evangelist Lena Shoffner was preaching in Oklahoma City in 1904, a man rose and proceeded to the platform. Disrupting the meeting, he shouted: "I rebuke thee in the name of the Lord." The individual insisted Shoffner leave the pulpit. In response, "she stopped her sermon long enough to place her hand on her hip, look the opposer in the eye and tell him that they had paid rent for the hall and furnished it and if he did not like what he was hearing he could rent a place and preach as he wished."[1]

In this incident Shoffner exhibited "holy boldness," a characteristic many Wesleyan/Holiness women possessed. Gifted by the Holy Spirit, women such as Shoffner broke through the invisible boundaries of "woman's sphere" and preached. The doctrine of holiness provided an alternative social ethic that challenged the ideology that woman's place was in the home. Recognizing that "woman's sphere" was a man-made construction, women appealed to a higher authority, quoting Bible verses such as "we ought to obey God rather than men" (Acts 5:29).[2] They rejected the confining strictures of "woman's sphere" and performed the public ministries God called them to accomplish.

Sociologist Bryan Wilson has observed: "The Holiness Movement in its varied forms brought women to the fore, perhaps more than any previous development in Christianity."[3] Emerging during the nineteenth century in the United States, the Wesleyan/Holiness movement affirmed the ministry of women from its inception.[4] It offers a usable past for the support of contemporary women clergy that is lacking in most mainline Protestant denominations which only recently have granted women ordination. The movement is distinguished by the emphasis on the second work of grace, also called sanctification or perfection, a distinct experience following salvation or being born again. Sanctification, an instantaneous experience accomplished by the Holy Spirit upon total consecration to Christ, results in holiness. Tracing its roots to Methodism, the movement values the writings of Methodism's founder, John Wesley, particularly *A Plain Account of Christian Perfection* (1739), a document which serves as a key reference.

This chapter will highlight the three largest groups associated with the Wesleyan/Holiness movement: the Salvation Army, the Church of the Nazarene, and the Church of God (Anderson), with reference to other smaller Wesleyan/Holiness denominations. The chapter begins with an introduction to Phoebe Palmer, who played a pivotal role in the formative years of the Wesleyan/Holiness movement. A brief overview of the origination of several Wesleyan/Holiness denominations follows. An examination of literary defenses of women clergy produced by writers in the Wesleyan/Holiness movement reveals the biblical foundation of their arguments. Wesleyan/Holiness women have answered the call to ministry, serving as evangelists, pastors, and church founders. Yet the percentage of women in ministry, with the exception of the Salvation Army, has declined dramatically over the years. The chapter concludes with analysis of this pattern and a summary of current efforts to reverse it.

PHOEBE PALMER: MOTHER OF THE WESLEYAN/HOLINESS MOVEMENT

Phoebe Palmer (1807–1874) was a lifelong Methodist who articulated and promoted the doctrine of holiness through her preaching and writing.[5] Her books, published in many editions, popularized her view of holiness. The National Camp Meeting Association for the Promotion of Holiness (known today as the Christian Holiness Association) promoted Palmer's theology of holiness. Palmer succinctly explained how sanctification could be achieved: "There are but two steps to the blessing: ENTIRE CONSECRATION is the first; FAITH is the second."[6] Entire consecration meant placing one's all on the altar of Christ. Palmer also believed that a person must testify publicly to the experience of holiness in order to retain it. This requirement often prodded women to make their first public utterances. Once empowered by the Holy Spirit to testify, women who had overcome their initial fear of speaking in public often took one step further and became preachers.

Palmer participated in public ministry from her sanctification in 1837 until her death. She conducted over three hundred meetings with her husband Walter's assistance in the United States, Canada, and Great Britain without official ecclesiastical credentials. Contrary to one author's contention that Palmer believed "it was improper for women to preach,"[7] she claimed that it was the duty of every Christian to prophesy, equating "prophesy" and "preach" by citing biblical passages as her justification. Palmer argued that "all Christ's disciples, whether male or female, should covet to be endued with the gift of prophecy; then will they proclaim or in other words, *preach* Christ crucified."[8]

DEVELOPMENT OF WESLEYAN/HOLINESS CHURCHES

While holiness doctrine emerged within Methodism and Palmer was the foremost spokesperson for holiness during the nineteenth century, it was not long before groups split from Methodism because they believed it had strayed from its holiness roots. Individuals opposed to Methodism's weak position against slavery formed the Wesleyan Methodist Connection (now the Wesleyan Church) in 1843. The Free Methodists separated from the Methodists in 1860 over slavery and other issues. The Salvation Army, another holiness group, traces its beginnings to a mission Catherine and William Booth founded in London in 1865.

During the early 1880s some preachers began to encourage people to leave their denominations. While many "come outers" were Methodists, others also responded and affiliated with what is known today as the Church of God (Anderson). Merrill Gaddis estimated that at least twenty-five holiness sects were founded between 1893 and 1907.[9] Mary Lee Cagle led an association of churches known as the New Testament Church of Christ which merged with another group in 1904 to become the Holiness Church of Christ. This church along with others around the country participated in other mergers in the early twentieth century, resulting in the Pentecostal Church of the Nazarene, now the Church of the Nazarene.

PROMISE OF THE FATHER

Wesleyan/Holiness advocates sought to emulate the primitive church described in the New Testament. They observed that the primitive church utilized women in leadership positions and proceeded to affirm an active role for women in their own churches. The minutes of the first annual conference of the Salvation Army in 1870 recorded its commitment to women preachers:

> Section XII. Female Preachers—As it is manifest from the Scripture of the Old and especially the New Testament that God has sanctioned the labors of Godly women in His Church; Godly women possessing the necessary gifts and qualifications, shall be employed as preachers itinerant or otherwise and class leaders and as such shall have appointments given to them on the preachers plan; and they shall be eligible for any office, and to speak and vote at all official meetings.[10]

Forerunners of the Church of the Nazarene likewise officially sanctioned women clergy. In 1899 members of the General Council of the New Testament Church of Christ "decided that under the gospel women had all the rights and privileges that men enjoy. Since there is neither Jew nor Greek, bond nor free, male nor female in Christ, a woman is eligible for ordination."[11]

Luther Lee of the Wesleyan Methodist Connection preached that "all antiquity agrees that there were female officers and teachers in the Primitive Church."[12] B. T. Roberts, founder of the Free Methodist Church, likewise discovered: "In the New Testament Church, woman, as well as man, filled the office of Apostle, Prophet, Deacon or preacher, and Pastor. There is not the slightest evidence that the functions of any of these offices, when filled by a woman, were different from what they were when filled by a man. Woman took a part in governing the Apostolic Church."[13] Leaders such as Lee and Roberts affirmed prophetic leadership that bases its authority on the Holy Spirit. This is in contrast to priestly authority that vests authority in ecclesiastical office. Phoebe Palmer exercised prophetic authority that does not depend on ordination by human institutions. She never sought licensing from her church because "she was divinely commissioned and ordained by the great Head of the church for the special work which she felt impelled to do."[14] The Holy Spirit rather than the institutional hierarchy of the Methodist Episcopal Church authorized Palmer's preaching.

When groups value prophetic authority, they recognize the gifts of the Holy Spirit regardless of whether men or women receive them. Prophetic authority fosters egalitarianism. Sarah Bishop in 1920 maintained: "The Bible does not teach a set of gifts for women differing from those for men."[15] F. G. Smith, in the same year, expressed the prophetic perspective in a Church of God periodical, *Gospel Trumpet*.

> Again, I call your attention to the organization of the church by the Holy Spirit. A man is an evangelist because he has the gift of evangelizing. It is not because he is a man, but because he has that particular gift. The gift itself is the proof of his calling. If a woman has divine gifts fitting her for a particular work in the church, that is the proof, and the only proof needed, that that is her place. Any other basis of qualification than divine gifts is superficial and arbitrary and ignores the divine plan of organization and government in the church.[16]

C. E. Brown, another Church of God leader, also emphasized prophetic authority based on the Holy Spirit's gifts. He declared that for early Christians, "the movement of the Spirit of God was the supreme authority in all the work of the church." Rather than a hierarchical institutional church structure, Brown advocated "spiritual democracy," which he defined as the "fundamental doctrine of spiritual equality and the universal priesthood of believers set forth in the New Testament."[17]

In the nineteenth and early twentieth centuries when most people cited biblical texts to prohibit women clergy, Wesleyan/Holiness students of the Bible produced numerous defenses of women's right to preach. Book-length apologies appeared such as Phoebe Palmer's *Promise of the Father* (1859)[18] and B. T. Roberts's *Ordaining Women* (1891).[19] Nazarene preacher Fannie McDowell Hunter compiled *Women Preachers* (1905).[20] Sermons such as Luther Lee's "Women's Right to Preach the Gospel" (1853) were printed.[21] Pamphlets included *Female Ministry* (1859) by Catherine Booth, *Woman Preacher* (1891) by W. B. Godbey, and *Woman's Ministry* (1921) by Alma White.[22]

Without fail, these writers highlighted the events of Pentecost recorded in Acts 1 and 2.[23] Palmer borrowed her title *Promise of the Father* from Luke 24:49 where Jesus told his disciples to remain in Jerusalem until they received the promise of the Father which he described as "power from on high." Jesus' promise was fulfilled at Pentecost when the Holy Spirit empowered those who had followed Jesus' instructions and men as well as women preached along with Peter in Jerusalem. Acts 1:14 documents the presence of women at Pentecost. Hunter observed: "The *women* as well as the men had tongues of fire—God's weapons for the spread of the Gospel."[24] Peter informed the crowds that Joel's prophesy that "your sons and your daughters shall prophesy . . . and on my servants and on my handmaidens I will pour out in those days of my Spirit; and they shall prophesy" was fulfilled at Pentecost (Acts 2:14–17). Roberts contended that "no distinction whatever is made between the 'sons and daughters.' . . . No higher ministry is given to the sons than is given to the daughters."[25] Booth claimed that Pentecost settled the question of women preachers.[26] Palmer held that the diffusion of the Holy Spirit was not a onetime event restricted to Pentecost but was available to all Christians in future generations. "The Father has not forgotten his ancient promise, but still pours out, in these the latter part of the last days, his Spirit upon his daughters and handmaidens, alike as upon his sons."[27] Pentecost ushered in the dispensation of the Holy Spirit during which men and women continued to claim the promise.

It is not surprising that each of these authors also quoted Galatians 3:28, "There is neither Jew nor Greek, there is neither bond nor free, there is neither male nor female: for ye are all one in Christ Jesus," to support their case for women clergy. Lee chose Galatians 3:28 as the text of his sermon, preaching that the verse "means that males and females are equal in rights, privileges, and responsibilities upon the Christian platform."[28] Hunter contended that Galatians 3:28 "removes the fetters from woman and leaves her free to serve Christ in any position she may be called to fill."[29] Writers challenged attempts to limit the application of the verse to the realm of conversion.

Hunter called Jesus "the woman's Friend" and observed that Jesus did not silence the woman at the well who was the first preacher to the Samaritans (John 4:28). Jesus also chose women to announce the news of his Resurrection.[30] Maintaining women's right to be ministers, Roberts contended: "We have never heard or read a single quotation from the words of Jesus against this right." In response to those who argued that because Jesus chose all males as his disciples then only males could be clergy, Roberts pointed out that Jesus' disciples also were Jews. It was inconsistent to argue that only men could be clergy while allowing non-Jews to assume this position.[31]

These defenses of women preachers included a litany of other women in the Bible who served as models for contemporary women. Prominent women in the Hebrew Bible included Miriam, Deborah, Huldah, and Isaiah's wife.[32] Turning to the New Testament, writers listed Anna, Philip's four daughters who prophesied, Eudia, and Syntyche.[33] They paid particular attention to Romans 16 where Paul greeted many coworkers, including ten women. They pointed out that the description of Phoebe in verse 1 had been mistranslated as servant rather than minister, thus minimizing her role in the church.[34] They also challenged the mistaken assumption that Junia (often mistranslated "Junias" in verse 6) was a man. Booth contended that since Chrysostom and Theophylact, early Greek leaders in the church, affirmed that Junia was a woman, subsequent translators should follow their lead rather than letting their prejudices get in the way.[35]

Wesleyan/Holiness writers challenged the interpretation of verses used by the majority of Christians to silence women in the church. Foes of women clergy relied on 1 Corinthians 14:34–35 and 1 Timothy 2:11–12. These passages which speak of women's silence in church appear to limit women's public role in worship. Because of the influence of these verses in excluding women from the pulpit, Wesleyan/Holiness adherents examined them closely to determine their intended meaning and to counteract their power in keeping women from the pulpit.

Holiness writers pointed out that these verses were the only ones from the entire Bible that opponents could produce in their attempt to build a case against women clergy.[36] Second, they observed that the verses were applied inconsistently in those churches that refused to ordain women. If churches really believed that women should be silent, they should be barred from teaching Sunday school, praying, or singing in the choir.[37]

Wesleyan/Holiness authors dismissed 1 Timothy 2:11–12 as irrelevant, claiming that it did not apply to women preachers. The verses state that women should be in silence and not "usurp authority over the man." Hunter contended that women were assuming lawfully invested authority rather than usurping authority.[38] Booth maintained that the prohibition of 1 Timothy 2:11–16 had "no bearing whatever on the religious exercises of women led and taught by the Spirit of God."[39]

Some writers interpreted 1 Corinthians 14:34–35 to mean that women were not to ask questions during worship. They further contended that the passage applied to a particular situation in the congregation at Corinth and was not a general rule. They quoted 1 Corinthians 11:5 which provides instructions for women praying and prophesying in public worship to establish that the prohibition was not intended to silence Corinthian women in all cases.[40]

Contemporary biblical arguments utilized by Wesleyan/Holiness supporters of women clergy parallel those produced during the nineteenth and early twentieth centuries.[41] Galatians 3:28 has continued to serve as the guiding principle for all arguments favoring women clergy. For instance, retired Church of God pastor Lillie McCutcheon quotes this verse in a recent article and affirms, "Our soul has no gender." She further claims, "God is an Equal Rights Employer. One standard is set for both female and male Christians."[42]

YOUR DAUGHTERS SHALL PROPHESY

The call to preach is often a dramatic spiritual event in a woman's life. Most women's accounts of their "calls" follow a similar pattern. Despite the numerous scriptural defenses of women clergy, women initially resist God's call, claiming ignorance, age (too young or old), or their sex. More than likely, they realize the opposition they would face as women preachers. Ministry is not a career they actively seek; but God persists and finally they yield. Lillian Pool's and Jonnie Jernigan's accounts of their calls provide representative examples. Pool reported: "I had no doubt about it being a call from God, for I recognized His voice saying: 'Lillian, go preach My Word to the lost.' " She demurred, "My argument against yielding to the call, was, that I was too young and had been deprived of educational advantages. And, too, the thought of leaving home and being separated from loved ones harassed me until at times it seemed I could never consent to do so." Eventually God prevailed and Pool began preaching.[43] Jonnie Jernigan felt called to preach as a girl but her Methodist family informed her that "it was masculine and unladylike for a woman to preach." As an adult, in 1895, she experienced sanctification when she finally yielded to God's call.[44] Her ministry focused on the poor, particularly prostitutes for whom she built a home in Peniel, Texas.

Rebecca Laird, studying the lives of ten women who pastored in the early years of the Church of the Nazarene, found that a common thread was their firm conviction that God had called them to preach. Susan Norris Fitkin's experience is typical. She spoke of her ordination (presided over by Phineas Bresee in 1907) as "only the human sanction to God's work." She described her call which preceded her ordination: "For years before [God] had definitely spoken these precious words to my heart, 'Ye have not chosen me, but I have chosen you, and ordained you, that ye should go and bring forth fruit.' "[45]

The empowerment of the Holy Spirit accompanied the call to ministry. Palmer's statement "holiness is power" explicitly connected the experience of holiness with the power of the Holy Spirit.[46] Numerous women testified that, once they experienced this power, they were enabled to launch their preaching careers and to withstand hostility to their preaching. Sarah Smith credited sanctification for enabling her to overcome a "man-fearing spirit" that had previously inhibited her.[47] Phoebe Palmer and Alma White also spoke of natural shyness which they overcame with the power of the Holy Spirit.[48] Vivian Pressley, who pastored a Nazarene congregation in South Carolina from 1946 to 1986, reported that when she was sanctified, "in place of my shyness,

[God] gave me holy boldness so that I am not afraid anywhere under any circumstances."[49]

Wesleyan/Holiness women called to ministry were empowered to serve not only as pastors but as evangelists and congregational and denominational founders. Historians, for the most part, have overlooked the hundreds of Wesleyan/Holiness women evangelists who were preaching at the turn of the century.[50] In the Church of God alone, at least eighty-eight women served as evangelists throughout the country during 1891 and 1892.[51] Initially most Church of God preachers traveled in teams from one evangelistic campaign to another. Women headed at least two teams or companies, as they were called. *Gospel Trumpet* reported in 1891 on the schedule of Mary Cole and Company, and Lena Matthesen advertised in 1905 for a woman to join a company consisting of herself and two other women.[52] The Pentecost Bands, founded by Vivian Dake and affiliated with the Free Methodist Church from 1886 to 1894, also offered opportunities for women evangelists and church planters. In 1892 two-thirds of the approximately 125 evangelists comprising the Pentecost Bands were women.[53] Traveling in teams or bands, they started over 100 churches, primarily in Pennsylvania and the Midwest, during their first ten years.

Women have played leading roles in establishing other Wesleyan/Holiness churches. The Salvation Army spread to the United States in 1879 when two women initiated a ministry in Philadelphia. Norman Murdoch contends that probably most Salvation Army corps were founded by women, and Alice Dise lists African-American women who started Church of God congregations throughout the country.[54]

Mary Lee Cagle played a leading role in the New Testament Church of Christ, founded by her first husband. Cagle began her ministry following her husband's death in 1894, starting at least eighteen congregations in Tennessee, Alabama, Arizona, and Texas. The roll of the second council of this group's churches in Texas listed five women ministers and nine males.[55]

Like Phoebe Palmer, Alma White (1862–1946) was a lay preacher in the Methodist Episcopal Church, but, along with many others of her generation, she believed Methodism had strayed far from its roots. Seeking to restore primitive Methodism, she established the Pentecostal Union (soon known as the Pillar of Fire) in 1901. White's church was highly sectarian: church members wore uniforms, worked for the church rather than in secular employment, and sent their children to Pillar of Fire schools. White explicitly founded the church to be an institution where "equal opportunities should be given to both men and women to enter the ministry."[56] Consecrated bishop in 1918 by William

Godbey, her spiritual mentor, Alma White became the first woman to hold this position in the United States and the only woman in the Wesleyan/Holiness movement to serve in this capacity. One goal of the Pillar of Fire was "to set the example of equality for the sexes, heralding a new era of religious freedom by breaking the shackles that have held women in bondage for ages."[57] White expressed her commitment to equality in the political arena by supporting the Equal Rights Amendment at its inception in 1923.[58]

SILENCING THE SISTERS

Given the initial strong affirmation of women clergy in the Wesleyan/Holiness movement and the many women who ministered during its formative years, an examination of current Wesleyan/Holiness clergy statistics presents a far more dismal picture for women than would be expected. The only exception is the Salvation Army, which has maintained a high percentage of women clergy. In 1896 the Salvation Army had over 1,000 women officers out of a total of 1,854 in the United States. Currently women still comprise a majority of the 24,779 ordained Salvation Army officers. Despite these impressive statistics, there are some practices in the Salvation Army that discriminate against women. For example, when a woman marries, she assumes her husband's rank if she outranked him prior to marriage.[59] A couple's allowance is based on the husband's years of service. Likewise, husbands receive appointments, and their wives serve under them.

In contrast to the Salvation Army, the percentage of women clergy in the Church of the Nazarene dropped from 20 percent in 1908 to 6 percent by 1973.[60] In 1989, 49 Nazarene women pastored churches in the United States. This is less than 1 percent of 5,129 American congregations.[61] In 1992 almost one-third (197) of the women clergy were retired, 56 pastored churches or missions while 121 served as associate pastors, and 61 were involved in other ministries or were students. The remaining women were unassigned.[62] Currently no women serve as district superintendents, and only 2 women have held this position throughout the history of the denomination.[63]

The highest percentage of women pastors in the Church of God (Anderson) was 32 percent in 1925. In 1992 the percentage of women clergy was 15.[64] Three Church of God women held executive positions in national agencies in 1989 compared to 45 men.[65] Jeannette Flynn became the first woman to direct an agency when she became director of Church and Ministry Service in 1994.

Sect analysis helps explain the reduction in the percentage of women clergy that has taken place in most Wesleyan/Holiness churches. In the early stages of development, sects value prophetic leadership and accept women preachers. As they institutionalize and shift from a prophetic to a priestly understanding of authority, the percentage of women in leadership positions declines.[66] Groups that earlier had readily approved the prophetic authority of women evangelists found it difficult to affirm women in a pastoral role that relied more and more on priestly authority.

The Church of God (Anderson) offers a clear illustration of what happens as a group undergoes the transition from prophetic to priestly leadership. In the early decades of the Church of God, evangelists traveled throughout the country seeking to spread the gospel as far as possible rather than to establish local congregations. One of the distinguishing features at the outset was the Church of God's anti-institutionalism that inhibited the proliferation of churches and the development of a national organization. However, by the 1910s congregations had evolved in some locations where evangelists had conducted revivals and a national structure emerged.[67] As itinerant ministry diminished, women lost an outlet for ministry.[68]

R. Stanley Ingersol points to institutionalization as one of the main causes of the decline in women clergy in the Church of the Nazarene. Males controlled the institutional development during the early decades while women remained charismatic leaders. The Cagles represent this pattern. C. G. Cagle, the second husband of Mary Lee Cagle, served as superintendent of the New Mexico district (1918–1920) and the West Texas district (1926–1936), while Mary Lee Cagle worked as district evangelist in these two locations.[69]

While most Wesleyan/Holiness churches ordained women from their inceptions, for the most part, they have yet to concede priestly authority to women at the highest institutional levels. This helps to explain why very few women hold executive positions at the national level in Wesleyan/Holiness churches. The Salvation Army is the exception; Eva Barrows became general in 1986, assuming responsibility for the Salvation Army throughout the world until her retirement in 1993.

Nancy Hardesty, Lucille Sider Dayton, and Donald W. Dayton attribute the decline in women clergy to the professionalization of leadership that has occurred in Wesleyan/Holiness groups, contending that a growing demand for seminary-trained pastors resulted in a reduction of women.[70] This is particularly evident in the Church of the Nazarene. Rebecca Laird credits increased ordination requirements for having a negative impact on the number of Nazarene women in min-

istry since 1950.[71] It was probably harder for women to relocate in order to attend seminary than it was for men.

A second reason for the decline of women clergy is acquiescence to
cultural stereotypes that support males in leadership roles and limit
women's participation in positions of authority. Lillie S. McCutcheon
has observed: "We have had decades when our culture influenced our
movement to discourage women in pastoral ministry. . . . It is disappointing that the church continues to remain with male domination
when it should have pioneered the equal status for women."[72]
R. Eugene Sterner states that the Church of God "has traditionally seen
women in a supportive rather than a decision-making leadership capacity. In this we have pretty much reflected prevailing social standards."[73] While these statements describe the situation in the Church
of God, accommodation to culture has occurred in other Wesleyan/
Holiness groups as well.

"Fundamentalist leavening"[74] also accounts for the reduction in
women clergy. Often, theological justification has been utilized to support cultural stereotypes. Fundamentalists who oppose the leadership
of women in the church attempt to support their position by keeping
alive the arguments derived from 1 Timothy 2 and 1 Corinthians 14,
insisting on a literal interpretation of these passages of Scripture. Just
as the movement has accommodated to culture, it has also compro-
mised its earlier convictions by adopting fundamentalist arguments
that support female subordination. Wesleyan/Holiness laypeople and
clergy who are unaware of their heritage embrace the fundamentalist
viewpoint expressed by such lecturers as Bill Gothard, who promotes
male headship in all areas of life, precluding any leadership role for
women in the church.[75] R. Eugene Sterner observes: "With what is an
apparent trend to more conservative thinking among our people, there
is a tendency to define, again, the women's place as in the home."[76]
Scholars have documented "fundamentalist leavening" in the Church
of the Nazarene and the Free Methodist Church as well as in the
Church of God.[77]

CRACKING THE STAINED-GLASS CEILING

Experts who research women's advancement in the workforce
coined the term *glass ceiling* to explain the fact that, despite the inroads
women are making in various professions, the top jobs in their chosen
fields elude them. In most Wesleyan/Holiness churches, a similar
humanly constructed barrier exists, more appropriately labeled a
"stained-glass ceiling" that adjusts to various heights depending on

the particular church. Some women never cope with the stained-glass ceiling because a stained-glass door prevents them from entering the church to assume a professional role. Other churches affirm women's right to serve as associate pastors while the position of senior pastor is off-limits. Many churches claim no ceiling exists within their communions, but statistics indicate otherwise. People in these denominations believe that they are absolved from any responsibility actively to promote women in ministry because their churches have always ordained women. They refuse to admit that prejudice against women might be the cause for the low percentages of women clergy in their denominations. They do not recognize that fundamentalist leavening and other forms of accommodation account for the large gap between theory and practice.

Others, however, comprehend this contradiction. In an editorial in the Church of God's *Vital Christianity*, Arlo Newell quotes C. E. Brown: "It is only when the church is in *deep spiritual apostasy* that the voice of her female prophets is silenced." Newell acknowledges: "It may be that while we have debated doctrinal purity and biblical authority, apostasy has overtaken us through sexual discrimination. Let us return to the apostolic church pattern and hear the voice of the Lord as we recognize and receive female prophets."[78] Newell wrote in a subsequent editorial: "In a time of social enlightenment when sexist barriers are being broken down, we in the church seem to have some spiritual blind spots. Prejudice and discrimination are never broken down or destroyed without corrective measures being willfully and intentionally implemented."[79]

At least two groups have recognized the inconsistency between their official support of women clergy and the low numbers of ordained women and have passed resolutions encouraging women in leadership. A resolution adopted by the Church of God in 1974 states in part: "in light of statistics which document the diminishing use of women's abilities in the life and work of the church, . . . RESOLVED, That more women be given opportunity and consideration for positions of leadership in the total program of the Church of God, locally, statewide, and nationally."[80] The General Assembly of the Church of the Nazarene issued a statement on women's rights in 1980 that includes the following: "We support the right of women to use their God-given spiritual gifts within the church. We affirm the historic right of women to be elected and appointed to places of leadership within the Church of the Nazarene."[81] Resolutions alone will not result in more women clergy, but awareness is the first step toward change.

Since Wesleyan/Holiness churches are generally non-liturgical, the uproar over the inclusive language lectionary in the early 1980s did not affect them. For the most part, a recognition of the theological importance of inclusive language is absent at the congregational level. In 1938 Mary Lee Cagle anticipated the contemporary concern for inclusive language when she raised the issue by refusing to complete a standard clergy form that consistently used male pronouns in reference to clergy.[82] Inclusive language has been adopted in a few instances. For example, the Church of God Division of Church Service (now renamed Church and Ministry Service) has removed male pronouns from its clergy registration form. Warner Press, the Church of God publication agency, adopted an inclusive language policy in 1975. Western Evangelical Seminary, a multidenominational Wesleyan/Holiness institution, began promoting inclusive language in the mid-1980s.

Thus far no Wesleyan/Holiness groups have implemented affirmative action policies to crack the stained-glass ceiling created by prejudice and discrimination. However, several have begun to address the problem in various ways. The Nazarenes, the Free Methodists, and the Salvation Army have established task forces to begin dismantling their respective "ceilings." The Church of the Nazarene started distributing the newsletter *New Horizons* to women clergy in 1992, while Wesleyan women established *Growing Together* the same year. Church of God women began publishing *Women in Ministry and Missions* in 1989. Denominational presses are publishing books highlighting their heritage and urging their churches and leadership to take a proactive stance to increase the number of women in professional ministry.[83]

Women clergy in the Wesleyan Church have met six times, while Church of God women in ministry have convened three times. Five Wesleyan/Holiness denominations cosponsored a conference for women clergy in April 1994 attended by over 375 participants.[84] A second conference will be held in April 1996. Denominational enthusiasm for this conference reflects a willingness to support and encourage women clergy.

Wesleyan/Holiness advocates of women clergy are challenging fundamentalist leavening and cultural accommodation with biblical defenses first articulated in the early years of their churches' history. By recovering their heritage, Wesleyan/Holiness groups are appropriating a usable past in their efforts to crack the stained-glass ceiling.

NOTES

1. John W. V. Smith, *The Quest for Holiness and Unity* (Anderson, Ind.: Warner Press, 1980), 129.
2. All texts are from the King James Version of the Bible, which was the primary translation used in the Wesleyan/Holiness movement during the nineteenth and early twentieth centuries.
3. Bryan R. Wilson, *Religious Sects* (New York: McGraw-Hill, 1970), 59.
4. Other formulations of holiness include one which centered around Charles Finney and Asa Mahan at Oberlin College in the mid 1800s and Keswick holiness, which originated in England later in the century. Keswick teachings were particularly popular among fundamentalists in the United States. These expressions of holiness permeated existing denominations rather than resulting in new groups as was the case in the Wesleyan/ Holiness movement.
5. Recent scholarship on Palmer's life and ministry has resulted in two biographies and a collection of her writings. See Charles Edward White, *The Beauty of Holiness: Phoebe Palmer as Theologian, Revivalist, Feminist, and Humanitarian* (Grand Rapids, Mich.: Francis Asbury Press of Zondervan Publishing House, 1986); Harold E. Raser, *Phoebe Palmer: Her Life and Thought* (Lewiston, N.Y.: Edwin Mellen Press, 1987); and Thomas C. Oden, *Phoebe Palmer: Selected Writings* (New York: Paulist Press, 1988).
6. Phoebe Palmer, *The Promise of the Father; or, a Neglected Speciality of the Last Days* (N.p., [1859]; rep., Salem, Ohio: Schmul Publishers, n.d.), 245.
7. Charles Edwin Jones, *Perfectionist Persuasion: The Holiness Movement and American Methodism, 1867–1936*, ATLA Monograph Series, no. 5 (Metuchen, N.J.: Scarecrow Press, 1974), 3.
8. Palmer, 34, 40–44, 36.
9. Merrill Elmer Gaddis, "Christian Perfectionism in America," Ph.D. dissertation, University of Chicago, 1929, 458.
10. *Minutes*, First Conference of the Christian Mission, held at the People's Mission Hall, 272 Whitechapel Rd., London, 15–17 June 1879; quoted in Norman H. Murdoch, "Female Ministry in the Thought and Work of Catherine Booth," *Church History* 53 (September 1984): 355.
11. M. E. Redford, *The Rise of the Church of the Nazarene* (Kansas City, Mo.: Nazarene Publishing House, 1948), 123; quoted in Janet Smith Williams, "The Impetus of Holiness Women for Preaching the Gospel, with Special Consideration Concerning Women in The Church of the Nazarene," unpublished paper written in 1981 for a course at the Conservative Baptist Theological Seminary in Denver, 23.
12. Luther Lee, "Woman's Right to Preach the Gospel," in *Five Sermons and a Tract by Luther Lee*, ed. Donald W. Dayton (Chicago: Holrad House, 1975), 91. Lee preached this sermon at Antoinette Brown's ordination in a Congregational church in 1853.
13. Benjamin Titus Roberts, *Ordaining Women* (Rochester: Earnest Christian Publishing House, 1891; rep., Indianapolis: Light and Life Press, 1992), 103.

14. *Guide to Holiness*, 78 (1880): 75; quoted in Charles White, 194.
15. Sarah Bishop, "Should Women Preach?," *Gospel Trumpet* 40 (17 June 1920): 9.
16. F. G. Smith, "Editorial," *Gospel Trumpet* 40 (4 October 1920): 2.
17. Charles E. Brown, *The Apostolic Church* (Anderson, Ind.: Warner Press, 1947), 138, 165, 30–31.
18. For summaries of *Promise of the Father*, see Raser, 202–208; and Charles White, 189–193.
19. Roberts wrote this book when his resolution to ordain women failed by two votes at the 1890 Free Methodist General Conference. See Linda J. Adams, "Stop Pushing the Sisters off the Scaffold!," *Light and Life* 124 (May 1991): 8–9. Free Methodists ordained women as deacons after 1907 but did not grant women full ordination as elders until 1974.
20. Fannie McDowell Hunter, *Women Preachers* (Dallas, Tex.: Berachah Printing, 1905).
21. Lee, 77–100.
22. Catherine Booth, *Female Ministry: Women's Right to Preach the Gospel* (N.p., 1859; rep., New York: Salvation Army Supplies Printing and Publishing Department, 1975); W. B. Godbey, *Woman Preacher* (Atlanta: Office of the Way of Life, 1891); and Alma White, *Woman's Ministry* (London: Pillar of Fire, [1921]).
23. The Wesleyan/Holiness movement identified closely with Pentecost, with many believing that the experience of sanctification was the gift bestowed on Jesus' followers at this time. Several groups, such as the Pentecostal Church of the Nazarene and the Pentecostal Union (the original name of the Pillar of Fire), incorporated the event in their names.
24. Hunter, 24. See also Lee, 86; and Alma White, *Woman's Ministry*, 2.
25. Roberts, 58.
26. Booth, 7.
27. Palmer, 176; see also 30.
28. Lee, 80.
29. Hunter, 40. See also Roberts, 37–40; and Godbey, 11.
30. Hunter, 96, 18–20.
31. Roberts, 37.
32. For representative examples see Palmer, 67; and Hunter, 13–15.
33. See Hunter, 18; Alma White, *Woman's Ministry*, 2; and Godbey, 8.
34. Roberts, 64.
35. Booth, 11. See also Palmer, 26; and Roberts, 53–54. The problem arose because Junia is among those whom Paul refers to as being "of note among the apostles." Translators refused to admit that Paul addressed a woman as an apostle.
36. Lee, 92.
37. Roberts, 40–41.
38. Hunter, 39.
39. Booth, 12–13.
40. Booth, 8; Palmer, 47, 6, 9; Booth, 11; Hunter, 36–37; and Lee, 94.

41. See Marie Strong, "Biblical Vision: An Interpretation of Acts 2:17–18" and Sharon Pearson, "Biblical Precedence of Women in Ministry," in *Called to Minister: Empowered to Serve*, ed. Juanita Evans Leonard (Anderson, Ind.: Warner Press, 1989), 1–33.

42. Lillie S. McCutcheon, "God Is an Equal Opportunity Employer," *Vital Christianity* 109 (May 1989): 14–15. Rev. McCutcheon pastored the Newton Falls Church of God in Ohio from 1945 until her retirement in 1988.

43. Lillian Pool, "Experience and Call to the Ministry," in Hunter, 68–69. For other examples, see 71–72 and 87–88.

44. Jonnie Jernigan, *Redeemed through the Blood or the Power of God to Save the Fallen* (Louisville, Ky.: Pentecostal Herald Print., [1904]), 6, 8. Rev. Jernigan was involved in the Independent Holiness group which merged with the New Testament Church of Christ to become the Holiness Church of Christ.

45. Susan N. Fitkin, *Grace Much More Abounding: A Story of the Triumphs of Redeeming Grace During Two Score Years in the Master's Service* (Kansas City: Nazarene Publishing House, n.d.), 46; quoted in Rebecca Laird, "A History of the First Generation of Ordained Women in the Church of the Nazarene," M.A. thesis, Pacific School of Religion, 1990, 71. Laird's thesis has been published as *Ordained Women in the Church of the Nazarene: The First Generation* (Kansas City: Nazarene Publishing House, 1993). It was unavailable at the time this chapter was written.

46. Palmer, 206. Hunter and Mary Lee Cagle also emphasized the power for service that accompanied sanctification. See Stanley Ingersol, "Burden of Discontent: Mary Lee Cagle and the Southern Holiness Movement," Ph.D. dissertation, Duke University, 1989, 253.

47. Sarah Smith, *Life Sketches of Mother Sarah Smith* (Anderson, Ind.: Gospel Trumpet Company, [1902]; rep., Guthrie, Okla.: Faith Publishing House, n.d.), 9. Smith was a member of the first team of traveling evangelists in the Church of God.

48. Susie Cunningham Stanley, *Feminist Pillar of Fire: The Life of Alma White* (Cleveland, Ohio: Pilgrim Press, 1993), 21, 23; and Anne C. Loveland, "Domesticity and Religion in the Antebellum Period: The Career of Phoebe Palmer," *The Historian* 39 (May 1977): 459, 461.

49. Nina Beegle and Wilbur W. Brannon, "Vivian Pressley Served Forty Years in One Church," *Grow* 3 (Spring 1992): 40. Pressley is a retired Nazarene pastor.

50. For two examples of historians who minimize the number of women evangelists, see Martha Tomhave Blauvelt, "Women and Revivalism," in *Women and Religion in America*, vol. 1: *The Nineteenth Century: A Documentary History*, ed. Rosemary Radford Ruether and Rosemary Skinner Keller (San Francisco: Harper & Row, 1986), 9; and Raser, 103.

51. "News from the Field," *Gospel Trumpet*, 1891–1892 issues.

52. *Gospel Trumpet* 2 (1 August 1891): n.p.; and 25 (26 January 1905): 5.

53. Howard A. Snyder, "Radical Holiness: Vivian Dake and the Pentecost Bands," Wesleyan/Holiness Church Leaders' Conference, 1–3 February 1990, Asbury Theological Seminary, 7–9. Members of the Pentecost Bands

did not seek ordination. The group became independent of the Free Methodist Church in 1895. Changing their name to Missionary Bands of the World in 1925, the group ultimately united with the Wesleyan Methodists in 1958.

54. Murdoch, 361; and Alice Dice, "Black Women in Ministry in the Church of God," in Leonard, *Called to Minister*, 59–63. Women founded many congregations in the Church of God and other denominations, but their contributions have not been fully documented.

55. Ingersol, 284, 205.

56. Alma White, *The Story of My Life and Pillar of Fire*, 5 vols. (Zarephath, N.J.: Pillar of Fire, 1935–1943), II: 364.

57. Alma White, *The New Testament Church* (Zarephath, N.J.: Pillar of Fire, 1929), 277.

58. Stanley, 111–14.

59. Murdoch, 349, 360, 358–59.

60. Donald W. Dayton and Lucille Sider Dayton, "Women as Preachers: Evangelical Precedents," *Christianity Today* 19 (23 May 1975): 7.

61. Ingersol, 258. This number does not include associate pastors.

62. Phyllis Perkins, "Clergywomen in the Church of the Nazarene: Who Are We?," *New Horizons* (Spring 1992): 1.

63. Maye McReynolds, who had managed the Spanish Mission in the Southwest, was officially recognized as district superintendent in 1911. Elsie Wallace filled a vacancy in the Northwest for four months in 1920. See Laird, 42, 54.

64. Susie Stanley, "Church of God Women Ministers: A Look at the Statistics," in Leonard, *Called to Minister*, 175. Statistics for 1992 were provided by Ilene Bargerstock, Division of Church Service, Church of God. The 1992 figure includes 113 retired women.

65. Juanita Evans Leonard, "Women, Change and the Church," in her *Called to Minister*, 162–64.

66. Barfoot and Sheppard trace this development in several pentecostal denominations. As the prophetic emphasis diminished in these groups, men increasingly assumed priestly functions. The Wesleyan/Holiness movement corresponds to this pattern. See Charles H. Barfoot and Gerald T. Sheppard, "Prophetic vs. Priestly Religion: The Changing Role of Women Clergy in Classical Pentecostal Churches," *Review of Religious Research* 22 (September 1980): 2–17.

67. John W. V. Smith, 148.

68. Joseph Allison, "Why We Encourage Women to Be Leaders," *Church of God Missions* 52 (January 1988): 9; and Joseph Allison, "An Overview of the Involvement of Women in the Church of God from 1916," in *The Role of Women in Today's World: Six Study Papers* (Anderson, Ind.: Commission on Social Concerns, Church of God, 1978), 27.

69. Ingersol, 277, 290.

70. Nancy Hardesty, Lucille Sider Dayton, and Donald W. Dayton, "Women in the Holiness Movement: Feminism in the Evangelical Tradition," in *Women*

of Spirit: Female Leadership in the Jewish and Christian Traditions, ed. Rosemary Ruether and Eleanor McLaughlin (New York: Simon and Schuster, 1979), 249–50. This article provides an excellent overview of women in the Holiness movement.

71. Laird, iv.

72. Lillie S. McCutcheon, "Lady in the Pulpit," *Centering on Ministry* 5 (Winter 1980): 5–6.

73. R. Eugene Sterner, "Women in the Church of God," in *The Role of Women*, 15.

74. Paul Bassett coined the term "fundamentalist leavening" to signify the influence of fundamentalism with respect to the understanding of the authority and inspiration of the Bible in the Church of the Nazarene, but "leavening" has influenced other theological positions as well. See Paul Merritt Bassett, "The Fundamentalist Leavening of the Holiness Movement, 1914-1940: The Church of the Nazarene—A Case Study," *Wesleyan Theological Journal* 13, no. 1 (1978): 65–91.

75. Williams agrees that Gothard's lectures are often accepted as "gospel," resulting in women's diminished role in the church. See Williams, 32. Gothard's teachings have made inroads into other churches as well.

76. Sterner, 15.

77. See Ingersol, 277–78; Laird, iv; and Adams, 9.

78. Arlo F. Newell, "Deep Spiritual Apostasy?," *Vital Christianity* 100 (8 June 1980): 5. *Vital Christianity* is a Church of God periodical, formerly called *Gospel Trumpet*.

79. Arlo F. Newell, "For Men Only?," *Vital Christianity* 109 (May 1989): 13.

80. Barry L. Callen, ed., *Thinking and Acting Together* (Anderson, Ind.: Executive Council of the Church of God and Warner Press, 1992), 66.

81. *Church of the Nazarene Manual*, 1980 (p. 346), quoted in Karen Schwartz, "And 'Your Daughters Will Prophesy,'" *The Preacher's Magazine* 59 (September 1983): 32.

82. Ingersol, 294.

83. Besides the 1992 reprint of Roberts's *Ordaining Women*, other recent books are *Called to Minister: Empowered to Serve*, edited by Juanita Evans Leonard, and Rebecca Laird's *Ordained Women in the Church of the Nazarene: The First Generation*. C. S. Cowles, *A Woman's Place? Leadership in the Church* (Kansas City: Beacon Hill Press of Kansas City, 1993) was published too late for inclusion in this chapter.

84. The denominations sponsoring the conference were the Church of God (Anderson), the Church of the Nazarene, the Free Methodist Church, the Wesleyan Church, and Evangelical Friends, International. The Salvation Army (USA Western Territory) was an official supporter of the conference. For coverage of the conference, see Timothy C. Morgan, *Christianity Today* 38 (16 May 1994): 52; and Stan Ingersol, *Christian Century* 111 (29 June–6 July 1994): 632. The Salvation Army has joined the other five denominations as a full sponsor of the 1996 conference, while the Brethren in Christ Church is an official supporter.

Women and the Baptist Experience

Carolyn DeArmond Blevins

INTRODUCTION

"Freedom!" was the cry of Baptists who emerged in the restricted religious climate of seventeenth-century England. Baptists in England and later in the American colonies fought tenaciously for freedom of religious expression for people of all religious faiths. The individual's religious freedom did not stop at the Baptist church door. Freedom within Baptist churches is a hallmark of Baptist theology. Ecclesiastical hierarchy is foreign to Baptist teachings. The doctrine of the priesthood of the believer, which asserts the individual's right to interpret scripture for herself, and the doctrine of the autonomy of the local church are cornerstones of Baptist doctrine. Congregational government, giving responsibilities and rights to every church member, is the polity of local Baptist churches. Great emphasis is placed on the individual's responsibility for her relationship with God. Historically, freedom has been treasured by Baptists—in their doctrine if not always in their practice.

Women took their religious responsibility seriously and were involved in significant ways as Baptists organized in England and America. Two of Baptists' most well known churches were founded by women. Dorothy Hazard led Baptists in Bristol, England, to form the Broadmead Baptist Church in the 1640s. Lucinda Williams led a small band of Baptists in 1868 to form the church that is now the First Baptist Church, Dallas, Texas. Women also served as deaconesses according to early Baptist documents. Some Baptist women preached: Hazard in England and Martha Marshall in America. But as Baptists became more structured, women's names as leaders began to disappear from church records and histories. Women were rarely noted except in accounts of membership or as the "wife of. . . ." Freedom within Baptist churches gradually became limited for its female members.

Freed slaves in the late nineteenth century found the Baptist emphasis on freedom and the individual very appealing. Many black Baptist churches arose as a result. Theologically, the same doctrines of individual freedom should have attracted large numbers of white women into Baptist churches as well. Pragmatically, however, by this time Baptist churches rarely deviated from dominant cultural patterns in matters pertaining to women. Between the seventeenth century and the nineteenth century men increasingly dominated church leadership positions. Like many of their Protestant sisters, Baptist women found effective but limited ways of ministering within the spoken and unspoken restrictions.

The nineteenth century was not the best of times for Baptists in \merica. Curious clashes were occurring in their culture: a religious ∕vakening, the swelling cry for abolition, regional tensions erupting into the Civil War, the difficulties of Reconstruction, and the growing frustration of women who discovered that because they had no vote, they lacked the power to bring about social and moral change. Turmoil also swirled among Baptists themselves soon after they established a national convention. Early in the century (1814), Baptists formed a national organization, commonly known as the Triennial Convention. By mid-century (1845) Southern Baptists split off primarily over the issue of slavery and formed a separate convention, the Southern Baptist Convention (SBC). In the last half of the century, during the period of Reconstruction, black Baptist churches emerged and eventually formed the National Baptist Convention in 1895. By the end of the century Baptists in the United States were divided into Northern, Southern, and Black Baptist groups. A national convention was a grouping of Baptists into national organizations to support programs too large for a local church or region, such as education, missions, and publishing.

Adding to the turmoil was the tension regarding women: their voting power, their roles, and their proper place. Uncertain about the growing influence of women, Baptist pulpits and presses warned of the dangers of any change in the traditional role of women. Baptist churches, schools, boards, and conventions allowed women to participate only in restricted and supporting roles. Baptist newspapers from this era clearly indicate that many Baptists would have agreed with the philosopher Pliny the Elder, who in his book *Natural History* insisted that women were to be quiet and inconspicuous so that when they died no one would even know they had lived.[1]

How does a woman who claims the doctrine of Baptists as her own respond authentically to her faith when the institutions of that faith erect barriers to her? How does she personally interpret her faith in a meaningful way? What avenues of ministry are open to her? What impact does her ministry have on the work and theology of her denomination? What is the experience of Baptist women who are called to minister professionally? What has been the response of Baptists to her ministry?

Before these questions are addressed, a crucial word of explanation is in order: No writer in her right mind would dare to speak for all Baptists. Because Baptists are a collection of autonomous churches, there are always Baptist churches or Baptist members who will disagree, in part if not altogether, with a position taken by another Baptist. Therefore, this writer claims only to speak for Baptists as they are on record historically or as they may be generally characterized. Be assured that some Baptists somewhere may take exception with any statement made here. That is a part of the freedom of Baptists!

WOMEN CLAIM BAPTIST DOCTRINE

Whenever Baptist men have difficulty controlling Baptist women, Baptist theology is often the culprit. Baptist doctrine places great confidence in the believer. Women find affirmation and support in these doctrines. Rejecting the overriding authority of bishops and priests, Baptists from their beginning laid spiritual responsibility at the feet of believers. This emphasis on the individual's responsibility before God is a cornerstone of Baptist theology. Three doctrines in particular are reassuring to women who are called to minister: the priesthood of the believer, the authority of the scripture, and the autonomy of the local church.

Priesthood of the Believer

The excesses of the Anglican Church (and the Roman Catholic Church before it) greatly influenced the direction of the young group called Baptists. One of the Anglican practices that Baptists strongly resisted was the control the clergy exercised over the people. Baptists agreed with the apostle Peter and Martin Luther that individuals were directly responsible to God.[2] No mediator was needed. Each believer had the right and the responsibility to be her own priest—going directly to God in prayer, being accountable to him, and responding to him.

On the basis of this teaching, a woman is responsible for how she responds to God. She does not need permission from any other source. A minister, a church, or a family member cannot determine the call of a woman. Only she is accountable.

Traditional Baptist doctrine does not address leadership in Baptist churches, institutions, or conventions. Because men were usually the church leaders, many Baptists assume that only men can occupy the highest positions. Many Baptist ministers are taken by surprise when the doctrine of the priesthood of the believer is taken seriously by women in their congregations. Frequently a woman hears messages from the pulpit which insist that people should listen to and heed God's call. The message from the pulpit does not stipulate that only men can answer this call. Yet, when a woman responds to the call of God to minister, she sometimes is told by the same minister that God does not call women to preach. These women insist that they are merely taking the message of the minister seriously. They also point out that ministers are not being fair in their preaching if they make no gender differentiation in their message but only accept male respondents. The theology is being preached, but parts of it are intended only for men—an unspoken limitation.

Theological confusion is created in other arenas of church life as well. Baptist organizations nurture a woman's faith and train her to express it, but these groups want her to express her faith only in ways approved by her immediate culture. In the nineteenth century Baptist women were encouraged to give their testimony and lead in public prayer. Mission groups educated women in mission needs, trained them how to meet those needs in various ways, gave them leadership training and experience, and eventually trained even young girls to learn the same skills. Today women continue to be trained in these methods. Churches devote much time to training their young women and teaching the stewardship of using one's gifts with an unspoken understanding that women will know which ones they cannot use in the church. When Baptist women choose to claim the full message of the church and use the church's fine training in ways that violate the unspoken message, the women's motives are usually questioned. This problem is not new; it has been with Baptists for over a century and still confuses women.

In Baptist doctrine stressing the priesthood of the believer, the term *believer* is not gender specific. In theory, a believer should respond positively to the call of God, whatever that task may be. Obviously this doctrine is a potent ally of Baptist women. Baptist practices, however, have usually assumed that a call to ministry leadership was the domain of men only. Doctrine as it is stated and doctrine as it is practiced therefore clash.

Authority of Scripture

Baptists, like other Christians, observed the abuses and fallibilities of the human religious authorities before them. Rather quickly Baptists made it clear that their authority would be scripture. For guidance on matters in question, Baptists ask, "What does the scripture teach?"

Since biblical translation and interpretation have been done predominantly by men, biblical materials could only reflect language and meaning as men saw it. Most men were sure that the scripture clearly taught that men should lead and women should follow. As women became more literate and more biblically informed, they discovered that some scripture clearly affirmed women's call to ministry. In their study of scripture, women found affirmation for their call to ministry. Scripture was *their* authority.

Using scripture as their authority, women claimed the call to ministry. Using scripture as their authority, opponents claimed that women could not be called to minister. Since the early 1970s the Southern Baptist Convention has made several attempts to use scripture to limit the roles of women in church life. The most blatant action was passage of a curiously reasoned resolution at the annual meeting in 1984 which states that those Baptists present recognized

> the authority of Scripture in all matters of faith and practice ... ; [that] The New Testament enjoins all Christians to proclaim the gospel ... ; [that] The New Testament emphasizes the equal dignity of men and women (Gal. 3:28) and that the Holy Spirit was at Pentecost divinely outpoured on men and women alike (Acts 2:17) ... ; [that] The Scriptures attest to God's delegated order of authority ... [that] The Scriptures teach that women are not in public worship to assume a role of authority over men lest confusion reign in the local church (I Cor. 14:33–36) ... ; and While Paul commends women and men alike in other roles of ministry and service (Titus 2:1–10), he excludes women from pastoral leadership (1 Tim. 2:12) to preserve a submission God requires because the man was first in creation and the woman was first in the Edenic fall (1 Tim. 2:13ff); ... Women are held in high honor for their unique and significant contribution to the advancement of Christ's kingdom, and the building of godly homes should be esteemed for its vital contribution to developing personal Christian character and Christlike concern for others.
>
> Therefore, be it *Resolved*, That we not decide concerns of Christian doctrine and practice by modern cultural, sociological, and ecclesiastical trends or by emotional factors; that we remind ourselves of the dearly bought Baptist principle of the final authority

of Scripture in matters of faith and conduct; and that we encourage
the service of women in all aspects of church life and work other
than pastoral functions and leadership roles entailing ordination.[3]

No wonder Baptist women are sometimes confused!

Autonomy of the Local Church

As a lifelong Baptist, this author is convinced that the invisible in-
scription above the pulpit of every Baptist church is, "No one can tell
us what to do!" That attitude can be quite frustrating at times, yet it
expresses a crucial Baptist doctrine. As the believer is responsible directly to God, so each church is accountable only to God. There is no
Baptist hierarchy to make Baptist churches conform to any practice. Of
course, Baptist organizations have ways of bringing pressure on local
churches, but ultimately a Baptist congregation can do as it pleases and
still call itself Baptist. The autonomy of the local church means that
some Baptist churches ordain and/or employ women as ministers,
while other Baptist churches adamantly denounce the practice as heresy. Baptist doctrine assures each church of that authority. Autonomy
is a unique freedom that Baptists treasure.

For a woman called to ministry, Baptist autonomy can be both a
liability and an asset. Local autonomy means that no one is capable of
making a church place a woman in a leadership position. On the other
hand, it means that the only people who will make that decision, her
church, are the people who know her well. Some churches who have
reservations about women doing ministry have no qualms about Ms. X
whom they know. So they ordain her. Although they may never hire
her or any other woman, they will proudly ordain her. The woman
needs only the approval of her congregation to become an ordained
minister. No hierarchical approval beyond her church is necessary.

Local autonomy does not protect a woman and her supporters
from opposition within the national convention or from area churches.
Male leaders opposed to women in ministry argue that in spite of Baptist doctrines, only men can lead since Jesus had only men among the
twelve disciples. Some Baptists insist that public ministry is not womanly. Two nineteenth-century Baptist leaders, A. T. Robertson and John
A. Broadus, were outspoken in their opposition to women speaking in
mixed assemblies.[4] In that era women were expected to lead only with
their influence, their purity, and their piety. They could never be the
figures that represented God. This idea has deep roots in Christianity.
Augustine taught that man by himself was the image of God; but

woman alone could not be in God's image.[5] Medieval churchmen were afraid that women's biological cycles would contaminate the altar. That fear in its many forms has not yet been obliterated.

In this century the old fears are topped with new layers of fear. The fear that Christianity will become more feminine and less masculine haunts some Baptists. Women's sexuality continues to be a major obstacle. And ministry is still viewed as a man's domain although nurturing, which is the essence of ministry, is perceived in our culture as a feminine characteristic.

Since Baptists began four hundred years ago, the men-only viewpoint of leadership has dominated Baptist life, inhibiting many women from even considering aspiring to the more powerful positions in their churches and denomination. At the same time a few women have claimed the doctrines Baptists taught as valid for women as well. These women prepared for ministry and sought, many times without success, to be professional ministers. The impediment to ministry for Baptist women has been Baptist culture, not Baptist theology.

Baptist doctrine is quite liberating for women. As Edna Snows said in 1978 in a letter to the editor of the Georgia Baptist paper, the *Christian Index*, "If the gospel, the good news, does not free women from bondage . . . , it is not good news for women."[6]

MINISTRY FOR BAPTIST WOMEN

Because of Baptist doctrine and in spite of persistent opposition, Baptist women find effective ways to minister within Baptist circles. Their contributions have been prevalent in the areas of missions, education, and denominational activities and through their local church ministries.

Missions

The greatest contribution Baptist women have made to ministry in the Baptist denomination is in the area of missions. From prayer groups to the mission fields Baptist women have been keenly interested in evangelizing the heathen. Mary Webb of Boston formed the Boston Female Society in 1800, gathering Congregational and Baptist women together to pray for and give financial support to missions. Webb's society was the first mission society in America. During the next few years, she was instrumental in encouraging the formation of similar societies in other states.[7] In the meantime Ann Judson sailed to India in 1812 with her husband, Adoniram. Their pleas to Baptists in the United States prompted Mary Webb's society to send money immediately. The Judsons' companion, Luther Rice, returned to America to secure more funds. As a result of Rice's work and the Judsons' repeated requests from the mission field, Baptists in America formed their first national convention, commonly known as the Triennial Convention, primarily for the purpose of supporting missionaries like the Judsons. Their commitment to missions has shaped Baptists. Women have shaped missions.

As Baptist churches were forming in greater numbers during the nineteenth century, men assumed the responsibility of hiring pastors and conducting the business of the church; women assumed the responsibility of missions education and support. Offerings were usually once- or twice-a-year events, often targeted to a time when money was plentiful, such as harvest time. One large contribution was made once a year. However, women had no income except perhaps the money kept in the sugar bowl from the sale of butter and eggs. Women could make no large contributions, so they decided to bring regular offerings of nickels and dimes from their sugar bowls to each meeting. To the astonishment of many, the regular small offerings of the women often exceeded the single large offering of the men. Gradually the women's method of giving became the accepted method for Baptists.

The nickels and dimes of the women from several states combined to provide steady financial support for missionaries serving in remote lands. Meanwhile the men appointed missionaries and controlled the mission boards. But Baptist women, black and white, were the backbone of financial support and missions education.[8]

Missions support improved as people were more informed. Therefore missions education grew in its importance. As the nineteenth century drew to a close, women were busy providing and improving missions education. Women wrote and published materials about mission work around the world. Groups of women, girls, and young children were organized to learn about, pray for, and give to missions. Women led these groups and trained new leaders. Mission organizations in Baptist churches have been predominantly, if not solely, led by women. As they gathered and taught mission information and encouraged members to pray and give money to missions, women in large numbers ministered within Baptist circles. Their ministry in missions support and education is valued but is often taken for granted.

For women, the missions were far away and also in their own backyards. Missionaries working in the United States also needed support. Native-American work often received strong support from Baptist mission societies. Local needs were also recognized. Histories of churches and missions organizations document repeatedly the community needs being met by various women's groups. Aid societies for uneducated girls, poor mothers, immigrant families, older citizens, or homeless men were common, especially in cities. Social ministries became a crucial part of missions for Baptist women. Many of these ministries were close enough for women to become personally involved in the work. Baptist women have been and continue to be involved in missions at several levels. The Baptist story of missions is a powerful story of the commitment of women.

Although the pastor's wife is held in high esteem, the woman in Baptist life who occupies the highest rung of the women's spiritual ladder is the missionary, especially a foreign missionary. For most Baptists there is no more noble goal for a Baptist woman than to be a foreign missionary, and Baptist women are proud of their sisters who have served or presently serve on mission fields. A married female missionary is often expected to serve as homemaker and active church member, cultivating the national women through women's groups. Single female missionaries are appointed to a specific task in fields such as medicine or education. However, it is not unusual for women to find they are needed for many other missionary tasks. Retiring female missionaries are known to complain that tasks they routinely perform on the mission field are frowned upon or prohibited in Baptist churches in the United States. For some women, being a missionary is more liberating professionally than working in a Baptist church in the United States.

Initially, Baptists did show discomfort with the role of women on the mission field. In the nineteenth century the Black Foreign Mission Convention paid both husband and wife salaries but sent the money to the husband. White Baptists were reluctant to appoint single women whom the boards viewed as defenseless.

In spite of obstacles, women repeatedly applied for mission work abroad and in the United States. Ann Judson and Henrietta Shuck blazed the trail for Baptists in foreign missions in the first half of the nineteenth century. Joanna P. Moore, a white Baptist, was highly regarded by black Baptists for her work among freed men and women, helping them in various practical ways to meet the new challenges of freedom. A letter from Lottie Moon in China inspired Southern Baptist women to increase their giving to foreign missions. Emma B. DeLaney of the National Baptist Convention led mission work in Liberia. Isabel Crawford was a spunky, talented American Baptist missionary who worked in Oklahoma among the Kiowa Indians in 1893.

The issue of women's roles on the mission field became a matter of concern that was addressed in some Baptist state newspapers. Some writers suggested that since woman was largely responsible for bringing sin into the world, she should do all she could to remove it. Working from a more positive viewpoint, many women's mission societies decided to use their financial clout. When one mission board showed reluctance to appoint single women as missionaries, some societies began to specify that their monies be used for the support of female missionaries. The mission board got the message. Women were then appointed with greater frequency and were assured of financial support by the board. The acceptance of women as career missionaries was given strong support by the women's mission societies.

The role of a missionary is the most familiar and most accepted professional role for Baptist women in ministry. For Baptist women in general, ministry has been and still is largely centered in missions: missions support, missions education, and career mission work.

Education

Teaching is perhaps the most common ministry of Baptist women. Sunday school teachers in Baptist churches are predominantly women. The faculty of Vacation Bible Schools (short-term summer programs) is staffed overwhelmingly by women. Most Baptists agree that Baptist churches could not function if the women withdrew their services. Women are the backbone of the educational programs of Baptist churches. In many cases men are in decision-making positions and women are carrying out the work. With few exceptions these women are happy and content to do the work. Many women have a strong sense of call and ministry regarding their work in the church and receive much satisfaction from it. There is no question that they make valuable contributions to the work of the church.

Outside the church Baptist women find professional teaching opportunities in denominational institutions. With the explosion of church-funded schools in the nineteenth century many women, especially single women, found respectability, income, and a sense of ministry in teaching. The proliferation of girls' schools at all levels gave women many teaching opportunities and a few administrative ones. Since women were so adept at molding the "plastic minds of the young," as one Virginia writer put it, women were allowed to teach girls at all levels as well as young boys.[9]

Eventually Baptist women became involved in several levels of education: the girls' schools, coeducational schools, schools in the mountains of Appalachia, schools in the villages of South America, women's colleges, coeducational colleges, and eventually seminaries.[10] A few women served as educational administrators. A notable leader in education was Nannie H. Burroughs, a National Baptist, who in 1901 stunned an assembly of black Baptist leaders when she proposed a school for black women. When black Baptists did not provide the funds, she raised the money to purchase land in Washington, D.C. In 1907 she announced to the National Baptist Convention that she had the land and needed fifty thousand dollars to build and launch the school. National Baptists did not have that kind of money and discouraged her efforts. Booker T. Washington told her that the nation's capital was not a good location. Burroughs believed that the border state location was indeed the best location. Although men gave no support, women believed in Burroughs's proposal, providing funds and encouragement—as was their pattern in educational matters.[11] She raised the money, and the school that opened in 1909 was known as the National Trade and Professional School for Women and Girls.[12]

For some women, teaching was simply a good career. For many others, the career was accompanied by a sense of ministry. Considering the low wages and long hours common in the field, ministry it was.

Denominational

As early as 1886 Baptist women were providing literature for Sunday schools; the women in Baltimore formed a Literature Department.[13] Teaching people in the local churches about the programs and needs on the mission fields and being involved in the work on various mission fields prompted women to design, write, and publish their own materials. Mission leaders needed literature giving missions information. Women teaching inner city or migrant girls to read wanted to use Bible study materials.[14] Publishing mission materials became the responsibility of the women. Women such as Helen Barrett Montgomery traveled to foreign countries where Baptists were involved in evangelistic work and wrote inspiring books about the work and needs there. Women such as Annie Armstrong produced materials on missions organizations. Missions education was a field ripe for women's talents and interests.

Denomination ministry outside women's groups has been more difficult for women. A common path taken by the denominational professional woman is movement from local church staff to state work to the staff of a denominational agency. As early as 1882 the Southern Baptist Convention (SBC) authorized its boards to appoint a "competent woman" to coordinate and strengthen the work of the women's committees in various states.[15] At the time there was tension in the convention over the woman-suffrage movement, and some feared a woman leader would face opposition. The "competent woman" was never employed. At that time the Foreign Mission Board and Home Mission Board of the Southern Baptist Convention were paying the heads of their agencies while Annie Armstrong worked without pay as the head of Woman's Missionary Union. After eighteen years she was pressed to accept a salary, although some in the convention were appalled that Miss Armstrong might commercialize her services by accepting pay and thereby "dim her glory."[16] However, Una R. Lawrence, mission study editor at the Home Mission Board of the SBC in 1926–1947, made it clear that "the pay you can afford to make will have much to do with the time I can give to the work."[17]

Women in the American Baptist Convention have found more opportunities for denominational involvement at upper levels than have women in the Southern Baptist or National Baptist Conventions. Helen Barrett Montgomery was elected president of the Northern (now American) Baptist Convention in 1921. Two black Baptist conventions have had women serve in denominational positions other than women's groups: in 1990 a woman served as the executive director of the Sunday School Publishing Board of the National Baptist Convention, Inc., and in the same year a woman headed the Congress of Christian Education in the Progressive National Baptist Convention.[18] In the Southern Baptist Convention, the president of the Woman's Missionary Union was not included as a member of the Executive Committee of the convention until 1953. Among Southern Baptists only two women have been elected to convention offices, Marie Mathis and Mrs. Carl Bates; they were elected as vice-president in 1963 and 1976 respectively. To date, neither the Southern Baptist Convention or National Baptist Conventions have elected women presidents.

One of the best denominational employers for Southern Baptist women has been the Woman's Missionary Union (WMU). From their organization in 1888 until after the turn of the century, the early officers of WMU declined pay. Like Miss Armstrong, they considered their work an offering to missions. Eventually professional specialists like Juliette Mather were hired in the 1920s to promote missions education. The result was an immediate leap in WMU membership which soon required more attention from central headquarters and therefore more professional workers. Today WMU employs more than two hundred women.[19] For many women a career with a state WMU or the national WMU office has been an effective route to careers in other Southern Baptist arenas.

In recent years a serious decline of women in leadership positions in SBC agencies and institutions has occurred. In 1952 14 percent of these leadership positions were filled by women. Thirty-two years later, in 1984, after a decade of emphasis on women's issues, women held 1 percent fewer leadership positions than in 1952. North Carolina's experience illustrates the serious decline in the numbers of women in denominational ministry. Between 1950 and 1980 the percentage of female directors of missions in North Carolina fell from 15 to 5 percent, and women ministers of youth and ministers of music dropped from 68 to 16 percent. Between 1950 and 1981 the percentage of female campus ministers in that state plunged from 63 to 7 percent.[20] The area of personnel that suffered the greatest decline in women employees nationwide by 1971 was the Book Store Division of the Baptist Sunday School Board. In the two-year period between 1969 and 1971, the percentage of female bookstore managers fell from 71 to 47 percent.[21] By 1993 the percentage had fallen further to 19 percent.[22] It is becoming more difficult for Southern Baptist women to serve in denominational positions. The "takeover leadership," a fundamentalist group of Southern Baptists who took control of the convention in 1979, does not approve of women serving in positions of authority.

Chaplaincy is another sphere of ministry for Baptist women. Some women know early that their call is to the chaplaincy, and their training is targeted to prepare them for that ministry. Other ordained women enter chaplaincy when they cannot find pastoral positions in churches.

Baptist women work in a variety of denominational positions, many of them clerical or support services. To many these jobs may seem insignificant to a study of ministry. However, to some women these are not merely nine-to-five jobs; they are crucial forms of ministry. A survey undertaken in 1978 of women employees of SBC agencies revealed that 38 percent felt God led them to work for him in that job. Sixty-eight percent felt called by God to do the work they were doing. The same survey uncovered substantial dissatisfaction with the ability of women to make a career advance in SBC agencies.[23]

A word must also be said about the unpaid denominational career of some Baptist women, such as some mission society presidents. These women have given their full attention to denominational work without a salary. For a season or two or more, they have been nonsalaried professionals. Much of the mission work of Baptists is indebted to the millions of hours volunteered by women across the nation. Many a Baptist woman has devoted a large portion of her time to missions organization, missions education, or missions involvement. Baptists' strength in missions overseas and at home is a direct result of the volunteer ministry of thousands of women.

Local Church Ministry

One of the earliest roles of public ministry for Baptist women was as the minister's wife. Leonard Sweet listed the "partner" role as one of the typical roles of ministers' wives in the nineteenth century. Sweet described the various ways these women were authentic partners in the ministries of their husbands. Baptist women, he noted, commonly prayed and spoke publicly. Some Baptist minister's wives energetically used their abilities and influence in evangelism and in the church. Sweet saw them as the forerunners of today's clergy couple.[24]

Some wives of ministers today feel called to be partners in ministry. All wives of ministers do not feel a call to such a partnership, nor should they. However, those who do sense that call and respond to it need to be recognized as women in ministry. Evidence of the contemporary partner role emerged in surveys done by the Baptist Sunday School Board of the SBC. The Research Services Department surveyed ministers' wives in 1976 and ministers' families in 1978. Over three-fourths of the wives felt called by God to be pastors' wives. Twenty-three percent of them described their role more specifically as "set apart." One-fourth of the wives assessed their involvement in the ministry of their husband as a teamworker, sharing in his ministry. Over a third of them thought wives should be trained for their special responsibilities.[25] Some pastors' wives have earned seminary degrees. The pastor's wife who follows the partner model is not listed on the church staff and receives no salary, but ministry is her career.

Salaried positions open to women have not been abundant or well paid. In the nineteenth century, women began to be employed as organist or music director at a salary of perhaps one hundred dollars a year.[26] Vocational options in the local churches continued to be limited well into this century. Data indicate that women initially entered church positions with low pay and few benefits. As the salary and benefits rose, women had fewer professional opportunities. In the early 1970s as the women's liberation movement was stirring, Norman Letsinger studied the movement's implication for the Southern Baptist Convention. His findings reveal an erosion of women's leadership in nonpastoral church staff positions between the 1940s and the 1970s. Women had often served in the positions of educational director or music director during the 1940s and 1950s. As more education was demanded and better pay provided, more men became interested in positions formerly held by women. As men in increasing numbers filled the positions, the titles were changed to minister of education and minister of music. Secretarial assistance, greater fringe benefits, better salaries, ordination, and opportunities to preach, which women usually were denied, were usually provided for men in the same job, although women's tenure on the job tended to be longer.[27]

Today the nonpastoral church staff positions in which women minister range from minister of education, minister of youth, minister of children, minister of activities, or minister of music to church hostess to secretary to counselor. However, in many churches the most powerful employee may be a woman, for the most influential person in the congregation is the church secretary, according to one survey.[28] Perhaps this view arises from the extensive knowledge church secretaries usually acquire about the workings of the church and the power that knowledge gives.

Preaching

Writing for the *Encyclopedia of Southern Baptists* in 1958, Juliette Mather said, "Southern Baptist women do not preach and are not pastors."[29] Mather was speaking the truth in 1958, but it had not always been so. Baptist foremothers in seventeenth-century England preached. During the first Great Awakening in the late eighteenth century in this country, three Baptist women preached in Sturbridge, Massachusetts. And few preachers anywhere matched the fire and zeal of Martha Marshall of the eighteenth century. She was even jailed in Windsor, Connecticut, for preaching and exhorting. Leonard Sweet said that she launched the southern tradition of women preachers among Separate Baptists.[30] Freewill Baptists in 1815 were the first Baptists to license women ministers in America.[31] Even though Baptist churches gladly heard women evangelists in the nineteenth century, there was debate within the Baptist community about the propriety of women speaking in public.

The doctrine of usefulness as taught by the Puritans and later by Charles Finney compelled women to use the gifts God had given them. Baptist and Methodist women were encouraged to tell of their conversions and lead public prayers. In fact, many Baptist women first learned to speak in public in the prayer meetings and class meetings of their churches. But Baptists were slow to ordain women. American Baptists ordained Edith Hill in 1894.[32] By 1925 dozens of American Baptist women were ordained.[33] Lansing Burrows, president of the Southern Baptist Convention in 1914, noted that the idea of ordaining women had excited many Christians and had significant support.[34] But the support must not have been too significant among Baptists in the South, since it was another fifty years before a woman was ordained by Southern Baptists. In 1964 Addie Davis was the first Southern Baptist woman to be ordained into the ministry, but she could find no Southern Baptist church to pastor. In 1972 Druecillar Fordham became the Southern Baptist Convention's first woman pastor and also its first black ordained female pastor. In 1979 the Black Ministers Conference of Baltimore and Vicinity admitted women preachers for the first time, which Leroy Fitts called a "shocking sign of change in the role of women in black Baptist life."[35] Since the early 1970s increased numbers of Southern Baptist and National Baptist women have made clear their call to preach and have prepared theologically to do so, but only a few have found churches willing to call them. As of January 1993 National Baptists had 311 women in pastoral positions (91 as pastors, 220 as associates), with 110 of them ordained. In 1995 there were 225 ordained women in the National Baptist Convention USA, Inc. As of April 1995 American Baptists had 831 ordained women, but 1,398 in ministry positions; Southern Baptists in 1995 had 1,130 ordained women, with 60 serving as pastors and 90 as associates.[36] Unfortunately, one woman's quip is all too true: "When I was a child I wanted to grow up to be a preacher. Then I grew up and decided I'd rather be a Baptist."[37]

Letsinger drew these conclusions regarding the Southern Baptist Convention:

> (1) that the status of women in Southern Baptist circles is considerably below that of men; (2) that many Southern Baptists have a limited view of the role women should fulfill in society and the church; and (3) that many Southern Baptists have attitudes that are in direct opposition to the goals of the WLM [Women's Liberation Movement].[38]

While some strides for women were made in the SBC during the 1970s and early 1980s (with an increased number of women serving as trustees of agencies, employed as theology faculty, or reaching new career heights), the fundamentalist takeover of the SBC during the 1980s severely slowed or reversed those trends. The 1984 resolution (referred to earlier) discloses the current leadership's view of women's limited role in religious institutions. Historically, the 1970s and early 1980s may well be the peak period of ordained women's involvement in the SBC. Women are given more opportunities to minister in the American Baptist Churches USA (formerly the American Baptist Convention). The National Baptist Convention, Inc., remains reluctant to provide women a full forum for ministry. As noted above, both National Baptists and American Baptists employ more women for ministry than they ordain.

INFLUENCE ON THEOLOGY

As discouraging as Letsinger's findings are, women and liberation theology are making some impact on the theology of Baptists. Those Baptists who see all authority resting in men are not open to the issues which concern women or to the theology taught by women. On the other hand, there are some Baptists who are listening and changing. For those attentive Baptists, women are beginning to influence theology. Evelyn Higginbotham in *Righteous Discontent: The Women's Movement in the Black Baptist Church, 1880-1900* provides a fine discussion of the influence of black Baptist women on the theology of their churches.

Like other Protestant women, some Baptist women find the solely male interpretations of God theologically limiting and oppressing. Like their Protestant sisters, some Baptist women find inclusive images, language, and theology to be liberating. As already noted, few Baptist women serve in pulpits where their theology can regularly be heard. Various Baptist women's groups do provide opportunities for women to hear each other speak or preach, to participate in inclusive worship services, and to share their theology. In small, but not insignificant, ways Baptist women have been influencing Baptist theology. As noted early in this article, Baptist theology is liberating. Therefore, Baptist women are challenging Baptists to practice the theology Baptists claim. That influence has come primarily from the following areas.

Literature

Because Baptist women have had few public forums in which to speak theologically to both men and women, their influence through public speaking remains limited. Their greater impact has been through their writing and publishing ministries. Women who wrote the early missions materials affirmed the use of women's gifts and were models of the professional use of women's abilities. Writing Sunday School and mission study curricula gave women opportunities to interpret or focus biblical materials in more inclusive ways. In some cases women used those opportunities to reexamine what it means to be human or to be woman. Through their writing women have quietly had some impact on Baptist theology.

One influence of Baptist women is subtle but powerful: their influence on the theology of the social gospel. As writers women emphasized the nurturing ministries of Jesus as their model for meeting needs in their own communities. The social gospel which came under strong attack from many pulpits was no problem for women whose mission interests and literature affirmed it as a crucial part of the gospel. While white Baptist pastors often portrayed personal salvation as the solution to all of society's problems, the women did not.[39] The women understood evangelism in more holistic terms; the person's physical and social needs must also be addressed. Salvation was of utmost importance, but as the women examined Christ's ministry they discovered that Jesus' ministry also was attentive to other needs.

Literature which identified needs and gave specific ways of meeting those needs influenced how those readers interpreted the gospel in their communities. As early as 1908 Baptist women saw medical missions as a natural model of Christ's ministry. The women insisted that treating people medically was a ministry in itself, not merely a bribe for evangelism.[40] In fact, the women believed that leading a community to be Christian in its beliefs and practices was more important than converting individuals to the Baptist faith. A belief in Christ could make a difference in every area of society—its education, its laws, family life, the rights of others, and the needs of others.[41] This theology motivated the work of Baptists among the needy in the inner cities. Literature written and published by women was instrumental in shaping this theology and action.[42]

At publishing boards, as women became editors the literature began to reflect some of their concerns. Family issues, inclusive language, scripture passages focusing on women, and contemporary illustrations reflecting women's interests became more frequent. Readers began to discover a Bible with more women than they had noticed before and a scripture which addressed issues of concern to women. Some readers objected to these new focuses, causing some publishing boards to move gingerly with the new trends.

Education

In the 1970s Baptist colleges and seminaries responded to the women's movement by incorporating some Women in Religion courses into their curricula. Women theologians such as Molly Marshall at Southern Baptist Theological Seminary in Louisville, Kentucky, taught seminary students theology from a woman's perspective. Some professors incorporated more material related to women in their courses. Other professors acknowledged sensitivity to inclusive theology and inclusive language. In some institutions these sensitivities were isolated; in others they were institutional policies. As a result of growing fundamentalist control, these trends are now in reverse in Southern Baptist institutions. Molly Marshall was forced to resign in 1994.

Increasing numbers of women and men are being exposed to more inclusive theologies in some Baptist schools. Some students resist the exposure, while others clearly have their consciousness raised. As the influenced students leave schools to enter positions of leadership, they carry with them a new understanding of misogynistic interpretations of scripture, and a new appreciation of inclusive theologies, of an androgynous God, and of the need to affirm and support female leadership.

Denominational Support

Organizations which support women in ministry have emerged in several Baptist conventions. The Spiritual Life Commission Women Auxiliary of the National Baptist Convention, Inc., tracks and encourages their female ministers. Women in Ministry of the American Baptist Churches USA provides similar services. In July 1995 Women in Ministry of the Southern Baptist Convention disassociated itself from the SBC and changed its name to Baptist Women in Ministry. Through these organizations, ordained women bring feminine influence on theology to a wider audience. In these various small audiences, Baptist women and men are hearing women ministers call attention to biblical passages that focus on individual women, feminine metaphors, or issues of interest to women. Obscure stories such as the courage of the Hebrew midwives in Egypt (Ex. 1:15–22) are used by women ministers to broaden understanding of Hebrew history, women's role in it, and God's actions through the lives of Hebrew women. Women ministers preach a Christology that emphasizes the nurturing, compassionate, ministering Christ. Baptist women give new focus to the stories about Jesus' encounters with women, the significance of those stories in first-century Jewish culture, Jesus' use of feminine metaphors, and his concern for the oppressed in society. In contrast, male Baptist preachers often favor Paul's teachings over Jesus', stressing authority of men in the home and church.

In the last decade the leadership of the Southern Baptist Convention has become more chauvinistic. The moderate wing of the denomination has formed the Alliance of Baptists and the Cooperative Baptist Fellowship. Both of these groups have listened to the concerns of women in ministry and have responded more positively to them. Both groups are careful to include women in planning, programming, and worship and in theological positions.

In all Baptist groups it is difficult to assess fully the impact of the female missions' leadership on the denomination's theology. It is also difficult to deny their influence. Baptists' keen interest in missions is largely due to the work and education of women's groups.

WOMEN AND THE BAPTIST EXPERIENCE

The gap between Baptist doctrine and Baptist practice creates tension for some Baptist women. In recent years some young women considering ministerial careers among Baptists have determined that the gap was too great for them to bridge. These women have chosen to leave the Baptist denomination for those denominations more hospitable to ministering women. Consequently, Baptists have lost some of their brightest and best-educated young women. The denomination that nurtured them, reared them, and invested significantly in their training has great difficulty finding a place in its theology for women to exercise gifts of ministry. American Baptists and Freewill Baptists encourage women in ministry more than Southern Baptists and National Baptists do. But in none of these Baptist groups do women occupy posts of leadership in proportion to their membership in the denomination. For example, the average black church has three times as many female members as male members. Yet leadership is overwhelmingly male. Once more, Baptists need to hear the address Nannie Burroughs gave to National Baptists in 1900, "How the Sisters Are Hindered from Helping."

Remarkably many Baptist women have found effective and varied ways of ministering. The denomination which in earlier days allowed women to be preachers and deacons, then retreated from that openness and severely restricted women is very slowly and reluctantly coming to terms with the new roles and expectations of women who take their Baptist faith seriously.

NOTES

1. Joan Morris, *The Lady Was a Bishop* (New York: Macmillan, 1973), xi.
2. 1 Peter 2:9 and Martin Luther, "The Freedom of a Christian," in *Three Treatises* (Philadelphia: Fortress Press, 1978).

3. *1984 Southern Baptist Convention Annual* (Nashville: Executive Committee, SBC, 1984), 65.
4. William P. Harvey, *Shall Women Preach?* (Louisville: Baptist Book Concern, 1906), 4–5, 18.
5. Angela M. Lucas, *Woman in the Middle Ages: Religion, Marriage and Letters* (New York: St. Martins Press, 1983), 5–6.
6. Letter to the editor, *Christian Index*, 30 November 1978, p. 12.
7. Leon McBeth, *Women in Baptist Life* (Nashville: Broadman Press, 1979), 75–78.
8. See Sandy D. Martin's *Black Baptists and African Missions* (Macon, Ga.: Mercer University Press, 1989) for a discussion of the numerous women's auxiliaries formed in connection with black mission boards.
9. "The Sphere of Woman's Usefulness," *Religious Herald*, 14 May 1868, p. 2.
10. See Evelyn Brooks Higginbotham, *Righteous Discontent: The Women's Movement in the Black Baptist Church, 1880–1920* (Cambridge: Harvard University Press, 1993) for an excellent discussion of the significant role black women played in establishing and supporting educational institutions.
11. See Higginbotham, chapter 6, for a more complete discussion.
12. Owen D. Pelt and Ralph Lee Smith, *The Story of the National Baptists* (New York: Vantage Press, 1960), 142–44.
13. McBeth, 106.
14. See Evelyn W. Thompson's article "Southern Baptist Women as Writers and Editors," in *Baptist History and Heritage* (July 1987), for a more extensive sampling of Baptist women in publication careers.
15. *1882 Southern Baptist Convention Annual*, 25.
16. *Christian Index*, 21 May 1903.
17. Una R. Lawrence papers (Historical Commission, SBC, Archives).
18. C. Eric Lincoln and Lawrence H. Mamiya, *The Black Church in the African American Experience* (Durham: Duke University Press, 1990), 45.
19. Catherine B. Allen, *A Century to Celebrate* (Birmingham: Woman's Missionary Union, 1987), 59.
20. Betty McGary Pearce, "SBC Women: Research Reveals Slow Progress," *Folio* (Spring 1984): 6.
21. Norman H. Letsinger, "The Women's Liberation Movement: Implications for Southern Baptists," Th.D. dissertation, Southern Baptist Theological Seminary, 1973, 157.
22. Telephone call to Book Store Marketing, Baptist Sunday School Board, 13 January 1993.
23. See Orrin D. Morris, "Survey of Women Employees of Southern Baptist Convention Agencies, April–May, 1978," Home Mission Board, SBC.
24. Leonard I. Sweet, *The Minister's Wife: Her Role in Nineteenth Century American Evangelism* (Philadelphia: Temple University Press, 1983), 115. See also chapter 8.
25. See Kenneth E. Hayes, "Pastor's Wives Survey," July 1976, and J. Clifford Tharp, Jr., "The Minister's Family," September 1978, p. 9. Both surveys

were done by the Research Services Department, Sunday School Board, SBC.

26. W. Harrison Daniel, "Virginia Baptists and Feminism, 1865–1900," *Virginia Social Service Journal*, 5/78 (November 1970).

27. See Letsinger, 194–208, for more complete findings.

28. "Secretaries Network," *Folio* (Summer 1986): 8.

29. Juliette Mather, "Women, Convention Privileges of," *Encyclopedia of Southern Baptists* (1958) II: 1,544.

30. Sweet, 115.

31. Janette Hassey, *No Time for Silence: Evangelical Women in Public Ministry Around the Turn of the Century* (Grand Rapids: Zondervan, 1986), 56.

32. *Honoring Our Heritage: Pioneer Women in Ministry* (New York: American Baptist Women in Ministry, 1987), 2.

33. Hassey, 62.

34. Lansing Burrows, "Woman's Position in the Church" (sermon, June 1872, Historical Commission, SBC, Archives).

35. Leroy Fitts, *A History of Black Baptists* (Nashville: Broadman Press, 1985), 310.

36. Telephone interviews on 13 January 1993 and 15 May 1995 with Elmorie Miller, National Baptist. Telephone interview on 28 April 1995 with Valentine Loyal, American Baptist. Telephone interview on 27 April 1995 with Sarah Frances Anders, Southern Baptist. Each woman collects data for her convention.

37. Carolyn Weatherford, "Shaping of Leadership Among Southern Baptist Women," *Baptist History and Heritage* (July 1987): 18.

38. Letsinger, 263.

39. A distinction is made here between white and black Baptist pastors since black Baptist ministers have more frequently preached a holistic gospel, believing that personal salvation should be evidenced in meeting crucial social needs.

40. "Medical Missions," *Our Mission Fields* (July 1908): 27.

41. "The Salvation of the City," *Our Missions Fields* (July 1909): 10–11.

42. For additional information regarding social impact see Gregory Vickers, "Southern Baptist Women and Social Concerns, 1910–1929," *Baptist History and Heritage* (October 1988): 3–13, and Catherine Allen, *A Century to Celebrate: History of Woman's Missionary Union* (Birmingham, Ala.: WMU, 1987), 211–62.

Women in the Evangelical Lutheran Church in America

Gracia Grindal

INTRODUCTION

When the American Lutheran Church (ALC) and the Lutheran Church in America (LCA), at their biennial conventions in 1970, approved the ordination of women, they did so for theological reasons. Although the rights of women were admittedly high on the social docket of the day and helped to push the question to the top of the denominations' agendas, the formulators of the recommendations in both churches cited mainly biblical and confessional motivations, not a secular commitment to women's rights. For Lutherans whose commitments to scripture and the confessional writings in the *Book of Concord* are fundamental, the debate about whether to ordain women had hinged on what scripture and the *Augsburg Confession* had to say on this issue. After sending the question of women's ordination to seminaries and other theological advisers, the committees of both denominations came to the conclusion that only traditional practice and ecumenical difficulties, especially with Rome, stood in the way. Scripture, they advised, gave contradictory signals, and nothing in the confessions advised either for or against calling women as pastors. For Lutherans, these theologians maintained, the speaking of the Word was prior in importance to the speaker, whether lay or ordained. It was the Word which had the authority, not the person.

Though the fact that women could be called as pastors in these two Lutheran denominations was a fundamental breakthrough for Lutheran women,[1] what has happened since for women, both lay and ordained, in the Evangelical Lutheran Church in America (ELCA) is more complicated as it includes a broader spectrum of women. Lutherans in this country are not a unified culture or group of people. Until 1960 their histories were ethnic and regional. There are many stories of influential Lutheran women in each of those various histories, and while it would have been simpler to report one such history, this would have given only a fragment of the background of Lutheran women. This messier, more bureaucratic history will show how Lutheran women still have significant cultural histories to share with each other before they can speak meaningfully of "the" Lutheran women's experience. It is difficult to compare the experiences of the typical upper midwestern Scandinavian Lutheran woman, whose more egalitarian culture and experience gave her more access to power in the churches, with a woman of the more patriarchal German Lutheran churches.[2] Significant for this article are the struggles of a wide variety of Lutheran women, lay and ordained, to be included in the structures of the Evangelical Lutheran Church in America (ELCA), a recently formed (1988) Lutheran denomination in America, one that was formed with the avowed intent to be inclusive. This chapter will explore how that rhetoric got started and whether or not it has resulted in any accomplishments for women.

WOMEN IN THE SAGA OF LUTHERAN UNION 1970–1988

As the ALC and the LCA voted to call women as pastors, the other large Lutheran Church in the United States, the Lutheran Church-Missouri Synod (LCMS), was entering a turbulent period which ultimately caused a split and helped to speed the 1988 merger of the ALC and the LCA with a splinter group from Missouri Synod known as the Association of Evangelical Lutheran Churches (AELC).[3] In the early 1960s it had seemed that the Missouri Synod under its moderate leadership was moving together with the ALC and the LCA to form one large Lutheran Church in America. Unaccustomed as LCMS had been to cooperating with other Lutherans in the United States, there were at that time fairly amicable relations between denominations forming the Lutheran Council in the United States (LCUSA), which included representatives from the ALC and the LCA, plus representatives of the conservative Lutheran bodies, the Wisconsin Synod and the Evangelical Lutheran Synod.

The ALC was the result of the 1960 merger of the American Lutheran Church centered in German Lutheran Ohio and Iowa; the Evangelical Lutheran Church, with its upper midwestern and western membership of largely Norwegian descent; the "holy Danes" in the United Evangelical Lutheran Church centered in Iowa and Nebraska; as well as the 1963 merger with the Norwegian Lutheran Free Church. The ALC was thought to be the middle church between the LCMS and the LCA. The LCA, formed in 1962, gathered together the United Lutheran Church in America (whose beginnings are prior to 1742 when Henry Melchoir Muhlenberg came to America to shepherd the German Lutherans on the eastern seaboard) with the Swedish Augustana Church centered in Rock Island, Illinois, the American Evangelical Lutheran Church "happy" Danes, and the Finnish Suomi Synod. Given the accidents of immigration and previous church mergers, the LCA consisted of Lutherans who were the most theologically liberal.

The LCMS,[4] whose American roots went back to the 1830s, was always seen as the most theologically conservative because of its concern for pure doctrine ("die reine Lehre"), which its founders brought with them from Germany. This concern for confessional purity made the LCMS much less interested in compromise and union than many of the other Lutheran bodies who, through years of mergers and schisms, had learned how to do these things well. In 1965 at its Detroit convention, the LCMS had upheld a declaration of women's suffrage in the congregations as long as it did not give women authority over men and it maintained the notion of the "created order."[5] What the declaration meant for local congregations, however, was not clear until the 1969 LCMS convention, which gave women the official right to vote and hold office in Missouri Synod congregations while specifically stating that women were not to "hold the pastoral office nor 'exercise authority over men.' "[6] For some LCMS theologians such as Robert Bertram of Concordia Seminary, who favored the ordination of women, the decision to give women voice in the congregations meant that the ban against women pastors had also been lifted. Once that had happened, Bertram argued, there was no way women could be denied their place as preachers of the Word.

In the late 1960s the theological conversations about women pastors, sponsored by the LCUSA, were going well when a furor began in the Missouri Synod regarding the interpretation of scripture. There had been harbingers of such a battle as early as 1962 when the moderate Oliver Harms was elected president of the LCMS by a convention which also had disciplined a Missouri Synod theologian for failing to hold to the strictest orthodoxy.[7] The conservatives, however, were in the minority, and the ruling moderates continued to forge closer relationships with other Lutheran bodies, especially the ALC. The work of the moderates became evident when in 1968 the ALC declared "pulpit and altar fellowship" with the Missouri Synod, which reciprocated at its biennial convention in 1969. This was also the LCMS convention which approved women's right to vote and hold office in the congregations. The same convention, however, elected as president Jacob Aal

Ottesen Preus, who opposed the historical-critical method of reading the Bible, and, consequently, women pastors.[8] This did not augur well for either LCMS proponents of church fellowship with the ALC or those who favored the ordination of women. Still, the declaration of fellowship was viewed as a remarkable step for both denominations.

As one might expect, in 1971 at the Lutheran Church-Missouri Synod's convention in Milwaukee, the question of the ALC's women pastors was posed. Kent Knutson, president of the ALC, spoke to the delegates of the LCMS convention and devoted a good portion of his speech to the question of ordaining women. In doing so he described the process the LCUSA had gone through to address the issue: "You have had your representatives involved every step of the way. Your representatives on the special subcommittee helped prepare the document which did not recommend ordination but said that each church in its freedom could make this decision within the freedom granted by Scriptures and without being divisive of fellowship. Your representative was chairman of the (LCUSA) division of theological studies at that time. One of your representatives objected. The three presidents at that time sent the study to the churches for their reaction. Many forums were held. Many of your people told us that although your church might make a different decision, it would not be divisive of fellowship."[9] Knutson urged the LCMS not to break fellowship with the ALC, which the convention did not do, although it did send a request to the ALC that it reconsider its action to ordain women, expressing its "strong regret" at this decision of the ALC.[10] This LCMS convention also passed a resolution calling for a report from President Preus "concerning doctrine and life at Concordia Seminary, St. Louis, Missouri." When the Preus report appeared, it contained a variety of interviews with Concordia professors, letters from Preus and Tietjen, declarations of the faculty, etc.[11] Among them was an interview with several Concordia professors concerning the ordination of women in the Missouri Synod. At issue in the interview was how one professor could read the Bible to find in it the approval of ordaining women. What the interviewers wanted was agreement with the theology of the "orders of creation" which taught that God, after the Fall, had commanded Eve to obey Adam, and thus "ordered" creation, indicating that God intended women not to have authority over men. This theologian, however, maintained that the "orders of creation" could not be found in the Bible, and thus the doctrine could not be used to prevent women from speaking in church, either as laywomen or as pastors.[12]

As the controversy began to build, some LCMS women in Illinois formed a group which soon became the Lutheran Women's Caucus

(LWC). Among them were: Christine Grumm, later vice-president of the ELCA; Gretchen Leppke, who would become president of the LWC; Sammy Mayer, who became coordinator of the AELC's Woman in Action for Mission (WAM); Olive Spannaus, an LCMS pastor's wife; Dorothy Stein, who became a director of gerontological ministries in the ELCA; and Carolyn Becker, a Missouri Synod deaconess and pastor's wife.[13] Their newsletter, *Adam's Rib*, later to be renamed *The Well Woman*, was read throughout the LCMS, and their tactics at the 1969 and 1971 Missouri Synod conventions and at district conventions—something like the street theater of the day—attracted notice. At first their goal was to advocate better working conditions and pay for women parochial schoolteachers, but it was not long before the calling of women pastors became an important cause for them as well.[14]

The 1971 request by the Missouri Synod that the ALC reconsider its decision to call women as pastors caused more theological debate within the ALC, which resulted in a repudiation of the orders of creation theology by ALC seminary faculties.[15] This reconsideration, however, did not affect the pace of change in the ALC or the LCA. After the decision to ordain women, both denominations realized that they needed to address many other issues related to the ordination of women as well as the questions raised by the burgeoning women's movement. The ALC in its 1972 statement, "Women and Men in Church Society—Toward Wholeness in the Christian Community," called for the 1972 ALC convention to establish the Task Force on Women in Church and Society, which the convention did. The statement noted that the faculties of the ALC seminaries had answered the Missouri Synod's questions about the ordination of women and the orders of creation clearly: "This firm response, with accompanying documentation, frees The American Lutheran Church to do that which justice and equity require in its teachings and practices concerning femaleness and maleness in the wholeness of the Christian community."[16]

The statement then offered some guidelines for action in the ALC: 1) nominating more women to positions of leadership; 2) making the language of the church more inclusive; 3) calling more women to theological leadership; 4) encouraging programs that would assist local congregations in dealing with these same questions; and 5) charging the denomination to review its progress in including women at the next convention in 1974.[17] The 1974 convention of the ALC showed that it had taken the resolution seriously: a task force on Women in Higher Education was appointed by the Board of College Education, the mission board urged the fuller participation of women on the mission field, and the general president, David Preus, first cousin of J. A. O. Preus of Missouri but of a different theological stripe, asked in his report that ALC congregations "give to women certified for call the same serious, prayerful consideration given to men."[18] That same ALC convention authorized by a vote of 431 to 307 "the establishment, for two years, of a task force on the full participation of women in the church."[19]

Although the LCA did not have to respond to the question put to the ALC by the Missouri Synod, it proceeded in much the same way as did the ALC after its vote to ordain women. At its 1972 convention in Dallas, the LCA adopted a recommendation that the Consulting Committee on Women in Church and Society (CCWCS) be established. Its charge was to: 1) survey the current participation and attitudes of women in the denomination; 2) develop guidelines for inclusive language in LCA's published materials; 3) design strategies to increase the proportionate representation of women in all decision-making bodies in the LCA; and 4) work with corresponding groups in the other two Lutheran denominations.[20] The language suggesting quotas for the representation of women was disputed at this LCA convention, although an amendment to remove it failed.

The Consulting Committee on Women in Church and Society (CCWCS) reported to the LCA convention in 1974. The CCWCS had chosen three goals: 1) the equalization between men and women in leadership; 2) an educational process for parish and seminary alike which would give full recognition to the concerns of women; and 3) the raising of consciousness "regarding images of men and women in church and society."[21] To reach these goals the committee had developed a long list of projects, such as "devising guidelines for evaluating images of women communicated through LCA materials and refer-[ring] these guidelines to churchwide staff for implementation."[22] Published with the report was a survey of the leadership of women in the LCA which gave a statistical picture of LCA congregations and the leadership of women. The most important recommendation adopted by the LCA convention was one having to do with inclusive language worship materials.

At this same time, the Inter-Lutheran Commission on Worship (ILCW), consisting of representatives from all three major Lutheran denominations—a remarkable event given the growing antipathy developing between the ALC and the LCMS—was mired in the work of preparing the *Lutheran Book of Worship*. Independent of these resolutions from either the ALC or the LCA, and to some extent unaware of them, the Hymn Text Committee of the ILCW had determined in 1973 that it would, wherever possible, change all texts which used "men" or "brothers" for human beings. At the time, these issues in the public mind were no larger than a cloud the size of a woman's hand on the horizon, but as the work was concluded in 1976 and the *Lutheran Book of Worship* went to press, these issues loomed larger as the LCMS began to withdraw from the project.

By the mid-1970s, the conflict over how to read the Bible embroiled the Missouri Synod and all of its institutions. Though the ordination of women was not the main issue, it certainly was an important one. The LCMS president, Jacob Preus, repeatedly challenged the president of Concordia Seminary in St. Louis, John Tietjen, to say unequivocally whether or not all of his faculty were orthodox Lutherans and faithful teachers of the Bible. This Tietjen could not do to the satisfaction of Preus or other conservatives in the LCMS. After the seminary's Board of Control suspended Tietjen on 20 January 1974, a large majority of the faculty and students declared a moratorium in classes to protest Tietjen's suspension.[23] The Board of Control then declared the faculty in breach of contract and no longer employees of Concordia Seminary, causing the faculty and students favorable to Tietjen to walk off the campus on 19 February 1974 in protest.[24] Thus Concordia Seminary in Exile, or "Seminex," was born.

The break with Concordia Seminary was a terrible blow to the faculty. When they and their families faced the loss of income and homes, they had to find support from sympathetic congregations in the LCMS. Months before the walkout, on 26–28 August 1973, a Conference on Evangelical Lutheranism met near Chicago and formed a "confessing movement" which began to gather funds to support and defend the dissenting faculty. This proved to be the beginning of the Association of Evangelical Lutheran Churches (AELC), which at its constituting convention in Chicago on 3–5 December 1976 commended to its synods "the action of the Pacific Regional Synod in approving the ordination of women to the ministry of Word and Sacrament" and urged the AELC regional synods to follow suit.[25] On 14 May 1976 Janith Otte became the first woman graduate of Seminex, and a year later she became the first woman pastor in the AELC.[26]

It is important to note that Seminex was in difficult straits, having only a small number of congregations to support a large theological faculty. After the original student exiles had graduated and gone on to ministries elsewhere, Seminex was unable to attract enough students to make it a viable institution. It had to turn elsewhere to save itself and its heritage. In the late fall of 1977 Elwyn Ewald, executive secretary of the AELC, and John Tietjen, president of Seminex, fashioned a proposal calling for the AELC to invite the ALC and the LCA to join with them in establishing a new Lutheran Church.[27] This decision was ratified by the AELC at its Milwaukee convention on 14–16 April 1978. The "Call for Lutheran Union" met with tepid response from the ALC and only a bit more enthusiasm from the LCA. However, the leadership of both churches finally relented, and in 1980 the resulting Committee on Lutheran Union submitted proposals to the three denominations asking whether merger was desired. The details of these negotiations are not pertinent here, but it is important to note that the break from Concordia Seminary had been caused mainly by the debate about historical-critical methods of reading the Bible, which had to a degree been complicated by the ALC's decision to call women as pastors based on its new reading of Scripture. The place the question of the ordination of women played in the events leading to the schism by the AELC from the Missouri Synod and the AELC's call for the formation of the ELCA should be clearly marked.

WOMEN IN THE THREE LUTHERAN CHURCH BODIES

In the spring of 1977, as the LCMS was preparing to hold its biennial convention in Dallas, seventy-four Lutheran women from around the world met for an International Consultation on Women and Worship in Madison, Wisconsin. Planned by the Women's Desk of the Lutheran World Federation and Lutheran World Ministries, this consultation included sixty-six women from the Lutheran denominations in the United States. The consultation was led by CCWCS member Constance Parvey, one of the first women pastors in the LCA, and Vivian Jenkins Nelson, an African-American ALC laywoman working in the ALC's Division for Life and Mission in the Congregation. The consultation approved a variety of resolutions concerning women and worship, which were then sent on to various bodies, including the Sixth Assembly of the Lutheran World Federation meeting in Dar es Salaam. The point of the resolutions was to insure that "the language of worship, the acts of worship, the theology of worship must be inclusive of the experience of women, the images of women, for all of us to be faithful to our Creator and to our baptismal call to ministry. If worship is not inclusive, the entire body of Christ, the church, suffers; it is less whole. The proclamation of the Gospel is diminished."[28] The resolutions addressed various points of difficulty for women and worship, from inclusive language, lack of women in leadership, and worship space to the sponsoring of workshops that would train both men and women in leading worship. The resolutions from the International Consultation received little mention in the Lutheran World Ministries Report at the ALC's 1978 convention. The LCA, however, with the leadership of Constance Parvey, and supported by Dorothy Marple, assistant to the LCA bishop, and Kathryn Kopf, executive director of the LCW (both members of the CCWCS), reviewed these recommendations and voted to transmit them to the appropriate church agencies with a request that they report to the LCA's Executive Council at the fall 1978 meeting.

If the conveners of the International Consultation of Women and Worship had hoped that their resolutions would have any effect on the language of the *Lutheran Book of Worship*, they were too late—the book was already being printed. Although the Inter-Lutheran Commission on Worship committees had been careful to remove almost all exclusively male language referring to human beings, they had left the pronouns and images for God, in the main, masculine. What the consultation did more than anything else, however, was to help create an "old-girls" network within Lutheran denominations.[29] Many women at the consultation found affirmation and the resolve to continue with their work. The consultation's resolutions, however ineffectual they may have seemed at the time, had considerable impact in the LCA and some in the ALC as well.

At the 1978 LCA Convention, the CCWCS noted with dismay that the liturgical texts in the forthcoming *Lutheran Book of Worship* had used more masculine pronouns for God in the liturgy. Since it had been the CCWCS's mandate to attend to the images of women in LCA materials, it asked the Office for Communication to "develop a set of guidelines for non-theological language" which would "assist persons to avoid generic use of masculine terminology, stereotypes of roles for women and men, and imagery which conveys less than full participation of women in church and society."[30] The CCWCS also reported that it had asked a representative, Kathryn Kopf, from the LCA women's organization Lutheran Church Women (LCW), to attend CCWCS meetings in order to create a stronger liaison between the two organizations. Printed at the end of the report were the results of a three-year study on the participation of women in the LCA. The main conclusion of the study was that vigilance needed to be maintained, especially concerning the calling of women as pastors and as employees in the church structures, so that women would be included in the LCA structures proportionate to their population in the LCA.

Along the same lines, the ALC's Task Force on the Full Participation of Women in the Church came forth with recommendations to the

ALC's 1976 convention in Washington.[31] The task force, led by Mabel Wold Sihler, an ALC pastor's widow, made recommendations concerning language, leadership, and leave policies for pregnant women. It also asked the *Lutheran Book of Worship* committees to use gender-inclusive language and requested that the ALC's general secretary develop uniform guidelines for use of language in ALC publications.[32] It advised that a smaller Task Force for Women's Concerns, including at least one person from a traditionally underrepresented community, oversee the progress of various jurisdictions in the church on the hiring of women. Perhaps the most consequential recommendation it made was one asking each district in the ALC to organize and fund a task force on the full participation of women.[33] It concluded its report with a survey on the participation of women in ALC congregations. This survey established a good baseline for further research on conditions for women in the ALC.[34] It concluded that the "variety and extent of the participation of women in the corporate life of congregations of The American Lutheran Church is considerably greater than was expected," noting with surprise that the larger congregations allowed for more involvement of women in lay leadership roles, and that over 25 percent of the ALC congregations had a woman treasurer.[35]

In 1978 the ALC Church Council reported to its biennial convention that it had dealt with many of these resolutions as required. The smaller committee of five people reported that same year on what it had learned from its studies, presenting numerous recommendations to the Church Council as to how it could further the progress of women in the ALC structures and review the language in ALC publications.[36] These recommendations were far reaching and gave the Task Force on the Full Participation of Women almost regulatory power over the ALC decisions, especially in matters of inclusive language.[37] One request, by the 1976 ALC Task Force on the Full Participation of Women, which became more important as the ELCA was being formed, was that liaison be established with both the LCA and the LCMS. In 1977 at the Dallas convention of the LCMS, J. A. O. Preus was once again elected president, and the hopes of many of the LCMS moderates were dashed. The LCMS voted to remain in "protesting fellowship" with the ALC, citing its disagreements with the ALC on biblical interpretation, the ordination of women, and other ecumenical issues as grounds for their protest.

With these events vivid in their minds, the leaders of the Lutheran Women's Caucus (LWC), which had formed in the LCMS in the late 1960s, saw that they had to enlarge their numbers and include women from all of the Lutheran denominations in America. To that end they

planned a convocation in Chicago in the spring of 1978 featuring
Margaret Wold, a popular speaker from the ALC and former executive
director of the American Lutheran Church Women, the women's organization of the ALC. Her presence at the Chicago convocation drew a
good number of ALC and LCA women, and that next fall the LWC
voted a board which included representatives from the four Lutheran
denominations. As noted before, this group was initially made up of
women trying to find their place as equals in the LCMS struggle, but
the character of the group gradually became more radically feminist as
the 1980s continued. As the prospects for women pastors began to dim
in LCMS, more women left Missouri for the AELC. The glue that
bound the LWC was *The Well Woman*, as well as biennial convocations
held in various places around the country. In time they adopted as
their mission statement "Lutheran Women's Caucus is a Christian
Feminist organization which works for full partnership of women and
men in the life of the church."[38] The LWC followed political developments in the several Lutheran denominations closely and sent resolutions to them from its biennial convocations. In 1978, after the AELC
called the ALC and the LCA to form a new church together with them,
the LWC, at its 1978 convocation, passed a resolution urging the denominations to include "large numbers of women in the total process"
of planning for the new Lutheran Church.[39] As the new Lutheran denomination, the Evangelical Lutheran Church in America (ELCA),
loomed on the horizon, the LWC continued to advocate the inclusion
of women in decision making.[40]

In 1980 both the ALC and the LCA conventions acted on issues
pertinent to women. The LCA pressed forward with the resolutions
coming to it from the 1977 Consultation on Women and Worship, publishing the booklets *Emerging Roles of Women and Men in Church and
Society* and *English Language Guidelines for Using Inclusive Liturgical Language in the Lutheran Church in America*. The ALC produced a similar set
of guidelines. ALC president David Preus, in his report to the ALC,
noted the progress being made toward the full participation of women
and commended women pastors for their fine work. He also praised
the participation of the American Lutheran Church Women in many
projects to support the mission of the ALC. American Lutheran Church
Women president Elaine Donaldson, and its executive director, Julie
Stine, wrote in their report to the convention that "there will continue
to be a healthy tension between feminism and the traditional image of
the organization. ALC Women reflect both in their persuasion and lifestyles. The organization, to maintain its integrity, must also reflect the

same. This is the hope and the strength for the future as we move into a new decade."[41]

Donaldson and Stine spoke to the new realities of those working with women's groups at this time and addressed them clearly. Since the ALC Women's group consisted of every woman who belonged to the ALC, it was necessary for the leadership to be inclusive of all the women in the ALC. The greatest accomplishment of the ALC Women had been the monthly Bible study published in its journal, *Scope*, the most widely read churchwomen's magazine in the country, with a peak subscription of 310,000.[42] ALC Women initiated and supported the SEARCH Bible studies, a highly successful Bible study published by Augsburg Publishing House, and ALC Women were officially involved with the work of Lutheran World Relief. The LCA's Lutheran Church Women consisted of those women who participated, and the LCW's leaders tended to be more politically active than the constituency. In 1978 they were joined by the AELC's Women in Action for Mission (WAM), led by Selma ("Sammy") Mayer as national coordinator. It was, however, not until 1982, when merger negotiations made it necessary, that the women's organization in each of the three denominations began to work and talk with each other about the kind of women's organization they wanted in the ELCA.

GETING IT TOGETHER

When it was finally determined that there would be a new Lutheran denomination and that it would be planned by a group of seventy people picked from all sectors of the three denominations, those with political commitments to equal justice in the church were ready. Of the seventy chosen in 1982 to constitute the Commission for a New Lutheran Church (CNLC), twenty-eight were women and fourteen minorities. At the time, the CCWCS, through its occasional paper *Wholenotes*, solicited names of LCA women who would be appropriate for "appointment to committees or other assignments within the church."[43] From the beginning the CNLC was pressed by a variety of groups to be *inclusive*.[44] In 1982 the editor of *The Well Woman* wrote, "because of pressure groups like LWC (Lutheran Women's Caucus), women are a prominent part of the group of 70," but worried that the women would be expected to agree on every issue.[45] The important issue facing women of the new ELCA was whether to have a women's organization in the new denomination or to abandon women's organizations as dinosaurs from a previous age. Women in the ALC and the LCA lobbied from the first for a women's organization, though one that would appeal to nontraditional woman as well as the traditional Ladies Aide type who was the backbone of the current organizations. This problem of definition would haunt them. The executives of the three Lutheran women's organizations had been meeting to get to know one another as they faced the future together. At their first meeting in Minneapolis, 7–9 January 1983, in what became a regular protest, they expressed regret that women and minorities and laity had not been adequately represented in all of the committees of the CNLC.[46] At a joint conference of ALC and LCA women in Omaha, Nebraska, titled "The Future of Women in the New Lutheran Church," held in late 1983, a statement was issued calling on the new denomination to establish quotas for the representation of women on national and regional boards and committees and affirming that there be a women's organization which would be self-supporting.[47] On 5 December 1983 Barbara Nelson, a member of the CNLC, presented to the CNLC Design Task Force an "Option for an Organization for Women in a New Lutheran Church" that suggested the new women's organization be self-supporting and that it be developed by a committee of people "involved and knowledgeable about women's organizations" and "selected by the organizations for women now recognized."[48] Bonnie Jensen, executive director of ALC Women, wrote a supporting letter indicating that there had been unanimous agreement at the Omaha conference on Nelson's proposal. Jensen made clear that the Omaha conference had not suggested that the new women's organization be "independent, separate, autonomous," but that the words used had been "partnership, interdependence," and that they were looking to create something "NEW and appropriate to the lives of women today" that was "participatory and non-hierarchical" and which could provide "programming for a wide, diverse constituency of women in the church."[49] Jensen reiterated these sentiments in an article she wrote for *The Well Woman*, in which she argued that the ELCA would need a women's organization to empower individual women by providing support groups and ecumenical connections with other women.[50] Jensen wanted an organization free from dependence on the ELCA's structure, mutually interdependent with other ELCA organizations, accountable only to the highest ELCA governing body which dealt with all structures on an equal basis. That meant to Jensen that the ELCA women's organization should be financially self-supporting.

On 3 February 1984 the executive committees of the three women's organizations, having discussed the new women's organization further and reacting to the report of the CNLC's Task Force on Theology, repeated their concern that an organization for women which limited its "relationship to one unit of the church" would not be good for ELCA women.[51] This complicated maneuvering had the purpose of avoiding ALC Women's perceived submission to the ALC's Division of Life and Mission in the Congregation. Signed by the twenty-five women in the three executive committees, including present and past presidents of the various women's organizations, the letter had an impact on both the CNLC and the ALC. Although ALC Women leadership was as adamant in its insistence on a self-supporting organization as the others, not everyone in the ALC bureaucracy was. The women's organizations executive committees' support for this proposal, seen as an LCA proposal by some in the ALC hierarchy, began an argument about the kind of women's organization there would be in the ELCA that revealed two different political cultures as time went on: the Lutheran Church Women with their political caucusing shocked many ALC Women who were used to making decisions by consensus, and who, on the whole, did not feel as alienated from the power structures as the LCA women did. Would women have more power in the new church if they were independent, as they had been in the LCA, or part of the structure, as they were in the ALC?

It can be seen that members of the CNLC and the leaders of all the women's organizations were affected by the growing political savvy of the Consulting Committee on Women in Church and Society (CCWCS). As early as 1983 the CCWCS had begun to make plans to have an impact on the outcome of the deliberations about the new denomination. The CCWCS endorsed a plan for the Coordinating Committee on Lutheran Women in Ministry that was to meet with representatives from the three merging denominations. More significant, the CCWCS laid out a plan for influencing the members of the CNLC. Each member of the CCWCS was to contact one person on the CNLC to "communicate general concerns."[52] They were to submit names for possible subcommittee members to Dorothy Marple, assistant to James Crumley, the bishop of the LCA. The CCWCS then mapped out a strategy to monitor papers submitted to the CNLC, particularly the Report of the Task Force on Societal Trends.[53] The CCWCS also sent a letter to regional synod task forces that included names of the CNLC members in their regions and the CNLC's time line and key dates.[54]

The intensive lobbying of CCWCS had its effects in nominations, but especially in the establishment of quotas for women and minorities in the ELCA structures.[55] Dorothy Marple, the LCA bishop's assistant, suggested in a report to the 1985 meeting of the CCWCS that the CNLC had not communicated effectively to the three merging denominations why concerns for quota and goals for achieving inclusiveness in hiring were important. The CNLC's progress report 6, in fact, had referred only to finding a good "balance" of women and men and people of color among ELCA staff, a phrasing more consistent with ALC preferences.[56] To remedy this failure of the CNLC, the CCWCS appointed subcommittees to work on certain areas of interest. Three people— Richard Priggie; Ann Kohler, the president of the LCW; and Christine Crist, who was later to be named director of the ELCA's Commission for Women—were to monitor the developments in the area of hiring for positions in the new denomination's structures. No less important to them was the issue of sexist language, both for humans and God.

The effect of the CCWCS's lobbying can be seen in the debate on whether to delete references to "Father, Son, and Holy Spirit" and refer to the Trinity only as "the Triune God" in the ELCA's constitution. The informally constituted women's caucus of the CNLC, led by Elizabeth Bettenhausen, an LCA representative who taught theology at Boston University, and Christine Grumm of the AELC, failed, by a vote of thirty to thirty-three, to have the first phrase deleted. This debate over God-language provoked worried comments from the constituency. A couple from Perham, Minnesota, asked in the ALC's *Lutheran Standard*, "Why was a deletion such as this even considered?"[57] This opposition to feminist theology increasingly centered in the independent journal *Lutheran Forum* attributed this vote to the "feminists" who had captured the mainline Protestant denominations.[58]

Most comments from the future ELCA constituency, however, had to do with the quota system being proposed by the CNLC requiring a minimum of 20 percent of the delegates at regional and national conventions to be from minority groups and 50 percent of the lay delegates to be women. In 1984 minorities constituted 1 percent of the membership in the ALC and 2 percent in the LCA. The proposal for what many regarded as unrealistic quotas met with opposition in the district and synod councils of the three denominations. At least seventeen districts and synods passed resolutions opposing the quota system. Over the summer of 1984, as the districts and synods of the three denominations met, the nearly eighteen thousand delegates were polled on the decisions of the CNLC. About one-third of all the delegates agreed with the idea of quotas in principle, and 15 percent agreed but thought it needed more work. Nearly 40 percent disagreed with the idea in principle, and 12 percent were not ready to express themselves.[59] The highest opposition to quotas was in the LCA, where 45 percent of the delegates opposed them, 29.2 percent agreed with them, while 12.9 percent agreed but wanted some change in the proposals. This debate unleashed a torrent of letters to the editors of church journals and opinion columns. Martha Ellen Stortz, assistant professor of systematics at Pacific Lutheran Seminary in Berkeley, California, wrote a column in the LCA's *The Lutheran* in which she argued that quotas had the effect of pitting groups against each other and prevented Christians from advocating for causes not their own. She longed for the day "when women will speak out for blacks, when the patriarchs will take up the cause of the poor."[60]

In the summer and fall of 1984, as the three denominations held their national conventions, the Lutheran Women's Caucus continued to advocate that there be an "equitable formula for representation" in the ELCA.[61] As could be expected, the quota proposal was once again contested at each convention. The LCA at its Toronto convention from 28 June to 5 July hotly debated quotas. By the end of the convention, the LCA approved "the implementation by means of specific formulas" of a commitment to inclusiveness in the ELCA's Churchwide Assembly: 50 percent of all delegates were to be women, 50 percent lay, and at least 10 percent persons of color or whose primary language was other than English. While these percentages were intended to apply only to the Churchwide Assemblies, they would become informal requirements for all committees in the ELCA. The ALC at its October convention in Moorhead, Minnesota, passed a milder resolution asking that the CNLC devise a way to include in the ELCA's governance structures "significant numbers of people from a variety of life experiences with an intentional balance between men and women."[62]

With the exception of the site for the ELCA headquarters and clergy pensions, the question of quotas and how the women's organization should be organized were the only issues that raised much passion in the final merger talks. Arguments about the kind of women's ministries there should be in the ELCA led Barbara Nelson to move at the 1 November 1984 CNLC meeting in Los Angeles that the "CNLC appoint a committee to initiate study of the concept of a board for Women's Ministries and make appropriate recommendations to the CNLC through the established channels."[63] Her motion passed and began the CNLC's formal process of deciding not whether but what kind of women's organization there should be. In a series of articles on the three denominations appearing in each denomination's magazine, H. George Anderson, president of Luther College in Decorah, Iowa, appeared to favor the proposal for a self-supporting organization favored by the women's leadership. He noted that letters were pouring into the CNLC "urging that the women's auxiliary in the new church have authority to (1) establish its policies and programs . . . , (2) manage its own assets, (3) relate to other churchwide expressions of the church, and (4) report to the highest legislative body of the church."[64] It is important to note here that the language of these proposals, consistent with good Lutheran theology, insists that all women in the ELCA would have "ministries" and that the ELCA would need to provide good support for the varieties of women's ministries that were already going on in the Lutheran churches.

On 21–24 February 1985 the board members of the women's organizations in all three denominations met at Techny, Illinois, to begin planning for women's ministries in the new church. There they discussed their common goals and different histories and asked that a "variety of organizational models be created to serve women in the mission of the church."[65] As it turned out, nine women representing the existing women's organizations (ALC Women, LCW, and WAM) and nine women who were not active in the organizations were appointed. These latter were included to give voice to those women who were not interested in the traditional women's organization. The eighteen newly appointed women met in May 1985 in Minneapolis with the Committee on Design, the most powerful committee of the CNLC.[66] Still, they could not achieve a resolution of their various agendas between a traditional women's organization and the less traditional idea of a board or commission for women that would not resemble a Ladies Aide group. The participants focused attention on what the Commission for Women would do to advocate for women in the ELCA, without being a traditional women's organization. Edgar Trexler wrote that the "advocates of justice" at this meeting, as the leftish proponents of quotas came to be called, could not agree with the leadership of the traditional women's organizations that there was a need to continue the old organizations.[67] The two groups of women, those from the traditional women's organizations and those who were not, could find no common ground. They did, however, agree that the CNLC had not been precise enough about how the hiring processes for the ELCA would "achieve inclusiveness." To this end, all eighteen of the participants signed a letter to the three bishops of the merging churches asking that attention be given to this concern. How to organize women's ministries was another matter. While they were contending about the shape of the women's ministries in the new denomination, however, the laity evidenced little concern. Many leaders remarked on the apathy of the constituency toward the new denomination and worried about it.[68] One opinion was that the laity's apathy let the advocates of quotas have their way. Lowell Almen, who was to be elected ELCA secretary at the 1987 Constituting Convention in Columbus, reacted to the organized lobbying for justice issues in his

5 May 1985 editorial in *The Lutheran Standard*. Marking the rise in the number of resolutions to the ALC Church Council, he criticized the "Working Group on Justice Agendas and the New Lutheran Church" for producing too many resolutions.[69] Although he acknowledged that the concerns of this group for justice for women, among many others, were valid, he feared that the ELCA was being moved "farther down the road to becoming little more than the ecclesiastical wing of the Democratic Party."[70]

In Kansas City, 23–27 September 1985, when the CNLC approved the structure for the ELCA, the Committee on Design chose not to make a recommendation about how to set up the women's organization, which it approved in principle, along with the Commission for Women.[71] Because the women were divided on the issue, the CNLC dared not dictate a solution for fear of seeming too patriarchal or hierarchical. The Commission for Women, however, with an office and staff in the headquarters, was to monitor the ELCA's progress toward the full participation of women and to advocate for women. The ELCA women's organization, on the other hand, was to be a more programmatic organization, providing women opportunities for Bible study, prayer, and theological reflection. The CNLC accepted the recommendation of the Committee on Design, as well as its suggestion that both organizations be evaluated after six years. This meant that the design of the women's organization still needed to be planned. In the fall of 1985 a new committee of fourteen women was named to help plan the women's organization of the ELCA.[72]

In November 1985 the newly named planning committee for the new women's organization met in Des Plaines, Illinois. Still trying to include the nonactive women in its organization, the new committee continued to plan a Lutheran women's organization that was independently funded and interdependently related with other ELCA churchwide units, and that would reach out to women who had not participated actively in the churches as well as those who had. The Transition Team for the New Lutheran Church had, by this time, assigned Staff Teams to develop a program and budget for the Commission on Women as well.[73] The CCWCS supported the plans of the Transition Team and hoped that the Commission on Women would immediately address questions of women and men in the workplace.[74]

Not everything went as well as the planning committee for the new women's organization had hoped. In March of 1986 the Board for ALC's Division of Life and Mission in the Congregation (DLMC) sent a resolution to the ALC Church Council requesting that the new women's organization not be incorporated and "that the Church Council support this resolution and commend it to the Commission for a New Lutheran Church."[75] Marlene Engstrom, president of ALC Women, reacted with astonishment: "Up to now there has been no concerted opposition to having the women handle their own funds."[76] Bonnie Jensen argued with great force that "the women planners from the three churches have been unanimous in their position that the woman's organization should be directly responsible to the church convention and church council, not to another board of the church."[77] There was much debate about this in the ALC, with opposing motions coming from its districts. After a day-long meeting at Techny, Illinois, on 11 April 1986, the ALC Women district presidents and executive board members passed two resolutions asking that the ALC Church Council adopt the proposal as made by the CNLC rather than keep it under another division in the new church.[78]

ALC Women, accustomed to a consensual style of making decisions, found this conflict over the structure of the new women's organization upsetting.[79] Though the leadership of ALC Women agreed on the need to be self-supporting, they found it much more difficult to agree on how to structure the women's organization that came to be known as Women of the ELCA (WELCA). Should WELCA devote itself, as the LCW had, to social causes? Or should it continue the strong emphasis on Bible study, which the ALC Women had as its tradition? At its May 1986 meeting, the Church Council of the ALC, eager to facilitate the merger, recommended that the ALC convention approve the motion that the women's organization be separately incorporated, and it passed.[80]

The only remaining obstacle to merger was how to constitute the ELCA's Church Council. The ALC, a more populist and rural denomination which had traditionally feared the dominance of the East, favored a council with one elected representative from each synod. The CCWCS, in its capacity as watchdog over the processes of the formation of the ELCA, viewed such proposals with alarm. The CCWCS argued that the synods could not be trusted to achieve the goals of electing people of color and women. Thus the CCWCS passed a motion urging that ELCA Church Council members be elected by the denominational assembly, so that the goals of having 10 percent persons of color, no fewer than 50 percent female, with 60 percent of the representatives lay would be reached.[81] The ALC lost on this issue. It was one loss that David Preus said he regretted the most,[82] because it kept the ELCA's Church Council from being popularly elected. Given the documented participation of women in ALC's structures, it is not entirely clear that the CCWCS was right that no women or people of color would be elected from the synods. The ALC saw this decision as a fear of democracy on the part of the LCA. One can note the irony in the fact that the LCA's fiercely feminist CCWCS delivered to its largely male hierarchy the thing the LCA bishops most wanted in their fight with the ALC.

As the conventions of the three denominations finished voting on all of the final documents, the issue of quotas caused the fiercest debate. LCA's North Carolina bishop, Michael McDaniel, made a spirited protest against quotas as an attempt to put people of color and women in positions of power to salve the guilty consciences of Lutheran liberals.[83] Robert Marshall, a former president of the LCA, and a leading member of the CNLC, sharply opposed McDaniel, and Marshall's position won the day. The final quotas set for the delegations to church-wide assemblies were: 60 percent lay, half of whom were to be women; and at least 10 percent persons of color and/or persons whose primary language was other than English. This was a remarkable event, in that thirty LCA bishops had opposed quotas before the LCA convention for the final merger deliberations. The LCA Executive Council, however, voted twelve to ten not to support the bishops.[84] Although other issues were serious, the question of quotas was most volatile, in part because it became a rhetorical trump card. Kathryn Marie Olson's study of the rhetoric of the CNLC showed persuasively that "inclusivity" became a term that white males felt that they could not criticize without being called racist or sexist.[85] Olson concluded that whoever could wrap their argument in the mantle of inclusivity, whether the issue was the selection of the headquarters or the composition of the new Church Council, would win. This rhetoric baffled the male leadership of the ALC and the LCA, who could not marshal arguments against it.

In the spring of 1987 at the ELCA's Constituting Convention in Columbus, a number of remaining issues were settled: the women's organization would be self-supporting; the Commission for Women would be established; and the quota system was in place. All that remained was the task of electing a national bishop. The foremost candidates were Herbert Chilstrom, William Lazareth, Barbara Lundblad, and David Preus. The first three of the candidates were LCA, and for a while the LCA split its votes among its contenders. In the caucuses swirling around the convention, the AELC delegates, who had suffered so much from J. A. O. Preus, could not stomach voting for another man with that name. There was much talk about the chances of Barbara Lundblad, a pastor from New York and the opening preacher of the Constituting Convention. With roots in the Swedish Augustana Synod, years of lay ministry in Minnesota, and her years of service in Lutheran campus ministry, she functioned as something of an informal bishop for the women pastors in the LCA. Her sermon, and then her surge in the ecclesiastical ballot, began to excite many at the Constituting Convention, especially those committed to the feminist agenda. She made it to the short list of four, which gave her a chance to make a speech to the Constituting Convention. Her speech attracted some votes, but she was eliminated, leaving Chilstrom, Lazareth, and Preus. She endorsed the LCA's Minnesota Synod bishop, Herbert Chilstrom, another heir of Swedish Augustana, who went on to win handily over David Preus. Later, AELC's Christine Grumm was elected vice president of the ELCA and thus chair of the ELCA's Church Council. When the delegates went home from Columbus, quotas were in place, as was WELCA and the Commission for Women. The goals of the CCWCS, among others, had been met.

WOMEN IN THE ELCA

Women have achieved significant stature in the ELCA from its beginning, with the election of Christine Grumm as vice president and a significant number of women on the ELCA's Church Council and other committees. When Grumm stepped down in 1991 to begin working with the Lutheran World Federation in Geneva, Kathy Magnus of the Colorado Synod of the ELCA was elected vice president of the ELCA. In 1992 the LaCrosse Area Synod elected April Ulring Larson as the first woman bishop in the ELCA. In 1993 other ELCA women pastors appeared to be nearing such elections as they gained the requisite pastoral experience to be considered.

The Women of the Evangelical Lutheran Church in America, however, has had difficulty from its inception. In 1987, during the original calling processes for the ELCA, three candidates, all ALC, contended for the position of executive director of WELCA.[86] When Bonnie Jensen was not appointed, for reasons that were never clear, the ALC Women's organization was thrown into turmoil which continued into the WELCA. The WELCA began its life with an executive director from the ALC, Betty Lee Nyhus, who resigned on 14 October 1988. The WELCA has since had one interim director, Doris Strieter of the former AELC, and is now directed by Charlotte Fiechter, formerly of the LCA. Nor has the WELCA-elected leadership been without strife. At WELCA's Constituting Convention in June of 1987 in Milwaukee, Ann Kohler, the LCA contender for president, was not able to win the election because the ALC Women, having experienced her political style, would not vote for her, and the convention finally elected by a margin of 252 to 148 Jeanne Rapp, a leader in the ALC Women's Illinois District. Since its turbulent beginning WELCA has been troubled partly because there was no carryover in its leadership from the membership of the planning committees which had spent five stressful years establishing the women's organization. The final design of the organization had provided for three foci, "Growth, Community, and Action: providing for leadership development, growth in faith and witness, support of one another in community, and service and development projects and programs, locally and globally."[87] The leadership of the Growth and Community teams has been in frequent flux, by default giving the Action team leadership of the organization, thus slanting its work toward the more politically active LCW style and putting the more conservative Bible study tradition of the ALC Women in some jeopardy.[88] Perhaps the goal of making the new women's organization both traditional and nontraditional at the same time was impossible.

The Commission for Women was the main achievement of the CCWCS, although the ALC's Task Force on the Full Participation of Women could find many of its goals fulfilled in the work of the Commission for Women as well. It was chartered in the ELCA to "enable this church to realize the full participation of women; to create equal opportunity for women of all cultures; to foster partnership between men and women; to assist this church to address sexism; and to advocate justice for women in this church and society."[89] The Commission for Women has a board of sixteen people, with seven executive staff members.[90] The board's membership has strong representation from the LCA's CCWCS and the LCA's Lutheran Church Women as does the staff. This gives the goals of the old CCWCS strong continuity in the new denomination, especially as the Commission for Women continues the work of monitoring the ELCA's progress in its attitudes toward women. Christine Crist, a laywoman in the LCA, began as the first head of the unit and then was followed by an interim director, Sylvia Pate. Since 1990 the director has also been a laywoman, Joanne Chadwick. The Commission for Women sponsors educational gatherings for Lutheran women, works for social justice, and has produced a variety of study documents on the place of women in the ELCA.[91]

The Commission for Women's most vocal opposition is the "evangelical catholic" wing of the ELCA, which espouses closer communion with Rome. *The Lutheran Forum* and its newsletter, *The Forum Letter*, have heaped scorn on Lutheran feminists who have, according to them, captured the ELCA and made it a typically Protestant mainline American denomination captive to the culture, especially feminism. The leaders of the "evangelical catholics," most notably Richard John

Neuhaus, and a number of women pastors want the ELCA to heal the schism with Rome by adopting Roman orders. They and Neuhaus, whose conviction on these issues caused him to leave the ELCA to become a Catholic priest, agree with the international Lutheran/Roman Catholic joint commission proposed in 1985 that Lutheran pastors be ordained and bishops be consecrated by Roman Catholic bishops so that Lutherans would be in "full communion" with Rome.[92] Their primary opponents, radical Lutherans generally out of the ALC, look upon such a proposal as unacceptable, not simply for what it would do to Lutheran ministry, but also for what it would do to women clergy. CCWCS feminists in the ELCA today regard these radical Lutherans' fear of the ELCA ecumenical strategy toward "full communion" with all churches and its possible effects on the ordination of women as sheer paranoia.

Several conclusions can be drawn from this story of women's place in the new Lutheran denomination. First, it can be seen that the political process worked for LCA women during the merger that produced the ELCA. The CCWCS organized and got results, mystifying especially the ALC old-boy's network which played the game with few glances at the distaff side and with a strong trust in democratic processes that had suited their needs for many years. The CCWCS stuck to its original objective of *proportional* representation in all decision-making bodies in the ELCA and obtained it. The CCWCS members were also skillful in their use of parliamentary procedure. By active lobbying they were able to achieve goals which were not necessarily popular at the grassroots levels, and they had an impact on the democratic processes which produced the new denomination.

Second, this story demonstrates that blood is still thicker than water. In the AELC, the ALC, and the LCA the women fought, as did the men, with loyalties to the political culture in which they had been born. Barbara Lundblad's endorsement of Herbert Chilstrom as bishop of the ELCA clearly proved that. More significant, it was the original ethnic groupings of Lutherans that held sway over loyalties. The dislike of the Norwegians, as represented by David Preus, due to old hurts from the 1960 ALC merger of the Norwegians, Danes, and Germans, caused especially the German and Danish Wartburg Seminary contingent of the ALC, as represented by Bonnie Jensen and others, to join with the LCA feminists against Preus.

Third, it can also be seen that in many cases women, who may have disagreed on many other issues, felt obligated to support the concept of inclusiveness at every juncture, even when it was beside the point of their particular discussion. It was, as Kathryn Olson demonstrates, a rhetorical trump card which prevented open discussion. To question inclusiveness of quotas was to court charges of being sexist or racist. As can be seen from the almost obligatory petitions urging quotas that were signed after every meeting of the women's executive committees, the issue of inclusiveness diverted attention from the more pressing issue of how the women's organization was to be structured and what agenda it should have. Any group that could link its cause to inclusiveness won whatever argument was being made, no matter how remote the connection was. This meant that Herbert Chilstrom, whose wife was an ALC pastor, was a more inclusive candidate than David Preus, who battled to desegregate the Minneapolis schools as chair of the Minneapolis school board in the 1960s.

Fourth, LCA women were able to take the high ground in the reshuffling of the various bureaucracies and use the appeal to sisterhood to their own ends, by assuming that ALC women would support them, even against ALC leadership, which on occasion they did. On the other hand, it is also clear that the more consensual and politically naive ALC women overly trusted the merger process. The ALC women nominated to serve on the CNLC, for example, were not organization women of the stature of the LCA women on the CNLC. Although the ALC's Task Force on the Full Participation of Women had stature in the ALC, it did not build the kind of lobbying network that was created by the CCWCS. As in society, there is a debate going on in the ELCA as to what is *the* "woman's position," if any. How these issues will be resolved in the ELCA is not entirely clear. Though the CCWCS made every effort to see that women did keep their power and were not marginalized in the new church, they did it at the expense of the loyalty and agreement of many of their ALC sisters. Though it is now obligatory to appoint women to all committees and task forces in the ELCA, the bureaucrats can manipulate these quotas to their benefit, and there is no democratically elected structure in the ELCA to monitor these manipulations. Quotas are not in and of themselves good for women if the power to appoint rests with male bureaucrats. The varieties of leadership styles evident here, and the growing awareness of many groups in the ELCA that they will have to learn to organize and caucus with the same skill and determination as did the CCWCS, should be instructive to ELCA women of all persuasions. In any event, women do play significant roles in the workings of the ELCA and are in more positions of public leadership than before. Without the lobbying efforts of various pressure groups in each of the merging bodies, this would not be so. What remains to be seen is whether or not all women, regardless of political persuasion, will be included in the processes of the ELCA in the future.

ABBREVIATIONS FOR LUTHERAN INSTITUTIONS

AELC	Association of Evangelical Lutheran Churches
ALC	American Lutheran Church
ALC Women	American Lutheran Church Women (ALC)
CCWCS	Consulting Committee on Women in Church and Society (LCA)
CNLC	Commission for a New Lutheran Church
ELCA	Evangelical Lutheran Church in America
ILCW	Inter-Lutheran Commission on Worship
LCA	Lutheran Church in America
LCMS	Lutheran Church-Missouri Synod (or Missouri Synod)
LCUSA	Lutheran Council in the United States
LCW	Lutheran Church Women (LCA)
LWC	Lutheran Women's Caucus
WAM	Women in Action for Mission (AELC)
WELCA	Women of the Evangelical Lutheran Church in America

NOTES

1. See Gracia Grindal, "Getting Women Ordained," in *Called and Ordained: Lutheran Perspectives on the Office of the Ministry*, ed. Todd Nichol and Marc Kolden (Minneapolis: Fortress, 1990), 161–79.
2. For example, some Norwegian-American women were allowed to vote at congregational meetings and the Lutheran Free Church in the 1890s. At this writing, however, some Missouri Synod congregations still do not permit women to vote or hold office in the local congregation.
3. To assist in keeping track of the abbreviations of names of Lutheran institutions, a summary of abbreviations is provided at the end of the chapter.
4. Lutheran nomenclature even for seasoned Lutherans is difficult. Synods usually refer to regional church jurisdictions in the LCA and ELCA. In the Missouri Synod, however, the name refers to the national church. Its regional jurisdictions are districts, as were those of the ALC. Lutherans did not adopt the term *bishop* in this country until 1970 when the ALC approved its use for its national president and the district presidents. The

LCA did not use the term until 1978. Both the ALC and LCA, and the ELCA, were and are governed by Church Councils.

5. "On the basis of 1 Cor. 14:34 and 1 Tim. 2:11–15 we hold that God forbids women publicly to preach and teach the Word to men and to hold any office or vote in the church where this involves exercising authority over men with respect to the public administration of the Office of the Keys. We regard this principle as of binding force also today because 1 Tim. 2:11–15 refer to what God established at creation." "Women Suffrage in the Church," *Committee on Theology and Church Relations Document*, no. 9.12022 (St. Louis: Concordia, 1969).

6. "Now that Women Can Vote in Church," *The Lutheran Witness* 88 (September 1969): 253.

7. E. Clifford Nelson, Theodore Tappert, H. George Anderson, August R. Suelflow, Eugene Fevold, and Fred W. Meuser, *Lutherans in North America*, rev. ed. (Philadelphia: Fortress, 1980), 528.

8. Kent Knutson in his speech to the LCMS in 1971 admitted that Preus had warned the ALC at its 1970 San Antonio convention that calling women to public ministry would be "troublesome" for the LCMS. *Lutheran Witness* 90 (September 1971): 215.

9. Ibid.

10. "ALC's Council Replies to LCMS On Ordination of Women Stance," *Lutheran Witness* 91 (2 July 1972): 285.

11. J. A. O. Preus, *Report of the Synodical President to the Lutheran Church-Missouri Synod in compliance with Resolution 2-28 of the 49th Regular Convention of the Synod, held at Milwaukee, Wisconsin, July 9–16, 1971*, p. 2. For another view of this process, see John Tietjen, *Memoirs in Exile* (Minneapolis: Fortress, 1991), 101ff.

12. Preus, 119.

13. Carolyn Becker, "Becker Tells of Caucus Beginnings," *The Well Woman* (Fall 1984): 1. The Missouri Synod, along with many other Lutheran churches in the nineteenth century, set deaconesses apart for work in the church in a ceremony of consecration.

14. Gretchen Leppke, "Prez sez," *The Well Woman* (Fall 1984): 3.

15. Duane Priebe, Inter-Church Relations Committee of the ALC, *1972 Reports and Actions*, Exhibit C (Minneapolis: The American Lutheran Church, 1986), 472.

16. "Women and Men in Church and Society—Toward Wholeness in the Christian Community," Exhibit E-1, in *1972 Reports and Actions* (Minneapolis: The American Lutheran Church, 1986), 1093.

17. Ibid.

18. David Preus, "Report of the General President," in *Reports and Actions of the Seventh General Convention of the American Lutheran Church (1974)*, ed. Arnold R. Mickelsen (Minneapolis: Office of the General Secretary of the American Lutheran Church, 1974), 776.

19. *1974 Reports and Actions*, 863.

20. LCA Consulting Committee on Women in Church and Society, "Minutes," *Sixth Biennial Convention of the Lutheran Church in America Dallas, Texas, June 30–July 6, 1972* (Philadelphia: Fortress, 1972), 632.

21. Ibid., 451.

22. Ibid.

23. Tietjen, 185.

24. Board of Control Concordia Seminary, "Board Resolution of February 17, 1974," Appendix I, in *Exodus From Concordia: A Report on the 1974 Walkout* (St. Louis: Concordia, 1977), 185.

25. "For the Ordination of Women: A Study Document prepared by the faculty of Christ Seminary—Seminex," *Currents in Theology and Mission* 6 (June 1979): 142.

26. Tietjen, 275.

27. Ibid., 299.

28. *Minutes Ninth Biennial Convention of the Lutheran Church in America July 12–19, 1978, Chicago, Illinois* (Philadelphia: Fortress, 1978), 720.

29. A partial list of participants includes: Lavonne Althouse, Rachel Conrad Wahlberg, Karen Bloomquist, Jean Bozeman, Norma Everist, Gracia Grindal, Doris Johnson, Nancy Knutson, Jean Lesher, Dorothy Marple, Robin Mattison, Susan Hedahl, Kathryn Kopf, Joan Mau, June Nilssen, Constance Parvey, Gail Ramshaw, Tecla Reklau, Anita Stauffer, Susan Thompson, and Sue Wendorf.

30. *Minutes Ninth Biennial Convention*, 396.

31. Members of the committee were William Adix, Gary Berkland, Bonnie Block, Karen Bloomquist, Eleanor Emch, Barbara Knutson, Marian Nickelson, Mabel Sihler, Mrs. Robert Spenn, and Evelyn Streng.

32. Task Force on the Full Participation of Woman in the Church, "Participation of Woman in the Church," in *Reports and Actions of the Eighth General Convention of the American Lutheran Church (1976)*, ed. Arnold R. Mickelsen (Minneapolis: Office of the General Secretary of the American Lutheran Church, 1976), 500.

33. Ibid., 502.

34. "Participation of Women in the Corporate Life of Congregations of the American Lutheran Church," Appendix 1-A, *1976 Reports and Actions*, 587–99.

35. "Findings of Sample Survey Participation of Women in the Corporate Life of Congregations of the American Lutheran Church," *1976 Reports and Actions*, 582–86.

36. The Task Force for Women's Concerns was made up of Gary Berkland, Eleanor Emch, Ann Francis, Lilette Johnston, and Mabel Sihler.

37. For example, see Task Force Recommendation number 19.C.1.a and b., in *Reports and Actions of the Ninth General Convention of the American Lutheran Church (1978)*, ed. Arnold R. Mickelsen (Minneapolis: Office of the General Secretary of the American Lutheran Church, 1978), 680–81. "#19.C.1.a. When reviewing the work of the following units: the Board of Publications,

... the Church Council should review the unit evaluations of: the curriculum materials, the constitutions, the official communications, b. Those specific review groups should also ask the following questions: 1) has all sexist language been eliminated? If not, what are the future plans to achieve this objective? 2) Do illustrations show that women and men can fulfill similar tasks in the church and the society? For example: both women and men should be illustrated as having responsibilities and capabilities of raising children, teaching classes, working on committees, or administering programs. 3) Do plans for material development include a strategy for growth in female and male consciousness? 4) When developing a publication plan, are women solicited as writers on all subjects including theology?"

38. See the masthead of any *Well Woman* after 1982.

39. "Actions by LWC Board," *The Well Woman* (June 1978): 2.

40. See Resolution 2 and 4 of the Lutheran Women's Caucus in Convocation, 13–15 July 1984, Seattle, Washington.

41. Elaine Donaldson and Julie Stine, "Into the '80s," in *Reports and Actions of the Tenth General Conference of the American Lutheran Church (1980)*, ed. Arnold R. Mickelsen (Minneapolis: Office of the General Secretary of the American Lutheran Church, 1980), 35.

42. H. George Anderson, "Three Church Women's Groups Reflect Mission Roots," *The Lutheran Standard* 24 (19 October 1984): 20.

43. *Wholenotes* (October 1981): 13.

44. On 4–6 May 1981 the National Assembly of Lutheran Social Ministries, which included over thirty social ministry groups and voluntary agencies, met in Cincinnati, Ohio. The Lutheran Women's Caucus held its board meeting there and, through its president, Gretchen Leppke, continued to support this group, working with it to assure the inclusiveness of the ELCA. See "Prez Sez," *The Well Woman* (Winter 1981): 2.

45. Gracia Grindal, "Viewpoint," *The Well Woman* (Fall 1982): 2.

46. Letter from Fern Gudmestad (ALC Women president), Dorothy Jacobs (LCW Executive Committee), and Selma Mayer (WAM Coordinating Council) to Arnold Mickelson (secretary of the CNLC), with copies to William Kinneson (chair of the CNLC), James R. Crumley (LCA bishop), William H. Kohn (bishop of the AELC), and David Preus (ALC presiding bishop), dated 17 January 1983.

47. "Equality Urged in New Church," *The Lutheran Standard* 24 (6 January 1984): 25.

48. Barbara Nelson, "Report to Design Task Force on Services and Resources for Congregational Ministry: Option for an Organization for Women in a New Lutheran Church" (5 December 1983).

49. Bonnie Jensen, "Background Information Regarding Joint Women's Proposal to Design Task Force on Service and Resources for Congregational Ministry" (23 December 1983).

50. Bonnie Jensen, "Women in the New Church," *The Well Woman* (Winter 1984): 1ff.

51. Letter from the executive committees of the three women's organizations to Arnold R. Mickelson, coordinator of the CNLC, dated 3 February 1984.
52. "Report of the Consulting Committee on Women in Church and Society," Division for Mission in North America, LCA, Exhibit A-3, 23–25 June 1983, 6.
53. Edgar R. Trexler, *Anatomy of a Merger: People, Dynamics, and Decisions that Shaped the ELCA* (Augsburg: Minneapolis, 1991), 66–68.
54. "Report of the Consulting Committee on Women in Church and Society," 7.
55. Edgar Trexler makes this the theme of his book *Anatomy of a Merger*.
56. "Minutes for October 4–5, 1985," Consulting Committee on Women in Church and Society, Division for Mission in North America, 4.
57. Harold and Betty Riemenschneider, "Letter to the Editor," *The Lutheran Standard* 24 (4 May 1984): 23.
58. *Forum Letter*, 15, ed. Richard John Neuhaus (2 May 1986): 3.
59. "Poll Results on New-Church Proposals," *The Lutheran Standard* 24 (13 July 1984): 19.
60. Martha Ellen Stortz, "Now, I Think," *The Lutheran* 19 (1 May 1985): 32.
61. Lutheran Women's Caucus in Convocation, "Resolution 4 Concerning a Formula for Representation in the New Lutheran Church," 13–15 July 1984, Seattle, Washington.
62. "Week of Hope," *The Lutheran Standard* 24 (16 November 1984): 7.
63. Barbara Nelson's motion 8, 1 November 1984. CNLC minutes.
64. H. George Anderson, "Three Church Women's groups reflect mission roots," *The Lutheran Standard* 24 (19 October 1984): 20.
65. "Inter-Lutheran Women's Planning Committee Report for CNLC/Women's Organization Meeting Regarding Proposed Board for Women's Ministries," 17 January 1985, 1.
66. Representatives from ALC Women were Marlene Engstrom, Maria Gomez, Bonnie Jensen, and Faythe Kalkwarth; ALC nonorganizational representatives were Barbara Ervin, Stacy Kitahata, Kathleen Kler Comsia, and Connie Sassanella Williams. Representatives from the LCW were Ann G. Kohler, Lois I. Leffler, Barbara F. Nelson, and Barbara Price. LCA nonorganizational representatives were Janis Goodman, Rafaela Morales, Elna Solvang, and Rachel C. Wahlberg. The representative of WAM was Selma ("Sammy") Mayer, and the AELC nonorganizational representative was Christine Grumm.
67. Trexler, 152.
68. See Marlene Engstrom, "Apathy toward the 'Wedding,'" *Scope* 25 (June 1986): 33.
69. This was an amorphous group of social ministries led by James Siefkes of the ALC's Division for Mission in North America.
70. Lowell Almen, "The Back Page," *The Lutheran Standard* 25 (5 May 1985): 30.
71. Exhibit E, 23–27 September 1985. CNLC Agendas, 55–59.

72. Jeanette Bauermeister (AELC), Marlene Engstrom (ALC), Margie Fiedler (ALC), Evelyn Frost (ALC), Janis Goodman (LCA), Victoria Hamilton (ALC), Stacy Kitahata (ALC), Ann Kohler (LCA), DeAne Lagerquist (ALC), Judy Lopez (LCA), Kathleen Morkert (AELC), Barbara Nelson (LCA), Barbara Price (LCA), Eloise Thomas (LCA), with staff persons Bonnie Jensen (ALC), Lois I. Leffler (LCA), and Sammy Mayer (AELC).

73. This group consisted of Lois Dekker (LCA), Susan Everson (ALC), Lois Geehr (LCA), Christine Grumm (AELC), Kathryn Lee (ALC), Cynthia Luft (LCA), Myrna Sheie (ALC), and Elna Solvang (LCA).

74. Consulting Committee on Women in Church and Society, Division for Mission in North America, "Minutes," 17–18 April 1986, 3.

75. "Board Opposes Separate Incorporation of Women's Organization in New Church," *The Lutheran Standard* 25 (18 April 1986): 25. See also *1986 Reports and Actions*, 867–68.

76. Ibid.

77. Ibid.

78. "Lutheran Church Women Start Unifying Process," *The Lutheran Standard* 25 (2 May 1986): 28.

79. Engstrom, 32.

80. *1986 Reports and Actions*, 1298.

81. Minutes, CCWCS, 17–18 April 1986, 10.

82. "ALC Seeks Council Change," *The Lutheran* 20 (August 1986): 20.

83. "Saying 'Yes' to Merger," *The Lutheran* 20 (17 September 1986): 19.

84. For a fuller account of this see Trexler, 165–77.

85. Kathryn Marie Olson, "Toward Uniting a Fellowship Divided: A Dramatistic Analysis of the Constitution-Writing Process of the Evangelical Lutheran Church in America," Ph.D. dissertation, Northwestern University, 1987, 107.

86. Faith Burgess, dean of Lutheran School of Theology, Philadelphia; Bonnie Jensen; and Betty Lee Nyhus.

87. ELCA Constitution 15.51.11-15.51.A87.a-i.

88. In 1988 the director for educational resources was Yvis J. LaRiviera-Mestre; director for community and organizational development was Inez M. Schwarzkopf; director for service and development was Doris E. Strieter; director for ecumenical and cross-cultural ministry was Kwang-Ja Yu; director for literacy was Faith Fretheim. As of 1993, only Strieter and Fretheim remained in these positions.

89. ELCA Constitution 16.22.B91.a.

90. In 1988 Doris Pagelkopf was the chair. Board members were: Alice Carter, Marcia L. Clark-Johnson, Ronald Good, Robert M. Holum, Jean Larson-Hurd, Ronald K. Jacobson, Nancy Jewell, Marcus R. Kunz, Selma ("Sammy") Mayer, Audrey Mortensen, Barbara F. Nelson, June Nilsson, Judy Jackson Pitts, Michael Sharp, Ronald Valenzuela, Loretta Walker; advisory members were: Lita B. Johnson, assistant to the bishop; David C.

Wold, bishop of southwestern Washington; and Charlotte E. Fiechter, executive director of women of the ELCA.

91. For example, Mary W. Anderson, "Call the Laborers: A Congregational Resource on Women and Ordained Ministry," ELCA Commission for Women, 1992.

92. Roman Catholic/Lutheran Joint Commission, *Facing Unity. Models, Forms and Phases of Catholic-Lutheran Church Fellowship* (Geneva: Lutheran World Federation, 1985), 45–48.

Women's Ordination in the Anglican Communion: Can This Church Be Saved?

Suzanne Radley Hiatt

It seems a curious fact that though the ordination of women in mainline churches has its roots in nineteenth-century America, twentieth-century debates on the topic almost never mention those beginnings. This phenomenon could be observed in 1970 at a World Council of Churches consultation on the ordination of women in Switzerland, where most participants, including the Americans, saw ordination as a newly emerging issue with a history dating back perhaps to the late 1950s in Sweden. More recently, a one-sentence summary of the nineteenth-century situation in *Time* magazine's cover article "God and Women" (*Time*, 23 November 1992) stated that the first woman minister in the United States was Antoinette Brown, a congregational women ordained in 1853 "who later became a Unitarian."[1] This was the only mention in the article of nineteenth-century women ministers, and it seemed as though the writer may have conflated Antoinette Brown with Olympia Brown, the first women ordained in the Universalist Church in 1863. True, the same surname is confusing, but it is possible to keep the various Adamses and Roosevelts of U.S. history straight, even though they were blood relatives, whereas the two Reverends Brown were not. Both were active in the woman suffrage movement later in their lives.

The problem in remembering these foremothers and others may be that they are associated with feminism. The various "movements for the ordination of women" with which I am familiar have always had an uneasy relationship with feminism. Indeed, feminists have historically had a hard time dealing with feminist roots, for we have grown up in a world where feminism is seen as strident and irrational and where historical feminists are portrayed not as heroines but as eccentric and amusing scatterbrains, "suffragettes" rather than suffragists, and "women's libbers" rather than freedom fighters.[2]

Those working for the ordination of women in Christian churches have an especially difficult time with our relation to feminism for we are immediately accused of lacking any true vocation to ordination but seeking instead and solely to move forward the feminist agenda by opening positions of power in the churches to women. Often the price of admission for women to institutional acceptance is the forfeiture of feminist ideas and identification. In this chapter I want to look briefly at how that price has been asked and continues to be asked in the various provinces (national churches) of the Anglican Communion in the struggle over the question of admission of women to Holy Orders. The struggle of women to make this change in the Episcopal Church has been one manifestation of the struggle of feminists throughout the world to open the Anglican Communion to women's voices in the late twentieth century.

To return briefly to the nineteenth century, the ordination of women was not an issue in the Episcopal Church, the United States province of the Anglican Communion. Of course, women were active in ministry as they have always been in the churches, but ordination was not even considered. There was agitation enough about allowing women to serve as nuns or deaconesses, but women simply did not present themselves for ordination. The educational paths to Holy Orders were not open to them.[3] Like other Protestant women, Episcopal women were active in missionary work both at home and abroad and in many reform movements. Curiously, not many of them were active in the temperance and suffrage movements; indeed the Episcopal Church usually weighed in on the anti–woman suffrage side in books and essays by clergymen, who saw the changes women were advocating as distinctly un-Christian. While women were indefatigable churchworkers and the clergy paid them gentlemanly compliments on their devotion, the limits of female authority were clearly drawn. The report of the Board of Missions to the General Convention of 1892 reflects well this prevailing attitude among churchmen:

> The Woman's Auxiliary has adapted itself, with the quickness of perception and delicacy of touch, which characterizes the sex which it represents, to the great variety of persons with whom it has had to do, and to the diverse and frequently changing conditions in which it has found itself. We think it of high importance that the Woman's Auxiliary should continue to be that which its name indicates, and which it has been in the past distinctly auxil-

iary to the Board, and that the Board and Woman's Auxiliary should thus realize, in their common work, that which is the true idea of the essential relation of the sexes. Should the present relations of the Woman's Auxiliary to the Board in this respect be changed, we think the change would involve the loss of elements of beauty/grace and strength which are quite peculiar and this loss would be incalculable.[4]

Episcopal women like Vida Dutton Scudder (1861–1954) were active and influential in the reform movements of the early twentieth century. Scudder, a professor of English at Wellesley College and a well-known champion of the rights of labor, clearly saw social reform as a requirement of her Christian faith. But she appears to have had little or no interest in temperance or woman suffrage.[5] In this she is typical of Episcopal women of her day.

It was not until the mid–twentieth century that the ordination of women became an issue in the Anglican Communion. The question was raised and a study commission issued a report, the first of many over the next fifty years following World War I and the enfranchisement of women in England.[6] The report suggested no reason not to ordain women but only that "the time was not right." A similar report again in the Church of England in 1935 reached essentially the same conclusion.[7]

But reports aside, it was an event that brought the matter to the attention of the Anglican Communion. In 1944, in war-torn China, the bishop of Hong Kong, the Rt. Rev. R. O. Hall, ordained a Chinese woman deacon, the Rev. Li Tim Oi (1907–1992), to the priesthood. Ms. Li ministered in Macao and in parts of mainland China as both war and revolution raged. When the war ended in 1945, Bishop Hall announced his intention to ask the next Lambeth Conference (a meeting every ten years of the Anglican bishops of the world at Lambeth Palace in London), scheduled for 1948, for permission to continue to ordain women to the priesthood on an experimental basis for twenty years. It was in this period that theological debate raged on the issue of women in orders, most notably in England.[8] In the end, the Lambeth Conference denied Bishop Hall's request and asked him to ask the Rev. Ms. Li to renounce her orders. Thirty years later when she retired to Canada, she admitted she had never done so but continued to minister in China where priests were few. She always considered herself to be a priest, and her ordination was officially recognized in 1970 in Hong Kong. Toward the end of her life, she concelebrated the Eucharist with the Rt. Rev. Barbara Harris at her consecration as the first Anglican woman bishop in 1989. But in 1948, the great debate appeared to be settled as women around the world were swept back into domesticity or a semblance thereof in the 1950s.

The issue reappeared in the late 1960s in various parts of the world. In the United States women had been admitted as students in a few of the Episcopal Church's seminaries in the late 1950s and early 1960s. In 1965 Bishop James Pike declared a deaconess, Mrs. Phyliss Edwards, to be a deacon, thereby putting her into Holy Orders and making her the Rev. Mrs. Phyliss Edwards.[9] Pike put her in charge of a parish. This raised the question of women's ordination (as deacons are considered ordained ministers in Anglican, Roman Catholic, and Orthodox polity), and the House of Bishops sent the matter to a study commission that was to report back to them at the 1967 House of Bishops.[10] When the commission reported at the 1967 General Convention that it could find no reason not to ordain women to all orders of ministry, another commission, the Joint (Bishops and Deputies) Commission on Ordained and Licensed Ministries, was appointed to study the question further and report back to the 1970 General Convention.

Meanwhile, the 1968 Lambeth Conference at the request of several provinces, including the diocese of Hong Kong, debated and resolved that women could be ordained deacons if the local province approved it. Several local provinces, including Hong Kong, New Zealand, Canada, and the Church of the Province of Kenya, began ordaining women deacons almost immediately. They also declared that deaconesses were within the diaconate and therefore ordained.

At this point feminism explicitly entered the debate—it had been hinted at in 1920 and 1948. For the first time women entered the fray as active proponents of the move. In the renewed wave of feminism in the United States, young women, many of them seminary-educated, older women who had long ministered as laywomen, clergy wives, nuns, deaconesses, and feminists who were also Episcopalians, came together and began to work for women's ordination.[11] The joint commission appointed in 1967 recommended to the 1970 General Convention that women be ordained to all ministerial orders immediately. Several women came forward to discuss their personal calls to ordination. The women of the church, voting in a separate convention of their own, approved the measure by a five to one margin. In the end, the commission's recommendation was defeated by a narrow margin in the clergy order of the House of Deputies. Before the convention adjourned, it passed legislation approving the ordination of women as deacons, and the supporters of full ordination began to organize for the next General Convention in 1973.

In 1970 the Anglican Consultative Council, an international body of clergy, bishops, and laity representing all the provinces (national churches) and meeting every three years between Lambeth Conferences, voted by a narrow margin that it would be acceptable for bishops who wished to go ahead and ordain women priests with the approval of their own province to do so. Hong Kong had requested this advice, for that burgeoning church was in as dire need of priests as it had been in 1944. In November 1971 yet another English bishop of Hong Kong, the Rt. Rev. Gilbert Baker, ordained two women deacons, the Rev. Jane Hwang and the Rev. Joyce Bennett, as priests. The matter began to be debated in the provinces of Canada and New Zealand as well. In these initial debates feminism was not an issue, for the need for ordained ministers in these three provinces was the most compelling argument for ordaining women. The women, by now ordained deacons, were already ministering in areas where no male priests were available. Indeed, Li Tim Oi had ministered as a priest in Macao before her ordination in 1944, as there were no male priests remaining there during the war. Women with clear vocations to ordination were presenting themselves to churches which clearly needed their ministries. Even so, in Canada the debate went on until 1976 and in New Zealand until 1977. Hong Kong was the first province to take the step without prolonged debate or objection.

In the United States opposing forces worked hard to get the upcoming 1973 General Convention to approve or reject women priests. In late 1971 the American bishops called for yet another study of the issue. A group of women, seminarians, and church workers, meeting at the same time to look at next steps, shot off to the bishops' meeting a letter listing the many studies in England and America since 1919—all of which had found no good theological reason not to ordain women. The women informed the bishops that they would not serve on another study commission and announced they were forming the Episcopal Women's Caucus to promote the ordination of women as well as other issues of equality for women in the church. The bishops proceeded with an in-house study by a committee of bishops. When the committee returned its report a year later in November 1972, the bishops voted by a narrow margin to support women's ordination when it came before the 1973 General Convention. The bishops cannot legislate without the concurrence of the House of Deputies, but this was what they call a "mind of the house" resolution.

Despite this vote and massive lobbying and educational efforts by the Women's Caucus and others, the resolution to ordain women as priests and bishops (they were already deacons) lost by a narrow mar-

gin at the 1973 General Convention. The opposition, too, had been organizing and lobbying for three years and was able to convince the
majority of voting members that if women were ordained, the church
would be wracked by schism and dissension from those clergy and laity who could never accept such a decision. On the other hand, the convention members were persuaded that the disappointed women
would continue to wait quietly for the institutional machinery to grind
toward acknowledging their vocations. After all, women had waited
patiently for twenty-four years between the time it was first proposed
(1946) and the time it was fully approved (1970) for women to be admitted as lay delegates to the General Convention. In political terms,
the 1973 General Convention decided it would be more trouble for the
church to ordain women than to continue not to do so.

The General Convention ended with the House of Bishops voting
for a resolution calling on member bishops not to ordain women
unilaterally (a strategy that had been suggested and was seen as a
possibility since church law did not expressly forbid the ordination
of women).[12] A large number of bishops signed a statement dissenting from that resolution on "collegiality." The newly elected presiding
bishop, in a move that post–Clarence Thomas might be considered
proof of his failure to "get it," called for yet another study of the
matter—a call that was quietly set aside.

Mindful of this long history of delay and parliamentary maneuvering to keep women in their place, Episcopal Women's Caucus members began to look toward new strategies in the early months of 1974.
An inconclusive meeting with supportive bishops in November 1973,
and the public refusal of the bishop of New York to ordain five women
deacons who presented themselves for ordination in December 1973,
helped women see that delay and legalisms could and probably would
effectively outlast their vocations. By the summer of 1974 a number of
women deacons and their supporters, male clergy, laywomen and laymen, and a scattering of bishops felt that the clear call to ordination
could be delayed no longer. On 29 July 1974 the feast of Saints Mary
and Martha of Bethany, three retired or resigned bishops (men who
were bishops but were not endangering their jobs) ordained eleven
women deacons to the priesthood at the Church of the Advocate, a
predominantly black parish in the heart of the north Philadelphia
African-American community. The bishops and deacons were all
white, but the parish's African-American rector (pastor), the Rev. Paul
Washington, was the master of ceremonies. The Episcopal Church's
highest-ranking lay leader, Dr. Charles V. Willie, an African American,
was the preacher. Another African American, Ms. Barbara Harris, later

to become the first woman bishop in the Anglican Communion, was the lay leader (senior warden) of the parish and led the procession carrying the cross.[13]

The women ordained in Philadelphia in 1974 were all feminists and willing to acknowledge that feminism as part of their vocation to the priesthood. All had been active in the civil rights movement (like their nineteenth-century feminist foremothers, many of whom had come to feminism by way of abolitionist activities). Five had been sponsored for ordination by predominantly black parishes, including one from the Church of the Advocate itself.[14] In a second "irregular" ordination in 1975, four more white women deacons were ordained priests by another retired bishop. This time the service took place in Washington, D.C., in the predominantly black church of Saint Stephen and the Incarnation. Those four, also, were feminists with essentially the same civil rights background as the Philadelphia eleven.

Of course, the reaction was swift and agitated. The bishops, meeting in emergency session in August 1974, voted that no ordinations had taken place. The women, in response to that judgment, began to function as priests wherever they could. Nearly two thousand people, mostly supporters, had attended the service and were quick to state that they did judge that eleven ordinations had taken place that day. In the ensuing months leading up to the 1976 General Convention, the women celebrated the Eucharist in many places. Two male clergy were tried in ecclesiastical court for allowing them to do so in their parishes. Meanwhile others were educating and lobbying for ordination to be approved at the 1976 General Convention. Several diocesan bishops declared their intention to ordain women after the 1976 Convention regardless of how the vote went.

It was small wonder, then, that the 1976 General Convention voted that women could be ordained to all orders of ministry (including the episcopate). The events of the intervening years had reversed the conventional wisdom of the 1973 Convention that it would be more trouble to ordain women than not. By 1976 it was clear that the more divisive course for the church would be to continue to deny ordination to women. At the 1976 General Convention, the bishops approved measures to admit the fifteen women priests to regular standing without reordination. Despite that, the House of Bishops has never revised its 1974 and 1975 opinions that no ordinations took place in Washington and Philadelphia.[15]

The first "regular" or "legal" ordinations of women priests in the Episcopal Church began in January 1977. These ordinations were generally greeted as "the first" by the church, and the official attitude was to play down the two "premature" ordinations of 1974 and 1975. The 1979 edition of *The Episcopal Clerical Directory*, a biannual biographical listing of Episcopal clergy, listed the fifteen women as having been ordained priests on the dates their ordinations were recognized by their own diocesan bishops. When the women objected to this rewriting of history, the 1974 and 1975 dates were acknowledged, but the ordaining bishops were not named. After a ten-year struggle with the record keepers, the women were listed in the 1989 edition as having been ordained in 1974 or 1975 and the ordaining bishops named, but a note of the date and name of the bishop who "recognized" them was left in each of their entries.

Officially, and in the conventional wisdom, women have been ordained priests in the American Episcopal Church since 1977. Women ordained in that year were commended for their patience and their devotion to the church. Feminism was quietly retired as a motivating factor for either the women or the church. As with the nineteenth-century ordained women ministers, inconveniently early ordinations linked with feminist aspirations were quietly forgotten.[16]

By 1992 nearly half the provinces of the Anglican Communion (fourteen out of thirty-four) had ordained women to the priesthood. Two provinces, the Episcopal Church USA and New Zealand, also had women bishops, both elected and consecrated in 1989. (Since that time five more women bishops have been elected in the United States and Canada. Three of the seven bishops are diocesans, meaning they are the head bishops in their dioceses.)

The Church of England had first approved women in priesthood "in principle" in 1973, but the forces of delay and procedure had kept things on a theoretical level. Women were admitted to the diaconate in England in 1987. In this matter, the "mother" province had fallen behind many of the "daughter" churches. Many of these provinces had started with ordaining women as deacons and then taken the next step of ordaining women as priests a few years later. Some had moved following provincial approval, and in these provinces (e.g., Brazil, Canada, New Zealand) women were "given" ordination because the church needed their priestly ministry. In other provinces (e.g., Uganda and Kenya), individual bishops began ordaining women without provincial approval, usually because they felt they could not delay the ordination of women who were asking any longer. In these churches the women "took" ordination. In both types of situation, women began serving as priests with minimal fuss and disruption. In nearly all these situations, feminism was carefully avoided as an argument for ordination.

The fall of 1992 saw a breakthrough in the ordination of women priests in the Anglican Communion. The issue came to a head in three key provinces, Southern Africa, England, and Australia, where it had been debated for many years, and where there had been feminist involvement in the debate. The measure was voted on—not for the first time—in each of the provinces' synods and finally achieved the required two-thirds majority.

In August 1992 the Province of Southern Africa voted to ordain women priests and proceeded with the first ordinations in early September. The key factor was Archbishop Desmond Tutu's strong support. He had issued a challenge in his opening address to the synod, which included this persuasive personal argument: "I cannot have struggled against an injustice that penalizes people for something they can do nothing about, their race, and then accept with equanimity the gross injustice of penalizing others for something they can do nothing about, their gender."[17] As it had been twenty years earlier in the United States, women's ordination was seen as a justice issue and linked with the racial struggle.[18]

For most of the previous twenty years, opponents of women's ordination in the various provinces had pointed out that the Church of England had not approved women priests. In the Japanese Anglican Church (Nippon Sei Ko Kei) this was indeed the primary reason bishops gave for voting against it in a 1991 debate. Although the provinces are self-governing, there is still the feeling in some Anglican churches that the Church of England is the "mother church" and must lead the way. This view is voiced especially strongly by conservatives when the Church of England takes a conservative position.

The Movement for the Ordination of Women (MOW) had been fighting for approval of women's ordination in the Church of England's General Synod since the movement's founding in 1979. The theological work was mainly done before that in the 1940s, and the approval of the ordination of women deacons in 1987 was a milestone. Finally, on 11 November 1992, the General Synod voted with a two-thirds majority in each house (bishops, clergy, laity) to approve the ordination of women priests. (As in Southern Africa, the primate [head bishop], the Archbishop of Canterbury, was strongly in favor of the measure.[19])

However, women could not be ordained immediately in England, as the measure needed parliamentary and royal approval, the Church of England being the established national church. Women priests finally began to be ordained in England in March of 1994. By midsummer there were close to a thousand women priests in the Church of England.

Ten days after the Church of England General Synod approved the ordination of women, the Australian Anglican Church voted for the seventh time in ten years at its provincial synod on a measure to remove the legal and canonical impediments to women's ordination. This time the vote was affirmative by a two-thirds margin in each order (bishops, priests, and deacons).[20] The Australian branch of MOW had been working for ten years on the issue. Legal maneuvering had led to the blockage by legal injunction of a diocesan-based ordination in February 1992. However, in March 1992, another diocesan bishop in another state in Australia had gone ahead to ordain ten women priests without having to defy a legal injunction. So the ordaining of women had begun before the vote. With that reality and the vote in the Church of England, the November 1992 Australian synod had little choice. The first women to be ordained with provincial approval were ordained in Adelaide on 5 December 1992. By year's end there were ninety-two women priests in Australia.[21]

So, as this is written in 1995, it looks as though the ordination of women to the priesthood is coming in all parts of the Anglican Communion. Though some provinces have had priests for as long as twenty-four years (fifty-one if one considers Li Tim Oi's lonely ministry), it was not until Southern Africa, England, and Australia finally accepted women's ordination that the balance was tipped. It will take some of the remaining provinces longer than others because of local church and societal circumstances, but the Church of England's change signals the future for the entire Anglican Communion.

Yet this great triumph for feminism, the ordination of women, has almost universally been won at the expense of feminism. In those provinces where feminists worked doggedly to bring about this change, at almost the moment it came the feminists who promoted it were sidelined and dismissed.

For many years the process of the ordination of women in the American Episcopal Church has been held up by opponents in other provinces as a horrible example of what happens when "militant feminists" fight for ordination and win. The opposition has effectively (if erroneously) portrayed the U.S. church as decimated and hopelessly and bitterly divided as a result of the mid-1970s fight over women's ordination. Schismatic groups are said to be rife and the Episcopal Church near collapse as a denomination. Though inaccurate and unfair, this picture of the Episcopal Church is widely accepted in other provinces.[22]

In some cases advocates of women's ordination have accepted this portrait and argued that this is precisely why their church should settle the matter in a timely and orderly way. Even Bishop Tutu, in arguing for women's ordination to his synod, felt called to remark: "We must not be scared that because in the USA this issue has been very divisive, it would be so here. It need not be so at all. It has not been so at all in Canada, in New Zealand, in Uganda and elsewhere. It will not be divisive here for we are very accepting of one another and very accommodating."[23] Portraying women's ordination as the mischief of an American (perhaps including Canada)[24] feminist cabal has been an effective strategy in resisting it in other parts of the world.

The antifeminist rhetoric of the opposition continues even after the vote is won and the churches scurry to accommodate the losers. The press reaction to the vote in England was sensationalist in pointing out that the question had won by the narrowest of margins in the General Synod, a mere two votes in the lay order. What they failed to report was the fact that the question had needed a two-thirds margin in each house to win at all, so that in fact this "narrow margin" was more than 66 percent of the votes. The same comment was made about the vote in Australia, where the two-thirds vote was also seen as a squeaker. Much was made in the British press of the pope's unfavorable reaction and his contention that the decision threw up a serious new obstacle to talk of reunion with Rome. Neither the pope nor the press mentioned the fact that Rome had already buried the report from the most recent Anglican-Roman Catholic talks. Neither did they note the fact that there have been Anglican women priests and tacit approval of them by the Anglican Consultative Council for over twenty years.[25] The British press was also quick to quote such feminist theologians as Dr. Daphne Hampson of Saint Andrew's University in Scotland who advised feminist women not to stay in the church and be ordained, as such a move was to capitulate to the male establishment by joining it. The press seemed eager to speed the parting gadfly on her way.[26]

After the debate on women's ordination, the Church of England General Synod spent many more hours discussing ways to accommodate those who disapproved and how to allow bishops and dioceses that cannot accept women priests to continue to exclude them. "The Archbishops of Canterbury and York issued a press statement immediately after the debate calling for 'a period of quiet reflection and deep prayer in which emotions are calmed, not further inflamed.... We pray that all those who opposed the measure will feel comforted by the great love for them in Christ felt by their fellow Anglicans with different views on this particular matter. What binds us together in God's love as a Church is vastly more important than a disagreement about women's ordination.' "[27]

As it had been in the United States and Australia, the first move of the Church of England after the vote was to reassure the traditionalists that allowing women into the priesthood would not make much difference. The women who had fought so hard and long were lost in the shuffle. In Australia the MOW women had been told that at the 5 December 1992 ordination in Adelaide they could process into the church with feminist banners and that the hymnody would be sensitive to sexist language. However, at this event, the MOW women were not allowed to process at all, nor were the usual liturgy and hymnody changed.[28] The effort not to offend the traditionalists ended up offending the feminists instead. Women were reminded that winners can afford to be generous.

But in the case of feminist churchwomen, can they afford it? The co-option of feminists and women called to priesthood has been going on in the American Episcopal Church for more than eighteen years, and it looks to be in full swing in England and Australia now. Perhaps Dr. Hampson is correct, and these Anglican churches, having decided they cannot lick the women, have instead invited women to join them—on their terms, of course. As in the American church, so in Great Britain and Australia, women can always be found to deny the feminist aspect of their call to ordination. The men in charge are quick to minimize and downplay the change and to point to the nonfeminist women priests as "truly called."

The question of whether women's ordination will change the ministry, and, by extension, the church, has been generally answered in the negative for a long time. This answer has been given even more by advocates of the change than by opponents, in order to reassure provinces and people who are still uncertain, and who fear and mistrust change in general, and in the church in particular.

Yet feminist advocates, by and large, do say that the ordination of women has changed and will change the ministry—that is, indeed, their fondest hope. One English bishop and theologian, a longtime supporter of women's ordination, answered the argument that women priests will simply be co-opted into the old boys' network: "The experience of other provinces is that it does not have to be so: that when the experience of women is valued and received within the ordained ministry of the Church, an inescapable difference starts to be noticed. We already see the signs: new styles, new language, a new concept of authority and service, all born out of the long struggle for women to receive the honor due to them as persons and as baptized members of the Body of Christ."[29]

There are still feminists at work in the Episcopal Church, U.S.A., some of them priests, female and male. Many other feminists have gone elsewhere, believing the Episcopal Church's insistence that women priests have not made much difference. The women and men of English and Australian MOW are wondering what to do next, where to go from here. There is pressure on them to disband because "the cause" is won or to turn to other "more important" issues. As was the case in the United States, it is hinted that their commitment to feminism has drawn them away from the "more basic" commitment to work against racism, the commitment that in many cases first drew them into the church struggle about women's ordination.

Yet history suggests that feminists declare victory too soon. We fight to enter patriarchal institutions and are so overcome with gratitude on our admittance that we fail to continue to work to change and humanize those institutions. Our nineteenth-century foremothers quit too soon in many respects, though the fact that they did not quit sooner is an emblem of their formidable strength. We Christian women who have fought for women's ordination are in danger of quitting too soon in this round of the feminist reformation. Our retreat would be a welcome relief to those who still hold power in the churches and who fear and distrust meaningful change. We must be vigilant not to allow what is presented as strategic retreat to develop into hasty and unwise accommodation to sexist patterns.

Our Roman Catholic sisters still struggle with questions of access to the hierarchy. Our Protestant sisters, having won that round, now struggle with issues of sexism in language, liturgy, and church governance, along with the many broader women's issues in the world that the churches must address. We Anglicans are somewhere in between. We have a foot in the door but are not yet sure how we will behave when the door finally opens wide. Let us hope that we will not forget where we came from and the people who are still outside.

NOTES

1. Richard N. Ostling, "The Second Reformation," *Time* (23 November 1992): 56.
2. See Susan Faludi, *Backlash: The Undeclared War Against American Women* (New York: Doubleday, 1991), for a broad and fully documented treatment of how women's concerns and history are systematically trivialized and

obscured in periods of antifeminist backlash. Also see Barbara Ehrenreich, *The Worst Years of Our Lives: Irreverent Notes from a Decade of Greed* (New York: Harper, 1991), where Ehrenreich comments in an essay on "Family Values" that "dissent is also a 'traditional value,' and in a republic founded by revolution, a more deeply native one than sunnyfaced conservatism can ever be. Feminism was practically invented here [in the USA], and ought to be regarded as one of our proudest exports to the world" (p. 11). I am indebted to this insight for stimulating me to think once again about how and why it is not so regarded.

3. For an excellent treatment of the ministry of women in the Episcopal Church in the late nineteenth and early twentieth centuries, see Mary Sudman Donovan, *A Different Call: Women's Ministries in the Episcopal Church 1850–1920* (Wilton, Conn.: Morehouse Barlow, 1986).

4. The Board of Missions Report to the General Convention of 1892. Quoted in Margaret Sherman, *True to Their Heritage: A Brief History of the Women's Auxiliary 1871–1958* (New York: National Council of the Episcopal Church, 1959), 7, 8.

5. See Vida Scudder's autobiography, *On Journey* (New York: E. P. Dutton, 1937).

6. Report of the Archbishop of Canterbury's Commission to Reconsider the Office of Deacons, *The Ministry of Women* (London: Society for the Promotion of Christian Knowledge/New York: Macmillan, 1919).

7. *Report of the Archbishop's Commission to Study the Ministry of Women* (London: Press and Public Board of the Church Assembly, 1935).

8. The issues were all laid out and explored in the debate of the 1940s. Theologians challenged each other for and against women priests; most notable were G. W. H. Lampe and M. E. Thrall (for), and Kenneth Kirk and E. L. Mascall (against). Even literary personages, who like most English people of their day happened to be Anglican, had something to say; most notable were C. S. Lewis (against) and Dorothy Sayers (for). In the fifty years since this period, in debates all around the world little theological or ethical wisdom has been added.

9. In Anglican polity there are three orders of ministry—deacon, priest, and bishop. Two Lambeth Conferences had debated whether women who had been "set apart" as deaconesses were in effect ordained women deacons. The 1920 conference said yes, 1930 said no, and until Bishop Pike's action it was an unsettled question with most Anglicans assuming deaconesses were not ordained but laywomen. Deaconesses had not functioned liturgically as deacons (in reading the Gospel at the Eucharist, administering the chalice), nor had they worn a deacon's stole or been addressed as "the Reverend" until Mrs. Edwards was put in charge of a parish.

10. The Episcopal Church is governed by a General Convention which meets every three years. This legislative body is bicameral, consisting of a House of Bishops and a House of Deputies. There must be concurrence of the two houses to enact legislation or change canon law. On weighty matters the

House of Deputies, which is half clergy and half laity, divides and votes "by orders," meaning legislation must be passed by a majority of both the clergy and lay orders. Changes to the church's constitution require the affirmative vote of all three orders (bishops, clergy, and laity) in two successive General Conventions—at least a six-year process. The bishops meet annually, but they cannot enact legislation or vote to change canon law except with the concurrence of the House of Deputies at the triennial General Convention.

11. The Episcopal Peace Fellowship called a conference of women on the status of women in the Episcopal Church at Graymoor Conference Center in New York in April 1970. The group issued a statement to the effect that women should be included in all church offices from incense bearers to bishop. Members of the group began organizing efforts to bring the matter to the attention of the next General Convention scheduled to meet in October 1970.

12. "Resolution on Collegiality and Loyalty," in *Journal of the General Convention of the Episcopal Church, 1973: Part II The House of Bishops* (New York: Seabury, 1974), 125. The resolution publicly affirming the bishops' "adherence to the principles of collegiality and mutual loyalty as well as respect for due constitutional and canonical process" passed by a margin of fifty-three to forty.

13. There has been a great deal written about the July 1974 ordinations. For further comment see Carter Heyward, *A Priest Forever* (New York: Harper and Row, 1976); Alla Renée Bozarth, *Woman Priest: A Personal Odyssey* (San Diego: Lura Media, 1988); Suzanne Hiatt, "How We Brought the Good News from Graymoor to Minneapolis," *Journal of Ecumenical Studies* 20 (Fall 1983); and Suzanne Hiatt, "July 29, 1974—*Kairos* as Paradigm Shift," in *No Easy Peace: Liberating Anglicanism: A Collection of Essays in Memory of William John Wolf*, ed. Carter Heyward and Sue Phillips (Lanham, Md.: University Press of America, 1992).

14. Betty Schiess from Grace Church, Syracuse, New York; Jeannette Piccard (1895–1983) from Saint Philips Church, St. Paul, Minnesota; Emily Hewitt and Carter Heyward from Saint Mary's Church, Manhattanville, New York; and Suzanne Hiatt from the Church of the Advocate.

15. At this writing (1995), one of the fifteen "irregularly" ordained women is deceased, three are retired, four are seminary professors, four are church-employed priests, and three are secularly employed. All were accepted as priests in good standing without reordination between 1977 and 1981.

16. In a 1992 general book on "women's firsts," the 1974 and 1977 ordinations were conflated and the first woman ordained in 1977 is listed as the first woman ordained in 1974. In *The Book of Women's Firsts*, ed. Phyliss Read and Bernard Wittleib (New York: Random House, 1992), see the entry on "Jacqueline Means," on page 285. Again, information on feminists and religion is widely "mis-remembered," creating confusion and doubt as to what happened when and by whose agency.

226 Protestant Women

17. Archbishop Desmond Tutu, "Opening Charge to the Triennial Provincial Synod of the Anglican Church in Southern Africa, Mbabane, Swaziland, August 11, 1992," *Bishopscourt Update* 5 (31 August 1992): 1. This newsletter is published by the Office of Archbishop Desmond Tutu of Cape Town, Republic of South Africa.
18. As in the United States twenty years earlier, in Australia for many years, and in the Church of England, women, most of them feminists, had been working hard to get the measure passed. See Denise Ackermann, Jonathan A. Draper, and Emma Mashinini, eds., *Women Hold Up Half the Sky: Women in the Church in Southern Africa* (Pietermaritzberg, South Africa: Cluster Publications, 1991). .
19. MOW and others produced volumes of educational material in the long struggle. Two of the most recent (and probably most influential) books are: Monica Furlong, *A Dangerous Delight: Women and Power in the Church* (London: SPCK, 1991) and Richard Holloway, ed., *Who Needs Feminism? Men Respond to Sexism in the Church* (London: SPCK, 1991). In June 1994 the Episcopal Church in Scotland, of which Holloway is the primate, approved women's priestly ordination.
20. MOW Australia had also produced volumes of material, including an occasional newsletter entitled *Balaam's Ass.* Among the most effective educational tools MOW circulated was a videotaped documentary of the debate at the 1987 General Synod entitled *The Fully Ordained Meat Pie*, Janet Bell, producer, Gillian Coote, director, Film Australia, 1988.
21. Janet Scarfe, "Letter to MOW Friends Overseas," 28 December 1992.
22. On a September 1992 trip to Japan, the first question I was asked by churchpeople everywhere concerned the depth and nature of the "split" in the American church.
23. Desmond Tutu, 4.
24. I was interested to read in the MOW Australia overseas newsletter published from Melbourne—*Ebb & Flow* 2 (November 1992): 2—the comments of an Australian woman, the Rev. Elizabeth McWhae, serving as a priest in Canada. "People here [Australia] have tried to suggest that the Canadian Church is splitting, or declining because of it [women priests]. That's rubbish! Women have been ordained in Canada for fifteen years. . . . It has never come up as an issue in any form."
25. The Roman Catholic Church is in a real dilemma as seen by the U.S. Catholic Bishops' inability to produce a pastoral letter on women in November 1992. The internal inconsistency of condemning sexism and insisting on an all-male celibate hierarchy would not fly and they knew it. Now that the Church of England has women priests, the Roman Catholic Church is more isolated than ever in its male priests–only posture. The pope's recent (May 1994) reaffirmation of the Roman Catholic Church's ban on women priests only compounds the difficulty as the issue has turned to papal authority now that theological argument has failed.

26. My comments on British press reaction are culled from a number of clippings that have come my way. For a somewhat ascerbic commentary on how the press handled it, see Paul Handley, "A Preference for Strife," *The Church Times* 6771 (20 November 1992): 17.

27. Press statement by Archbishops of Canterbury and York (Rt. Revs. George Carey and John Habgood) quoted in *The Tablet: The International Catholic Weekly* 246 (21 November 1992): 1486.

28. Janet Scarfe, "Ordination of Women in Adelaide," *The Church Scene* (11 December 1992). *The Church Scene* is a newsletter of the Australian Anglican Church.

29. The Rt. Rev. Peter Selby, "At Last!," *Signs of the Times* Special Issue (11 November 1992).

Roman Catholic Women

Roman Catholic Women

Ministry of American Catholic Sisters: The Vowed Life in Church Renewal

Marie Augusta Neal, SND de Namur

It is not ordination that distinguishes the ministries of Catholic Sisters but the vows of poverty, chastity, and obedience lived today without the historical confines of cloister. Catholic Sisters are such by reason of their experience of being called to the vowed life within the Catholic Church. Eighty-nine percent report that they have experienced this call.[1]

Historically women and men following this unique call to the vowed life, usually formalized into the three vows of poverty, chastity, and obedience, were labeled "nuns" or "monks" depending upon their sex. Before the industrial era, they all lived a contemplative life apart in monasteries, mostly in silence, working the land for subsistence in days and nights punctuated by chapel attendance to recite or sing "The Divine Office," a series of psalms, other biblical excerpts, and prayers which constituted the official prayer of the Catholic Church. By vow they committed themselves to live a simple lifestyle and share all resources in common, to abstain from all sexually stimulating interpersonal behavior, and to seek the will of God as expressed for them in the constitutions of their order and the will of their "superiors," that is, the persons in charge of the house, the region, and the whole institute. In the religious community the vowed member, faithful to work and sharing, could be free of anxiety about subsistence and free too of greed, lust, and willful use of power in one's own self-interest.

All kinds of unique adaptations developed in time resulting in some unintended consequences. For example, facilitating the inclusion of the sacramental liturgy of the Eucharist into this life of withdrawal from the world was the reason that some monks became ordained priests, a quite separate vocation and a role open to them because they were men. (In the Roman Catholic Church only ordained priests can

celebrate the Eucharist.) This added role of ordained minister, however, linked the monks formally with the Roman Catholic hierarchy because priesthood, historically, became the entrée to decision making.
Roman Catholic institutional structures were based on the belief in a
direct male line of authority from Christ. This arrangement gave some
monks access to decision making in church structures not open to
nuns. Monks and nuns, as such, did not and still do not belong to the
line of formal decision makers in the church. One consequence of this
arrangement was that nuns were left dependent on monks and other
priests for the liturgy and were more isolated by cloister from what
was happening in the outside world.

This cloistered style of monastic spirituality still exists today and
attracts about twenty-five hundred women in the United States to
complete enclosure and to a monastic lifestyle with emphasis on community life.[2] But how do we get from nuns to Sisters? As early as the
sixteenth century, with the coming of industrialization and, with it, the
migration of peoples to urban areas, some nuns felt called to live outside of the cloistered life, to serve and work with the dispossessed
poor, i.e., with those lacking access to food and shelter, land ownership, and care when ill—accelerating problems stemming from the
breakup of the serfdom of feudal Europe. There were ordained priests
out in the world already doing what they do today, providing the sacraments, preaching and teaching the good news of salvation, and administering in the institutional church as pope, bishops of dioceses,
and pastors of parishes, each with territorial jurisdiction within which
he served and reached out to help the poor with the aid of dedicated
laity. As is the case now, they did this with great unevenness of effectiveness. Some cloistered nuns saw serious needs not being attended
to. They felt called to action and supported by the vows, but they
needed to be free of the cloister which since 1298 c.e. was imposed in
the strict form on all women who chose the vowed life.[3]

Several attempts were made to start new active women's groups
with vows from 1500 onward, but these efforts were opposed by episcopal or papal prohibitions, which decreed either the cessation of the
good works and return to the cloister or laicization, that is, a command
to withdraw from the formal vow commitment. Efforts toward some
compromise continued because a vowed support community remained for some a deeply felt need. There are many historically recorded accounts of nuns trying to expand their outreach to the poor
within the parameters of the restrictions of cloister and of inventing
new lifestyles for those in the vowed life. To cite here but one model
imagined by Louise de Marillac and Vincent de Paul and described in

an exchange of letters between them: "They shall have no convent but a hospital, houses of the sick or an asylum; no cell but a hired room, no chapel but the parish church, no cloister but the streets of the town; for enclosure they have only obedience, for a grille the fear of God; for veil, holy modesty."[4] About 1750, finally, these newly founded Daughters of Charity were recognized but only with temporary vows that they must renew each year, so certain were the church fathers that women could not be faithful to a lifetime commitment to poverty, chastity, and obedience outside of a cloistered life.

By the nineteenth century, thousands of women were choosing a semicloistered life even though categorized as "not real nuns" for so doing. Literally hundreds of new congregations of women religious were founded, some caring for orphans left abandoned in the anonymity of new urban shantytowns that sprang up near factories whose owners underpaid workers and felt no responsibility to provide housing. Others cared for the sick and wounded from local battlefields and epidemics. Many opened schools for children and working young women. In response to the migration of poor workers to the United States, in the mid-nineteenth century many chose to join the migration to settle in American towns and cities to minister among the working class.

Working within a modified cloister to keep within canon law, thousands of Sisters did follow the call to take simple vows and work to provide education, health care, and other human services to needy human beings in the new world. To distinguish them from cloistered nuns, they came to call themselves and to be called by others "Sisters."[5] Today the term *nun* is reserved for cloistered women religious; *Sister* is more accurately used for those actively involved in ministry in the world and who seek to develop a spirituality relevant to their chosen ministries. The Roman Catholic Church today formally distinguishes the contemplative vowed life from the vowed life of those responding to human needs by classifying the latter as members of "Institutes of Apostolic Life."

There is, however, a further story associated with the emergence of the Sisters of today. Only recently have many Sisters, for the first time, lived as Louise de Marillac and Vincent de Paul imagined their group would live, namely in ordinary neighborhood dwellings without standard religious garb or with some modified form of religiously identified dress and/or symbol. And the authorities in Rome are still reluctant to condone this lifestyle. The current acceleration to nonuniform dress is associated with the emergence of a new mission for Sisters and that, in turn, with the Second Vatican Council of 1963–1965. This link will unfold in this account of the Sisters.

Related to the recent changes in living style, Sisters are finding that newly developing problems are threatening their ministry. These current problems include some pragmatic and fundamental ones, namely lack of funding, unemployment, aging, and recruitment. These problems threaten the very existence of some apostolic institutes of Sisters. Yet they are related to some of the creative aspects of the Second Vatican Council called by Pope John XXIII in the mid-1960s. It would be unfortunate to miss the complexity of this reality.

The Second Vatican Council was called to update the Roman Catholic Church when it became evident that, like many other religious institutions, it had become too closely linked with established economic and political centers of wealth and power to the neglect of its primary function of bringing good news to the poor.[6] This showed up clearly in the early 1960s. The United States began to feel the influence of the civil rights movement, and the whole world was affected by the coming of age of the colonized third world as various African, Asian, and Latin American groups tried to throw off the shackles of colonization with its accompanying political, social, economic, and cultural oppressions. Sadly, oppression has often contaminated missionary ventures, as seen in the link between religious education and apartheid in South Africa.

Pope John XXIII's call to *aggiornamento* (update), a call to update commitment to mission, was addressed in a direct way to the apostolic institutes. A special decree mandated apostolic institutes to update their way of life, in order to provide effectively for the new direction in mission that the Second Vatican Council was mandating.[7] What was being mandated, in brief, was the visible presence of the Roman Catholic Church standing with the poor as they learn to take what is rightfully theirs. This stand, recognizable now as a significant part of the evangelizing mission, was termed by Vatican II "the special option for the poor."[8]

But was not this concern for the needs of the poor the very reason for the original foundation of apostolic institutes, distinct from the contemplative lifestyle of monks and nuns? Yes, but over the centuries the lifestyle of Sisters had become so enclosed by rules of cloister that the Sisters failed to do the critical social analysis needed to keep the needs of the poor central in their educational, health, and welfare ministries. Because of this and other interacting factors, unwittingly for the most part, their institutions gradually tended to become the preserve of the nonpoor who could afford the fees levied for the services rendered.

Their services often served specific immigrant ethnic groups in whose struggle for upward mobility they played a significant role historically. By 1960, however, many communities of Sisters were connected to the poor by sympathy expressed in acts of charity to alleviate the results of poverty but seldom by effective social action for eliminating its causes. So real was this situation that, when surveyed in 1967, 83 percent of the 172,100 apostolic Sisters in the United States alone were working with the nonpoor, and 65 percent had never worked with the poor or in their interests as a conscious part of their calling.[9] As were many other well-intentioned religious efforts to render service, the unintended consequence of the unexamined religious life was co-optation into the status quo. This in itself is no evil if the society is organized justly. But the cries of the poor coming from missionary centers in the third world suggested that this was not the case.

The Second Vatican Council was called and did its work based on the growing conviction that the majority of the world's peoples were being systematically deprived of their just share of the world's resources which a hundred years of Catholic social teaching claimed was not only their right to share but also their duty to seek.[10] Furthermore, when sought, their share was discovered to be held, in many cases, by wealthy elite membership in churches including their own Roman Catholic Church.[11] This growing awareness of their rights by the poor of the world was shared at the Second Vatican Council. It was linked to the development of the United Nations' human rights covenants as noted in Pope John's encyclical entitled *Pacem in terris* that was published just before the opening of the Second Vatican Council in 1963. *Pacem in terris*,[12] which claims that peace, poverty, and human rights should be the central concerns of all committed Christians, endeared this old peasant pope to many, while it led others to see him as a doddering old man and the dupe of Communists. These conflicting images of Pope John XXIII, as minister of the gospel versus dupe of Communists, are central to an account of what happened to the Sisters during the decade before, during, and after the Second Vatican Council. In 1965 Sisters were mandated to update their rules and customs and to revise their constitutions accordingly. The revised constitutions were subject to papal approval through what is now called the Vatican Commission on Institutes of Consecrated Life (CICL).[13] Beginning with an obedient response to this mandate, changes within the communities of Sisters accelerated.

Accounting for the dynamics that characterize the ministry of Sisters today requires some understanding of what Sisters had been doing during the previous century. Sisters came to the United States in large numbers beginning in the 1830s, the early years of the huge European immigration. The Sisters began working in schools, orphanages, and later in hospitals, where they were a bridge to assimilation for thousands of Irish, Germans, Italians, French, Polish, and other ethnic groups of impoverished European Roman Catholic exiles. Speaking the language of the same country of origin as those to whom they ministered, they became a part of the establishment of ethnic parishes in the United States. All this was good in itself as an adaptation to a new and somewhat hostile environment, but for many of the Sisters it created an enclave or cultural ghetto.[14]

Sisters began moving out of this enclave slowly, some to take university degrees and to staff their newly founded colleges. A more noticeable move out came in the early 1950s with the founding of the first international and national organizations of the leaders of religious institutes, the International Union of Superiors General and the Leadership Conference of Women Religious, and of the Sister Formation Conference.[15] The former two provided opportunity for comparison of experiences among institutes, the latter for the widening of opportunity for college degree completion while a Sister was still young and at low cost by sharing college resources.

There were still other changes at midcentury. Theology, of course, was a central part of the education of Sisters, and in the 1950s the theologians writing theology were the men who would be the experts called to Rome to guide the Second Vatican Council in the mid-1960s. The younger Sisters were the first to receive training in this new theology as part of a newly planned concentrated study time before they went out on mission. The older Sisters had received their training often on mission. Traditionally, Sisters were educated over several years and as apprentices in training in the schools, hospitals, and homes for orphans. Beginning in the 1950s, these younger Sisters studied full-time and often on a college campus where they experienced campus life and issues.

In the late 1960s Sisters on campuses could hear and see and, in some cases, join in with the socially concerned laity. The laity themselves had a strong mandate from Vatican II to transform the structures of society according to principles of social justice and peace.[16]

Older Sisters—those who had entered religious life before 1950, who had lived the semicloistered style of life that had become characteristic of the apostolic communities, saw the accelerated education of the "junior Sisters" as a major change in lifestyle. These junior Sisters often lived in a separate housing unit and did not get to know their older colleagues during their formative years. This tended to weaken ties of community during the coming period of rapid change. When the renewal (referring to the mandate of the Second Vatican Council given to religious institutes of women and men to update their constitutions in order to carry out more effectively the Council's decrees) began in 1965, the trickle of Sisters leaving religious life before making their perpetual vows accelerated from the occasional leave-taking in the late 1950s, to a few hundred in the 1960s, to thousands in the early 1970s.

The reasons for leaving are complex. Many claimed that the Second Vatican Council introduced too many innovations too soon. Research finds several other reasons, some pragmatic and some value-related: the desire to move more quickly to action for social change; the security of having a college degree in hand; disenchantment with the divisions within the religious community between groups with differing opinions on the process of renewal; a feeling that nothing was going to change; a desire for a democratic model on the part of some and, when democracy was implemented, a distaste on the part of others that too much time was spent in deciding unimportant things. The whole list of reasons for leaving is longer, but these main items indicate a period of intense unrest. Those seeking a contemplative space within which to live and work had their lives disrupted. For most it was a time of trial but, at the same time, of hope. Evidence from the next two decades shows the growth of efforts to find satisfying community lifestyles that provided Sisters with energy, renewal of spirit, and opportunities for effective action for social justice.

What alerted the leadership of those semicloistered communities of nun/Sisters to take action so simultaneously to review their life and work? This question calls for a look back to the mid-1960s and the formal beginning of the renewal. First of all, the Second Vatican Council mandated a renewal of every aspect of life in institutes living the vowed life and doing apostolic service. The council recognized the need for updating so that those dedicated to the gospel call to help the materially poor could do this work more effectively. By using new technology, poverty, now, could be eliminated, but the will to get involved in this task was lacking. Furthermore, this council made it clear that although thousands were involved in providing education, health care, and other human services, these efforts were not, as was morally demanded, done on behalf of the poor, whose needs should primarily be served by the church. Why should the Roman Catholic Church devote its resources to serving the poor? Because that is the gospel mandate and the now-current need. *The Decree on the Renewal of Religious Life* expressed in detail the sort of renewal that should be carried out.

By what may have been an accident of history, the president of the organization for the leaders of women's religious communities that is now called the Leadership Conference of Women Religious (LCWR), Mary Luke Tobin, a Sister of Loretto and a member of the board of the LCWR, Mary Daniel Turner, a Sister of Notre Dame of Namur, and several other Sisters met at the Grail, a conference center in Loveland, Ohio, in 1964 to spend a week studying change in the church. I was there also. A draft copy of the *Decree on Renewal* was examined in detail. Together we planned a proposal to survey the readiness of Sisters for their participation in fulfilling the mandate to give first place in ministry to attending to the needs of the poor in a more effective way.[17] The Sisters' Survey of 1967 was the end result of that 1964 meeting. The survey questionnaire included themes from the Second Vatican Council, thus raising them to consciousness and accelerating their implementation in some cases. It was sent to 157,000 Sisters, and 139,691 responded.[18] This survey with its 649 questions was one of the factors accounting for the amazingly vigorous and critical response of the American Sisters to the call of the Second Vatican Council to make an assessment of the life of their communities and ministries. It was not done without internal conflict which resulted in the anguish of some in having to let go cherished practices. Certainly there were some overhasty and unwise initiatives. There was also great anguish at the loss of some treasured members who chose to leave the community.

Since the renewal mandated by the Second Vatican Council was initiated, the number of Sisters has declined precipitously. Of the 181,100 Sisters in the United States in the peak year of 1966, with some 5,000 more entering each year, there remain, in the 1990s, about 99,000. Of these only 1 percent is under thirty years of age compared to 22 percent in 1967; and 28 percent are over eighty compared to 8 percent in 1967, the year the renewal began in earnest.[19]

Although the decline in numbers is at present a critical concern due to the needs of the older Sisters, the decline itself is indicative of a new division of labor within the Roman Catholic Church. The laity has been invited to respond to a call to action, and they are responding in large numbers.[20] Much of the work done by Sisters for the past century is now being enthusiastically shared by the laity. What Sisters are being called to has changed and is expressed in the mission statements in the revised constitutions of most of the over six hundred congregations of Sisters in America. They are being called to participate in the work of societal transformation rather than only addressing the immediate needs of the poor. It is also reflected clearly in three nationwide studies that explore the dimensions of the experience of Sisters in the institutional church and the innovations introduced. These three studies are the 1993 Leadership Conference of Women Religious study of ministries, the *Third Sisters' Survey*, and the Religious Life Futures Project.[21]

Although money and members are pragmatic issues facing Sisters today, their inspiration comes from their commitment to mission within the context of the Bible, the product of their many years dedicated to renewal. There is a question of who is going to do the work and why this is an issue today. The mission to which the Roman Catholic Church calls Sisters today, to be on the cutting edge of societal transformation, is a frightening mission—beautiful and inspirational to articulate in song, dance, and prayer but hard to analyze into the segments of action which it demands,[22] and life-threatening to carry out now in many parts of the world. Think, for example, of Dorothy Kazel, Maura Clark, Ita Ford, and Jeanne Donovan, killed in El Salvador in 1981, as was Archbishop Oscar Romero in 1980. Sisters are ordinary people with an extraordinary mission to take the good news where most fear to tread. Their greatest challenge is associated with the keeping of the vow of obedience when consensus is lacking among the Roman Catholic leadership concerning the centrality of the special option for the poor.

Today books are written naming "the call to action" to transform social and institutional structures that oppress the poor "our best kept secret."[23] Some people wonder why these social teachings failed to find a place in seminary training, theology and social science in higher education, religious education materials, and parish life until the 1990s. Since they were mandated by such an official gathering as a Vatican Council, why, in fact, even today are efforts being made to reverse this emphasis of the Second Vatican Council in favor of a more otherworldly emphasis in church teaching? The answer is that the implementation of this mandate requires that the nonpoor let go both wealth and power. Many church-sponsored institutions providing services for the poor rely on the donations of the nonpoor. For example: for Roman Catholics high costs are associated with the funding of schools, hospitals, and social services in poor inner-city neighborhoods. This demand tends to drain diocesan funds.[24] Some church leaders conclude that these services are becoming too costly. The temptation is to abandon the central city and to concentrate on the needs and interests of suburban parishes where the more successful Catholics move, and/or to fail to emphasize the gospel value of the "special option for the poor" lest the donors become alienated from a church that is always asking for money. When apostolic institutes of Sisters discover that they have been a part of a policy of abandoning the poor, now, enlightened through the renewal, they feel moved to stand with the poor in their manifest need. This is a challenge that must be faced when an institute commits itself to a "special option for the poor."

As seen earlier, the mandate to do the justice agenda comes from the Second Vatican Council. It was incorporated with remarkable clarity and accepted with enthusiasm in the revised constitutions of many religious congregations, particularly of women. The decade of the 1970s deeply involved Sisters in renewal "chapters." These were policy-making meetings recognized officially by the authorities in Rome who had mandated the Sisters to revise their constitutions to update their effectiveness through greater contact with the world. Few of the hierarchy, however, realized the extent to which experimentation would go. Rome tried but failed to stem the tide of change, and, as a result, many experiments were initiated. Perhaps the most striking of these experiments was with Sisters' responsible participation in decision making. It was practiced in assemblies in order to develop a skill the poor would need once they were involved in seeking their human rights and making their just demands. The Sisters' decision to adopt democratic forms of governing themselves came to be called "government for mission." The goal was to address the social justice issues of racism, disarmament, poverty in a rich world, and sexism that were mandated by the Second Vatican Council. Trying to do this agenda encouraged experimentation with a participatory model of institute governance.

The renewal stimulated the establishment of institute archives preserving documents indicating the intent of the founders of religious communities and the reason for the institute's being. This concern for their historical roots, in turn, stimulated Sisters' study to prepare for specific ministries in community organizing or teaching, particularly in inner-city schools, to cite but two of many fields of human service, in order to invent effective means of community action. The reactivation of the original charism[25] of the founders of their institute led many Sisters to question their current commitment to schools, hospitals, and welfare works that did not incorporate in practice the founder's intent. The questioning, as with each dimension of religious life that was reflected on in assembly, loosened long-standing ties to customs and practices that had lost their original reason for being. Because all these changes came about rapidly, there was little time for corporate reflection in order to sort the good proposals for action from the naive.

Although Sisters had opted to work with the poor, they discovered that a good intention was not enough and that special skills were needed. They saw the need of critical social analysis. For them, this meant awareness and analysis of the dynamics of political, economic, and social oppressions of the poor and taking action to change those conditions. This proved to be a different agenda from the earlier one of providing a human service for a class or ethnic enclave. The process of discernment—that is, reflecting together on the causes and consequences of their proposals for renewal—changed Sisters' corporate commitment to specific private and parochial schools, hospitals, or social service agencies. They now asked how each work provided for the needs of the poor. In researching for answers, some Sisters discovered deep layers of poverty they did not know existed in our society.

The intent of renewal became clearer as Sisters were encouraged to study the content of their original charism and to examine critically the effects of their ministry in the local community where they lived and worked, always asking what effect their institute had from the point of view of the poor. Asking this question and looking at the new migrations of peoples to make a multiethnic America suggests a direction Sisters may choose, but that is a story of the future.

Currently, in 1993, Catholic Sisters are still in transition from a semicloistered to an active life. American Sisters are still experimenting with more relevant forms of apostolic spirituality. They are still wondering why their remarkable obedience to incorporating into their mission statements the commitment to the social justice agenda, with its special option for the poor, as mandated by the Second Vatican Council, was perceived by some of the hierarchy as a violation of their vow of obedience. They continue to wait for the approval of their plans for more democratic forms of community government, because such forms bring their lives into conformity with their teaching. They still believe in the vowed life as a form of Christian witness but are reflecting seriously on the question: In whose interests do we serve?

NOTES

1. All references to survey data in this essay are taken from my *Report on the National Profile of the Third Sisters' Survey*. It contains the frequencies and percentages from surveys on Catholic Sisters in the United States for 1967, 1980, and 1989. Currently it circulates only in xeroxed form. It can be found in the archives of the University of Notre Dame, Notre Dame, Indiana.

2. Calculated from *The Official Catholic Directory* (New Providence, N.J.: P. J. Kenedy & Sons, 1993).
3. Eileen Power, *Medieval English Nunneries* (Cambridge: Cambridge University Press, 1922), 344.
4. Letters of Saint Vincent de Paul quoted in the current Constitutions of the Daughters of Charity.
5. See Sister Marie Augusta Neal, SND de Namur, *From Nuns to Sisters: An Expanding Vocation* (Mystic, Conn.: Twenty-Third Publications, 1990).
6. See John XXIII, *Mater et Magistra* (Christianity and Social Progress) (New York: America Press, 1961).
7. Vatican Council II, "Decree on the Renewal of Religious Life" (Boston: St. Paul Editions 1965).
8. See Donal Dorr, *Option for the Poor: A Hundred Years of Vatican Social Teaching* (Maryknoll, N.Y.: Orbis Books, 1983).
9. See the *Third Sisters' Survey*.
10. John XXIII, *Pacem in terris* (Boston: St. Paul Edition, 1963), 44.
11. See Dorr; see also David O'Brien and Thomas A. Shannon, *Renewing the Earth: Catholic Documents on Peace, Justice and Liberation* (Garden City, N.Y.: Doubleday, 1977); and Michael J. Schulties, Edward de Berri, and Peter J. Henriot, *Our Best Kept Secret: The Rich Heritage of Catholic Social Teachings* (Washington, D.C.: Center of Concern, 1987).
12. See John XXIII.
13. This commission reviews the rules of all religious institutes in the Catholic Church.
14. Because rules of cloister still held by custom, though loosened in 1907, many Sisters lived their whole lives outside the mainstream and within the local, often ethnic, parish.
15. Both leadership organizations were initiated from Rome; the Sister Formation Conference was developed by the Conference of Major Superiors of Women Religious (the original name of the Leadership Conference of Women Religious).
16. See "The Decree on Apostolate of Lay People" in Austin Flannery, ed., *Vatican II: The Conciliar and Post Conciliar Documents* (Northport, N.Y.: Costello, 1975), 766–98.
17. Because I was a sociologist, when the proposal for the survey was approved by the Board of LCWR, I was asked to organize the study and was given a wonderful team of fourteen Sisters, five major superiors and nine specialists, to work on the project.
18. There were in the United States in 1968 about 172,000 Sisters not counting the contemplative orders. By using the membership lists of the LCWR, which was at that time named the Conference of Major Superiors of Women Religious (CMSW), we could reach about 157,000 women religious.
19. Data from the *Third Sisters' Survey*.

20. See Paul VI, *Octogesima Adveniens* (*A Call to Action*: Apostolic Letter on the Eightieth Anniversary of *Rerum Novarum*) (Washington, D.C.: United States Catholic Conferences, 1971).

21. These three national surveys have all been completed since 1990. The LCWR study is authored by Anne Munley IHM and is called *Threads for the Loom*. It is the LCWR planning and ministry study, available in spiral notebook form from the Leadership Conference of Women Religious, Silver Spring, Maryland. The Neal study, *A Report on the National Profile of the Third Sisters' Survey*, published in spiral notebook form, is in the archives of the University of Notre Dame, Notre Dame, Indiana. The third study, by Miriam D. Ukeritis C. S. J. and David J. Nygren C. M., entitled *Religious Life Futures Project*, was funded by the Lilly Foundation and is an extensive survey and interview study of both women's and men's institutes. It was published as *The Future of Religious Orders in the United States: Transformation and Commitment* (Westport, Conn.: Greenwood Press, 1993).

22. See Synod of Bishops, *Justice in the World* (Boston: St. Paul Edition, 1971), especially the sixth paragraph.

23. See Schulties et al. See also Dorr.

24. The Roman Catholic Church is divided into dioceses presided over by a bishop. The bishop is responsible for its financial stability. Most of the funding is collected at the local parish level. Parishes are the subdivisions of dioceses, the local churches. Poor parishes have to be subsidized by the diocese. The parish school, the local hospital, and other services for the poor are a financial strain on the diocese in times of recession. If the diocese makes decisions as if it were a business firm, services to the people in poor residential areas are curtailed in hard times.

25. In reference to the founding years of a religious community, the common belief is that the Holy Spirit inspires and blesses the intention of the founder(s) and that this intention becomes embodied in a unique spirit or charism worthy of preservation and a source of inspiration for renewal.

Ministerial Attitudes and Aspirations of Catholic Laywomen in the United States

Virginia Sullivan Finn

INTRODUCTION

Perhaps the best evocation of ministry today, embracing main denominations in the United States, is Nancy Werking Poling's delightfully illustrated children's book *Most Ministers Wear Sneakers*. The sentence surrounding an illustration of male and female clergy with vestments states: "Sometimes ministers wear special clothes to work such as robes or collars or shawls." This is followed by male and female ministers in street clothes: "most of the time they wear ordinary clothes—such as suits or dresses or even jeans. Most ministers even wear sneakers to work at one time or another." The text explains: "Some ministers work in big houses of worship" and then later points out: "Some ministers don't have jobs in churches or temples. Chaplain Hung works in a hospital. . . . Sara Jenkins is a minister who works at a counseling center. . . . Some ministers teach in schools. Others work at prisons."[1]

Such a wonderfully inclusive definition of ministry reflects a contemporary American reality, but it is not the primary perception of ministerial leadership of most Catholics. The sometimes strident declaration of the Roman Catholic tradition is that ordained priesthood is the definitive model of pastoral shepherd and is the paradigm of authority. Consequently, the Catholic laywoman minister is often perceived as peripheral and inconsequential.

Ambiguity is another burden the Catholic laywoman minister bears. Although vowed women religious (Sisters and nuns) are juridically considered "lay," they are the Catholic women traditionally permitted certain ministerial responsibilities. The search for identity and meaning among laywomen who are not in ecclesial vowed life and who are called to ministry has not been an easy journey. But what will you *do*? is a question that often plagues the laywoman who experiences a call to ministry. She herself may be asking a number of questions: What are Roman Catholic laywomen who answer a call to ministerial leadership accomplishing? How do we prepare for ministerial leadership? Where are we ministering? How are we evaluated? What responsibilities and what authority can we expect to have?

The purpose of this chapter is to disclose not only where laywomen are ministering and what they are accomplishing but also the significance of preparation and of ministerial setting to a sense of accomplishment and confident leadership. It is based on research data available and on my own experience in the field for over twenty years.

The term *laywoman minister* represents no one typology; it encompasses feminists and traditionalists, leaders and followers, single and married women, all serving within an institution in which ministry and male celibacy have long been fused in an exclusive way. In spite of the past, the answer to the question Where are laywomen ministering? is the same as the answer to the old Baltimore Catechism question Where is God? Everywhere.

The *breadth* of settings and involvements of Catholic laywomen in ministry is astonishing. The number of women entering vowed religious life and of men entering seminaries to prepare for ordained priesthood has been more than halved in recent decades. This diminishment and the disinclination of most laymen toward ministry means that the laywoman minister may be the paradigmatic Catholic ministerial figure of the future.

Even today, as mentioned above, she is everywhere—in parishes and schools, prisons and hospitals, diocesan offices and missions, theology departments of higher education and campus ministry offices, social justice and spiritual life centers. The simple fact is that most ministry in the Catholic Church in the United States is the fruit of women's labors. For married and single laywomen this phenomenon was initiated in the late 1940s and the 1950s through involvement in parish religious education for children.[2] In the 1960s Vatican Council II opened new horizons for lay participation and leadership within the church. Sisters, by assuming diversified leadership roles within and beyond their religious congregations and colleges, modeled and mentored attitudes and a process of aspiration among grassroots women.

INVOLVEMENT OF LAYWOMEN IN PARISH
VOLUNTARY MINISTRY

Evidence that laywomen in ministry is a nationwide reality is found in the major research project *The Notre Dame Study of Catholic Parish Life*, which states, "Probably few of us are fully aware of the extent to which we depend on women to conduct the ministry, programs, and activities of Catholic parishes in the United States."[3]

Thousands of women parishioners, according to the study, have assumed parish responsibilities, as the following percentages of ministerial activities done by women reveal: altar preparation 85 percent, teaching 80 percent, social caring and justice ministries 85 percent, parish council leadership 52 percent. Over 50 percent of ministries related to worship (Eucharistic liturgy) are carried out by women; 80 percent of the Catholics surveyed welcome this involvement by women in altar ministries.

Initiated as a quiet phenomenon, the broad diffusion of laywomen into voluntary parish ministries became the impetus for a remarkable ministerial revolution. Laywomen who subsequently assumed professional leadership often started by participating in voluntary parish ministry. This broadening wedge into the ministerial enterprise may lead to an eventual lay leadership diffusion within all levels of the institutional church. But there are complications.

POPULAR AND PROFESSIONAL ROUTES TOWARD
MINISTERIAL LEADERSHIP

Before Vatican Council II, Roman Catholicism was sometimes referred to as "the sleeping giant." Today in the United States there are approximately fifty-three million Roman Catholics, representing a rich multicultural diversity as well as varied socioeconomic and educational backgrounds. The enormity in size offers striking contrasts and multiple models of organization—from cloistered communities who live in silence, to Catholic Worker Houses, to national organizations like Catholic Charities and the National Association of Church Personnel Administrators, to diocesan offices, to parishes, to major universities.

Even among the ordained, differences are noted. For example, seminarians preparing for the cultic priesthood enter through the auspices of dioceses and through membership in vowed religious orders such as Franciscans and Jesuits. Research studies conducted by Katarina Schuth, OSF, and studies by Dean Hoge and Eugene Hemrick reveal that religious order seminarians tend to be oriented toward community and to reveal a desire to collaborate with lay-people. On the other hand, diocesan seminarians seem to be more institutional in approach, perceiving themselves "as set apart, distinct, and separate from the laity." Commenting on this Rev. John Gerber, C.S.C., wonders if there is developing "an ecclesial reality resembling two churches within the one Catholic Church."[4]

Whether laywomen who minister with religious order priests or with diocesan priests experience different ecclesial realities would be an interesting query. Another question, however, will be posed here. Do Catholic laywomen leaders who are compensated for ecclesial ministry experience themselves as similarly competent and confident? Two types of ecclesial ministerial leadership by laywomen are currently apparent: laywomen ministerial leaders indigenous to parish; and lay alumnae of graduate programs in ministry who assume more varied leadership positions.

According to a new study, the former initiate their roles in ministry along a "popular route," e.g., parish leadership without prior graduate theological studies; the latter initiate their leadership roles along a "professional route," e.g., after graduate-level studies.[5] The popular/professional dialectic sets the framework for the investigation that follows. Both popular and professional ministerial trajectories will be examined from three perspectives: motivation and initiation into ministry; formation and education for ministerial leadership; and responses of the laywomen ministers to their ecclesial leadership roles, responsibilities, and authority.

Types of ministerial responsibilities vary in Roman Catholic settings. In addition, official, juridical policies are often interpreted in varying ways within the dioceses of the United States.[6] For example, I was present at the National Conference of Catholic Bishops (NCCB) gathering in Washington in November 1988 when the bishops, by a narrow margin, voted to forbid women and laymen from preaching at the Eucharistic worship service. A few months later I preached a week-long parish mission, with the permission of the bishop of the diocese, that included preaching at the worship services on Palm Sunday, Holy Thursday, Good Friday, and Easter Vigil. Bishops vary in their attitudes toward the ecclesial empowerment of women. A few have publically endorsed the ordination of women; the majority have not. Women do serve, however, in major institutional offices, but this development is sporadic rather than uniform and consistent.

LAYWOMEN LEADERS IN PARISH MINISTRY

The new study mentioned above, designed and implemented by the National Pastoral Life Center (NPLC), located in Manhattan and directed by Rev. Phillip Murnion, a diocesan priest, offers significant insight into the situation of laywomen who are compensated for parish ministry. Two factors make this study of particular importance: the research was commissioned by the institutional church through the Committee on Pastoral Practices of the NCCB; and breadth was a deliberate component of the project's design.[7] Survey questionnaires were sent to 40 percent of the nation's Catholic parishes, and in-depth study through site visitation was carried out in two parishes within two dioceses of each of the thirteen NCCB regions (fifty-two parishes). The project's valuable statistical data corroborates *The Notre Dame Study of Catholic Parish Life* regarding the extent of women in ministry. For example, in addition to the diffusion of voluntary ministry by women cited above, there are approximately twenty thousand nonordained parish leaders compensated for at least twenty hours of ministry weekly within half of the nineteen thousand Catholic parishes in the country. Of these twenty thousand ministers, 85 percent are female and 15 percent male; 60 percent are lay, with there being 45 percent laywomen and 40 percent women religious. Although 40 percent of the women religious in parish service are over the age of sixty, only 8 percent of the lay ministers are over age sixty. The divergence in age reinforces the prediction that future ministerial leadership will be the province of laywomen.

INITIATION INTO PARISH MINISTRY

The NPLC study found among parish lay ministers considerable relationship between participation in ministry and prior participation in lay spiritual movements such as Cursillo, Charismatic Renewal, Marriage Encounter. Motivations cited by lay ministers parallel involvements in religious education before Vatican Council II: call to church service, the desire to be active in church life, relationship with the pastor. For 90 percent of the compensated lay ministers, prior voluntary parish ministry provided the primary initiation process.

The most striking initiation finding was that 82 percent of the pastors who hired ministers recruited them "from people they already knew." In particular, laywomen were "invited by a pastor to take a position." In this popular approach to hiring, more than half of the pastors gave preference to laywomen for the following reasons: their lay experience was felt helpful, and they brought fewer needs to the ministry.

EDUCATION/FORMATION FOR PARISH MINISTRY

According to Catherine Mowry La Cugna, between 1976 and 1986 the total enrollment of Roman Catholic women in advanced educational programs leading to ordination (such as the M.Div. degree) rose by 110 percent.[8] These are not the new parish lay ministers of whom only 1.4 percent had an M.Div. degree. Although 75 percent of the women religious in the NPLC study had master's degrees, only 30 percent of the lay ministers held this degree. One-third of the lay ministers included in the NPLC study lacked any college degree. How were these lay ministers prepared to minister? Reliance on nondegree training sponsored by dioceses, universities, or professional organizations was extensive: 87.3 percent participation with 60 percent in certification programs.

Was this sufficient education and formation for ministerial leadership? Perhaps it was not, for the responsibilities assumed typically included teaching, supervising volunteers, leading prayer, organizing projects, administration, and counseling. In its report the NPLC warned that, with the decline in the number of Sisters, a supply of laypeople with good theological and ecclesial preparation for ministry would be needed but could not be taken for granted.

RESPONSE OF THE LAYWOMEN PARISH MINISTERS

Even more disquieting is how the laywomen parish ministers evaluated themselves as ministerial leaders. Entrance through the popular route, according to evidence in the study, engendered feelings of inadequacy. Although over 60 percent of the ministers felt adequately prepared in scripture and in doctrine, only half felt adequately prepared in moral theology, family life, and youth development. Preparation for dealing with justice concerns and social service also lagged. "A significant portion of the parish ministers feel ill prepared to supervise and train others. . . . Yet, the majority are called upon to do some training and supervision." Only 37 percent felt competent in managing conflict, 30 percent felt competent in counseling, and 13 percent felt competent in preaching.

Telling gaps exist between the limited ministerial preparation available to many parish laywomen compensated for ministry and the challenge of the ministerial responsibilities delegated to them. In addition, the NPLC study revealed that over a quarter of the lay ministers did not feel close to either the parish or the broader church. Although the majority felt that ministry enabled them to feel closer to God and "to develop and use my talents in service of the church," the lay-women were fourteen points below the Sisters in encouraging others to enter ministry.

How do feelings of inadequacy influence aspirations for leadership roles? In the project's preparatory process it was felt significant to ascertain opinions about visible public roles for the new parish ministers. Consequently, the new ministers, the ordained pastors, and the parishioners were queried about nonordained ministers assuming more visible leadership roles in the parish. After the data was gathered, the report stated: "Oddly enough, the parishioners and the pastors tend to think this (expansion of visible role) is a good idea, but the majority of parish ministers are not quick to agree." Some remarkable gaps appeared between the expectations of both parishioners and pastors and the aspirations of new parish ministers. When they were asked "Which of the following do you think the Lay/Religious Ministers ought to be able to do or share in the doing?" the parishioners, the ordained pastors, and the new nonordained parish ministers responded as follows:

	Parishioners	Pastors	Parish Ministers
Marriage Prep	86%	77.5%	19%
Lead wake service	61%	70%	24%
Lead role/Eucharist	73%	70%	39.5%
Parish Council participation	97%	84%	60.7%
Preach	55%	46.5%	26.5%

The data above indicates timidity on the part of the new ministers in fully embracing ministerial responsibilities; what accounts for this? The extent of inadequacy expressed by respondents in the study coupled with a reticence to assume visible leadership roles pose questions needing further research. Were more docile women candidates favored in hiring? Was ministry sought to bolster the women's self-esteem? Had the lack of theological education and ministerial formation led instead to less esteem, to the women turning in on themselves in a negative way that evoked feelings of inadequacy? Had earlier formation in belief and faith led to a self-identity that favored *service* but at the cost of confidence in capacity for *leadership*?

Although the popular approach gave many grassroots laywomen an opportunity for ministerial leadership in a familiar setting, it may have also undercut, through lack of thorough preparation and mentoring, the potential the laywomen brought to the ministry. The NPLC study concluded, "All in all, the education and formation for lay ministers may be too important to be left as unorganized as at present." Because parishes are "largely on their own regarding personnel issues (and) unaccountable to the diocese," there exists "a relatively 'free market' approach—freelance ministers accepting positions from autonomous pastors." Although this may be symptomatic of a broader pattern of contemporary Roman Catholic church life in the United States, the NPLC report strongly suggested a need for greater investment from diocesan leaders in the theological education, ministerial preparation, and personnel organization of new parish ministers.

The question remains: Are laywomen ministers victimized by what appears to be enabling? According to John Boucher, in commenting on a National Association for Lay Ministry (NALM) study of longevity patterns in lay ministry, *self-esteem* is a major factor in whether lay ministers persevere in their ministerial roles. Boucher cited "four major norms on which we base self-esteem: significance, competence, virtue and power." Lack of a sense of significance, competence, and power characterizes many laywomen serving in parish ministry.[9]

THE ROMAN CATHOLIC INSTITUTION AND LAYWOMEN MINISTERS

Do the institutions within Roman Catholicism encourage laywomen to become ministerial leaders? The "new parish ministers" who are laywomen were invited by ordained pastors in half the nation's Catholic parishes to assume leadership. The American bishops unanimously welcomed professional lay ministry in their 1980 statement "Called and Gifted." The National Conference of Catholic Bishops (NCCB) in 1992 refused to adopt a conservative pastoral letter on women. All this sounds an encouraging note. But the role of laywomen in ecclesial ministry still seems obscured by gender and by definitions of lay identity. As Georgia Masters Keightley notes, "Historically . . . the laity were thought of as being 'in' the world and only marginally 'in' the church. In practice, the laity have long been treated as though they were ecclesial outsiders, and, as the experience of women in the United States confirms, this is, in many respects, still true today."[10] As recently as spring 1992, a high clerical official within Roman Catholicism in the United States asserted that the ordained priest promises

lifelong service to the church, and, in return, the church promises to
take care of him. The cleric then asserted that lay ministers are no more
than lay employees.

This juridical perspective is not only insulting to innumerable lay
ministers who contribute their talents to the upbuilding of local and
diocesan communities, but it fosters a concept of dependency and pas-
sivity, of "being taken care of," that is the risk when open hiring is rejected in favor of personal appointment and invitation. Passivity/
dependency and self-esteem seldom walk in hand-in-hand. This may
be the Achilles heel of the popular route to ministerial leadership.

Other recent evidence of attitudes within official Roman Catholicism is no more encouraging. For example, among the thirty interven-
tions concerning laywomen at the 1987 Synod on the Laity in Rome,
only one was from an episcopal leader from the United States. Archbishop Rembert Weakland urged a greater role for laywomen in
governance by opening various decision-making roles to them. "Christifideles Laici," the papal exhortation that was "meant to be a faithful
and coherent expression" of the Vatican Synod on the Laity, states:
"The Lord Jesus chose and constituted the apostles . . . to form and
rule the priestly people." It continues: "(ordained ministries) express
and realize a participation in the priesthood of Jesus Christ that is different, not simply in degree but in essence, from the participation given
to all the lay faithful through baptism. . . . The lay faithful, in turn,
must acknowledge that the ministerial priesthood is totally necessary
for their participation in the mission of the church."[11]

LAYWOMEN WHO PREPARE FOR MINISTRY IN
GRADUATE DEGREE PROGRAMS

The institutional setting where affirmation of women's aspirations
for ministry have been affirmed is within Catholic higher education.
Does a portrait colored by self-esteem, confidence, and zest for leadership emerge when contemplating laywomen ministers with professional credentials for ministry? Initiation into ministry, education/
formation for ministry, and responses of the laywomen ministers to
their ecclesial leadership will also serve as the lens for viewing laywomen ministers who entered ministerial leadership through professional graduate studies.

Garnering information beyond the anecdotal about Catholic
women who are professionally trained for ministerial leadership has
not been easy. In 1983 Rosemary Radford Ruether attempted to gather
such information and later deplored the lack of follow-up of women

ministerial graduates from both Protestant divinity schools and Catholic seminaries and theologates.[12] Even more scant is data on *laywomen* Catholic ministers, as distinctions are seldom made between females and males in commentaries on lay ministry, yet laywomen overwhelmingly outnumber laymen ministers.

INITIATION: MOTIVATION FOR GRADUATE MINISTERIAL STUDY

Dr. Joseph P. O'Neill, director of a current study of fifty-five hundred seminary students, cites frequency data for entering women students at three Roman Catholic theological schools in California. Within this group 46.9 percent are laywomen. Primarily full-time students, 77.6 percent of the women surveyed had been active in a parish. Among the categories offered, the women chose the following as "important" and "very important" motivators: desire to serve others, 79.6 percent; experienced a call from God, 65.3 percent; intellectual interest, 52.7 percent; promise of spiritual fulfillment, 57.2 percent; opportunity for study and growth, 69.4 percent. In contrast to the women in the NPLC study, clergy encouragement (32.7 percent) was not a strong motivator for these women.[13]

EDUCATION/FORMATION WITHIN PROFESSIONAL STUDIES

What happens as a result of preparation for ministry through professional degree programs? Ruether, in criticizing the lack of follow-up of women ministerial graduates, cited one major exception—the Weston School of Theology in Cambridge, Massachusetts. Among degrees granted to women between 1977 and 1992 at Weston, twenty-eight laywomen earned the master of theological studies (M.T.S.) degree and sixty-six laywomen received the master of divinity (M.Div.), the degree most commonly sought by candidates for the ordained priesthood. Within their preparatory process at Weston, M.Div. laywomen candidates participate with candidates for the ordained priesthood in supervised field education placements, theology coursework, comprehensive examinations, community leadership, prayer, and worship. They also elect various opportunities for spiritual formation.

Women who aim for lay ministerial leadership though graduate programs desire to continue to grow spiritually, as more than half of the entering California students stated. Not able to rely on the institutional affirmation, support, and security accorded to ordained status, many laywomen ministers seem to need and tend to seek depth in relationship with God. Some find it in feminist spirituality, others in more traditional forms of Christian spirituality. Institutional structures to support spirituality are warmly welcomed by these women.

From the beginning of their studies, laywomen students at Weston meet individually or in groups (often with Sisters, priests, priest candidates) in a process facilitated by seasoned spiritual guides. For individual spiritual direction, laywomen may choose to have a male or female, lay or vowed religious guide. Most concur with the laywoman who said, "Spiritual direction is essential to my ministerial identity and theological development." In addition, the institution sponsors activities such as days of reflection and the Weston Guided Prayer Experience, in which degree students, male and female, lay and vowed religious, meet to discern in small groups how God is present in their journey and in their personal prayer. To encourage a further and deeper unity with God, Weston offers a partial subsidy to any lay student who desires to make a week-long retreat. Each year many laywomen accept this support, joining women graduates as well as other students on retreat. Arrangements are also made for women graduates to return to reflect with women lay students on the ministerial journey that each is traveling.

During theological studies, without support for spiritual formation provided by the institution of higher education, a sense of God's call and God's sustaining love may be replaced by self-doubt and skepticism, defeating the purpose for engagement in ministerial studies. Institutions have a responsibility to offer resources that enhance self-esteem and faith. Among laywomen ministers the desire for structures for spiritual supports does not end with the preparatory process for ministry. In 1990 the National Association for Lay Ministry issued a report on the spiritual needs of currently active professional lay ministers, the majority women. The report was based on a query sent to over four hundred lay ministers through a project supported by the Raskob Foundation for Catholic Activities. The project, *On-going Formation Resource Use by Lay Ministers*, breaking new ground as its design, part of a twenty-thousand-dollar grant, was developed entirely by Catholic laywomen ministers; it revealed that laywomen ministers utilize many paths in the sustenance of their relationship with God, including some considered nontraditional such as meditation with music, keeping a journal, or participating in small support groups with other women, sometimes ecumenically with other ministers. Although most respondents cited institutional support for ongoing ministerial education, they found that activities to promote spiritual formation were often neglected in their settings. In particular, there was too little time and too little support for retreats and for spiritual direction. Al-

though 84 percent of the respondents felt that having a spiritual director was important, only 49 percent were currently able to receive this
support.[14]

WESTON LAYWOMEN GRADUATES AND
THEIR CAREER TRAJECTORIES

Formation experience prior to graduation, both ministerial and
spiritual, enables the integration of personal identity, ministerial identity, and spiritual identity. Intentional reflection on the variety of ministerial careers open to laywomen and laymen is encouraged at Weston
as a means to enable freedom in response to the call from God to ministry and as a way to discern one's gifts and talents. This kind of activity is a strength of the extended process that professional graduate
degree study affords. To help insure prudent postgraduate choices, lay
students meet regularly during studies in the school-sponsored placement process.

A review of seventy Weston laywomen graduates reveals the following ministerial placements: higher education—teaching or doctoral
studies, 17 percent; teaching religion in secondary school, 7 percent;
campus ministry, 14 percent; hospital chaplaincy, hospice, bereave-
ment ministry, 15 percent; ministry of spirituality, 5 percent; social
justice/secular helping profession, 15 percent; parish ministry, 13 percent; institutional leadership, 11 percent.

Do the laywomen who have been professionally prepared for these
ministries at Weston feel adequate in assuming responsibilities and engaging in leadership? Do these laywomen graduates believe that God,
through the Holy Spirit, is bearing fruit through their ministries? Responding to a query, many described their competencies and this fruit:
"I provide some responses to people's very deep theological questions, which are extremely relevant to their relationship with God; or I
enable them to think about the questions in new ways. God is most
definitely at work in this." "In the past, I was able to be a caring witness to grieving men, women and children who were coming to terms
with their losses. I was also a presence of hope with victims of domestic violence who were picking up the pieces of their broken lives."

A number of women cited gifts brought to ministry that included
compassion, the ability to gather the community and bring people together, skill in reconciliation (including among staff members), and a
sensitivity in helping persons focus on their worth and dignity. "I've

been there to be supportive and as a sign that God is with them, often in times of crisis."

One minister perceived herself as a model for commitment to ministry: "I bring a great dedication to ministry in a peaceful way, and I challenge fellow ministers to do the same." Another saw her visible leadership as having potential for reform of structures: "My ability and skills in management and administration have resulted in a recognition among individuals in the clergy that laywomen are competent and can be trusted. My hope is that this will work towards reforming strucures that need reform." Another laywoman in ministerial leadership for five years as associate director of a diocesan peace and justice office (until she left the position to start a family) put it this way: "The image of seeds that have taken root is apt for the fruit of my ministry. In my diocesan leadership position I feel I planted many seeds and persistently cared for and guarded some small sprouts . . . of these I was fortunate enough to see some fruit. One kind that comes to mind is attention to process and participation."

It is not unusual for a laywoman graduate to preach and/or preside at Catholic communion services: "The Spirit has gifted me with ability to preach, though I do less of it now. In this dry spell, the Spirit has gifted me with a presence of compassion that is recognized by students through their increased trust of my ministry."

The context of professional preparation at theology schools like Weston must not be underestimated when considering components that lead to fruitful ministry. For example, the Weston experience enables lay students to rub shoulders day after day with over forty Sisters and ordained priests in a continuing education program, with candidates for the priesthood, and with Sisters in degree programs. In other words, the context of studies mirrors in some ways the context of colleagueship they will encounter in their future ministerial positions. The laywomen leave studies holding an advantage over those without graduate-school preparation as well as over those with preparation from a divinity school that is nondenominational. Not only have the laywomen created a network of invaluable Catholic ministerial friends and leaders, they have also developed savvy in distinguishing between and dealing with ordained clergy who desire to enable others to minister and those who are addicted to clericalism.

The strength of this kind of graduate preparation for ministry is the opportunity to develop a creative path within ministerial leadership. Is there evidence that Weston's laywomen graduates have taken advantage of this opportunity?

EVALUATION OF MINISTERIAL LEADERSHIP

To provide support for graduates, as well as to discern whether lay graduates are becoming leaders with effective voice and influence, four means are utilized at Weston. The first is to stay in close contact with graduates and to keep track of shifts in ministerial positions. For example, of Weston laywomen graduates who are at least four years postgraduation, 36 percent have remained in the same settings, 55.6 percent have made several ministerial shifts, but only 9 percent have made lateral moves (same ministry, different setting).

A second means of support and data gathering is to trace shifts that have led to either greater responsibility and authority or a deepened sense of mission. Among the Weston laywomen ministerial graduates, 42 percent have moved from entry-level placements to positions with greater leadership potential—some from doctoral student to college teacher and theologian, others from a staff position, such as chaplain, to administrator (such as director of pastoral care).

A third criteria related to leadership and influence is publishing. Since 1980, of the thirteen books and contributed chapters authored by Weston women graduates, twelve are by laywomen graduates who have also published thirty magazine or journal articles. Other professional activities range from serving on national boards of Catholic organizations to presenting papers and workshops at national Catholic conferences.

Finally, Weston maintains a sensitivity to feelings of inadequacy or of low self-esteem on the part of laywomen graduates. For example, in the mid-1970s many of the women preparing for ministry at Weston felt inadequate about moving into ecclesial settings without the authority and credential value of ordination. More recently, when queried about the challenges they face, fear was replaced by a healthy anger at injustices perceived at institutional levels of Roman Catholicism. Responses to a query about "the greatest challenge or frustration in ministry" included: "the continued failure of the hierarchical church to recognize and value the tremendous growth in lay vocations to ministry, especially of laywomen"; "the lack of recognition in this diocese of my ministry"; "bad management"; "institutional priorities, especially in regard to how money is spent"; and "dealing with incompetencies and dysfunctions in the institutional church."

CREATIVE MINISTERIAL PATHS

A look at the creative ministerial journeys of two Weston graduates reveals something about the aspirations engendered by professional preparation for lay ministerial leadership: One Weston laywoman

graduate, whom I will call "Molly," initiated her postgraduate ministerial leadership on a Methodist college campus, where she was the
first campus minister for Catholic students. In a house donated by
Catholics from a parish in the nearby city, Molly created a center for the
students as well as its worship space. After two years, seeking "more
depth," Molly participated in a year-long advanced Clinical Pastoral
Education program. Feeling drawn to hospice ministry, Molly felt she
was not yet ready to assume that work full-time. She became, instead,
archdiocesan director of young adult ministry in a southern diocese
and engaged in voluntary hospice ministry. Molly also enrolled in
part-time studies leading to an M.S.W. degree in order to be more flexible in choices for the future. A few years later, still seeking "the
More," Molly was appointed archdiocesan director of hospital ministry with responsibility for thirty hospital chaplains. She has also initiated a research project to study the impact of clergy sexual abuse and
exploitation on spirituality. The preliminary findings were published
in the premier issue of *The Journal of Sexual Addiction*. Molly is also one
of six women serving on a national board with a focus on clergy sexual
abuse.

Campus ministry in the Midwest was Anne's first placement after
graduation. With a Sister on staff, Anne designed programs to attract
Catholic commuter students at a state community college. After two
years Anne became the diocesan director responsible for mentoring
vocations of the laity in the church and in societal settings. During this
time she taught occasionally in a Catholic college, wrote a few articles,
married, and had a baby. Now the mother of two, Anne is archdiocesan
director of campus ministry in a major midwestern city but is moving
on to doctoral studies, having received a full fellowship at the University of Chicago.

Few Weston laywomen graduates have been terminated from their
ministry positions. After a lengthy grievance process, one did resign,
but she was rehired and returned shortly to direct the office when the
priest director, who had been instrumental in her difficulties, left. In a
setting a thousand miles away, a graduate resigned, along with four
other staff members, when a dynamic and enabling pastor was replaced by a domineering, clerical-type pastor.

The few firings that have occurred reveal the brutality that sometimes exists within institutions. For example, a pastoral associate in a
parish was terminated when a married deacon threatened to leave if
she did not. Currently she is working as a pastoral associate in another
parish within the same city. A campus minister, after two years of service, received word that she "would be happier elsewhere." To add

insult to injury, the letter from the priest terminating her appointment arrived on Holy Thursday, the feast day often used to celebrate the institution of priesthood. Told by the priest director a week prior to his firing her "What I like least about you is that you are a woman," the campus minister received considerable support from the administration of the secular college and from Weston, but little help from diocesan institutions. After a bleak period of despair, the graduate regained her self-esteem and went on to a successful ministerial career. The cleric also went on—to fire, consecutively, three more women in different ministerial settings.

Self-esteem appears to be a pivotal quality for women lay ministers. Professional ministerial education and formation seem to be key factors in developing feelings of esteem that enable ministers to envision aspirations and to pursue them. If suitable education and formation are missing, the needed confidence and self-esteem to interiorize aspirations may never develop. When resources that provided necessary preparation and ongoing education are terminated, the Roman Catholic people as well as Catholic women lay ministers seem to suffer. One example was the closing of the Institute for Pastoral Life in Kansas City, Missouri, a place originally supported by a number of bishops for the training of lay ministers from rural dioceses (where the means to educate professionally for ministry are unavailable).[15]

ASPIRATIONS, COMMUNITY, AND COLLABORATION

A number of Catholic laywomen leave ecclesial ministry in anguish and rage. Some channel their energy and hope into Women Church, a movement to provide an alternate, feminist model of church, one committed to bonding with minority and poor women. According to Rosemary Radford Ruether, "Women Church understands leadership as a ministry of function rather than of clerical caste. Such an understanding of ministry can allow the true variety of the needs of particular communities to be defined and addressed." Ruether further explains that the practice of "lumping all ministry into one ordained caste has meant that many of the community's needs go unmet, because no one person possesses all these skills and capacities."[16]

Some Roman Catholic laywomen have sought ordination in other Christian churches. Others are active in the Women's Ordination Conference, a group of activists for the expansion of ordination and for the reform of the priesthood. Other women channel their energies into church-sponsored women's organizations that come together through the National Council of Catholic Women, an umbrella organization that has provided leadership training to nearly two thousand Catholic women.[17]

In creative and communal ways innumerable Roman Catholic women echo Karen Doherty in Jane Redmont's interview book, *Generous Lives*: "I care enough to want to shape the church that shaped me."[18] Because they are women, the way they gather together and organize for governance is often hospitable to linking the empowerment of women ministers with the empowerment of those to whom they minister. The desire for a more collaborative model of local church governance is one that sociologist Ruth Wallace discovered in her study of Catholic women pastors (currently called pastoral administrators) in parishes without resident ordained priests. Wallace included nine parishes headed by laywomen ministers and eleven headed by women religious in her study. Among these women pastors Wallace found that collaboration with the people of the parish was a central aspiration. "Women pastors tend to be very sensitive about the problem of usurping the parishioners' authority, even in seemingly small ways."[19] The emerging ministerial model, disclosed in Wallace's study, is one that empowers both the people and the ministerial leaders. Out of conviction, not cowardice, many women ministers reject governance by authoritarianism within their pastoral roles in favor of governance through collaboration with the people.

Aspirations of laywomen working in the Roman Catholic Church vary enormously—from having a bureaucratic job to being a minister of God with full sacramental leadership. In reality, laywomen are housekeepers, secretaries, voluntary ministers, professional pastoral leaders, theologians, and pastoral administrators (pastors of priestless parishes). According to Gilbert Brim, director of a MacArthur Foundation research network, "The line between ideal aspirations, on the one side, and grand illusions, on the other side, may be thin, but it is there."[20] In democratic societies many believe it is a grand illusion to think that one can be a true leader without identifying with the people, but the plague of continuing clericalism proves that attempts to do just that still exist in Roman Catholicism. Yet, in spite of tepid encouragement and even veiled discouragement from those at hierarchical levels of the institution, women ministers persist in aspiring to leadership in order to enflesh a vision of a collaborative church within American Catholicism.

Brim claims, "Some aspirations are of little importance to us, and we can reduce them with ease. Others mean more to us, and we may never get over our failure to fulfill them."[21] Denial of ordination may block an aspiration from which some Catholic women never recover.

What is striking, however, in the career paths of many laywomen ministers, is the number who initially experienced a strong call and desire for ordained priesthood yet who have moved forward, steadily and sensitively ministering and exercising leadership without attaining that ideal. Some have been fired from positions in ways that can only be called devastatingly cruel, yet they go on ministering in other settings, some Catholic, some societal.

Rather than despair, many Catholic women will continue to renew the struggle. What is known today—that was not known two decades ago, before the presence of Catholic laywomen in ministry became widespread—is that women who have the opportunity for professional, graduate-level preparation for ministry offer a model for ministry that works, one that has the potential to be a transformative witness for both governance and creative ministerial leadership. To insure continuing vitality within American Catholicism, it is crucial that the hierarchy act on what is being learned by eradicating existing injustices through empowering new forms of governance and by pressing for a broadened entrance to ordination.

The splendid courage of so many lay Catholic women ministers indicates that they are responding to and sustained by a call from God, a call that supersedes the prejudice and injustice found in some leaders who officially hold institutional authority. Challenge and accomplishment converge in a way that enables perseverance in being prophetic despite the seemingly impenetrable institutional prohibition against a right to a substantial role in governance and a place in the cultic priesthood, the latter officially denied women because they do not physically resemble Jesus Christ.[22]

The results of this perseverance, undreamed of twenty-five years ago, Catherine Mowry La Cugna points out, are ironic. "The first irony of not ordaining Catholic women is the high number who have become educated and employed as professional theologians, who now hold tenured positions in colleges, universities and seminaries . . . , who now educate the future adult laity and future priests and bishops. The second irony arises out of the fact that most feminist theologians are Roman Catholic." La Cugna cites the laicizing of the theological enterprise as the third irony.[23]

On the Feast of Pentecost, 22 May 1994, although offering no new or original evidence, Pope John Paul II reaffirmed *"Inter Insigniores,"* the ban on the ordination of Catholic women. The focus of reactions to his apostolic letter has been on one section of the letter: "Wherefore, in order that all doubt may be removed regarding a matter of great importance, a matter which pertains to the church's divine constitution

itself . . . I declare that the church has no authority whatsoever to confer priestly ordination on women and that this judgement is to be definitively held by all the church's faithful." Response has ranged from
the bishop of San Diego writing to staff that "Anyone who even thinks
of dissenting should resign with integrity," to the bishop of Juneau,
Alaska, suggesting that "If, in fact, women can never be ordained and
the subject itself is no longer open to review, should the church continue limiting all final and ultimate authority to the ordained and
therefore to males only?"

What is significant is that educated commentary is challenging the
binding power of papal authority that has neither the prior, worldwide
consensus of the bishops nor of the *sensus fidei*, the universal consent of
the whole people of the church. Nonetheless, the potential muting
even further of the prophetic voice of courageous theologians, bishops,
priests, and women ministers, if it occurs, will further keep hidden the
reality of women's ministerial leadership that already exists.

REMOVE THE VEIL

Greater attention to what is actually taking place in the careers of
laywomen ministers is desperately needed as women's ministerial
leadership shifts from vowed religious to lay. Most lay ministers are
women. Some are convinced that disparaging lay ministry is no more
than a veiled way to continue to discriminate against women.[24] Laywomen ministers are so often rendered nearly invisible by their service
role that little attention, even by feminist and by more mainline Catholic women's organizations, is given to their situation and its risks—an
enormous ecclesial error when one considers that the future vitality of
faith within North American Catholicism depends on laywomen who
currently hold leadership positions in ministry.

How laywomen ministers deal with their aspirations, how they
utilize the freedom and the strictures that are their lot, how they grow
spiritually and change psychologically, how they manage responsibilities and authority—all this is a rich field for exploration. Close, ongoing analysis of these elements, particularly in ministries other than
parish, may reveal a new and creative model—one that genuinely un-
folds, one that is interiorly motivated, one that will eventually benefit
the formation of all ministers, including the ordained who even now
experience elements of transformation as they collaborate with
women. Evidence of this was expressed at the Thirty-fourth General
Congregation of the Society of Jesus in Rome in 1995 in the statement
"Jesuits and the Situation of Women in Church and Civil Society." This

document calls for individual Jesuits and their institutions "to align themselves in solidarity with women," for example, through "genuine involvement of women in consultation and decision-making in our Jesuit ministries."[25]

The Roman Catholic Church in the United States must remove the veil that hides so many of its female members in obscurity. Catholic media as well as national women's associations, feminist movements, and diocesan offices are key in bringing to the forefront laywomen who *already* hold leadership positions. Too many Catholic believers do not know the extent and creativity of this leadership. Too many, in all forms of institutional leadership, including the media, seem to feel that saying "Oh, yes, we're for women's ordination" settles the issue of their involvement in empowerment and in acting on behalf of women in ministry. The current leadership exercised by laywomen would be enhanced if associations on the national, regional, and diocesan levels (including women's organizations, commissions, and feminist movements) offered scholarships for theological study, and if Catholic magazines and newspapers regularly featured stories of laywomen engaged in leadership.

Widened opportunities for governance by lay ministers and women religious at every level of church life are key to eradicating injustice within the institutional structures of Roman Catholicism. In addition, a drastic improvement in diocesan-sponsored personnel offices and in preparatory programs, dovetailed to the ministerial needs of laywomen leaders, is in order. Is it too much to hope that the American bishops who defeated the conservative pastoral letter on women would be the first to implement what is desperately needed?

THE VOICE OF LAY WOMEN MINISTERS ON ORDINATION AND AUTHORITY

Listening to experiences voiced by laywomen ministers is the most imperative step of all. This chapter concludes with some of these voices.

A startling new story of faith and freedom has broken through. Within professionalized lay ministry comes a freedom of movement not found within other designated ecclesial identities. Diocesan priests, for example, are confined ministerially to a particular ministry and a particular geographical area. Although religious orders may offer more scope, many vowed religious minister within the limits of a congregation's mission and the need to live within community. Narratives of the courageous journey of laywomen in ministerial leadership, with

neither the security of ordination nor the support of institutionalized
religious life, need to be heard from diverse platforms and pulpits, as
well as in university classrooms and religious education settings—not
only because these are stories of women but also because they reveal a
fresh paradigm of God's call to dare to live out faith in new and bold
ways.

In response to a query last year, laywomen graduates of Weston
shared their aspirations, experiences, and perspectives. Included here
are some of the responses received in relation to questions on authority
and on ordination. Some of these laywomen have been active in ministerial leadership for a decade. They minister in all regions of the
United States; some are single, some married; most are between thirty-
five and forty-five years of age.

Authority: What is its source for you in your ministry?

Three sources of authority were mentioned by many of the women
for their ministry: an interior, spiritual sense of God's call, baptismal
call, and confirmation by others:

> "Sense of authority can only come from within."

> "Our/my authority comes from baptismal call. Initiation into
> the Christian community is a call to ministry, a shared ministry
> with others that is diverse."

> "My sense of authority for ministry is primarily internal al-
> though I find it confirmed repeatedly by others, by my ministry
> experiences, in my prayer and through spiritual direction."

The issue of exercise of authority has been for some a thorny path:
"For me the question of authority is a delicate one because my authority seldom goes unchallenged."

> "Don't expect any institutional authority. Whatever there is comes
> at the will or whim of the pastor. I do what God has called me to
> do and I have a sense of being able to do it. Others give you au-
> thority that you earn. This is time-consuming, not guaranteed, and
> usually a gift or surprise!"

For some a sense of authority is a steady factor in their ministry,
and for others there have been shifts and cycles:

"I still maintain a deep belief that I was called by God and a belief that future paths will be open to me."

"The authority issue is a hard question for me to answer because it changes. Sometimes I sense my authority coming from personal prayer, scripture and reflection. Sometimes from friends, and colleagues, from those who taught and mentored me. Sometimes, I don't get a sense of it at all, and I forge on in emptiness hoping that light, hope and direction will open up again. I cling to the Gospel mission."

"My authority comes from the people who hunger for compassionate ministry. From baptism. From my own need to live the Gospel. From Jesus. From being 45 and a lot less inhibited."

Ordination—What are your desires regarding ordination?

Although many laywomen who have the opportunity to prepare professionally for ministry have discovered that ordination is not necessary for them to be effective ministerial leaders who are trusted by the people they serve, the issue of ordination does not fade. As more ordained women gain in leadership within other denominations, the cost of remaining a disciple within the Roman Catholic tradition may seem even more sacrificial. What the amazing story of Catholic laywomen in ministry during the past two decades tells us is that denial does not mean death:

"I spent many years believing I should be ordained, but I now enjoy the freedom of being outside of that hierarchy. My presence without ordination empowers others to work for justice."

"The longer I do my ministry, the less I see my work up against the ordained model. What I have to offer is distinctive and timely in this historical moment."

For some laywomen ministers the issue of ordination has been their central challenge:

"I struggle with the clerical model of ministry a lot, and lately I have abandoned it. Why? Because I would have to deny my true self in order to operate out of that mode of being. Now I try very hard to be true to the Gospel. My experience of God, my companionship in the christic mission and the gifts and strengths I have and wish to offer to the Christian family sustain me."

"I do feel painfully excluded from the sacramental ministry of the Catholic Church . . . I often struggle with witness at the front or in the back of the flock; role modeling in strength vs. role modeling in weakness. But I am the first woman to hold this leadership position, and the reception of my colleagues is positive. It has pushed my colleagues to invite not just clerics to lead prayer but more and more Catholics, Protestants and Jews outside the rabbinic and priestly tribes."

"Ordination matters less and less. . . . At times I regret not being ordained because I yearn for a more complete, sacramental ministry. But at the moment I feel strongly that I am exactly where God wants me to be. Also I feel freer not being ordained—especially to speak out the truth."

"Not all priests operate 'clerically,' but there is a sense of ministering *with* rather than *to* in most women ministers. Also women ministers know they have to be good. Priests can cruise in their status. We never can."

"In my former, progressive diocese I was able to do pastoral ministry without ordination, and I was not interested in being ordained. Now I'm in an ultraconservative diocese where that is nearly impossible. Here, there's clericalism even among voluntary lay ministers. I now find I think about ordination often."

The journey of laywomen ministerial leaders serving in an American Catholic setting is a valiant one. Not to bow down in submission and become self-effacing, to witness boldly yet not arrogantly to one's call from God, requires "experiencing in your own being the power of love and unity in God." By listening to stories such as these, priests, Sisters, Brothers, and bishops can learn more not only about ministry but also about God's Spirit working in our time. To close this chapter on lay Catholic women ministers one more eloquent voice speaks: "The point of all this is to say that I felt a Call to Christian ministry, and I have tried to answer that Call. I feel I must answer that Call whether or not the Catholic Church permits it because the Call isn't to the Catholic Church; it is to the work of Christ. In my awareness there should not be a discernible difference between the two. Right now there is; one of the ways it is seen is in the way the church has refused to empower me fully as a minister of Christ. But that is its sin, not mine. Mine would be not to answer the Call."

NOTES

1. Nancy Werking Poling, *Most Ministers Wear Sneakers* (New York: Pilgrim, 1991).

2. See Debra Campbell, "The Struggle to Serve: From the Lay Apostolate to the Ministerial Explosion," in *Transforming Parish Ministry—The Changing Roles of Catholic Clergy, Laity, and Women Religious* (New York: Crossroad, 1989).

3. David C. Leege and Thomas A. Trozzolo, "Participation in Catholic Parish Life: Religious Rites and Parish Activities in the 1980's, in *Notre Dame Study of Catholic Parish Life* Report 3, Notre Dame University (April 1985).

4. Karen Sue Smith, "Today's Seminaries, Tomorrow's Priests," in *Progressions—A Lilly Endowment Occasional Report* (Indianapolis: Lilly Endowment Publication, 1989), 14. See also Katarina Schuth, *Reason for the Hope: The Futures of Roman Catholic Theologates* (Wilmington: Michael Glazier, 1989).

5. Rev. Phillip Murnion, David DeLambo, Rosemary Dilli, S.S.N.D., and Harry A. Fagan, *New Parish Ministers—Laity and Religious on Parish Staffs* (New York: The National Pastoral Life Center, 1992).

6. A diocese is a Roman Catholic polity structure under the jurisdiction of a bishop who is mandated to report directly to the Vatican in Rome.

7. Rev. Murnion et al. The data and citations which follow on "new parish minister" are from this study, funded by the Lilly Endowment.

8. Catherine Mowry La Cugna, "Catholic Women As Ministers and Theologians," *America* 167 (10 October 1992): 241.

9. John Boucher, *Lay Ministry*, 9 (April 1992). See also Rebecca A. Proehl, William Coy, and Jill L'Esperance, *Longevity Project for the National Association for Lay Ministry* (Chanhassen, Minn.: The National Association for Lay Ministry, 1990). This project was one of several related to lay ministry funded by the Raskob Foundation for Catholic Activities.

10. Georgia Masters Keightley, "Women's Issues Are Laity Issues," *America* 159 (13 August 1988): 80.

11. John Paul II, *Christifideles Laici—Apostolic Exhortation on the Laity, Origins* 18 (9 February 1989): 571.

12. Rosemary Radford Ruether, *The National Catholic Reporter*, 21 October 1983.

13. Correspondence from Dr. Joseph O'Neill, Education Testing Service, Princeton N.J. See also *Ministry Research Notes* (Spring 1991) for data on the significance of age difference. See also Rev. James M. Utendorf CSP, "Motivations for Enrolling in Lay Ministry Training Programs: A Research Overview for Adult Religious Educators," in *Insight: A Journal for Adult Education* (October 1987).

14. Pamela Thibodeau Hardiman and Madelein Provost, *On-going Formation Resource Use by Lay Ministers* (Chanhassen, Minn.: The National Association for Lay Ministry, 1990). For a summary of the report see "NALM Studies Formation of Lay Ministers," GIFTS (Winter 1990).

15. Fortunately, the Institute for Pastoral Life is now sponsored by the Loyola Institute for Ministry at Loyola University, New Orleans, where it is

known as the Loyola Pastoral Life Center. Another noteworthy effort in the education and formation of lay ministers, particularly those from more remote areas, is an institute for lay ministry sponsored by the Diocese of Portland and Saint Joseph's College in North Windham, Maine, under the direction of Sr. Bernadette LaFlamme. Here over one hundred ministers, mostly women, gather for a week of spiritual renewal and ministerial education. The bonding engendered by the program has drawn some women to return for more than five summers.

16. Rosemary Radford Ruether, "The Women-Church Movement in Contemporary Christianity," in *Women's Leadership in Marginal Religions: Explorations Outside the Mainstream*, ed. Catherine Wessinger (Urbana: University of Illinois Press, 1993).

17. The National Council of Catholic Women, which originated when two hundred Catholic women convened in Washington, D.C., in 1920, now provides a national and international focus for its more than seven thousand local Catholic women's groups.

18. Jane Redmont, *Generous Lives* (New York: Macmillan, 1992).

19. Ruth A. Wallace, *They Call Her Pastor—A New Role for Catholic Women* (Albany: State University of New York Press, 1992), 79. See also Peter Gilmour, *The Emerging Pastor: Non-ordained Catholic Pastors* (Kansas City, Mo.: Sheed and Ward, 1986). According to Gallup survey results in May 1992, 63 percent of those polled favor expansion of the priesthood to include women to alleviate the priestless-parish problem.

20. Gilbert Brim, *Ambition—How We Manage Success and Failure throughout Our Lives* (San Francisco: HarperCollins, 1992), 176.

21. Brim, 155.

22. Congregation for the Doctrine of the Faith, "Declaration on the Question of the Admission of Women to the Ministerial Priesthood," *Catholic Mind* 75 (May 1977): 52–64.

23. La Cugna, 248.

24. See Ellen G. Lahr, "Women on the rise in the United Church of Christ—They Are Pastors at Half the Denomination's Churches in Berkshires," *The Berkshire Eagle*, 26 December 1991. For a more general discussion of Catholic women in ministry and mission see also Virginia Sullivan Finn, "Lay Formation for Mission," *Origins* 21 (11 November 1991): 375; "Generativity and Church—The Power of Shunning," in *Pilgrims in This World* (New York: Paulist Press, 1990), 144–59; and Finn, "Laity: Mission and Ministry," in *Vatican II: The Unfinished Agenda* (New York: Paulist Press, 1987), 146–59.

25. Thirty-fourth General Congregation of the Society of Jesus, "Jesuits and the Situation of Women in the Church and Civil Society," *Origins* 24 (13 April 1995): 742.

Jewish Women

Are Women Changing the Rabbinate? A Reform Perspective

Janet R. Marder

In 1921 a seventeen-year-old girl set out to become the first woman rabbi in America. That spring Martha Neumark, a student at the Hebrew Union College and daughter of an HUC professor, petitioned the faculty for permission to lead High Holy Day services the following fall, should a pulpit be available. She let it be known that her ultimate goal was rabbinic ordination. Martha Neumark's quest did not go very far. Though the faculty narrowly approved her petition "providing that the congregation in question had no objection," they reversed their decision a few weeks later when Neumark failed one of her courses. But the larger issue of women's ordination could not be dismissed so easily, and for two years the college faculty and Board of Governors debated the issue, as did the Central Conference of American Rabbis (CCAR). Among the records of that debate are the earnest words of Rabbi Ephraim Frisch: "I have been wondering whether we are not denying ourselves a new source of strength, a new source of inspiration, by our reluctance to admit women to the rabbinate. I recognize the handicaps, but I believe that the women who surmount the obstacles will be greater spirits than the men who are in the rabbinate today. . . . If we get women into our midst as rabbis, I believe that we will be enjoying some of the inspiration and strength which we feel we need."[1] Though both the faculty and the Central Conference of American Rabbis concluded that women "cannot justly be denied the privilege of ordination," in the end the Board of Governors voted to maintain its policy of "limiting to males the right to matriculate

A shorter version of this chapter appeared as "How Women Are Changing the Rabbinate" in the Summer 1991 issue of *Reform Judaism*, published by the Union of American Hebrew Congregations. The conversations reported in this chapter took place in 1991.

for the purpose of entering the rabbinate."[2] It was not until 1972 that Sally Priesand fulfilled Martha Neumark's dream by becoming the first woman rabbi.[3] In 1991 as the first generation of Reform women rabbis enter middle age, it is time to ask if Rabbi Frisch's hopes have been fulfilled. What kind of impact are women rabbis having on the profession?

As of June 1991, 168 women have been ordained by the Hebrew Union College. Forty percent of them were ordained in the previous five years, 80 percent in the previous ten years. The 1990 Central Conference of American Rabbis salary survey (which does not include the 1991 graduating class) reveals that 57 out of 153 women rabbis work full-time in congregations affiliated with the Union of American Hebrew Congregations (16 as assistants, 10 as associates, 31 as solo rabbis).[4] The CCAR does not include part-time positions in its salary survey, but my own informal count (again excluding the 1991 class) suggests that at least another 38 women rabbis serve in congregations. Most of the others serve as Hillel directors or chaplains, teach, pursue graduate studies, or work in various Jewish organizations.

Since most women rabbis have entered the field so recently, is it too soon to discern trends in their career paths? Probably not, according to Rabbi Mark Winer, who has analyzed the CCAR salary survey results for the last nine years. "Certain patterns begin emerging early, and they have become more pronounced over the years. Women and men start out in the same kinds of entry-level positions at similar salaries, but the longer women are in the rabbinate the more they behave differently from men. As the years go by, women make less money, they're more likely to work part-time, and they're far less likely to move into large congregations.[5]

At first glance in 1991 it seems that women have not made the kind of dramatic impact that Rabbi Frisch envisioned. No woman heads a thousand-member congregation; only three serve as senior rabbis of congregations larger than three hundred. Women are not, apparently, following the conventional path of upward mobility in the rabbinate, according to which a rabbi becomes a leader in the movement by progressing from smaller to larger and "more prestigious" synagogues until he reaches the pinnacle of success: an "E" congregation of more than nine hundred members.[6]

It is true that women rabbis have not thus far assumed prominent positions of leadership in the Reform movement; they are not, by and large, the visible spokespeople and opinion shapers in the rabbinic "establishment." But it would be a mistake to draw the conclusion that women's impact on the rabbinate has been minimal. On the contrary, one senses in conversations with women rabbis that our generation is witnessing the beginning of a profound and pervasive transformation in the nature of the rabbinate—a change brought about by the distinctive values and goals women have brought to this once exclusively male enterprise.

What follows is the result of conversations in 1991 with sixty-five colleagues, fifty of them women, about the new perspectives women are bringing to the rabbinate.[7] This sample includes rabbis who are young and old, married and single, with and without children. Some have from the outset worked in noncongregational settings; some after several years in synagogues have left the congregational rabbinate; most serve as assistants, associates, or solo rabbis in congregations of various sizes. A remarkable number of Reform women rabbis see themselves as agents of change, consciously struggling to reshape the role of the rabbi in our society. Despite the differences in their personal and professional situations, most of the women share a commitment to three fundamental values, which they describe as crucial to their rabbinate: balance, intimacy, and empowerment.

BALANCE

In 1922 Rabbi Jacob Lauterbach, professor of Talmud at Hebrew Union College, composed a *responsum* (legal opinion) entitled "Shall Women Be Ordained as Rabbis?" The *responsum*, provoked by Martha Neumark's ill-fated application to the college, contained the following remarkable passage:

> If there is any calling which requires a whole-hearted devotion to the exclusion of all other things and the determination to make it one's whole life work, it is the rabbinate. It is not to be considered merely as a profession by which one earns a livelihood. Nor is it to be entered upon as a temporary occupation. One must choose it for his lifework and be prepared to give to it all his energies and to devote to it all the years of his life. . . . It has been rightly said that the woman who enters a profession, must make her choice between following her chosen profession or the calling of mother and homemaker. She cannot do both well at the same time. This certainly would hold true in the case of the rabbinical profession.[8]

Many of the Reform women rabbis interviewed seem determined to carve out careers that will prove Lauterbach wrong. Speaking of their need for "a balanced life" and their desire to be "a whole person" whose life is not circumscribed by the synagogue, they argue that the rabbinate need not consume all their time and energy "to the exclusion of all other things." "I want to have a life apart from my work," says one busy congregational rabbi. "The idea of having my entire life given over to the temple is not appealing." The concept of the rabbinate as an all-consuming lifetime calling is not even authentically Jewish, according to Rabbi Elka Abrahamson. "In fact, this is a model best exemplified by the Catholic tradition, in which the clergy are quite literally 'married' to the Church." Male rabbis in general tend to take pride in how many hours they devote to their work. Being overworked appears to be a point of honor with most, and those who are clearly not workaholics do not advertise this fact to their peers. Women rabbis, on the other hand, emphasize the ways in which they manage to use their work time efficiently so as to make room in their lives for other priorities.

Part-time work is a subject on which many women rabbis disagree. Some contend that there are no real part-time congregational jobs—only part-time salaries—and that women who take these positions may be exploited. Others insist that a part-time jobs allows them to delineate their work hours more clearly and gives them more control over their lives. Rabbi Mindy Portnoy, whose job is defined as three-fourths-time associate rabbi at Temple Sinai in Washington, D.C., says this structure allows her to be home every day from 3:30 to 6:30 P.M.—a condition that helps provide balance in her life.

The quest for balance led Rabbi Constance Golden to exchange her full-time position as assistant rabbi in a large congregation for two very small synagogues in Arkansas and Mississippi which she serves on a monthly basis. "I had just gotten married, at age 42," she explains. "I decided that I didn't want to work those kinds of crazy hours while trying to make a new marriage work." Rabbi Golden acknowledges that her career choice may confirm some people's worst fears about women rabbis—that they are not seriously committed to their profession: "Senior colleagues in the CCAR have told me how I've disappointed them by failing to live up to my potential—they wanted me to become the first woman rabbi of an 'E' congregation. But I said, 'That's your dream, not mine.' The fact is, my marriage is the most important thing to me now; that's my priority . . . I've reached the point where I'm at peace with myself. I know how happy I am. I don't feel I'm a failure, and I don't really care what the values of the CCAR are. I know that I'm doing what's right for me. I'm doing good work for my congregations—and they are thrilled to have a rabbi!"

Rabbi Ellen Dreyfus, mother of three young children, has held a series of part-time positions during the twelve years since her ordination. At the time of the interview, she serves Temple Beth Sholom, a small congregation in Park Forest, Illinois. "There have been times over the years," she says, "when I've been frustrated—I've felt my career was going nowhere. But then I think . . . it's not such a bad thing to take ten or twelve years out to be with my kids. I can't do that for them ten years from now; now is when they need me."

A few colleagues are openly critical of women like Rabbi Dreyfus, who have limited their work hours in order to spend more time with their children. "A lot of women are on the 'Mommy track,' " says one woman rabbi, herself single and childless. "They've opted not to kill themselves professionally. They've accepted a lower salary in exchange for a lighter schedule. I understand why they do it, but I don't think it's good for women. Men who have children still manage to have a full-time career. Why can't women? I think they should get a housekeeper or do whatever it takes. Because as long as women rabbis stay on the 'Mommy track,' they'll never set the world on fire."

But most women rabbis who choose to work part-time say a housekeeper would not solve their problems. They are acting out of a deeply felt need to participate intimately in the lives of their children—a sense that they can give their children something that no housekeeper can. "I used to feel strongly about mothers working full-time," says Rabbi Randy Musnitzky, a three-fourths-time associate at a large congregation in New Jersey, "but that was before I had kids. Until you're a mother you don't know what it's going to be like. Now I remind myself that they can always find someone to replace me on the job—but my children can never find another mommy. I'm always expendable to the congregation, but never to my kids." Rabbi Aliza Berk, mother of two and part-time rabbi of Temple Beth Solomon of the Deaf, puts it poignantly: "I don't want to be 60 years old and say, as I've heard so many older colleagues say, 'I wish I had spent more time with my children.' I don't want my grown children to say to me, 'You were out saving the world but you were never there for me.' "

Most women rabbis in congregations work full-time, but they too, say they refuse to be swallowed up by their jobs. Many of those who struggle to combine hectic professional schedules with the needs of young children say they can only achieve this balance by minimizing all activities and interests outside of work and family. "I don't get a lot of sleep," says Rabbi Shira Stern of Monroe Township Jewish Center of Spotswood, New Jersey, "and there are friendships I cherish that I haven't been able to keep up. But those are the sacrifices I've made." Rabbi Elizabeth Stern, mother of three children (ages seven, five, and one and a half) and just completing her five-year term as associate at

Temple Emanu-El in Dallas, says that a full-time housekeeper has been essential. "When I took this full-time job I completely gave up house-keeping. I just decided it was not a priority. I gave up all non-essentials. I decided that I could do only two things at this point in my life: do my job and love my family."

"It's very stressful," says Rabbi Elyse Frischman matter-of-factly, "because there is no question that I'm doing two full-time jobs." Rabbi Frischman, the mother of three children (ages eight, six, and three and a half months), has served the 240-member Reform Temple of Suffern since her ordination ten years ago "While I work very hard," she says, "I don't sacrifice my family or my personal needs for the sake of the job." Rabbi Frischman has developed a support staff (a full-time educator and a rabbinic intern) unusual for a congregation this size. Her day off is "sacred." She usually comes home at 3:15 to meet her children when they arrive from school, gets back to the office by 4:00 for *bar/bat mitzvah* training, and is always home for dinner, though often out again for an evening meeting. She leads worship every Friday night and Saturday morning, but keeps her Saturday afternoons free. "I almost never go to a *bar* or *bat mitzvah* reception. My congregation understands that that's one of my few times to spend with family."

Rabbi Susan Talve, mother of three young children and full-time rabbi of Central Reform Congregation in St. Louis, says she has developed a creative approach to serving the needs of her 260-member congregation while still making her children (two of whom have chronic illnesses) her first priority. Rabbi Talve leads services only one Friday night a month (members conduct services on other weeks), and Saturday morning has become the primary time for congregational worship and study. How do the members of Rabbi Talve's synagogue feel about this rather unorthodox definition of a full-time job? According to Roger Goldman, founder and first president: "We started out several years ago without a rabbi. So this kind of shared responsibility seems very natural to us. We are incredibly devoted to our rabbi. We want to create a work environment that's supportive of her needs, because we value her so highly. But it goes both ways. We are great for each other—and we know it!"

Sometimes, despite their best efforts, some women rabbis have found it impossible to arrive at a satisfying balance between work and family demands. For them, the best solution has been to leave the congregational rabbinate, at least until their children are older. Typical of this group is Rabbi Eve Ben-Ora. Ordained in 1986, Rabbi Ben-Ora has had "a wonderful time" in her five years at Congregation Emanuel of Denver. While working full-time in this large congregation, she and her husband, Rabbi Avi Schulman, have reared two children ages five and sixteen months. Rabbi Ben-Ora has worked hard to fulfill her commitments to job and family. When her second child was born she hired a babysitter to care for him in the temple building all day so that she could work full-time while continuing to nurse her son until he was eight months old. But in 1991 she said that she can no longer combine congregational service with motherhood—for a while at least. "I'm an obsessive-compulsive worker; I don't know how to stop. I was feeling that I was missing so much of what my children were doing; I experienced a greater pull than ever before. I just didn't feel that I could do my job justice and still give my family the attention it deserved." Rabbi Lenore Bohm, who in 1991 stepped down from one of the largest pulpits occupied by a woman rabbi (about 450 members), seems motivated by a sense of urgency similar to Rabbi Ben-Ora's. In many ways, Rabbi Bohm's departure from the synagogue was a result of her success. During her six years with Temple Solel of Encinitas, membership increased ten-fold. That explosive growth and the growth of her own family (two children under five) made increasingly intense demands: "It was becoming apparent that the congregation, to its credit, was getting more sophisticated and more demanding—in the best sense of the word—of the quality of programs and services. Meanwhile, I was getting pulled more and more. As my children were getting older I felt they wanted me and I wanted them, too. My husband really didn't want me to leave the job; it's my need to be less hassled, less frenetic, less pulled." Both rabbis react strongly to those who would view their choice as characteristic of all women who attempt to combine motherhood with a congregation. "There's a tendency to take the experience of one woman rabbi and generalize it to all women," says Rabbi Ben-Ora. "That kind of attitude makes me angry. There are male rabbis who do all kinds of immoral things, and yet no one ever says, 'Let's not hire a man.' " Rabbi Bohm echoes her words of caution: "This is not a commentary on women rabbis. This is what happened in *one* situation in which a woman rabbi's personal life and professional life grew dramatically and simultaneously."

Male rabbis, of course, are used to balancing the competing demand of career and parenthood, but many women rabbis believe that mothers feel the conflict more intensely than fathers. "I'm much more obsessed with trying to create family time than my husband is," says one congregational rabbi whose husband is also a rabbi. "I feel much more guilt than he does about not being with the kids. I'm always trying to be a model parent." Other women contend that male rabbis may have the same "parenting needs" as women, but society gives them less permission to express those needs. "Men just don't talk about these things much," says one. "They want private time, too—but they don't feel as comfortable saying so. Women are more honest about asking for what all rabbis want." Rabbi Jason Edelstein agrees that the tensions women rabbis experience are also felt by men. Rabbi Edelstein, director of the CCAR's confidential hotline for rabbis and their spouses, describes the kinds of calls he receives: "Most of them revolve around the question of balancing the multiple demands that rabbis face. The question they all ask is 'How do I harmonize the pulls of professional life with the pulls of family life?' This dilemma is reflected in problems such as marital conflict, larger family conflicts (often involving children), addictions of various kinds, and generalized stress and anxiety."

Surprisingly, the quest for balance is not confined only to those rabbis who are caring for young families. Several women who are single or childless also spoke eloquently on this subject. Rabbi Carole Meyers, who recently married after serving Temple Sinai in Glendale, California, for five years, says: "I've been protecting myself and my time all the years I've been single. I've never accepted the traditional model of giving oneself over entirely to the synagogue." Rabbi Meyers tries to limit her workweek to forty hours, primarily as a way of maintaining her strength and effectiveness on the job. "I am very conscious of this when I make decisions about community activities and outside speaking engagements. It's so easy to say yes and yes and yes . . . until you lose yourself. In the end, it does the congregation a disservice, because you get too wiped out, too burned out, and you're not able to give the congregation the best that's within you."

Women react strongly to the suggestion that their desire to set limits on the job means they are less committed to their work. "I think my women colleagues work incredibly hard," says one, "and they are as intense and passionate about their work as any man. But a congregation can't keep depleting the resources of a rabbi and still expect something to be there. I'm not sure that rabbis who are workaholics and ignore primary relationships in their life are doing their congregations any favor."

Rabbi Rosalind Gold, who has served Northern Virginia Hebrew Congregation since 1981, suggests another reason for rabbis to set limits—one that was echoed by many others: the need to be a healthy role model for the congregation. Rabbi Gold, married with two grown stepchildren, says, "when I work, I devote 100 percent effort to my job. But I also want to be a well-rounded person. Often, I think, we rabbis send a crazy double message to our congregations. We say: 'Your marriage is sacred, your relationships with children are sacred. But don't do as I do—I'm out at a meeting every night and don't work on my family relationships at all.' We need to model the kind of behavior we want to see in our congregants—that of being well-rounded individuals."

While some women criticize congregations for making excessive demands on their rabbis, "insisting that the rabbi be eternally available and accessible," others say the problem often lies within rabbis themselves. "I think I have less need to be needed than many of my colleagues," says one. "I don't need to have the phone ringing all night. My real sustenance comes from other sources—from family, friends, my own Jewish practice. But with some rabbis this sense of needing to be needed, needing to be present all the time, running the temple as their own little fiefdom, can become pathological."

The quest for a balanced life is often a particular challenge for women who work as assistants or associates, for the senior rabbi's concept of the rabbinate may differ significantly from theirs. "This is an all-consuming job," says one young rabbi. "My ability to put limits on my job has been like hacking my way through a jungle. My senior rabbi is the quintessential workaholic. For me, insisting on the rightness of another model has been very difficult."

Rabbi Shira Milgrom, a full-time associate at the Jewish Community Center of White Plains, structured her job so that she leads worship every Shabbat morning but is home three Friday nights out of four—an arrangement she says the senior rabbi and congregation have accepted well. "This is very important to me as Jewish mother. To structure the synagogue in a way that undermines family life is not healthy for anyone—rabbis or congregants. But it takes a certain amount of flexibility on the congregation's part. If there are two rabbis, why must both of them be on the pulpit every Friday night? If there is only one rabbi, why not occasionally have services led by lay people, or guest rabbis, or other synagogue professionals? Why not offer early Friday evening services so that people can go home and be with their families? If we start to develop synagogue life in a way that supports Jewish families, rabbis won't be the only beneficiaries."

INTIMACY

Rabbi Arnold Sher, director of the Reform movement's Rabbinic Placement Commission, reports: "I have no statistical way of proving it, but my gut feeling is that most men in 'A' congregations [up to 120 members] aspire to move into larger ones. It's very clear that women in 'A' and 'B' congregations [166–300 members] are not seeking larger pulpits."

Why are women who are solo rabbis disproportionately clustered in smaller congregations? Why are some women spending five or ten years in an "A" or "B" congregation, rather than seeing it, as many men do, as a stepping-stone to something bigger? Before attempting to answer, it is important to remember that the vast majority of congregations in the Union of American Hebrew Congregations are small. In 1991 temples with fewer than three hundred members make up about 60 percent of the UAHC synagogues, while only 13 percent have more than seven hundred members. Obviously, then, most Reform rabbis, whether male or female, are not heading large congregations. It should also be noted that since rabbis must be at least ten years out of the seminary before they are eligible for an "E" congregation, it has been only recently that significant numbers of women entered this category. As of 1990 there were only thirty-seven women in the country eligible to serve as senior rabbis in the largest synagogues; three years previously there were only seven. Add to this the fact that only a limited number of "E" positions are open in any given year (two were available in 1990), and it becomes not at all remarkable that as of 1991 no women have yet achieved this position. Still, a larger number of "C" congregations fall vacant in any given year (in 1990 there were about ten), and given a larger pool of potential applicants (ninety women were eligible in 1990), it is rather striking that in 1991 only three women served these synagogues of between three hundred and six hundred members.

There are many factors that account for women rabbis' tendency to remain longer in smaller communities. Some are committed to staying in a particular geographic location—because of a husband's well-established career (few spouses with lucrative careers are giving up their jobs in a recession), child custody arrangements, other family ties, or simply a strong affection for the area. Some women simply state, "I'm happy here; I don't feel any need to move on." They claim not to experience with much intensity the itch of restlessness or ambition that periodically provokes many men to try to climb up the career ladder. Some do not experience the financial pressure to move to a better-paying job because theirs is not the primary income in the family. And some women clearly prefer to remain in a congregation that is less programmatically demanding while their children are young.

But one factor is cited more than any other when women are asked "What do you like about being in a smaller congregation?" Again and again they answer: "In small congregations you have the opportunity to form intimate relationships." Thus Rabbi Sally Priesand, who has spent a decade in a congregation of about two hundred members (Monmouth Reform Temple in Tinton Falls, New Jersey), praises the sense of community in her congregation: "As the first woman rabbi, I always thought it was my obligation to become senior rabbi of an 'E' congregation. But to me, success doesn't necessarily mean bigger. I appreciate very much the sense of family we have here. In a large congregation you reach a bigger audience, but in a smaller place you have the opportunity to make a greater impact on individuals." Says Rabbi Elyse Goldstein: "For women, it's *quality* of relationships that counts, not quantity. I'd rather have quality, substantial relationships with 200 families than fleeting, superficial relationships with 1000." Another woman, reflecting on her eight years with a small congregation, says, "I've never envisioned myself as senior rabbi of a large synagogue. . . . The types of relationships that one forms in a small congregation are more satisfying. You have a better chance of building community, and I personally find prayer in a smaller setting more meaningful." Another woman rabbi, working as associate in a large temple, says when asked if she would like to be senior rabbi of a comparable synagogue: "Not a chance! I've lived it—I don't want it. You have to be an extraordinary person to be able to maintain some intimacy with your congregation when you have 1400 families. There's no way you can know even half of them well. I don't like looking out at a sea of unfamiliar faces on the High Holy Days. The choice I see most senior rabbis making is to distance themselves from the congregation and to be more involved in community work. There is a place in this world for large congregations. I've had some amazing opportunities to grow here that I would not have had in a small congregation, and any idea I had for a program I could fulfill; the resources seemed limitless. But it's not for me."

Several women comment that they were not daunted by the amount of work done by rabbis of large congregations, for rabbis of small congregations often work just as hard since they have no staff support. It is the *nature* of such rabbinic work that they find unappealing. "I wouldn't put a numerical cap on the size of congregation I could serve," says one who is in a small temple, "but I am wondering what the rabbinic job really is in these mega-congregations. You don't really know your congregants. It's a different job; it's more an organizational, administrative job—setting priorities for the organization, leading the organization."

It will be wrong, however, to conclude that all women rabbis interviewed are "antigrowth" and abhor larger synagogues. Indeed, many of them speak proudly of how their membership has expanded over the years and express the hope that it will grow larger still— mostly because they yearn for more financial and human resources to enhance the temple program. "It would be nice to be in a place with some money," says one young rabbi wistfully. "It's hard to work in a temple that has to worry about every paper clip." Others confess that they do sometimes "feel the itch" to move on to a larger place: "At times I think that the resources of a large congregation would be just wonderful, and the idea of having some influence on the lives of a larger number of people can sound very appealing, too." What is significant is that even those women who aspire to larger congregations stress their wish to form close connections with their congregants. One rabbi speaks of creating "nurturing sub-groups" within the larger community, another of her wish to "build religious community by spending time in small learning groups." And some insist that large synagogues need not be cold, impersonal institutions. One woman serving in a "B" congregation says: "I'm happy here; I want to see the kids grow up and maintain the relationships that we've developed. I'm not going to move to a bigger place just for the added prestige. But if this congregation were to grow into a "D"—terrific. I don't think intimacy is impossible in a large congregation; I know a couple of large synagogues that seem to be very intimate places. Intimacy is built over time. I wouldn't experience it during the first few years, but I could develop it gradually."

Will a woman ever become senior rabbi of an "E" congregation? And how important is it for that to occur? Rabbi Joseph Glaser, executive vice president of the CCAR, says, "Although I firmly adhere to the maxim that 'Small is beautiful,' I'm afraid that the mark of success in our rabbinate is to be rabbi of a large congregation. Given the values of our society, that 'Big is beautiful,' it would be an act of great symbolic importance for a woman to attain this position." A woman who is an associate comments, "I think it's important that a woman get one of those jobs. That's what it will take to show that we can really do the job as rabbis." [In July 1994, Laura Geller became senior rabbi of Temple Emanuel, an 850-member Reform congregation in Beverly Hills, California.]

Several women remark that while they have no interest in an "E" congregation, they believe that a talented woman who aspires to such a position will have little difficulty being hired. Others are not so sanguine: "There is so much hidden resistance to the idea of a woman as authority figure. The male authority is still the model. People will deny those feelings, but they're there. You know, in large congregations the leaders are the movers and shakers in the community—people with money and power. And many of them have negative feelings about women as authority figures. Also, the board is often a reflection of the senior rabbi. It would take a senior rabbi who is *truly* a feminist to lead his board in the direction of a female successor." Another woman commented, "I'm not sure that women are ever going to get up to those large congregations until male senior rabbis say to their search committees: 'This woman has been my associate for a number of years and she deserves a chance to be the senior rabbi.' Until that happens, I'm not very optimistic." One UAHC regional director is a bit less gloomy:

> If a very talented woman were on the panel, I think most large congregations would give her serious consideration. However, if it came down to two equally qualified candidates, one male and one female, I think the woman would be at a disadvantage—at least at this point in time. There would have to be something extraordinary about her for her to get the job. Our congregations tend to be conservative institutions. If other congregations hadn't yet taken this step I think they might be a little reluctant to be the first. There is another factor, as well. What I hear from time to time is anxiety about the "feminization of the synagogue"—the perceived difficulty in attracting good, strong male lay leadership to the synagogue—a problem that some think would be compounded, were the head of staff a woman. The fact is, there are more men who have difficulty working with a woman than vice-versa.

It remains to be seen how accurate these speculations are. Though few women have sought "E" congregations and most say they will never aspire to the job, a few spoke forthrightly about their wish to serve in "a larger arena." One woman, an associate rabbi in a large congregation, says, "I would like to head a synagogue like this one someday. I have made the decision to devote myself primarily to my career. [Since] I have the time and energy and interest, I think that might be a real possibility for me. And my feeling is that it would be possible for me to bring my ideas and insights into a large congregation, and exert some influence on the nature of the institutions. Serving as rabbi of an 'E' congregation doesn't mean I can't have a day off or set boundaries so I have some personal time."

An interesting and little-discussed factor in some women's reluctance to serve as senior rabbi in "D" or "E" congregations may be the negative experiences some have had as assistants in these synagogues—either because of a difficult relationship with the senior rabbi or because they perceive his life as so unsatisfying. Several young women tell of unpleasant experiences with their senior colleagues. One explains: "It's made me believe that there's tremendous hidden prejudice among some of our older male colleagues. All of the women in our class were offered assistantships before the men were, and all of us who have been really unhappy are working with men who have tremendous egos. I think they were eager to hire a woman assistant because they thought they could be more dominant over us. They thought they could maintain their power and not be threatened. They expected a woman to be compliant and docile."

While others speak warmly of their senior rabbis, several comment that the lives of senior rabbis appear frenetic, unhealthy, and unfulfilling. One, reflecting on her experience in a large temple, states, "I don't want to have a heart attack at an early age." Another remarks "You see these rabbis of big congregations smoking two packs of cigarettes a day, running around constantly, driving themselves crazy, often acting out sexually. It's a very, very stressful life." And another comments simply, "I feel sorry for my last senior. I don't think he has much of a life outside the congregation."

Tension between senior and assistant rabbis is nothing new, and is certainly not confined to cases where the assistant is female. But senior rabbis who genuinely want women to aspire to jobs like theirs might think carefully about what kind of impression their younger colleague is receiving of the life of an "E" senior rabbi. In the end, says Rabbi Deborah Zecher, each woman will take the path that seems best to her—dictated by taste and temperament and personal circumstances. "There need to be all kinds of women rabbis. Some will take jobs that leave them lots of time for family; some will be assertive go-getters who aim for large congregations. Both are fine. All options should be open to any rabbi."

EMPOWERMENT

Reconstructionist Rabbi Sandy Eisenberg Sasso wrote in 1984: "Women in the rabbinate, all Jewish women for that matter, contribute the most to Judaism when they do *not* fashion themselves out of a masculine mold. Women come to the rabbinate with a different set of experiences. The findings of feminist sociologists, psychologists and moral theorists teach us that we come with different priorities, versions of reality and relationships. Women's center of focus is on people rather than principles. . . . Women's version of reality is not a hierarchal model where one's goal is to move up, to be alone at the top, but rather a network model where the goal is to connect with others, to be together at the center."⁹

Not all women rabbis interviewed accept Sasso's view that there is a distinctive woman's style within the rabbinate. Many, however, do echo some of her language, expressing the wish to "make synagogue life less hierarchical." They point out, with some irritation, that the rabbinic "establishment" still promotes the idea that congregational rabbis are superior to those who do not work in synagogues, and that rabbis of large congregations are superior to those serving smaller temples. One points out that the presidents of the CCAR are almost exclusively from large synagogues. Several mention that "when you go to a CCAR convention, the first thing the men always ask is, 'Where are you now, and how big is it?' It's all about power. It's the phallic obsession: bigger is better."

Many women rabbis express the desire to break down some of the traditional power structures within the synagogue, too, and create a more egalitarian system. Some speak with distaste of the notion of rabbi as "CEO" or "chief of staff"; they suggest instead the idea of staff members working together in genuine partnership. Says one associate rabbi: "One of the incentives I'd have to work in a large congregation would be to have the opportunity to develop a different kind of professional structure—one that's less hierarchical than this or any other synagogue I know. I'd like to see the rabbi, cantor, executive director and education director all receive the same basic salary and work together as a 'care-giving team.' Each would have ideas of special expertise; all would make a full-time commitment but have time for their own families. The rabbi would not be 'chief of staff'; decisions would be made jointly by the team."

Several other associates speak with interest about the possibility of forming a long-term partnership with a senior rabbi—what some congregations call a "permanent associate track"—provided they can work with a senior who will not be threatened by this arrangement. Rabbi Judy Shanks, who decided in 1991 to leave the congregational rabbinate for a time, describes the kind of arrangement that is appealing to her: "I'd love to share a congregation of 300–600 families with a colleague. Both of us would benefit from the interaction and the congregation would benefit from the combination of our strengths. It would be great to create a co-rabbinate, rather than a hierarchical situation with senior and assistant."

While some greet Rabbi Shanks's idea with enthusiasm, the notion of two co-rabbis sharing a congregation arouses considerable skepticism among many other colleagues, male and female, who insist that such an arrangement will never work because "there is too much ego involved" and "ultimately there has to be one person who's in charge." A co-rabbinate, albeit on a smaller scale, does seem to be working effectively for Rabbis Linda Motzkin and Jonathan Rubenstein, spouses who share a full-time position at Temple Sinai of Saratoga Springs, New York. Both also hold separate part-time hospital chaplaincy positions. Rabbi Motzkin praises her congregant's openness and flexibility, saying: "Fortunately they didn't adopt a very rigid approach by insisting that we tell them right at the beginning how we were dividing up the job." Temple president Howard Gunther confirms that "the arrangement is working very very well. None of the possible problems we imagined have arisen. One of them is always there. The accessibility is great. We enjoy both perspectives, and we feel very lucky to have two such fine rabbis."

In addition to creating new, less hierarchical staff structures, some women speak with passion of breaking down the hierarchical relationship between rabbi and congregant by "Jewishly empowering our members." In part, this seems to be related to a sense of profound weariness in the face of an ignorant and apathetic congregation. One rabbi explains: "For years and years when I was in rabbinic school I was filling myself up with study, creative pursuits, religious growth. Now I feel like all I do is give and give and give. I'm wrung out! I don't have time to fill up anymore. I want people to do Jewish things for themselves. I'm tired of being a surrogate Jew, a surrogate Mom." Another woman explains that one factor in her decision to leave the congregational rabbinate is her feeling that congregants prefer to be dependent on the rabbi, rather than take an active role in their own religious lives:

> I believe in the "round" model of the rabbinate—the partnership model—but so many congregants still want the "ladder" model, where the rabbi is the boss. Women rabbis want to empower, not officiate. The rabbis we grew up with did everything for their congregants; that was one way of exerting control. You don't need a rabbi to do an unveiling! You don't need a rabbi to lead a *shiva minyan*! People say: "But aren't those things the rabbi's job?" I say: "My job is to empower you to be Jewish in your own life! Let me teach you how to run a Saturday morning service. Let me teach you how to read the Torah. Let me help you to take on a *mitzvah* in your home! I want to turn away from the system where the rabbi is the repository of all Jewish knowledge—the only one who knows how to do things, and the one who does them on everybody else's behalf. That's a priestly role.[10]

Since the Jewish tradition does not regard the rabbi as representing God or as a God-like figure, it is particularly open to the sharing of ritual leadership roles. The rabbi is regarded as a learned Jew who is empowered to teach other Jews.

CONCLUSIONS

There is an obvious connection between the three concepts that so many women are trying to introduce into their rabbinic work: balance, intimacy, and empowerment. In teaching and sharing Jewish skills with her congregants, the rabbi draws closer to them and forms an intimate bond of real partnership. By sharing her skills, she also frees her members to take responsibility for the religious life of the community, thus lifting from her own shoulders the burden of being the congregation's surrogate Jew. The synagogue now becomes a *shared* enterprise, with the rabbi no longer bearing sole responsibility for *mitzvot* (commandments) incumbent on *all* Jews: prayer, study, visiting the sick, comforting mourners, etc. Having taught her congregants to develop their own rich, satisfying Jewish lives—to function, in a sense, independently of her—the rabbi is free to live a balanced life, finding strength and refreshment in private pursuits, able to give back to the community the best that is within her.

Such, at any rate, is a picture of what congregations guided by women might look like. It is not only women, of course, who espouse the values described in this chapter—nor do all women subscribe to them equally. But quietly, without fanfare, a community of women rabbis has come into being which seeks to transform the landscape of Reform Judaism. The question on most of their minds is: Will women reshape the rabbinate, or will the rabbinate mold them, instead, in the traditional male image?

Certainly women's voices will be heard more clearly as their proportion within rabbinic ranks increases. In 1991 women constituted about 10 percent of all Reform rabbis, but recent Hebrew Union College graduating classes have ranged from 30 to 50 percent women, and in 1991 women constituted 40 to 50 percent of all applicants to the rabbinic program.

Rabbi Peter Rubenstein, in a 1990 essay on the future of the Reform rabbinate, suggested that the increasing numbers of women will have a profound influence on the profession, causing male rabbis to reexamine the traditional definition of success and to consider alternative job structures that will allow them more time with family. "Rabbis who have children, or who are intent upon spending substantial time with a spouse, will face the decision of either working part-time, . . . taking time away from careers, or demanding that a full-time rabbinic position be viewed within the 40-hour work week framework."[11] UAHC regional director Lennard Thal of Los Angeles questions the practical reality of such a vision: "It may well be that some limits will have to be set on the demands placed on rabbis. The question is: Who decides what reasonable limitations are and how those limits will be set? Given today's economy, will many congregations be willing to pay the price of hiring additional staff so the rabbi's job can be more limited? Will many rabbis be willing to accept lower compensation in return for fewer demands being placed on them? It remains to be seen."

Other male rabbis, however, speak hopefully of the "feminization of the rabbinate"—not a condition in which woman dominate the profession but one in which men adopt some of the values and concerns of their female colleagues. There are some signs that this change is occurring. Many younger male rabbis speak emphatically of their efforts to make family time a priority. According to one, "I keep reminding myself that, of all the families I serve, the primary one is my own. I can't be a decent role model for my congregation unless I'm a good husband and father." Others, like Rabbi Arthur Gross Schaefer of Congregation B'nai B'rith of Santa Barbara, say that feminist principles have influenced the way they relate to their congregants: "My goal is to form a relationship with the lay leaders in which we work as a team. I'd like to form a community in which God and Torah are at the center—not the rabbi—and in which the members feel challenged and empowered to become knowledgeable Jews."

Most rabbis, male and female, agree that rabbis alone cannot reshape the profession. A rabbi states, "I'd like to see the congregations struggle with these issues for a while. I'd like to see them re-think the demands they place on rabbis, the roles they cast for rabbis, the relationships they have with rabbis."

Women, it seems, have been the catalyst for this complex and wrenching process of re-thinking the congregational rabbinate. Some have abandoned congregational service—at least temporarily—physically and emotionally drained by stresses they never envisioned in the seminary. But many more are enduring, bringing strength and inspiration to congregations—as well as more creative disruption than Ephraim Frisch ever expected. How proud he would have been to hear the words of Rabbi Shira Stern: "Of course there are frustrations—I don't deny that. But I entered the congregational rabbinate because I felt that if I could touch people from womb to tomb, if I could have an impact on people's lives, it would be tremendously fulfilling. I still feel that way. I love being close to people at times of joy and sorrow. I love watching people's eyes light up when I teach. I love having my words give comfort. I love so many things about this work ... I'm willing to put up with the frustrations, I'm willing to put up with the nonsense—because I really love what I do. You have to love it. It's too hard a job to do if you don't love it."

NOTES

1. Walter Jacob, ed., *American Reform Responsa: Collected Responsa of the Central Conference of American Rabbis* (New York: Central Conference of American Rabbis, 1983), 37. Also found in J. Gordon Melton, ed., *The Churches Speak on: Women's Ordination, Official Statements from Religious Bodies and Ecumenical Organizations* (Detroit: Gale Research, 1991), 310–11.
2. Michael A. Meyer, *Hebrew Union College-Jewish Institute of Religion at One Hundred Years* (Cincinnati: Hebrew Union College Press, 1976), 98–99, 263.
3. There were a number of steps taken in the Reform movement that led up to Priesand's ordination and even to Neumark's earlier ambition to become a rabbi. From its inception in Germany, the Reform tradition attempted to include women more fully in Jewish religious life. The Breslau Conference meeting in 1846 had committed the Reform movement to "the equality of religious privileges and obligations of women insofar as this is possible." To accomplish this, Reform Jews included women in the *minyan*, or quorum, needed for worship; the daily prayer in which a Jewish man thanks God for not having been created a woman was abolished; women were admitted to formal religious instruction; and women and men were seated in the congregation together. Rabbi Isaac Mayer Wise, who founded the Hebrew Union College in Cincinnati in 1875, worked for the rights of women. During his twenty-five years as president of Hebrew Union College, women were encouraged to attend, but none of these sought ordination. See Ellen M. Umansky, "Women in Judaism: From the Reform Movement to Contemporary Jewish Religious Feminism," in *Women of Spirit: Female Leadership in the Jewish and Christian Traditions*, ed. Rosemary Ruether and Eleanor McLaughlin (New York: Simon and Schuster, 1979), 339; J. Gordon Melton, ed., *The Churches Speak on: Women's Ordination*, cited above, presents documents issued by the Central Conference of American Rabbis on women's ordination dating from 1922 to 1975.
4. There are (in 1991) 1,544 members of the Central Conference of American Rabbis: 780 members serve UAHC congregations; 119 serve non-UAHC congregations; 44 serve congregations overseas; and 943 altogether serve congregations. There are also 220 members of the CCAR who are classified as "retired"—many of them from congregational life. Excluding retired rabbis, 71 percent of CCAR members are in the congregational rabbinate.

5. Rabbi Rosalind Gold, who chairs the CCAR Task Force on Women in the Rabbinate, says that the CCAR leadership as well as the Women's Rabbinic Network (an organization of women Reform rabbis) are "very concerned about the salary gap issue. First we need to understand why it's happening—why women and men in comparable positions are not being paid the same. Then, together with the UAHC, we want to take serious steps to address the problem."

6. The Category System of the Rabbinic Placement Commission follows:

A   Up to 120 members. There were (in 1991) 297 congregations in this category.

AB   From 121 to 165 members; 67 congregations.

B   From 166 to 300 members; 145 congregations.

C   From 301 to 600 members; 184 congregations.

D   From 601 to 900 members; 72 congregations.

E   More than 900 members; 70 congregations.

7. It should be noted that due to the candid and sensitive nature of these conversations, several colleagues requested anonymity in this report.

8. Jacob Z. Lauterbach, "Shall Women be Ordained Rabbis?" in Melton, 306.

9. Quoted in *Jewish and Female*, ed. Susan Weidman Schneider (New York: Simon and Schuster, 1984), 49–51.

10. Unveiling is a service performed six months or a year after the funeral that consecrates the gravestone. A *shiva minyan* is a seven-day mourning worship service that takes place in the home. *Mitzvah* refers to a religious obligation. The only rituals that must be performed by a rabbi are marriage and conversion.

11. Peter Rubenstein, "The Next Century," in *Tanu Rabbanan: Our Rabbis Taught*, ed. Joseph Glaser (New York: Central Conference of American Rabbis, 1990), 149–51.

Women in the Reconstructionist Rabbinate

Rebecca Alpert and Goldie Milgram

INTRODUCTION

Unlike other branches of American Judaism, Reconstructionism originated in the philosophy of one individual, Mordecai Kaplan (1881–1982). Kaplan was a principal architect of women's equality in Judaism in the United States. While the philosophy of the movement based on his teachings has undergone significant changes over the past several decades, the equality of women remains a central tenet and hallmark of the newest movement in Judaism. This chapter will first present the philosophical and historical framework of Reconstructionism which created the opportunity for women's equality in the rabbinate. Next will follow a discussion of the findings of interviews with approximately half of the women rabbis who graduated from the Reconstructionist Rabbinical College from 1974 to 1991 regarding the nature of their rabbinate and their distinctive concerns and commitments as women rabbis. Significant changes in the nature of the training and socio-historical circumstances facing the next generation of women Reconstructionist rabbinical students will then be assessed.

KAPLANIAN INFLUENCES

Kaplan's Philosophy of Women's Equality in Judaism

The concepts and teachings of Mordecai Kaplan form the basis for understanding Reconstructionism's pioneering role in admitting women into the rabbinate. Kaplan's commitment to the equality of women was an essential part of his life and thought. Kaplan's upbringing was Orthodox, and as a young man he served a traditional congregation as their rabbi. He left this position in 1922 in part because of the membership's insistence on retaining the traditional practice of separate seating for women and men, and its refusal to set up a women's organization in the synagogue.[1] When Kaplan founded the Society for the Advancement of Judaism in New York the same year, he demanded mixed seating at services and achieved his goal despite significant protest. The following fall, Kaplan orchestrated the now-famous "first *bat mitzvah*," during which his eldest daughter, Judith, pronounced the blessings and read from the Torah at Sabbath morning services. Up until that event, there had been no puberty ceremony for girls comparable to the boys' *bar mitzvah*.[2]

Kaplan sermonized frequently in the 1920s in support of women's political participation, using biblical texts to prove his point. In 1936 Kaplan's blueprint for women's equality in Judaism, including ordination, was published in *The Reconstructionist Papers*. Perhaps his most insightful comment in this essay was that equality could only come about through women's "own efforts and initiative. Whatever liberal-minded men do in her behalf is bound to remain but a futile and meaningless gesture. The Jewish woman must demand the equality due her as a right to which she is fully entitled."[3]

In addition to Kaplan's commitment to the equality of women in Judaism, several other elements of his philosophy play a significant role in the way Reconstructionism approaches women's equality and other feminist principles and innovations.

Religious Naturalism

Reconstructionism is distinguished from other branches of Judaism by its base in Kaplan's theology. Influenced by the popular religious naturalism of his time, Kaplan did not accept the concept of God as person, but understood God as the power in the universe that makes for righteousness and salvation. Kaplan understood God as a process inherent in nature and humanity that can be accessed to bring about good in the world. Kaplan's God is not an actor, controlling history, but rather can be perceived in the world through the best endeavors of human beings, acting *b'tselem elohim*, in the image of God. Although Kaplan never removed anthropomorphic God language from the traditional prayers, his concept at least philosophically renders God gender-neutral.

Living in Two Civilizations

Kaplan believed that to function effectively, American Jews need to live in what he called two civilizations, the Jewish and the American. He was convinced that Jewish life would flourish if immigrant Jews understood that they did not have to give up their heritage and traditions to consider themselves fully American. In this regard Kaplan became an early proponent of cultural pluralism. He was able to look back on Jewish history and see the continuous interpenetration of the ideas and norms of the larger civilizations in which Jews dwelled and the accommodations which Judaism made to these realities. He taught that Judaism is a continuously evolving civilization, not a static, immutable religious system. It was this understanding that allowed Kaplan to make innovations in women's roles, and to embrace philosophies, like democracy, that had not previously been dominant in the Jewish experience. This worldview has been translated to an openness to such contemporary issues as feminism and environmentalism among Kaplan's next generation of followers.

Jewish Law

Kaplan understood *halakhah* (usually translated as Jewish law) as a component of the nonbinding but sacred inherited traditions of the Jewish people. Kaplan was observant of traditional ritual practices, but he also held Jewish law accountable to contemporary ethical standards. It was on this basis that Kaplan had no problem calling for the full equality of women, despite the clear problems with this in the traditional *halakhah* and norms of Jewish practice at that time. He also vigorously supported creative approaches to ritual. Because of Kaplan's affinity for Jewish tradition, however, the changes he made in his own congregation and recommended in his writings were much less radical than those of the Reform Jewish thinkers of his era, who usually dismissed halakhic considerations. Even so, his attitude eventually proved too flexible even for the denomination which would come to be called "Conservative," into which he had moved after his early years in Orthodoxy.

Not the Chosen People

By far the most significant element in Kaplan's thought that would turn out to be consistent with general feminist principles was his passionate opposition to hierarchy. This was most boldly expressed in his decision to remove the chosen people doctrine from Jewish liturgy. Kaplan maintained that such a claim to divine election was inseparable from a claim to superiority. He advocated the recognition that all peoples have unique and important destinies, which inherently invalidates the idea of one particular chosen people.

Kaplan's opposition to hierarchy was also manifested in his removal of the traditional distinctions of class within the Jewish people.

These distinctions comprise the categories of "Cohen," "Levi," and "Israel" which were carried over from the time when the Temple stood in Jerusalem. Representing categories of Temple service among the people, these class referents were passed on to males through their fathers. When called to witness the Torah reading, men would receive this honor in the hierarchical order of Cohen, Levi, Israel. The maintenance of this tradition was originally intended to hold in place these class identities for the future, when the sacrificial system would be restored in a rebuilt "Temple on the Mount" in Jerusalem. Within Orthodoxy and Hasidism the doctrine of the restoration of the Temple system is taken seriously. By Kaplan's time, within the more liberal movements these distinctions had become folk custom. Kaplan's elimination of the maintenance of this class system, coupled with his religious naturalism, also led away from one of the traditional forms of Jewish messianism, the expectation of the restoration of Jewish hegemony in Israel under the leadership of a divinely approved male descendent of the House of David, including the restoration of the sacrificial system. In its place the vision of a nonhierarchical messianic time of peaceful human coexistence brought about by ethical human labor took hold in Reconstructionist philosophy.

The Need for a Separate Movement to Achieve the Kaplanian Ideals

In fact, Kaplan opposed the idea of creating a separate movement in Jewish life based on his philosophy. His goal was to create a unified American Judaism without denominational factionalism. Yet it became clear to his followers that if Kaplan's visions were to be realized, a separate movement was needed. The debate over becoming a movement lasted for several decades, during which time more and more small groups around the United States and Canada began to develop and label themselves Reconstructionists, after the title of Kaplan's influential journal, *The Reconstructionist*. The decisive move to upgrade to the status of a formal denomination was made in 1967 when a convention of Reconstructionists took the bold step of deciding to open a college for training rabbis in Philadelphia.

WOMEN'S ACCESS TO LEADERSHIP IN THE MOVEMENT

Any analysis of women rabbis' access to power within Reconstructionism as a movement requires a view which includes its three major structures: the Reconstructionist Rabbinical College (RRC), the Federation of Reconstructionist Congregations and Havurot,[4] and the Reconstructionist Rabbinical Association. Without exception every graduate interviewed felt they had full access to opportunities to lead and serve the denomination in the manner of their choosing. With one exception, all had served in some movement-related capacity—giving courses or seminars at the college, mentoring students, as a Rabbinical Association committee member or chairperson, on search committees, or in fund-raising capacities.

The Reconstructionist Rabbinical College

Decision to Ordain Women   The question of the ordination of women to the rabbinate certainly was in the public consciousness at the time the Reconstructionist Rabbinical College was founded in 1968. The women's liberation movement was compelling people to ask questions about women's equality that had not seriously been considered previously. Although none was yet ordained, several women candidates were then studying at the Reform movement's Hebrew Union College. Despite the open discussion of this issue, the disappointing fact is that the founders of the Reconstructionist Rabbinical College decided not to create added controversy by seeking out women for its first class.

In its second year, when the founders advertised for students they received one inquiry from a woman. Sandy Eisenberg (Sasso) was accepted without debate or subsequent controversy.[5] For the next several years, only a few women applied, and all were accepted. The class that entered in 1974, the year of Sandy Sasso's graduation, was half women, and that trend has continued ever since.[6]

Several of the graduates remember instructors who were opposed to women entering the rabbinate. One Talmud instructor was notorious for being unwilling to instruct women he did not assess to be sufficiently serious students, though he made no such distinction about the men. Several recalled an episode of resistance to a rabbinic text instructor who would place his *yarmulke*[7] on the head of a bare-headed man who was about to read from the Talmud, but who did not do so when bare-headed women would read. On one occasion a male student protested the inequity after reading by then placing the professor's *yarmulke* onto the bare head of the woman beside him who was to read next. In the early years there were also professors who were unwilling to sign the ordination certificates of the women students.

New problems surfaced in the 1980s when more women were pressing for changes, especially in the area of liturgical expression. Feminist concerns about theological gender language were trivialized by some faculty members. Some of the graduates who defined themselves as radical feminists described encounters with the faculty which they term "persecution." One was brought up for possible dismissal based on reports of her explorations into goddesses. Another recalled being publicly chastised at school for wearing a T-shirt with a women's religion message. By the 1990s it became apparent that experimentation with women's religions, just as earlier graduates had with Eastern religions, in combination with Jewish traditions could yield powerful new Jewish forms of spiritual practice.

Lesbian Rabbis In 1987, in an article on women in the rabbinate, Anne Lapidus Lerner credited the Reconstructionst movement with being the "first to champion egalitarianism as an underlying principle." The main issue for Reconstructionism, she asserted, was that the movement also "openly espoused non-heterosexuality" and would have to come to terms with the presence of lesbians in the rabbinate.[8] In 1978 the faculty of the RRC unanimously voted not to admit gay or lesbian applicants. However, when a vote was taken again in 1984, a substantially reconfigured faculty voted overwhelmingly to reverse the original decision, although not to publicize the new policy aggressively. In the past decade, the presence of one or two lesbians who openly declared their sexual orientation met with open hostility from other women rabbis. They feared that the presence of these women would ultimately raise questions about the sexual orientation of all Reconstructionist women in the rabbinate and would be a detrimental influence on the ability of Reconstructionist rabbis to obtain positions and be accepted by the mainstream.

Due to the courage of the lesbian women and their allies, and the insightful leadership of the past president of the Reconstructionist Rabbinical College, Ira Silverman, and faculty member Rabbi Herschel Matt (may their memories be for a blessing), lesbian rabbis have become an accepted part of the Reconstructionist rabbinate. Of the six open lesbians, two currently hold positions in Reconstructionist settings and a third is the rabbi of the largest American gay and lesbian congregation, located in New York City. The lesbians who are currently closeted in more mainstream positions do not believe that they can maintain their current positions and be open about being lesbian.

It was lesbian rabbis who reported the greatest feelings of censure. Issues over lesbian rabbis ranged from whether RRC could politically "afford" to have more than one lesbian faculty member to the resignation of a lesbian rabbi from her congregation when the issue became divisive. At the time of this writing, Reconstructionism is engaged in an educational process to facilitate inclusiveness and sensitivity to gay and lesbian rabbis and congregants.

Pedagogical Innovations   The founders of the Reconstructionist Rabbinical College took pride not only in admitting women but in providing radical innovations in rabbinic education. The initial norms decided upon for instruction at RRC presaged current feminist approaches. Classes were held in small groups. No grades were given, and an atmosphere of cooperation rather than competition was fostered among the students. Students were encouraged to work together on projects and assignments; traditional examinations were rare. The program is still largely non-competitive.

Women's Studies   In its early years, occasional courses were taught about women in Judaism and women's issues were raised in some courses at RRC. In 1990 a course in Jewish Feminist Theology developed by Rabbi Linda Holtzman and Dr. Tikva Frymer-Kensky[9] was offered as one of RRC's intensive summer courses and drew many participants. Despite its success, the course has yet to become part of the regular curriculum.

The rabbis in this study were more often busy with adjusting to rabbinical school and the attention focused upon them as "first women rabbis" than questioning the curriculum. Most acknowledged a near total absence of women's studies in their training, noting, however, that they "didn't really know what questions to ask."

The next generation in the RRC is comprised of men and women who went through college during the establishment of women's studies as an accepted discipline. These students are requiring the rabbinical college to adopt the secular world's acceptance of women's studies as normative. A joint student-faculty initiative launched in 1988 has developed a process for curricular and programmatic modifications at the Reconstructionist Rabbinical College. Intended primarily to redress the relative absence of women's studies in rabbinical training, the Jewish Women's Studies Project (JWSP) is a carefully managed process of institutional change. Founding student chairperson Rabbi Gail (later Goldie) Milgram organized a student-faculty task force to press for curricular reform. A proposal for planned change was adopted by the full faculty and the Reconstructionist Student Association within the year.

Four years later, in 1993, the Reconstructionist Rabbinical College had in place two women's studies student internships, an annual lecture in women's studies, an award for excellence in Jewish women's studies, extensive library and liturgical collection development efforts in women's studies, and a national juried art exhibition to encourage images of Jewish women in spiritual leadership. In addition, faculty in-service training is provided to teach cutting-edge developments in the fields of women's studies and feminist hermeneutics. Exploration of new models for Jewish feminist prayer-leading, music, and liturgy is a vital aspect of the project. In addition to advocating for the inclusion of women's history and works throughout the core curriculum, the project offers and funds elective courses in women's studies.

Women's Access to Academic and Administrative Leadership To date, no woman has served as president or dean at the Reconstructionist Rabbinical College, while middle-level administrative posts have been held by women, many of whom are RRC graduates. That there have yet to be women at the highest levels of administration has been attributed by several graduates to a "subtle and complex sexism that is not at all on a conscious level."

The first full-time woman professor was Dr. Shulamit Magnus, who was hired in 1978. There have been at least one and as many as three women on the full-time faculty since that time. The chairman of the board of the college has always been a male, although there are a few women board members. The Reconstructionist Student Association leadership has shown no evidence of gender barriers at any level, although the presidency of the association has most often been held by male students.

The Reconstructionist Rabbinical Association

New Models for Rabbis Based on Kaplan's passion for democracy and antipathy toward hierarchy, Reconstructionism encourages new and diverse models for the rabbinate. The Reconstructionist rabbi is not prepared to be the distant "father figure" or authoritarian leader. Reconstructionist rabbis are trained to see themselves as facilitators in Jewish life. The congregational rabbinate is not stressed as the only option. Reconstructionist rabbis are encouraged to serve the Jewish community in many ways: on college campuses as professors and as staff for Jewish campus organizations; as chaplains in long-term care, military, psychiatric, and hospice settings; as leaders of communal service organizations, through educational positions in day schools and afternoon religious schools; and in the performing arts. The Reconstructionist rabbi is still "the teacher" but one who understands the importance of learning from and listening to students. The goal is to promote the growth of others as knowledgeable Jews, to empower them to engage fully in Jewish life, able to bring the strengths of their secular world into creative and productive encounter with Judaism.

For those early graduates who chose synagogue work, it was likely that their congregation comprised a small group of Jews committed to Kaplan's egalitarian principles and eager to participate in the ritual decision-making. Reconstructionist groups had existed for many years without rabbis; congregants expected that the young RRC graduates would be their partners in Jewish life brought on board for their knowledge base and not to serve as authorities. The rabbis' relational skills and knowledge base for teaching, pastoral counseling, and community organizing were most emphasized.

Women rabbis reported that they were often praised for being "more approachable and sensitive," a perception which congregants would attribute to the rabbis' gender. However, Reconstructionists generally consider their rabbis to be more informal and approachable regardless of gender. The women are conscious of their desire not to step into the male rabbinic model they had been exposed to in their childhood. They are interested in networks and do not want to be alone at the top of a hierarchy. They favor listening and discussing over lecturing and homilies.

A number of the rabbis experienced their attempts at maintaining democratic, participatory processes in the congregation as a struggle. Several mentioned a desire for greater rabbinic authority, particularly in the area of ritual. Rabbi Barbara Penzner notes that "It's important for the rabbi to have a position and people to be aware of it." Rabbi Susan Shifron agrees that people expect rabbis to exercise authority and power, but she emphasizes that "women rabbis need to work at new ways to do this because empowering those around us is critical."

Rabbi Rebecca Alpert conjectures that part of the initial resistance to women in the rabbinate was the challenge to the notion that the rabbi is a symbolic representation of God. Rabbi Joan Pitzele Sacks notes that in her chaplaincy work, older clients sometimes have initial difficulty with accepting her as a rabbi. Not only does this concern abate after a short time, but from the older women she hears "about what it was like not being able to study Hebrew, how painful and difficult their status often was." And so it is that the identification of the rabbi with the feminine has often proven to be an asset. In the words of Rabbi Marcia Prager: "Just by virtue of being a woman rabbi I represent a paradigm shift. When I speak about the feminine aspect of the Divine I'm actualizing that in my very being; it's as if my presence becomes a manifestation of the presence of that very teaching." As women take on higher profiles in Jewish spiritual matters, an influence can be detected in the contemporary Jewish understanding of the divine. For example, increasingly the term *shechinah*, a rabbinic expression for God's immanence that mystical Judaism associated with God's feminine dimension, is achieving currency in song and prayer.

Feminism   All of the rabbis interviewed who commented on the subject understood the importance of the feminist movement in Judaism and saw women in the rabbinate as a result of feminist changes in the secular culture. By "feminist," most of our interviewees meant giving women full opportunities for self-expression and full human rights. Others went further and saw themselves as activists for feminist causes. Rabbi Sharon Stiefel was able to set up a Jewish Feminist Collaborative at the University of Pennsylvania Hillel. Rabbi Gail Diamond has done significant work on domestic violence issues. Many voiced concern about and work actively on women's issues that are not exclusively related to Jewish interests—reproductive choice, violence against women, electoral issues, and issues of lesbian rights. These rabbis understand feminist philosophy not merely as equal rights but as a way of understanding justice and communications among people.

Some saw political commitments to feminism as alien. These rabbis "do not view feminist as a defining characteristic of self or work" and find the "single issue focus" of feminists problematic. They resist making feminism the litmus test for Jewish values and want to define their rabbinates in other ways. One disliked what she perceives to be the individual rights focus of liberal feminism and viewed herself as more focused on community as a concern.

The rabbis in this study are serving an older generation of Jews that is one of the most traumatized in Jewish history, having lived during the Holocaust, while at the same time, the younger generations they serve are among the most assimilated in Jewish history. For most of these rabbis, feminism is an important strand in their rabbinate, but one that is closely interwoven with other concerns.

Current rabbinical students have had greater exposure to feminist theory during their rabbinical training. Taught by concerned members of the first generation of rabbis such as Linda Holtzman, Rebecca Alpert, Nancy Fuchs-Kreimer, Jacob Staub, and Leila Berner, they are exploring the prospects for an intentional integration of feminist and Reconstructionist hermeneutics in regard to prayer, text, and social action.

Professional Association   The Reconstructionist Rabbinical Association is the rabbis' professional association. The board is elected by the membership. Gender was not seen as a barrier to participation by any of our interviewees, and women have served at all levels of office. Two women have served in the capacity of president of the Reconstructionist Rabbinical Association, Rabbis Sandy Sasso and Joy Levitt. The professional positions of executive director and placement director have been held exclusively by male rabbis. Firm policies have been established prohibiting discriminatory hiring practices based on race, gender, family status, or sexual orientation. Contract recommendations include substantial paid maternity and paternity leave. A rabbi serves as the part-time professional staff person for the association; however, all such staff, to date, have been male.

It is interesting to note that of its many issue-focused task forces, there is not a Reconstructionist rabbinical task force on women in Judaism. Despite its large female membership, the first formal RRA recognition that women in the rabbinate might have particular needs and issues took place at a one-day session, "Issues Facing Women in the Rabbinate," added onto its 1992 annual convention at the instigation of the Jewish Women's Studies Project. Focus group discussion led conference organizers to select a panel to discuss how gender socialization impacts on the style and effectiveness of women rabbis. Concurrent workshops then explored such issues as "Rabbis and Their Families," "New Liturgy and Rituals," and "Gender and Power."

At the conference mentioned above and throughout the interviews, discomfort with occasional congregant trespassing of physical and gender-related boundaries was mentioned. Many received comments at *bar/bat mitzvah* receptions or weddings such as "I've never danced with a rabbi before." Most women rabbis reported the experiences of being told "I've never touched/hugged/kissed, etc., a rabbi before" by a stranger who proceeded to do exactly that. Often these gestures were prompted by well-meaning impulses. Nevertheless, these rabbis experienced such comments and actions as subtle forms of gender harassment. Such comments imply the objectification of the women involved and allow the speakers to engage in touching which may not have been desired by the rabbis. After a while, for some rabbis, such experiences have a cumulatively stressful effect. Discussion at the convention included the sharing of coping strategies for such situations in ways which would not undercut the important pastoral rapport between rabbi and congregant.

Job and hiring discrimination based on gender came up as an issue when graduates sought positions outside the movement. Several early graduates reported losing positions in Jewish communal educational institutions when they refused to go by "Ms." rather than the title "rabbi." Some were not admitted to local boards of rabbis, where acceptance is usually automatic upon rabbinic ordination. Two women who do campus work within the Hillel Foundation reported struggling with the issue of using the rabbinic title because of the deleterious effect this had on their ability to be effective with Orthodox students, who would not accept a woman as a rabbi. Comments such as that reported by Rabbi Sandy Sasso, who was told that she was "destroying Judaism" and that "when she grew up and had children she would change her mind about being a rabbi," were not infrequent experiences of early graduates. Rabbi Linda Holtzman talked about congregants who assumed that she would be unable to deal with men's problems and some who refused to have her do their funerals. Rabbi Goldie Milgram, one of the movement's most recent graduates, described a scene at a hospice, where she met an elderly parent dying of cancer. The ninety-three-year-old man hoisted himself up on his elbow and announced: "I'd rather be dead than buried by a woman rabbi!" "Pa," his daughter whispered, "I'm afraid you're going to get your wish." Most interviewees agreed with Rabbi Vivian E. Schirn, who reported a decreasing incidence of being the first woman rabbi that anyone had met, or of experiencing significant resistance to her status or overt discrimination.

Federation of Reconstructionist Congregations and Havurot (FRCH)

Many of the women with congregational assignments serve FRCH congregations. These congregations understand the equality of women as a central tenet of Reconstructionist philosophy and have been comfortable places for women rabbis to serve and introduce feminist innovations. This has not uniformly been the case for the acceptance of lesbian rabbis, which has been a slow educational process. The FRCH leadership has always included a higher percentage of women, and several women have served as presidents of FRCH. The professional directors of FRCH have always been men, although Rabbi Joy Levitt served for several years as editor of the *Reconstructionist* magazine, which FRCH publishes.

WOMEN RABBIS RECLAIM TRADITION

The traditional dictum "kol isha erva," "a woman's voice leads to sexual enticement," describes the background against which the efforts to define a public role for Jewish women has to be created. Reconstructionist women rabbis have been instrumental in the creation of rituals, stories, music, and theologies that have begun to give women's experience a voice in Judaism. In the words of Rabbi Sandy Sasso: "What makes a difference is not just counting women in the *minyan* [quorum necessary for prayer], but counting women's perceptions as a valid way of looking at the world."[10]

Ritual

Most women in the Reconstructionist rabbinate have been involved either in creating, interpreting, or using new feminist rituals. Most of the focus has been upon life-cycle events, the area that Jewish ritual has needed the most work with regard to the equality of women.

Judaism has always celebrated the birth of sons with the covenantal ceremony of circumcision; no parallel ceremony existed for daughters. Rabbi Sandy Sasso set a powerful example in 1975 with one of the first new ceremonies for naming baby girls. Other early ceremonies were developed by Rabbis Linda Holtzman, Nancy Fuchs-Kreimer, and Rebecca Alpert. Most of the rabbis interviewed mentioned baby namings as an expected part of their rabbinate. The routinizing of the ritual has led to its legitimacy. Many, like Rabbi Sandra Berliner, mentioned that they attempt to bring equality to life-cycle rituals, such as weddings. Reconstructionist women rabbis have tried such innovations as creating egalitarian *ketubot* (marriage contracts); removing the betrothal blessings, which stigmatize same-sex couples, those who are single, and those who cannot conceive; and such actions as having both partners break the glass at the end of the ceremony.[11]

There has been a lot of creative work in inventing new rituals for women's life-cycle events. Rabbi Sasso has been an early innovator in writing prayers for women's transitions, such as weaning and miscarriage, and a healing ritual for women recovering from abuse. Rabbis Barbara Penzner and Amy Zweiback Levenson published premarital *mikveh* ceremonies.[12] Rabbi Jane Litman has developed birthing rituals. Most of the respondents saw the use of these and other feminist rituals, like women's Passover *seders*, as crucial to their rabbinate. Many were also involved in organizing *Rosh Chodesh* women's groups (celebrations of the New Moon), which often function as consciousness-raising groups in synagogues.

An important impetus to new ritual development is given by Rabbi Linda Holtzman, who teaches the life-cycle ceremonies courses at the RRC. She encourages students to pioneer and explore the potential of feminist, gender-sensitive rituals such as commitment ceremonies for gays and lesbians, menopause and menarche ritual celebrations, new blessings for contemporary issues such as the first time one ceases using contraception in order to allow for conception, and egalitarian divorce rituals and documents.

Women Rabbis and Jewish Texts

We are at the advent of a generation of North American Jews who will not remember a time when there were not women rabbis. Almost everyone interviewed experienced as a responsibility of their generation not only to have broken through the barriers to women in the rabbinate but to begin the process of adding women's voices to the recorded tradition.

Rage at the sometimes heinously oppressive messages in Jewish texts toward women certainly exists. In 1988 the first program of the Jewish Women's Studies Project at RRC was the creation of the Scroll of Ire. Students pasted photocopies of texts that provoked their anger and rage during their studies onto a huge blank canvas scroll and in the margins inscribed their opinions of these texts. However one may inveigh against one's ancestry, family is still family. Alongside their rage, these women rabbis have voted with the dedication of their lives to repair their inheritance which had too long been deprived of their vital participation.

Jewish tradition provides many channels for the continuing creation of sacred text. The primary methods undertaken by this first generation of women rabbis were as follows.

Interpretation   *Midrash* is a technique whereby one's religious imagination engages with a particular line, character, word, or story in the text and a tale evolves which unleashes new potential inherent in the text. Reconstructionists often see themselves as partners in creation with God, and this task of unmasking the power of the text to speak to each generation is experienced as a *mitzvah*, a holy task. In publications and sermons women rabbis are increasingly using *midrash* as a way to uncover and add the experience of women to the tradition. Many mentioned that they frequently include such *midrashim*, written by themselves or other Jewish feminists, to help amplify the voices of their female ancestors. Rabbi Sheila Weinberg described the telling of such stories as a spiritual act. She pointed out that "women have been accused of telling old wives tales. The truth of our stories has not been included." Rabbi Linda Holtzman noted that "It is through *midrash* that we touch and rebuild the text."

Archiving and Documentation   Women rabbis expressed their commitment to preserve the lives of Jewish women of the past. New research techniques for uncovering the lives of Jewish women across history are being taught at RRC. Archives exist for preserving documentation of the evolving Jewish women's movement.

Liturgical Innovation   Some of the women in the Reconstructionist rabbinate have written and spoken eloquently in favor of changes in the liturgy to promote not only inclusive language, to which the Reconstructionist movement as a whole is committed in their new prayer books, but changes that include referring to God as "he" and "she" when using anthropomorphic language in reference to God. Rabbi Sandy Sasso has also written on the value of using female God language and sees the theological issue as paramount. "Male God language," she pointed out, "legitimates a society which values male dominance." Rabbi Reena Spicehandler, who serves on the Reconstructionist Prayerbook Commission, noted that through such vehicles as the denomination's new series of prayer books, the liturgical contributions of women are entering into Jewish practice and history. The strategic importance of this was poignantly expressed by Sandy Sasso: "Jewish feminism makes its greatest contribution when women's stories and prayers become tradition, when they find their way between the hard bound covers of a book that is kissed when it falls."[13]

Women rabbis are also making important contributions in the field of Jewish music. Numerous performance artists are currently rabbinical students, and Rabbi Leila Berner is the first of the graduates studied to release a tape of feminist Jewish prayers set to music. Under the leadership of a student rabbi, Cantor Elizabeth Bolton, a choir has been set up at the RRC dedicated to performing the musical works of women rabbis and rabbinical students.

Halakhah   Rabbi Mordecai Kaplan's understanding of the nonbinding nature of Jewish law is one area in which Reconstructionist women rabbis particularly feel the confluence of Reconstructionist and feminist thought. Rabbi Nancy Fuchs-Kreimer assumes her nonhalakhic perceptive to be related to gender as "the world of observant Jews is closed to me [as a woman rabbi]." She sees *halakhah* as a " 'male game' that some women do seem to enjoy, nonetheless." Several rabbis mentioned their inability to imagine being governed by laws written by men and about men. Some expressed their interest in pursuing the question "What would a woman's Talmud[14] look like?" Others feel halakhic approaches are useful in some cases, citing funeral practices in particular.

A number of rabbis expressed the confusion of a nonhalakhic approach and would like to see some community norms more strongly articulated in ritual and ethical issues. The current rabbinical students may also prove to be heavily influenced by a new curricular emphasis on enhancing competence with rabbinic texts. Recent graduates now see themselves as actively engaging in a dialogue with the Talmud and other traditional texts.

Homiletics and Social Action   Reconstructionist women rabbis have also found their voice through raising consciousness in their congregations and schools about issues related to women's lives. Some have focused on secular issues like domestic violence or reproductive rights as these affect the Jewish community. Others have devoted energy to helping Orthodox women gain the right of divorce in Israel in traditional communities. Many have spoken out for the right of Jewish women to pray aloud and read from the Torah when at the Western Wall in Israel. Most said it is common for them to discuss or preach on women's issues, but for only a few has this become the focus of their rabbinate. The majority of women in this study do not wish to be focused on women's issues alone. They became rabbis because of their love of Jewish texts and the Jewish people and see their interest in women's issues as only one dimension of being a rabbi. Issues also of great concern that were mentioned include Jewish identity, Jewish-Christian dialogue, addictions, and Israel. They may approach these issues in certain ways because they are women but do not see gender as central to the questions themselves. Some wish to be known primarily for making a contribution to the changed role of women in Judaism, but most wish to be known for their abilities and commitments as rabbis in Israel.

THE RABBINATE AS A WOMAN'S CAREER CHOICE

By far the most difficult problem facing women in the Reconstructionist rabbinate today is finding a balance between their professional and personal commitments. The most poignant comments in our interviews were about this subject. As Rabbi Bonnie Koppel said, "My personal and professional lives are enemies." Yet others found the rabbinate congenial because "motherhood is expected of Jewish women and the community actively accommodates." What for some is a positive synthesis of their professional and private lives is for others an experience of living without healthy limits and boundaries. Most experience the dilemmas common among women who have taken on professional commitment while at the same time attempting to raise children, run a household, care for elderly relatives, or have a meaningful life outside of work. The problems of balancing career and home life are particularly acute in a calling such as the rabbinate, which is still defined and experienced as much to be a personal commitment as it is a professional commitment.

The rabbis we talked to have made a wide variety of professional and personal choices. Approximately one-third of the women graduates have worked predominantly in synagogues as the rabbi, compared to half of the men. The question arises as to whether there is some underlying gender distinction here. Are women less interested in the pulpit? Keeping in mind that most of these rabbis are premenopausal, have they avoided pulpit responsibilities because these demand the kind of hours that are not consonant with the care of children? (The deepest satisfaction was expressed by those women who had their families before entering rabbinical school.) Were they rejected by congregations in favor of their male counterparts? Most pulpit positions available to Reconstructionist rabbis are in small congregations with one rabbi. Two rabbinic couples have for a long period of time shared pulpit responsibilities. Other women rabbis have juggled their lives by working part-time. This option usually requires the support of a partner working full-time. Rabbi Ilene Schneider commented on this phenomenon: "It bothers me that women have the 'leisure' to quit the work force for a few years without anyone questioning the gaps in their resumes, while men cannot do the same."

Those in other rabbinic careers experienced many of the problems reported by the pulpit rabbis and others. Those who worked as educators often felt treated as though they are not "real Rabbis," despite Reconstructionist efforts at broadening rabbinic career options. As Rabbi Andrea Gouze suggested, being an educator sometimes feels like a "betrayal of the feminist struggle." Yet those in education know the importance of what they do, and understand the implicit sexism of the idea that somehow educators are less important because they work in traditional female roles. Those in Hillel and in educational administration are most aware of the glass-ceiling phenomenon as pertaining to them. Chaplains reported the most consistent job satisfaction. Women rabbis have yet to attain major leadership positions in national Jewish organizations that work on political, social, and cultural issues of concern to Jews.

Even Rabbi Mordecai Kaplan's forward-looking philosophy did not encompass an analysis of the family that would be helpful to this generation of women. The majority of Reconstructionist women rabbis are in heterosexual marriages and have children. There are several single parents and lesbian couples with children, as well. Some of the rabbis who work part-time or temporarily left active rabbinical work to care for their children have been criticized by supporters of the Reconstructionist movement for taking up spaces in rabbinical training programs that might have gone to those willing to make a full-time commitment to their rabbinical careers.

For those who have remained single or childless, their choices have been complicated by pressure from the Jewish community to follow the Genesis 9:5 injunction to be "fruitful and multiply." Although the technical commandment to continue the survival of the Jewish people is addressed to men, women in the rabbinate feel the responsibility as heavily incumbent upon them. While accepting their choices or lack of them in some cases, most have internalized the sense that to be complete as Jewish women they must have children. There is little support for the idea that they are in fact building up the Jewish people through their contributions as teachers of children rather than necessarily as biological parents.

In the sample were several rabbis who have chosen to work outside the Jewish community, primarily for personal reasons. Some lost prior rabbinic positions as a result of coming out openly as lesbians. Others have gone on to different areas of interest—career counseling, carpentry, and veterinary medicine. Several are unemployed due to the soft job market or by choice to engage in intensive early childhood parenting.

CONCLUSIONS

For the past two decades, women have been an integral part of the Reconstructionist rabbinate. They have given articulate voice to their concerns as Jewish women and feminists. The ease with which they have been accepted in the Reconstructionist movement obscures tensions which do exist for them. They face the same dilemmas of balancing work and family as other professional women in the United States, and often are forced to make difficult choices between their personal lives and careers. Lesbian rabbis have yet to achieve full acceptance. Awareness of the need for feminist liturgical innovations and the value of Jewish women's studies have yet to be integrated into the movement at large. Efforts at collective solutions to these problems would enhance the prospects of finding solutions. What is obvious to those with experience as Reconstructionist rabbis is that the Reconstructionist movement will accept the challenge to face and solve many of these problems, as the integration of feminism and Judaism continues into the twenty-first century.

NOTES

1. These events are recorded in Kaplan's unpublished diaries, 1922, *passim*, Mordecai Kaplan Library of the Reconstructionist Rabbinical College, Wyncote, Pennsylvania.
2. Since the Middle Ages, *bar mitzvah* has been the ritual marking a thirteen-year-old boy's entrance into adult religious ritual responsibilities, expressed by his assuming for the first time the honor (called an *aliyah*) of blessing and/or reading from the Torah at services. Puberty rites for girls existed in some eras in Europe. Kaplan himself saw one in Rome, Italy, and remarked about it in his diary (August, 1922). But these ceremonies were unheard of in the United States. Because Reform Judaism had also done away with *bar mitzvah* in this period, such an innovation would not have taken place in that context. Since *bar* and *bat mitzvah* are no longer biologically concomitant with puberty or adult status in society, these have rather become ritual passages related to the level of Jewish education attained and to those Jewish responsibilities and privileges to which the youngster will have access. Onset of menstruation rituals for girls have been developed and are attaining some currency in the Jewish community. Examples of these and other new rituals are available in the Jewish Women's Studies Resource File at the library of the Reconstructionist Rabbinical College.
3. Mordecai Kaplan, "The Status of the Jewish Woman," in *The Jewish Reconstructionist Papers* (New York: Behrman House, 1936), 129.
4. *Havurot* are often a precongregational phase of group development, where common interests have led to the regular gathering of a small group, most commonly for worship and/or study. A full-time rabbi, ownership of a synagogue building, and a religious school are unlikely to be associated with a *havurah*. However, in a few cases, larger full-service congregations, seeking to promote greater closeness among congregants, have developed internal interest groups that are similar to and often called *havurot*.
5. Sasso comments: "My first day at the Reconstructionist Rabbinical College one member of the staff called me into his office. What could I possibly

have done? I hadn't even gone to my first class! I entered the office. He looked at me for a moment and said, 'You look like a normal American girl!' " (private communication, 1992). Apart from that comment, and the absence of other women until her third year, Sasso found the RRC to be a "safe haven" for women, particularly when compared to the Jewish community at large.

6. Because the Reconstructionist Rabbinical College is small, proportions of women have varied. Some years the students have been all male. Other years they have been predominantly female. Of the 130 current RRC graduates, 50 are women.

7. *Yarmulke*, referring to a skullcap type of head covering, derives from the hebrew *yarei m'Eloka*, "one who fears God." Worn by Orthodox Jewish men at all times except while bathing, it signifies one's active commitment as an observant Jew. While many Reconstructionists, male and female, choose to wear them, it is considered an elective practice and does vary by individual preference.

8. Anne Lapidus Lerner, "Judaism and Feminism: The Unfinished Agenda," *Judaism* 36 (1987): 170.

9. The first, and to date only, tenured woman professor at the RRC.

10. Sandy Sasso, "Women in the Rabbinate: A Personal Reflection," *Reconstructionist* (March 1984), 19.

11. This ancient Jewish custom has many explanations, the standard being the commemoration of the destruction of the Temple in Jerusalem by the Romans in the year 70.

12. Traditional women use the *mikveh*, a ritual bath facility, prior to the wedding night, at the end of their monthly menstrual periods. It is also used during the ceremony of conversion to Judaism by men and women. The premarital ceremonies written by these rabbis proved helpful to those liberal Jewish women seeking to endow the practice with an accessible spiritual message, rather than that of ritual purity, with which it had been primarily associated.

13. It is common practice for Jews to kiss sacred texts such as the Bible, Talmud, or prayer book should they inadvertently fall to the ground.

14. The Talmud is the fifth-century compilation of Jewish legal and interpretive texts wherein a great deal of the *halakhah* and *midrash* can be found.

Faithful Daughters and Ultimate Rebels: The First Class of Conservative Jewish Women Rabbis

Sydell Ruth Schulman

INTRODUCTION

In 1984, amid conflict and apprehension, the faculty of the Conservative Judaism's Jewish Theological Seminary opened its gates to admit eighteen women for rabbinical training. Each of these chosen women could be described as the ultimate faithful Jewish daughter, loving the tradition, joyously participating to the extent women could, and longing for greater involvement and more intense learning. Yet many must also be described as dissenting rebels, claiming their inclusion within the central requirements of male status in Judaism—ritual, study, and law. They wanted to participate fully in public prayer, to take on the responsibility to perform the commandments, and to study religious legal texts. They chose to root themselves as fully obligated adults within the prescribed and historical rituals and laws, and to become rabbis.

These Conservative Jewish women struggled to reconstruct a more enabling vision of themselves, their traditions, and their possibilities for spiritual leadership. Yet even while striving to achieve basic changes in the interpretation of the religious law and its view of women, they pledged themselves and their life's work to observing and transmitting that system of law. Each entered the seminary committed to the religious law and its commandments, yet many knew themselves as outsiders who wrestled with a rigid tradition and a static revelation. This chapter is based on information gathered during intensive interviews with fifteen women, members of the first class of women admitted for rabbinical training in the Jewish Theological Seminary (JTS) in 1984.

To understand the personal and political tightrope walked by these women one needs a synopsis of the system of Jewish law, the *halakhah*, and a brief outline of the origins of Conservative Judaism in the United States.

HALAKHIC MODIFICATIONS AND INTERPRETATIONS

The shorthand definition of the word *halakhah* is usually given as the body of religious laws, but this is inadequate. The literal meaning is "the path," a total way of living that has defined, guarded, guided, and legislated what it means to live a Jewish life across thousands of years of history in every town where Jews have lived. Obeying the *halakhah* meant sanctifying and transforming every act of behavior, with the goal of bringing about the perfection of the world, the messianic age. For traditional Jews, the entire system of *halakhah* is divine revelation, the everlasting covenant with the Creator; therefore, the process by which any modification is considered becomes most critical in sustaining the entire system.

It is this legal code which has defined and perpetuated the role of women within the community, specifically excluding women's input in its content or its methodology for analyzing change. A masculine hegemony legislated women as not eligible to acquire the knowledge of texts which is a necessary requirement for credentialing. Although there are no written qualifications for determining who merits the status of legal interpreter or *posek*, an Orthodox scholar has explained: "Anyone can become an outstanding scholar, professor, or rabbi. But few can become a posek. . . . His decisions are . . . all filtered through his exquisitely trained mind and sensitive heart . . . the conviction and humbling knowledge that (his) decisions are an extension of Torah law and an expression of G-d's will."[1] Blu Greenberg, an Orthodox feminist scholar, notes, "what was a sociological truth about women in all previous generations—that they were the 'second sex'—was codified in many minute ways into *Halakhah* as religioethical concepts, binding upon future generations as well."[2]

Men and women are each obligated to fulfill specific commandments, many of which are sex delineated. Traditionally, women's obligations include lighting Sabbath candles at home, baking the Sabbath bread, and adhering to laws of sexual purity. These have reinforced a separate and powerful role for women, but one located entirely within the private and domestic sphere of the family. Women have no access to the public domain within Orthodoxy.

All traditional Jewish women were exempt from the central religious obligations concerning the relationship between the individual and the Creator: the requirements to study religious texts and the performance of time-bound rituals, including the three daily communal services with the recitation of creedal prayers. Time-bound commandments are those required to be performed at designated periods of the day, the year, and/or the life cycle in the attempt to entwine the secular and religious, the physical and spiritual aspects of life.

For a male child, the first time-bound commandment occurs when he is eight days old; his father, or male surrogate, performs the circumcision, initiating the male infant into the covenanted community at a public, hence male, service. Traditionally, at age thirteen each male becomes a *bar mitzvah*, fully obligated to live by the commandments. After this ceremony, males may be temporarily excused from performing time-bound commandments only under certain conditions: during the first week of mourning, or if too physically or mentally ill. Criminals may be excluded during the period of servitude. Always exempt, historically, are children under thirteen, slaves, and women. Male children would, of course, become juridical adults at age thirteen, slaves when freed. Only women could never participate fully in the public sphere, exempted by the tradition on the basis of biology. Today many girls from all branches of Judaism do have a *bat mitzvah* ceremony, but this liminal moment does not change their status within the Conservative or Orthodox traditions from exempted to that of obligated to perform the commandments. Reform and Reconstructionist Judaism do not view *halakhah* as binding, neither exempting nor obligating women or men.

Theoretically, the justification for disallowing women to serve as rabbis was based on the universal female exemption and the interpretation that only persons who are themselves obligated to observe the time-bound commandments can lead prayer services for equally obligated others. The public community, the congregation, has been tacitly understood as a male arena covenanted to God through maleness.

The seemingly natural and neutral moral imperative of the religious law exempts women from the public community of prayer and study—no matter what their level of commitment, scholarship, or marital status. Over the millennia, exemption has come to be interpreted as exclusion from the public domain, with women relegated to the category of religiously other than normative Jewish humanity.

THE DEVELOPMENT OF CONSERVATIVE JUDAISM

In 1886 the Jewish Theological Seminary (JTS) was founded in the United States as an institution for the training of religious scholars. Critical analysis and Western scholarship is used in studying sacred, classical texts, even while faculty are expected to accept the authority of the *halakhah* in their daily behavior. Thirty-two years after the seminary's founding, in 1918, the full framework for a Conservative movement included a network of affiliated synagogues, grouped under the rubric of the United Synagogue of America, and a professional association for its ordained rabbis, the Rabbinical Assembly. Today the Conservative branch of Judaism is the largest in America, claiming 1.2 million affiliated Jews.

Conservative Judaism defines its mission as confronting "the challenge to integrate tradition with modernity,"[3] evolving a blend of historical precedent and religious law with contemporary mores and knowledge. But this blending must grow out of the authority of the *halakhah*, the Jewish law, "which has never been monolithic or immovable."[4] But who shall be entitled to interpret which of the laws are immutable, the direct word of God, and which laws may be subject to reinterpretation, containing God's intent as understood by humans?

Legitimation of *poskim* (decision makers) and the process of explication are zealously guarded. The Rabbinical Assembly established a twenty-five-member Committee on Jewish Law and Standards to consider and advise on *halakhic* questions. Based on the logic and precedent of previous generations of rabbinical *poskim*, the Law Committee decides which laws and practices may be reinterpreted in light of modern considerations. However, its decisions are nonbinding; each member synagogue decides whether to accept the Law Committee's recommendation. For example, in the mid-1970s the Law Committee approved a *responsa*, reinterpretation, permitting women to be counted in the quorum of ten adults (*minyan*) needed to constitute a public prayer group. Yet two decades later one of the official religious services located in the seminary still refuses to count women in its quorum, one of the very few conservative services in the United States which also requires men and women to sit separately. A second seminary service was formed after women's entry into the rabbinic program, but it only counted women who publicly acknowledged all religious obligations including wearing previously traditional male prayer garments, the prayer shawl and phylactery. It took another ten years before a third *minyan* started, one which now allows all women to participate equally in the service.

A CALL FOR CHANGE

In 1972 a group of Conservative women issued a "Call for Change" at the annual Rabbinical Assembly (RA) convention to redress what was later described as "the terrible choice between their identities as woman and as Jews."[5] Five years later, in 1977, RA members approved a new constitution which deleted the mention of sex in qualifications for membership. The RA had already accepted male rabbis ordained by other branches of Judaism into its midst; it seemed it might now consider women ordained by Reform and Reconstructionist seminaries. The RA also asked the JTS to study the contentious question of ordaining traditionally observant women by its own Conservative seminary. The Law Committee and the Rabbinical Assembly ceded their authority on *halakhic* reinterpretation to the JTS Faculty Senate.

At JTS traditionalist faculty vigorously objected to giving the power of a *posek* to other than eminent Talmudic scholars, whom they considered the authentic methodological gatekeepers. Even the most learned or pious woman was excluded from becoming a *posek* by the traditionalists' minimally acceptable criteria: publicly acknowledged *halakhic* scholarship and full public obligations. Women were exempted, historically disenfranchised by the very institution that provided credentialing.

To assist the Faculty Senate, the seminary chancellor established a commission of rabbis and laypeople, including women, to examine the question of whether the *halakhah* could permit women's ordination and to make a recommendation to the JTS Senate. A number of seminary scholars wrote *responsa* addressing the question of whether it was possible within the framework of Jewish law for women to share full membership in the religious community.

In 1979 the commission issued a positive recommendation to the chancellor. However, on 20 December 1979 the seminary faculty voted twenty-five to nineteen to table a decision, explaining: "The question has provoked unprecedented divisions at every level of the Movement. The bitter divergence of opinion threatens to inflict irreparable damage. . . . we move that the question be tabled until such time as a balanced committee of talmudic scholars, to be appointed by the Chancellor, has completed a systematic study of the status of women in Jewish law."[6]

The chancellor offered the possibility of a quasi-rabbinical program to those women who had petitioned for admission to the rabbinical school, a program which would allow women to take all rabbinical courses but receive only a para-rabbinical credential. If a positive decision were made at a later time, the women might be retroactively eligible for ordination; however, this could not be guaranteed. The program was not established as only one woman accepted this alternative.

Four years after the vote to table, on 24 October 1983, the seminary faculty voted to admit women into its rabbinical school the following fall. A fifty-page *responsa* with twenty-three additional pages of endnotes, written by Rabbi Joel Roth, was accepted as the basis for the decision.

This *responsa* reiterated the two fundamental legal objections to the ordination of women: women are exempted from positive time-bound commandments; and a person who is not obligated cannot serve as an intermediary to help fulfill a commandment on behalf of one who is obligated. Since public prayer is a required, positive time-bound commandment, a woman cannot serve as a prayer leader or emissary for male congregants.

However, Roth reasoned, earlier generations of rabbis had allowed people, who so wished, to assume voluntarily obligations from which they had been exempted. Therefore, if certain women were to state they wished to assume full responsibility to observe all the obligations, then they might be able to serve in the rabbinical role of congregational prayer leaders.

One interviewee described this as a negative and reluctant basis on which to admit women; this reluctance was an issue the seminary never acknowledged or addressed during their years as students. In 1993, ten years after the Faculty Senate accepted this *t'shuvah*, interpretation, another interviewee noted that most current rabbinical students do not believe this logic can ultimately serve as the underpinning, the source of authority for the decision.

One rabbi remembered her feelings of estrangement and alienation from the logic that a woman had to overcome her fixed female nature in order to become equal to a male who attained status simply by being born male: "Women are now free to become men, as opposed to women now able to be rabbis. We're not equally valid. Women can be equal with men as long as we're just like men, only *less so* because men have the option of choosing to be traditional or non-traditional. Women *only* have the option of choosing non-traditional [that which is not the accepted role for religiously observant women]." Conservative Judaism still categorized women as a group as qualitatively defective, needing consciously to transcend their womanhood if they were to become religious leaders.

Roth's *responsa* opposed declaring that all females over thirteen were as equally obligated as men. He rejected arguments of equality,

of justice. "Ethics is not the issue, nor is egalitarianism . . . being ha-
lakhicly serious is."[7]

THE FIRST CLASS OF SEMINARY WOMEN

The remainder of this chapter looks at fifteen of the eighteen
women admitted to the rabbinical program in 1984, women who developed a dialectic of acceptance and resistance enabling them to be
ready to enter rabbinical training at that historic moment. It examines
their early years within the family and schooling, the mediating effect
of spirituality, and some of their experiences as rabbinical students at
the seminary.[8]

Each woman interviewed was thoughtful and articulate, projecting
strong values, passionate commitments, and a determination to find
her way through the contradictions and stresses in which she lived.
Most spoke of needing a deeper, more personal commitment than that
provided by their parents; all told of searching for individual meaning
and purpose. They depicted the early development of a religious and
cultural identity: a nuclear and sometimes intergenerational family
which connected them to timeless historical memory or myth, and to
an extended geographic tribal family.

Family and Early Schooling

Demographically these women were all Jewish by birth. Each had
siblings, none were children of Holocaust survivors, and no one's parents divorced or separated when the children were living at home. Social problems such as abuse, teen pregnancies, and drugs were not
mentioned.

Most grew up in large cities with extensive Jewish communities,
but two lived in small towns where theirs was the only Jewish family.
While there were differences in social class, geography, extent of politi-
cized lifestyle within the family, and degree of ritual practice, each
grew up in a family which acknowledged its religious identity and
marked itself off from the majority culture. Almost all described an
early connectedness to Judaism which occurred as a natural and ongoing part of their childhood. Each had extensive knowledge about her
extended family and previous generations' devotion to or struggles
within the Jewish tradition. Grandparents were important contributors
to the early religious life of many, fostering a caring relationship. For
most, there was a powerful sense of a family community and an integration of that family within the larger ethnic community.

A few described parents with a conflicted response to traditional Judaism, or families which were dysfunctional for periods of time. But even in these latter families, ethnicity was an integral piece of family life, not a disconnected add-on. As youngsters these particular women reached out to an extended network of relatives or found deeply formative relationships with a surrogate family—sometimes the community rabbi and his family—and immersed themselves in the synagogue, the historical community. At an early age, they chose to strengthen their own individual religious practices and commitment, perhaps in an attempt to heal family fractures by revivifying once-meaningful rituals, but certainly to connect themselves to a powerful historical tradition, or to a caring and supportive community.

All recounted family myths of noble actions, and also of traumatic adventures, of family members who were exemplars or rebels. The integration of family histories with cultural and/or religious traditions and ceremonies, and the implied responsibilities to their community of memory were literally ingested with their food. Each portrayed a cultural embeddedness, a network of multiple relational patterns— familial, peer, and intergenerational—which both facilitated and impeded their personal and religious growth.

Most had positive relationships with their parents. They discussed fathers or significant father figures in greater detail than mothers and with more affect—greater identification or more unresolved conflict. They characterized the conflicts as dealing with fairness and justice within family relationships. Ten related stories of mothers who were role models helping them learn to have confidence in themselves; three others found additional motherlike nurturers with whom they developed close ties.

The tradition exalted knowledge of the past, their homes were filled with books, and they entered school with a strong desire to learn. Each was achievement-oriented, excelling in her academic settings. Many spoke of class leadership positions, but others detailed lives bifurcated from that of their schoolmates, of constructing a parallel and totally separate Jewish environment of study and extracurricular Jewish youth leadership activities. None saw formal education as either peripheral or irrelevant. Even when experiencing anti-Semitic or sexist incidents in secular or religious school, they accepted the necessity of remaining committed to the educational process. They competed with and frequently exceeded the achievements of male peers, yet many were still dealing with feelings of academic inadequacy during their graduate studies at the seminary.

This strongly felt kinship and allegiance to their cultural and reli-gious ancestry encouraged a sense of belonging and trust within the ethnic community. Their emotional involvement and lived commit-ment enabled them to affirm their religious and personal identity and authenticity. As with most young women, there was continuous rein-forcement for attachment and connection to family and community, rather than for separation.

Within the family they absorbed the lessons of argumentation, questioning, multiple conversations, and the art of negotiation be-tween and within generations and cultures. This has been an accepted art throughout Jewish history, with dissenting opinions of religious scholars recorded alongside interpretations accepted as normative. For many of these women, discussion and dissent were reasonable tools for growth when expressed within the stability of the family and reli-gious community.

While accepting the strictures of both Jewish and American cul-tures, they increasingly understood that one need not be disloyal to disagree with the dictates of authority. Conflicting views could be equally committed to finding truth. Astute in the art of reflective and critical thought, they discovered how to test social limits and to take public stands without fear of being totally ostracized from their vari-ous communities.

They needed these strengths. Crises of trust emerged by their teen years. The interviews were filled with stories of limiting bound-aries, contradictions. Issues of gender and ethnicity, inclusion and ex-clusion, separation and connection multiplied as they grew older. Each struggled to find a balance between cultivating a healthy and creative individual integrity, and a deeply ingrained sense of responsibility to continue the historical ethnic memory. How to hold tight to a tradition which both hobbled and nourished spiritual growth was a typical issue.

They evolved a variety of strategies to circumvent restrictions to their personal legitimacy. Some learned they could retain private feel-ings and understandings which disagreed with given public truths, even while remaining in a school or synagogue setting which they per-ceived as trying to diminish them. A few created an inner world struc-tured to allow for private feelings, questions, or searchings to confirm their own authenticity; others developed an additional dimension of activity to supplement the sanctioned area.

This separation and resistance was negotiated within relationship and connectedness to the public sphere. Fourteen women recounted painful experiences of individuation, contesting family or peers and willing to be different, sometimes to the point of describing herself as having two separate personae at a particular time. These experiences resonated with stories of other family members who had also rebelled, who had wrestled with dissonance while working toward developing their own individuality. Each constructed an identity which reached toward change within continuity, toward healing within family relationships, toward maintaining and reinforcing the religious community, toward developing her own growth as an educated, spiritual, committed Jew.

They adjusted the male model of successful independent functioning, reframing it with connectedness. They covertly challenged the hierarchy embedded in secular education and religious law and custom by viewing themselves as created in the image of the divine.

The Mediating Effect of Spirituality

Only four of the fifteen women interviewed grew up in families rooted in traditional ritual observance; three of these were daughters of Conservative congregational rabbis. Five women saw their families as involved positively within their ethnic communities—belonging to a synagogue, wanting them to have some religious education, culturally celebrating their religious identity—but not as fully observant or knowledgeable as these daughters wanted to be. A few families were not affiliated within a local ethnic community, but did have a strong sense of extended family and provided some religious education which their daughters supplemented. Two women sought their own religious education during their precollege years. One searched for spirituality and political attachment within her secular community, while holding onto positive memories of grandmothers' spirituality, finding a religious community and education in her junior year in college.

Most described their siblings as being much less committed to and less passionate about religious education, ritual observance, or synagogue attendance. Despite the possible risk of detachment, at least five women, as teenagers, bound themselves to stricter ritual obligations than was comfortable for their parents. Their mothers acquiesced to the additional work of cooking separately for their daughters' observance of *kashrut*, respecting and supporting their daughters' efforts to become self-directed, and strengthening the bonds of family and religious connectedness.

Taking on the commandments seemingly reinforced their ability to rely on their own feelings and insight, allowed them to be responsible for creating their own synthesis of intellectual and religious experiences. They had equipped themselves to take risks, to chance that some disruption of family norms would not imperil family stability.

Judaism never barred women from praying in the synagogue; therefore, each had some exposure to public prayer services. In the few families which rejected synagogue affiliation the daughters found religious service through a grandparent or within a Jewish camp setting. Those who grew up immersed in the religion accepted the authority of the tradition; they went to synagogue and became emotionally committed to prayer and ritual as young girls. Before college they taught junior congregations of youngsters under thirteen, led youth group services to the extent possible, and even instructed their brothers in conducting services for adults.

But Conservative Judaism would not allow their participation as equals in the adult congregation at the age when their male peers became obligated to enter the adult community. They experienced not merely discouragement but an inviolable prohibition against taking on rituals and wearing prayer garments tied to male privilege. Their most basic identity, as females on the verge of menarche, forbade them from any contact with the Torah, the prayer shawl, or the phylacteries.

As they became both more knowledgeable in Jewish scholarship and more understanding of their own spiritual and psychological needs, there was an increasing awareness of and chafing against contradictions and disenfranchisement. Yet these observant young women remained connected with traditional Judaism, initially internalizing the sacral ban against their connection with the basic symbols of public affirmation. Appropriating these forbidden symbols would have been an empowerment of self above the *halakhah*, an act potentially destructive to Judaism, and their Jewishness was as integral a part of them as their being female. Later, as rabbinical students, many were able to reflect on these contradictions, alluding to an ongoing search for balance, the dialectic tension between individual identity and the dicta of family, community, and religion.

Perhaps to relieve dissonance, two-thirds of the interviewees had decided to take on many of the traditional obligations by the time they had completed their undergraduate studies. There was an intense need to unify the religious and secular parts of their lives. Some became strict Sabbath observers; many prayed on a daily basis. A few wore ritual prayer garments, *tallis*, *kippah*, and/or *tefillin* (prayer shawl, head covering, and phylacteries which had been restricted by custom to men) during public prayer services well before the legal decision to admit women into the Conservative rabbinical seminary. As one interviewee said, "I knew women were exempt from the *mitzvah* of *tallis* and *tefillin* as part of a larger network of exemption. If I *reject* that exemption for myself—I'm a woman who shares equally with men in every facet of Jewish obligation—then I shall be entitled, a powerful word psychologically, entitled to expect equality of rights in return. That was an important decision I made when I was eighteen."

Tying themselves to the religious law, more than half the interviewees studied, prayed, or lived within Orthodox communities for a period in their teen or adult lives to obtain the knowledge and imbibe the spirituality of that community. Ultimately, after intense struggle, they were not able to give up the feminist elements of their own identity: "In the Lubavitch community I saw many very happy, strong, totally satisfied women. They gave up access to the central areas of the synagogue and *halakhic* decisions. . . . They chose a level of spiritual intensity over feminism, not a choice I could make."

The women described an internal world of personal insights, of experiences of self-enlightenment, of self-actualizing openness, which enabled them to cope with familial or institutional inconsistencies: "I formulated it [the issue of women in the rabbinate] as competing Jewish values: the Jewish value that all people are created in the image of God versus the Jewish value of how we relate to and preserve the tradition. This idea of 'being created in the Image,' that I was basing myself on something that was Jewish, that could justify the direction in which I was moving."

Another described her sense of the deity which had helped in the quest to unify the disparate pieces of the self: "My Jewish search has also been a search for wholeness as a woman. For me, God is that entity, the One that tells us that we are whole when people are telling us we're not. God is the reference point that allows for human wholeness."

Another spoke of the presence of a "guiding hand" in her life, a religious way of living in the world through discerning the miraculous in everyday events, patterns which permeated and reinforced her understanding that humans live rooted in a community within the care, the blessing, the struggle, and finally the mystery of the divinity.

However, most theological metaphors were distinctly nontraditional, describing God as "a process," and "entity," even a human creation: "Community has permeated my theology of why Judaism needs to exist. I am traditional in my beliefs. I put value on ritual; I believe it's very important to conserve. But even when I was very young and would sit in services singing, my feeling was that we brought God into existence almost by our being together, praying together. A flip version of the creation story—we've created God." Another also alluded to the urgency of community: "My primary connection, primary reason for being Jewish, observant, or wanting to become a rabbi probably didn't have to do with God. It had more to do with community and being of service. I was disturbed by the failure to include women in a communal way."

All who described their vision of the rabbinate spoke in terms of a nonauthoritarian relationship with the community. They strongly believed in their capacity to effect the world positively, that they have something of value to offer.

Perhaps because Judaism has always put less emphasis on theology or creed and more on behavior, many of these Conservative women described spirituality in terms of study, law, and empowering themselves and others to find connectedness within the tradition. One said, "*Halakhah*'s a process that God gave to us to improve the world. It evolves as our sensibilities evolve; it can't be a stagnant *halakhah*, or it doesn't command our allegiance."

Another described spirituality in terms of love and confrontation with biblical and rabbinical texts which ground the law: "I can be studying a page of Talmud and get lost in the page; it becomes a spiritual experience detached from all my other baggage. And then I take three steps back and say, 'I can't believe how they are looking at women.' Everywhere I turn, textually, I'm in trouble. I feel torn when I deliver sermons. It's always a battle how to introduce congregants to the text, to Judaism, and, at the same time to critique what is going on."

A third found positive growth in her own *halakhic* practice, both a deepening of meaning and a flexibility in observance: "I get very frustrated by the hierarchy of Judaism that says Orthodoxy is the most, Conservative Judaism second most. The most what? Who shelters the most homeless? Most is a quantitative word that doesn't apply; religion is not about racking up the maximum *mitzvah* points. It can be about being the deepest, or the most expert in the one *mitzvah* you choose to devote your life to. For this reason I am much more forgiving of myself about changes, lapses in observance than I ever was."

Their spirituality contains a moral vision, a passion for justice and rights, care for those who are treated as different, problematic, or excluded. How to revivify the tradition, transform a Judaism which objectifies, subordinates women in ritual, language, image, and text? Are women Jews? Another said: "I can help to create that new tradition, but I'll always be straddling two worlds. Women need to be able to read the *siddur* (prayer book) and have a vision of God that isn't all masculine. Women need to know, to believe that God is not male. Men need that too. We need to think beyond the patriarchal system of Judaism and give it new life." But for most Conservative women rabbis, this must be accomplished within the framework of the *halakhah*: "This tradition has been culled through time, the wisdom of the ages. There's something that transcends what any one person, any one generation can contribute. To me, that is divine. There are elements of ritual that are so powerful and important and valuable that we don't understand consciously; we do not have the right to deprive future generations of those rituals. We have the right to reinterpret them, to understand them differently, using the sources to write *t'shuvot*."

Diverse and Invisible within the Rabbinical Program

Only three women entered the rabbinical program directly upon graduation from an undergraduate college. Even the youngest had worked in the Jewish community; the others had spent years working as Jewish professionals. Many had taken additional years of Jewish studies. Amy Eilberg entered the rabbinical program having previously completed all the course work for a doctoral degree in Talmud. She had decided that a life of research was not her passion and left the graduate school to get a master's degree in social work. Nine of the fifteen had been enrolled in the seminary's graduate school or had taken some courses at JTS prior to their admission into the rabbinical program; these had been unequivocally positive experiences.

Their years as rabbinical students contrasted dramatically. For some, the problems started with the legitimizing *t'shuva* that allowed their entry into rabbinical school. One described the *t'shuva* as "the most meticulously researched and reasoned from a *halakhic* point of view, and also the closest to saying that you couldn't do it."

Interviewees described faculty and administration's lack of comprehension that the different socialization patterns women had experienced might clash with the forms of knowledge, values, and social relationships prevailing in the rabbinical school. They portrayed an administration which fully believed that the hitherto male rabbinate was gender-neutral, that women could become professionalized in the same way as male students into a seemingly androgynous model.

But these women had no role models, and the seminary did not understand that many had been struggling for years with searching critiques, histories of conflict with issues such as sexist language, sexist liturgy, and text which viewed women as peripheral. However, these tensions and questions were not on any agenda. One woman told of making an announcement after the opening breakfast on the first day of rabbinical school and the reaction to her statement: "I really wanted to ask the women to get together, but do you dare do such a thing in this place the first day. I said, 'If any women would like to stay afterwards, we'll have a chat.' I can't tell you the *extreme* feedback from that, the craziness, the sense there was a *conspiracy* to *overthrow* the *Chancellor*; people were so horrified!"

The women in the first class were diverse individuals in age, previous level of religious observance, and feminist consciousness. Many spoke of episodes of social injustice or personal discrimination at the rabbinical school, and ways they had individually tried to modify patriarchal strictures; others assumed there was equal access for women and goodwill, and they had confidence in the authority of the received truths of teachers and tradition. One attributed adjustment problems to her own "short-comings," seemingly unaware of systemic problems.

There was a fragile women's group that never evolved into a recognized or effective presence. The women who participated felt too uncomfortable to put up notices, let alone meet at the seminary. Most discussions dealt with venting personal issues, such as handling sexism in a class; macro solutions, on the institutional level, were beyond the capability of the group. The pressure of time, the structure of the curriculum and scholastic demands, and the diversity of their personal lives were among the factors that hindered them from sharing, listening, and developing an activist agenda or systemic approaches for change.

Perhaps there were unstated, unexamined reasons as well. Did they perceive that any critique might possibly shatter their still tenuous individual goals? Some seemed to feel unduly responsible for the comfort of the larger community. After the acrimonious divisions created in allowing women into the program, was any seeming challenge so threatening to the hegemony of the seminary and the tradition that the women themselves feared that Conservative Judaism, their home, might not survive the encounter with modernity and feminism?

Members of the first class of women were not able to find answers from their own lives on how to build cooperatively and responsibly in order to confront values which deprecated and undermined their authenticity. Similar to other women who have pioneered nontraditional positions without female role models, their commitment came from family or community roots, from individual confrontations with inequity. There was an absence of conscious, cohesive, and collective strategies for change. While students they found no theoretical or conceptual binding to unify their needs or concerns.

UPDATE

A meeting convened by the author with women attending the annual RA Convention in 1992, and conversations with other members of the first class the following year, reveal that there have been no collaborative or regularly supportive efforts among the women since ordination. Indeed, the breakfast meeting at the RA Convention was the first time that some of the women had been together since their student days. Although one woman did start a newsletter to try to keep all women rabbis and cantors in touch with each other, she was not able to continue this on her own; an ongoing official mechanism had not yet been established by the seminary or the women themselves. At the RA breakfast meeting there was no general agreement about how or whether to use their abilities and increasing power to transform their institutions and the public domain.

One person, comparing her first-year class with current students, saw her peers as having a "historical binding-together" which did not seem to be present in their seminary days. She suggested even that minimal tie is apparently absent for today's women students. Many women still feel besieged, and that it is necessary to censor their comments in class; there is little tolerance for those students who think differently. As late as 1993, women in the rabbinical school had no common conversation; their differences were wide-ranging, encompassing traditionalists, lesbians, feminists, and radical feminists. A nascent women's *Rosh Chodesh minyan* (biblical holiday for women, resurrected in modern times by Jewish women, especially Jewish feminists, as a time to meet and celebrate together) which started in September 1991 split apart in spring 1993 over the issue of men being invited to participate without the consent of the entire group.

In questioning the RA's Placement Bureau in 1993 about the percentage of graduates who take pulpit positions upon ordination, it was explained that the office was not yet equipped to answer such questions. The bureau stated that it did not keep any statistics and did not study placement patterns, although it acknowledged that this "should be looked at." A hand count was made of the 20 rabbis who graduated in May 1993; 5 of the 9 males took a pulpit position; 6 of the 11 women also took a pulpit position. The year 1993 was the first in which a larger number of women than men were ordained (55 percent). However, the rabbinical class which entered in September 1993 was composed of 25 men and 9 women (26 percent). This brought the student body in the rabbinical school to 137, including 55 women (40 percent).

A total of fifty-two women were ordained between May 1985 and May 1993. According to conversations with women from the first class, their best guess is that perhaps five or six of their number currently hold part-time or full-time pulpit positions. Most of these are as solo or assistant rabbis in small congregations, one of whom had "grown her congregation" above two hundred members. With no mechanism for the women to keep in touch with each other, and without statistics from the Placement Office, one would have to search through all members of the Rabbinical Assembly to determine their counterparts who are pulpit rabbis.

Those in pulpits who are married and have children struggle to balance the needs of congregation, family, and self. One rabbi felt it became a bit easier the longer she was with her congregation: "They now know me and trust me if I tell them a problem can wait until I'm in the office in the morning." Another problem which some mentioned was finding a congregation which met their religious needs but, at the same time, was lenient enough to accept their husbands' needs, since in some cases they were much less observant than their wives.

Women in the Rabbinate: Dynamics of Change was the title of a conference held at JTS in October 1993 to mark the tenth anniversary of the decision to admit women to the rabbinical school. One stated goal was to "help the Seminary understand what happens ritually, behaviorally, emotionally to students; what it means to educate a person to become a rabbi." Plenary topics included: historic models of change and resistance, the challenge of women's rabbinic careers, Judaism and the spiritual life of women, and ministry for the next generation.

Many attended the conference with some expectation that it would celebrate ten years of women in the rabbinate. But the seminary organizers planned a balanced scholarly conference which included presentations by opponents of women's ordination. Rabbi Joel Roth, whose *t'shuvah* was used to open the *halakhic* restriction, stated that in retrospect, because of divisions which subsequently occurred between factions within the Conservative movement, it was a mistake to have allowed women to enter rabbinical training.

Toward the close of the conference, at the end of another presentation of panelists which left almost no time for discussion or processing, an unscheduled event occurred. One rabbi stood up and announced that there needed to be a ritual to connect and honor large numbers of those in the audience. As she called different groups, including rabbis and educators, to the front of the auditorium to participate in the ritual, there was an elation and enthusiasm which engulfed the conference. In breaking the hierarchical model of panelists talking to a passive audience, the conference was animated as communities of people joyously connected with one another. Within a year of the conference, a new, third religious service started at the seminary, the first truly egalitarian service which allows women to participate fully.

SUMMARY

Conservative women rabbis, like their Reconstructionist and Reform sister rabbis, struggle to maintain a healthy and creative individuality, balancing the public and the private, the secular and the spiritual aspects of their lives. However, Conservative women are additionally committed to live within the strictures of *halakhah*. All tacitly accepted a limit to their position of equality at the time of the interviews: *halakhic* restrictions prevent women, even those who have taken on all the obligations of the law and who are ordained as rabbis, from serving as legal religious witnesses. All accepted the *halakhic* process as the appropriate method to modify systemic injustices.

Entry into the rabbinate focused on the desire for personal authenticity and equality of obligation and authority within the system. They did not link this access to a radical critique of the system. They wanted to defend the integrity, the conserving force of *halakhah*.

As maturing young women, many evolved an emotional understanding that it could not have been God's plan to exclude them from the sacred aspects of the religion because of their biology. They came to the conclusion that the human authors of the Bible and of rabbinic texts, submerged in the cultures of their time, had written down flawed misunderstandings of God's word.

Although the women did not speak about a feminist theology, their experience of God was not literal, not described with human attributes, not visualized as a dichotomy between human and divine. Imagery encompassed connectedness, "a unity of wholeness and holiness" or "experiencing the divine spark that's in human beings." The spiritual or sacred was not separate from everyday life and behavior, not abstract theologizing, but "finding God when we reach out to each other."

Spirituality seemed to enable each woman to insist on the right to mark out her own separate path to individual piety and devotion, but as one who refused to relinquish her profound immersion in and emotional commitment to the collectivity of the Conservative Jewish community. Each strained to remain a loyal adherent to that community of belief while searching for her own personal, existential encounters with revelation. Intertwining ritual and revelation like a double helix,

each patterned herself in a reflection of the unity expressed in the Hebrew word *Echad*, an image of the undivided wholeness of the Creator.

However, in their rabbinical training they discovered a multiplicity
of practices, norms, and imperatives which fostered gender barriers
and hierarchies of male privilege and power relationships. They
wanted an educational process that would include a search for meaningful personal understanding along with the acquisition of facts. The
seminary should "model the rabbi as questioner. It's an egalitarianism; saying we're all searching together. Rabbis have to deliver a message about how to become better human beings. It's not preaching to
people what they should do, but how you and I, together, can work
towards that goal."

Although many wanted to revitalize or transform the seminary, in
actuality there was little change during their years there. The first class
of women completed the program in different years, as separated individuals who did not know many of their female peers on an intimate
basis, who rarely encountered a supportive, nurturing community of
women or men.

Yet, despite institutional obstructions and personal anxieties, they
dedicated themselves to strengthening the Jewish community. They
continue to relearn their early lessons of tolerating uncertainty, sup-
pressing negative reactions, and interweaving attachment and autonomy. Separately, each strives in her life's journey to fulfill the
potential for leadership and her concern for equality and justice, and to
deepen and share her love for Judaism.[9]

NOTES

1. Emanuel Feldman, "The Torah, More G-d's Law than Ours," *Sh'ma* (6 October 1987): 148–50.
2. Blu Greenberg, *On Women and Judaism: A View from Tradition* (Philadelphia:
   Jewish Publication Society, 1981), 4, 5.
3. Robert Gordis, *Emet Ve-emunah: Statement of Principles of Conservative Judaism* (New York: The Jewish Theological Seminary of America, 1988), 10.
4. Ibid., 15.
5. Conversation with Rabbi Amy Eilberg.
6. Seymour Siegel, "Conservative Judaism and Women Rabbis," *Sh'ma*
   (8 February 1980): 49–51.
7. Simon Greenberg, *The Ordination of Women as Rabbis: Studies and Responsa*
   (New York: The Jewish Theological Seminary of America, 1988).

8. Quotes in the remainder of this chapter are taken from interviews held in late 1988 and early 1989 with fifteen of the eighteen women who entered the rabbinical school in 1984. At the time of the interviews, one-third of the women were ordained; another third were in their final year of training; and the remaining five were ordained the following year, including one woman who had transferred to Reform Judaism's seminary, Hebrew Union College.

9. This chapter is based on the dissertation by Sydell Ruth Schulman, "Empowerment and Ordination: A Study of the First Class of Women Admitted to Rabbinical Training at the Jewish Theological Seminary," completed in May 1992 at Rutgers, the State University of New Jersey.

Women's Voices: The Challenge of Feminism to Judaism

Sue Levi Elwell

INTRODUCTION

Jewish women have never been silent. The Bible records the words of Eve, Sarah, Hannah, Rebekah, Rachel, Leah, Miriam, Hulda, Ruth, and others. The Talmud introduces us to the sages Beruriah and Ima Shalom, Yalta and an elusive Matrona. For most of Jewish history, however, Jewish women's voices have gone unheard.

In the last hundred years, there have been several attempts to give women's stories a wider hearing, an expanded audience. In 1910 scholar and social reformer Bertha Pappenheim translated the memoirs of her distant relative Gluckel of Hameln (1646–1724) into German, but this important work was ignored by historians until sixty years later.[1] Henrietta Szold's pioneering work on women's devotional prayers was treated as a curiosity.[2] And in the early 1980s a professor in rabbinical school warned this author that focusing attention on Jewish women would render her an ineffective historian.

Today, Jewish women's voices are finally being heard: in the pulpit, in the classroom, and in the academy. Jewish women's words are being read by scholars, by students, and by schoolchildren. Jewish women's prayers, songs, and petitions are finally being incorporated into the liturgy. The influence of Jewish women's insights, political commitments, and deep religious convictions is propelling Jewish women into both Jewish and secular arenas in greater numbers and with more focused energy than ever before in history.

After a brief historical introduction, this chapter will explore six discrete areas in which Jewish women—professional and lay, ordained rabbis and invested cantors, and leaders in synagogues, community centers, and voluntary organizations—have taken the lead in challenging and changing Judaism. These are: prayer, context and content; study; Jewish law; life cycle; holiday cycle; and coalition building.

JEWISH WOMEN LEADERS: HISTORICAL REFLECTIONS

"And Miriam the prophet . . . took her timbrel in her hand and all the women followed her lead" (Exod. 15:20). Since the time of the Bible, women leaders have set the pace and the tone for the forward march of the people of Israel. It is clear from texts as early as the second century that the words of the scholar Beruriah were honored by men and women alike. Bernadette Brooten's path-breaking scholarship on women leaders in ancient synagogues dispelled previously held theories that the synagogue has always been an exclusive men's club.[3] Because of the inability to transcend the sexist norms of the peoples among whom Jews have lived for so much of their history, however, it has only been in the recent past that women's leadership has been recognized as essential to the continued health of the Jewish community.

However, there have always been exceptional women whose leadership has been acknowledged by the Jewish community. Beatrice de Luna Mendes, called Dona Gracia Nasi, fled the persecution of the Inquisition and then used her wealth and influence to arrange passage for thousands of Portuguese Jews to safe harbors. She was a patron of arts and literature in Ferraro, Italy, and later in Constantinople she became known as a leading merchant and a generous philanthropist.[4] Gluckel of Hameln was a respected businesswoman in the early years of the eighteenth century in Hamburg, Germany.[5] Hannah Rachel Werbermacher became a Hasidic teacher in the Ukraine in the mid–nineteenth century. In 1904 social reformer Bertha Pappenheim founded the Judischer Frauenbund, the German Jewish Women's Organization, to lobby the Jewish community for full religious rights for women. In addition to her political work, Pappenheim also established a home for young Jewish immigrant women, many of whom had turned to prostitution as their only means of survival.[6] More recently, Lily Montague helped to create the liberal Jewish movement in England, and in America both Hannah Greenebaum Solomon, a founder of the National Council of Jewish Women, and her contemporary Henrietta Szold, Zionist pioneer and founder of Hadassah (the Women's Zionist Organization of America), were acknowledged as extraordinary women of their time.[7]

But for every woman who was honored for her work in the community, the contributions of many others were overlooked, undervalued, or ignored. Without women's work, Jewish communities in

Europe and America could not have functioned, but it has been only recently that women have begun to serve as rabbis, cantors, and lay leaders in synagogues; as presidents of Jewish communal welfare and defense organizations; as administrators in schools for children; and as teachers in schools and seminaries for adolescents and adults. What is important about these changes, however, is not simply that women are finally moving into positions of leadership but, rather, that their leadership styles and goals and intentions often differ from the men with whom they have trained. Many of the women now moving up in the contemporary Jewish community are challenging the operational assumptions of a community that solidified in the 1950s and 1960s. Rightly assessing that the last decades of the twentieth century demand a very different response, they have questioned the hierarchical structure of the community and created new models of cooperative leadership. Some insist that the community welcome into its midst not only women but also Jews from non-European backgrounds, interfaith families, families of divorce, gay and lesbian Jews, and others who have felt marginalized. Some challenge accepted definitions of Jewish professional success by their work in hospices, in homes for the elderly, in prisons, among the homeless, and in nonurban areas, and by their insistence on bringing themselves to their work in a deeply personal way. For many contemporary Jewish women leaders, the model of Bertha Pappenheim, the scholarly social activist who lived among the immigrant women whose lives she saved by offering them shelter, support, and then job and language training, is a more potent model than the distant, learned rabbi and teacher or the politically motivated communal official. Acknowledging the imperative and the challenge of combining the personal and the political, bringing together commitment to family with commitment to the community, women leaders are helping the Jewish community see itself with new eyes.

PRAYER

On Friday evenings and Saturday mornings, Jews gather in synagogues and centers to celebrate the Sabbath with psalms, songs, and prayers, and, depending on custom, by the public reading or chanting of biblical texts. In the past twenty years, in non-Orthodox *minyanim* (prayer quorums) around the world, both the content and the context of these Sabbath prayers have changed. In most liberal congregations, men *and* women lead the congregation in prayer, chant or read from the Torah scrolls, and teach through sermons and stories. And in increasing numbers of congregations, change has extended not only to those who lead and those who respond but to the language of prayer as well. Following the lead of the liturgical revisions pioneered first in Europe and then in America,[8] feminist liturgists have successfully introduced a number of innovations into the Sabbath, daily, and holiday liturgy.

One change replaces exclusively male God-language with gender-neutral or gender-balanced references to the divine.[9] A correlative of this is the pioneering work by Marcia Falk which challenges Jews to reconsider the traditional blessing formulation. She suggests that instead of addressing the divine with "Blessed are You, Our God," we can acknowledge our role in blessing: "We bless the Source of Life. . . ."[10]

Another change includes the matriarchs when the patriarchs are invoked. The traditional prayer that begins "God of our fathers, God of Abraham, God of Isaac, and God of Jacob" becomes "God of our ancestors, God of Abraham, God of Isaac, God of Jacob, God of Sarah, God of Rebecca, God of Rachel and God of Leah." Some are now questioning whether the "other" matriarchs—Hagar, Bilhah, and Zilpah—should be included in this prayer.

A third innovation recognizes that Hebrew's limitation of either male or female verb forms makes women invisible as ones who pray. By offering a choice for one of the first morning prayers—for example, not only *modeh ani* but also *modah ani*: "I thank you, God, for returning my soul to me"—women can speak in a feminine first person that enables us to hear our own voices as never before.

The integration of prayers and poems written by women, including women's interpretations of traditional texts and new "texts" composed by women, has changed the liturgy,[11] as has creating worship experiences that focus on interaction of individuals with one another and individuals with the community rather than on the exchange of the service leader with the members of the congregation. This latter innovation includes but is not limited to: empowering a range of individuals to share leadership of worship; intentional spatial arrangements; making the services linguistically accessible to all (in some communities the Hebrew of prayer is a barrier to women's participation even more than it is for men); building a shared base of knowledge of songs and responses; and the institutionalization of portions in the service for individual prayer as well as for some kind of dialogic or shared experience.[12]

STUDY

Traditionally, Jewish text study has been a field of endeavor closed to all but a few, handpicked Jewish men. Jewish women's studies, a field of academic inquiry unimagined two decades ago, is now attracting graduate students to programs of Bible, history, anthropology, sociology, literature, the arts, and traditional Jewish texts. Each year dissertations are written that open new areas of inquiry or explore newly discovered texts, or study older sources that illuminate previously obscured women's lives and the contexts of those lives. The publication of Judith Plaskow's *Standing Again at Sinai: Judaism from a Feminist Perspective* (HarperCollins, 1990) challenges the androcentric vision of normative Jewish theological discourse. Judith Romney Wegner's *Chattel or Person? The Status of Women in the Mishnah* (Oxford University Press, 1988) provides a comprehensive and sophisticated reading of essential Talmudic texts, and makes many of those arguments available in English for the first time. Judith Z. Abrams's work *The Talmud for Beginners* (Northvale, N.J.: Jason Aronson, 1991) also opens the world of rabbinic discourse to the non-Hebrew reader and is one of the first guides to the Talmud to be written by a woman, who, in Abrams's case, is trained both as a rabbi and as a Talmud scholar. Abrams's *Women of the Talmud* (Northvale, N.J.: Jason Aronson, 1995) focuses on the depiction of women in these ancient texts. Rabbi Susan Grossman and Rivka Haut bring together feminist and Jewish scholarship in their able editing of *Daughters of the King: Women and the Synagogue* (Jewish Publication Society, 1992), which offers a comprehensive and moving account of Jewish women's spiritual search from the time of the Jerusalem temple until the present. The basic text for an increasing number of courses in Jewish women's studies has become Ellen Umansky and Dianne Ashton's comprehensive *Four Centuries of Jewish Women's Spirituality: A Sourcebook* (Beacon, 1992), for it includes diary entries, letters, poems, prayers, and sermons composed by Jewish women since 1560.[13]

What is the impact of these works and others on traditional curricula of Jewish studies? In the Orthodox world, works that have been influenced by feminism have little impact, but the number of women studying texts that were formerly studied only by men continues to increase. A recent article by Orthodox feminist Blu Greenberg mentions four institutions that exist solely for women's study of traditional texts.[14] Surely, as an increasing number of women study in such programs and institutions, these "new" texts will find a place in students' homes, if not in traditional classrooms. Greenberg points out that the mere fact that these women are studying, regardless of the fact that they are studying only traditional texts in a traditional context, has the power to change both the institutions which they study and the community in which these women live, in addition, of course, to changing the women themselves.

JEWISH LAW

Jewish law and its interpretation stands at the center of traditional Jewish life. For traditional Jews, *halakhah*, the law, is of divine origin and guides every aspect of a Jew's life. Liberal Jews consider the law to be part of the vast textual legacy of the ages and may respect but reject its tenets and direction. For the first time in history, women are now studying and becoming proficient interpreters of *halakhah*. As students and teachers of the Talmud, the codes, and the *responsa* literature, women are now becoming fluent in a language of discourse that has determined many of the attitudes, behaviors, and mores of the traditional Jewish community. And as women take their place at the study table and behind the teacher's lectern, they are challenging long-held notions of women's credibility. Traditional Jewish law explicitly states that women are not admissible witnesses, yet as Orthodox feminist Blu Greenberg has pointed out, both in Israel and America, more and more religious courts are finding ways for women's voices to be heard, if not directly, then through male interpreters and intermediaries.[15] Other legal standards that are being challenged by women are the prohibition against women initiating divorce and the prohibition against women forming a *minyan*, or prayer quorum. Traditional women are now banding together and taking to the streets, through organizations such as Getting Equal Treatment (G.E.T.) and Agunah, advocacy groups for women unable to procure religious divorce, and challenging the traditional community to begin to take action to equalize the inherent discrimination against women in Jewish law. In small prayer or study groups, other women are taking smaller steps to challenge the traditional status quo. Using newly acquired study and liturgical skills, they are teaching other women and their own daughters. Still others, including scholars Judith Romney Wegner, Judith Z. Abrams, Rivka Haut, and Rachel Adler, are adding to the legal literature, and their thoughtful essays and books are influencing a widening circle of Jewish thinkers.[16] As Greenberg asserts,

> these changes are . . . nothing short of revolution. Though when taken item by item none is earth shaking, when measured together

they add up to the redefinition of women's role in the liturgical, spiritual, and intellectual life of the community. . . . *Halakah* will again open itself to interpretation, and we will see within it a defi- nition of equality, as well as distinctiveness of male and female, that will carry us faithfully forward into the next four thousand years of Jewish life.[17]

LIFE CYCLE

Traditional Jewish life-cycle rituals focus on the life cycle of the in- dividual in the context of the family and the Jewish community. Begin- ning with birth and covenant rituals (for boys through *brit milah*, or ritual circumcision), the ritual cycle continues with *bar mitzvah* and then on to marriage and then death.

Following the lead of women lay leaders, rabbis, and cantors, con- temporary Jews are challenging the limited opportunities for celebrat- ing significant points of transition in their lives. For the last twenty-five years, Jews have been welcoming daughters with an explicit articula- tion of bringing these Jews into the covenant, but without circumci- sion. Since 1922 liberal Jews have been following the lead of Judith Kaplan Eisenstein, who became the first American Jewish girl to cel- ebrate becoming a full member of her Jewish community by being called to the Torah at age thirteen. It is now commonplace in liberal (Reform, Reconstructionist and Conservative) synagogues for girls to prepare for a *bat mitzvah* ceremony sometime between the ages of twelve and thirteen.[18] In addition to the *bat mitzvah*, Jews are also ac- knowledging other rites of passage in the adolescent years with me- narche ceremonies and rituals for leaving home.

Marriage ceremonies have been profoundly influenced by egalitar- ian approaches to partnership, and most liberal Jews choose an alter- native text to the traditional *ketubah* (marriage document), which transfers ownership of the bride from one party (traditionally the fa- ther) to another (the husband). The scholar Rachel Adler has devised a *brit ahuvim*, a partnership document that can be used by heterosexual and gay and lesbian couples that focuses on the mutual responsibilities of each party in the relationship.[19] Some rabbis have adapted tradi- tional marriage ceremonies for gay and lesbian couples, and others have suggested new rituals that acknowledge the particular challenges of establishing gay and lesbian partnerships in a heterosexist world.

Rituals and ceremonies have been developed that transform the traditional immersion in a *mikveh* (ritual bath), which preceeds a mar- riage and then is used each month following the completion of men- strual bleeding. These new rituals, which can be used as part of healing after rape, acknowledgment of childhood sexual abuse or incest, abortion, hysterectomy, or divorce or the end of a relationship, focus on restoring the integrity of the individual who immerses herself, not on her sexuality in relationship to another. Intentional immersion, accompanied with formulaic words and blessings, is reclaimed as a powerful vehicle for personal transition and transformation. Rabbi Elyse Goldstein first suggested using the *mikveh* before rabbinic ordination. When a candidate for the rabbinate immerses herself on the eve of ordination, s/he is preparing herself or himself for a life of service to her/his people rather than for a life of conjugal happiness with a spouse. Rather than denying one's sexuality, however, the immersion can celebrate the integration of sensuality and essence with spirituality.

Other new rituals include *simchat hochma*, the celebration of wisdom, which is often connected to a sixtieth or seventieth birthday. This new ritual, pioneered by women, is a celebration of age and achievement and an acknowledgment that the individual is now facing the end of her/his life. The community gathers to honor each elder, and by doing so reinforces the traditional Jewish value of respect and honor for the senior members of the Jewish community.[20] Other new rituals acknowledge the range of families that now make up Jewish communities: blended and step-families, intentional families, gay and lesbian families, adoptive parents, and more.[21]

HOLIDAY RITUALS: THE EXAMPLE OF PASSOVER

While women's voices are beginning to be heard in holiday rituals throughout the year, Passover seders that incorporate inclusive liturgy and song are now celebrated in many homes across America, Europe, and Israel. The primary liturgy for the annual Passover celebration is the *haggadah*, literally the "telling" of the Exodus story. For centuries, Jews have adapted the *haggadah* to reflect the norms and needs of individual communities and families, retelling the story of liberation and redemption through the lens of their own experience. The *haggadah* is ordered according to the tradition, but within its proscribed framework the feminist liturgist has many opportunities for reinterpretation, reconstruction, and innovation.[22] Women's voices and perspective were first expressed in *haggadot* compiled for use in women-only seders, privately circulated and passed hand-to-hand from woman to woman.[23] Later, gender-inclusive *haggadot*, written for mixed communities, began to appear.[24] In many non-Orthodox households, the following correctives have become a part of the Passover ritual: the "four sons" have become the "four children"; Miriam, Yoheved, the midwives Shifra and Puah, and Pharaoh's daughter are acknowledged as central to the telling of the Exodus story; an enumeration of contemporary plagues includes an acknowledgment of women's historic invisibility in Jewish history and silence in the seder ritual; the central narrative of the ritual (*maggid*) now includes the stories of women throughout Jewish history, or rewrites the ritual through women's eyes; and the traditional *hallel*, or praise portion, has been expanded with contemporary women's poetry to complement the traditional psalms.[25]

COALITION BUILDING

Historically, Jewish women have connected to other women in many of the contexts and cultures in which Jews have lived. Today, however, building coalitions between women across the chasm of differences demands a particular intention and commitment.

In *Deborah, Golda, and Me: Being Female and Jewish in America*, Letty Cottin Pogrebin relates a dream/fantasy of standing up in front of a "huge feminist conference" where "an increasingly rancorous debate between African-American women and Jewish women" is brewing. She imagines herself quoting words of Sojourner Truth, delivered at the Women's Convention of 1851, "Ain't I a Woman?," appealing to the commonalities between women as a more powerful force than their differences.[26] Her fantasy is grounded in the history of American Jewish women, who have often taken the lead in building and maintaining coalitions between women across the barriers of religion, class, and race. Recent scholarship has begun to explore Jewish women's participation in movements for social change in this country and in England.[27]

In small circles and in larger groups, Jewish women continue to reach out to other women, to talk, to share common concerns, and to form coalitions that reach beyond the barriers of race, religion, and culture. There are a number of such examples in cities across the country. In preparation for the 1985 mid-decade conference for International Women's Decade, the writer E. M. Broner and Palestinian Anina Rahman met regularly in New York, and once they arrived in Nairobi they worked together to create a dialogue between Israeli and Palestinian delegates. In *Deborah, Golda and Me*, Pogrebin describes her efforts to build trust and to bring together the personal and political in Black-Jewish dialogue in New York. In St. Louis, Missouri, Rabbi Susan Talve initiated an interfaith women's clergy dialogue where Jewish,

Christian, and Muslim religious leaders come together to share common concerns and to strengthen one another as change agents.

The interfaith Women's Coalition Against Ethnic Cleansing was established in Los Angeles in December 1992 by representatives of the Catholic, Muslim, and Jewish communities following press revelations about Serbian rape camps and the use of rape as a weapon of genocide and war in former Yugoslavia. Following the lead of the religious representatives, over twenty community women's organizations banded together to speak out and take action on behalf of the victims of the atrocities in Bosnia-Herzegovina with a specific focus on acts of violence against women. In the first year after its creation, the coalition implemented campaigns to raise awareness, lobby, and raise substantial funds for direct relief. Two delegations of rape crisis workers and others traveled to the war zone, carrying medical supplies, essential clothing and personal items, and funds for grassroots women's support services. Women Against Gun Violence, another interfaith, interethnic coalition of women in Los Angeles, was also catalyzed by the work of Jewish women. The group, which includes representatives from fifty women's organizations in Los Angeles, works with antigun and firearm control groups nationwide to educate people about the dangers of firearms and to eliminate gun violence from our society.[28]

CONCLUSION

Jewish women are no longer silent, and women's voices are transforming Judaism. Over the course of the last twenty years, Jewish women across the world have begun to come out of the kitchen and the nursery and out from behind the *mehitza* (curtain that separates sexes in a traditional synagogue) to claim the classroom, the study hall, and the synagogue as their rightful domains. The texts, the liturgy, and the rituals that have defined Judaism have begun to be transformed by the addition of women's voices on the page and in the pew. Changes that began in liberal Jewish communities have reverberated through the most traditional communities, and women are now taking leadership roles that until recently were reserved for men. Women's voices, now raised, will not be silenced. The new song of which the psalmist speaks is the song that includes *all* voices. Jewish women are demonstrating that this song, a song of inclusion and hope, is the song that will heal the world.

NOTES

1. *The Memoirs of Gluckel of Hameln*, trans. Marvin Lowenthal, with an introduction by Robert S. Rosen (New York: Schocken Books, 1977).
2. See Szold's lead article, "What Our Grandmothers Read," in the 5 April 1907 *Hebrew Standard*. Her impressive erudition and thoughtful analysis evoked little response.
3. Bernadette J. Brooten, *Women Leaders in the Ancient Synagogue* (Chico, Ca.: Scholar's Press, 1982). See also Hannah Safrai, "Women and the Ancient Synagogue," in *Daughters of the King: Women and the Synagogue*, ed. Susan Grossman and Rivka Haut (Philadelphia: Jewish Publication Society, 1992), 39–49.
4. See Sondra Henry and Emily Taitz, eds., *Written Out of History: Our Jewish Foremothers* (New York: Biblio Press, 1988), 139–143, and Cecil Roth, *The House of Nasi: Dona Gracia* (Philadelphia: Jewish Publication Society, 1948).
5. See *The Memoirs of Gluckel of Hameln*.
6. See Marion A. Kaplan, "Bertha Pappenheim: Founder of German-Jewish Feminism," in *The Jewish Woman: New Perspectives*, ed. Elizabeth Koltun (New York: Schocken Books, 1976), 149–63.
7. See Ellen Umansky, *Lily Montague and the Advancement of Liberal Judaism: From Vision to Vocation* (New York: Edwin Mellen Press, 1984); Faith Rogow, *Gone to Another Meeting: The National Council of Jewish Women, 1893–1993* (Tuscaloosa: University of Alabama Press, 1993); and Joan Dash, *Summoned to Jerusalem: The Life of Henrietta Szold* (New York: Harper and Row, 1979). For a more detailed historical study of the precursors of women in the rabbinate, see Ellen Umansky, "Women in Judaism: From the Reform Movement to Contemporary Jewish Religious Feminism," in *Women of Spirit: Female Leadership in the Jewish and Christian Traditions*, ed. Rosemary Ruether and Eleanor McLaughlin (New York: Simon and Schuster, 1979), 334–54.
8. The first reform prayer book was the *Hamburg Temple Prayer Book*, published in 1818. In 1854 Abraham Geiger compiled a prayer book that was "regarded as highly authoritative." It was followed in America by Isaac Mayer Wise's *Minhag America* (1857) and David Einhorn's *Olat Tamid* (1858). See Abraham Millgram, *Jewish Worship* (Philadelphia: Jewish Publication Society, 1971), 583–86.
9. See Alpert and Milgram's chapter in this book. See also Judith Plaskow, *Standing Again at Sinai: Judaism from a Feminist Perspective* (New York: Harper and Row, 1990), 121ff.
10. Marcia Falk, "Notes On Composing New Blessings," in *Weaving the Visions: New Patterns in Feminist Spirituality*, ed. Judith Plaskow and Carol P. Christ (New York: Harper and Row, 1989), 128–38; see also Marcia Falk, *The Book of Blessings: New Jewish Prayers and Rituals for Daily Life, the Sabbath, and the New Moon Festival* (San Francisco: HarperSanFrancisco, 1996).
11. See Alpert and Milgram's chapter in this volume.

12. *Or Chadash: New Paths for Shabbat Morning* (Philadelphia: P'na Or Religious Fellowship, 1991), which was edited by a feminist team of women and men, pioneers in providing context and examples for all these innovations.

13. These works were preceded by the groundbreaking collections *Jewish Women: New Perspectives*, ed. Elizabeth Koltun (New York: Schocken Books, 1976) and *On Being A Jewish Feminist*, ed. Susannah Heschel (New York: Schocken Books, 1983). Judith Baskin has edited an outstanding collection of essays that must be included in any serious study of Jewish women's history: *Jewish Women in Historical Perspective* (Detroit: Wayne State University Press, 1991). Paula E. Hyman's recent *Gender and Assimilation in Modern Jewish History* (Seattle: University of Washington Press, 1995) models how our understanding of Jewish history changes when gender is factored into the analysis.

14. Blu Greenberg, "Feminism Within Orthodoxy: A Revolution of Small Signs," *Lilith* (Summer 1992): 11–17.

15. See Greenberg.

16. In addition to the works mentioned above, the work of Rachel Adler, published as essays in periodicals and collections, is crucial for understanding the feminist critique of *halakhah*.

17. Greenberg, 16–17.

18. Tradition teaches that boys attain religious and legal maturity at the age of thirteen, and girls at age twelve. See also Alpert and Milgram, in this volume, and Barbara Goldin, *Bat Mitzvah* (New York: Morrow, 1995).

19. A full treatment of this document can be found in Adler's forthcoming *Engendering Judaism* (Philadelphia: Jewish Publication Society).

20. Savina Teubal's *simchat hochma* ritual is included in Ellen Umansky and Dianne Ashton, eds., *Four Centuries of Jewish Women's Spirituality* (Boston: Beacon, 1992), 257–65.

21. Selected rituals are available from the American Jewish Congress Feminist Center, 6505 Wilshire Boulevard, Suite 417, Los Angeles, CA 90048; the Reconstructionist Rabbinical College, Church Road and Greenwood Avenue, Wyncote, PA 19095; or the Jewish Women's Resource Center, 9 East 69th Street, New York, NY 10021. See Rebecca Alpert's excellent essay "Exploring Jewish Women's Rituals," *Bridges* 2/1 (Spring 1991), 66–80; Debra Orenstein, ed., *Lifecycles: Jewish Women on Life Passages and Personal Milestones* (Woodstock, Vt.: Jewish Lights, 1994); and Rela Geffen, ed., *Celebration and Renewal: Rites of Passage in Judaism* (Philadelphia: Jewish Publication Society, 1993).

22. See Lee T. Bycel, " 'To Reclaim our Voice': An Analysis of Representative Contemporary Feminist Passover Haggadot," *CCAR Journal: A Reform Jewish Quarterly* (Spring 1993): 55–71.

23. *The San Diego Women's Haggadah* (Women's Institute for Continuing Jewish Education, 1986) was one of the first to be available beyond a circumscribed locality. E. M. Broner's *The Telling* (San Francisco: HarperCollins,

1992) is the first feminist *haggadah* to be published by a mainstream publishing company.

24. See, for example, the *haggadot* compiled by Dov ben Khayyim, *The Telling: A Loving Hagadah for Passover* (Oakland, Ca.: Rakhamim Publications, 1983); New Jewish Agenda, *The Shalom Seders: Three Haggadahs* (New York: Adama Books, 1984); and Richard N. Levy, *On Wings of Freedom: The Hillel Haggadah for the Nights of Passover* (Hoboken, N.J.: B'nai B'rith Hillel Foundations in association with Ktav Publishing House, 1989).

25. See *V'Hayinu Kulanu Shama: And We Were All There* (Los Angeles: American Jewish Congress Feminist Center, 1993).

26. Letty Cottin Pogrebin, *Deborah, Golda and Me: Being Female and Jewish in America* (New York: Crown Books, 1991), 275.

27. See, for example two excellent studies: Linda Gordon Kuzmack, *Woman's Cause: The Jewish Woman's Movement in England and the United States, 1881–1933* (Columbus: Ohio State University Press, 1990); and Faith Rogow, *Gone to Another Meeting: The National Council of Jewish Women, 1893–1993* (Tuscaloosa: University of Alabama Press, 1992).

28. For further information on these coalitions, contact the American Jewish Congress, 6505 Wilshire Boulevard, Suite 417, Los Angeles, CA 90048.

Chronology

Key Events for Women's Religious Leadership in the United States—Nineteenth and Twentieth Centuries

Compiled by Catherine Wessinger

The following is a chronology of events important for women's religious leadership in the United States from about 1800 through 1995. This chronology is not exhaustive; facts will continue to be filled in as a more complete picture of women's religious leadership in the United States becomes available. The chronology documents that the process has not always been progressive—there have been steps taken backward as often as there have been steps forward.

Events that do not directly concern women's leadership in religious institutions but are nevertheless important landmarks along the way, such as mergers of denominations and significant secular and religious events, are italicized. Purely statistical information is also italicized.

This chronology includes some key events concerning women's religious leadership in other countries, because these have influenced events in the United States. Future studies must indicate more clearly the international connections in the saga of women's struggle for full inclusion in their religious institutions. In the past, women have often crossed boundaries to work for women, and will increasingly do so.

This chronology was constructed by combining data contained in this book with information taken from a variety of other sources.[1] Statistical data that are not referenced are taken from chapters in this book. The sources are indicated for other statistics given.

Blank pages have been provided at the end of the chronology, so that the reader may note additional significant events for women's religious leadership. The story continues.

1795–1830   The revival enthusiasm of the Second Great Awakening prompts
            Protestant Christian women to seek actively the salvation of
            themselves and others.

1796–1821   Mother Lucy Wright is the primary leader of the Shaker
            communities of celibate men and women.

1800   The Boston Female Society, the first women's missions society in
            America, is founded by Mary Webb and Congregationalist and
            Baptist women.

1809   Jarena Lee asks Rev. Richard Allen, who would later found the
            African Methodist Episcopal Church, that she be licensed to
            preach. Her request is denied.

1814   Abigail Roberts is converted by a woman preacher, Nancy
            Cram. Roberts founds numerous Christian churches until her
            ministry ends with her death in 1841.

1815   Free Will Baptists become the first Baptists in America to license
            women as preaching ministers.

1816   The African Methodist Episcopal Church is officially
            organized in Philadelphia with Rev. Richard Allen as its bishop.
            The AME women organize themselves as Daughters of
            Conference.

1817   Jarena Lee again asks Rev. Allen that she be licensed to preach.
            He directs her to hold prayer meetings in homes and exhort
            people to convert to Jesus.

1829   The first American Sunday school for children is founded by the
            First Baptist Church of Boston. Women come to predominate as
            Sunday school teachers in Protestant denominations, but not as
            supervisors.

1830s–   A mother and her daughter, both known as Marie Laveau, reign
1880s   as voodoo priestesses in New Orleans.

1832   Maria Stewart, an African-American abolitionist, addresses men
            and women in Franklin Hall in Boston. She is heckled so badly
            that she ceases public speaking, but she subsequently earns
            teaching credentials and opens a school.

1833   Lucretia Mott, a Quaker minister, helps to organize the
            Philadelphia Female Anti-Slavery Society, with black and white,
            Quaker and non-Quaker members.

1836   Sarah Lankford (Methodist) begins to hold the Tuesday Meeting
            for the Promotion of Holiness in her home. Phoebe Palmer
            assumes leadership of the meetings in 1840. These meetings,
            which average an attendance of about 200 and include
            Methodist bishops and clergy and laity from several
            denominations, are the beginning of the Holiness movement.

1836   Mary Lyon founds the Mt. Holyoke Female Seminary to train
            women to be teachers and missionaries. Female "seminaries"
            are increasingly founded for imparting higher education to
            American women.

1836–1837   Sisters and former slaveowners from Charleston, South Carolina,
            and members of the Female Anti-Slavery Society, Sarah and
            Angelina Grimké, on the basis of their Christian convictions,
            lecture to public audiences in New England advocating abolition
            of slavery. The Grimké sisters find that they must additionally
            advocate for the right of women to address public audiences
            and to function outside the domestic sphere. Ministers,
            including those who are abolitionists, are among those most
            agitated by the Grimké sisters' move into the public domain.
            Male abolitionists urge the sisters to drop their outspokenness
            for women's rights as detracting from the more urgent cause of
            abolishing slavery. Angelina writes in 1837, "*The time* to assert a
            right is *the* time when *that* right is denied." Sarah defends their
            actions and advocates for women ministers in *Letters on the
            Equality of the Sexes and the Condition of Women*, published in
            1838.

1837–1847   Shaker communities experience "Mother Ann's work," in which
            Shaker women are "instruments" or prophets who receive
            messages from Mother Ann Lee and Holy Mother Wisdom.
            Holy Mother Wisdom, however, advises Shaker women to keep
            to the traditional feminine virtues and not to assert themselves
            against male authority.

1839–1874   Methodist Phoebe Palmer publicly preaches at Holiness revivals,
            stimulating the widespread Holiness movement and numerous
            camp meetings. Her popular book, *The Way of Holiness*, is
            published in 1843. By 1867 the book is reprinted for the fiftieth
            time.

1840	Lucretia Mott, Elizabeth Cady Stanton, and other women, mostly Quakers, are not allowed to participate in the World's Anti-Slavery Convention in London. Mott and Stanton pledge to hold a women's rights convention in the United States.

1844   "The Great Disappointment" occurs on 22 October when the end of the world does not come as predicted by Millerite Adventists on the basis of the Book of Revelation. The young Ellen G. Harmon (later White) begins to have visions of the heavenly realm.

1844   The General Conference of the African Methodist Episcopal Church decides to admit laymen as delegates. Women are not admitted. A petition to authorize women to preach and exhort is rejected.

1845   *Southern Baptists split from Northern Baptists over slavery and form the Southern Baptist Convention (SBC). The Northern Baptist Convention later was known as the American Baptist Convention and is currently (1995) known as the American Baptist Churches USA.*

1846   The Breslau Conference (Reform) in Germany states that women are equal to men in Judaism in terms of "religious privileges and duties." The result is that in Reform Judaism women are counted in the *minyan* or quorum needed for public worship service, the daily prayer in which a man thanks God for not having made him a woman is dropped, girls and women are taught Torah and Talmud, and women and men sit together in the congregation.

1846   Ellen G. Harmon (later White) receives a vision that the Sabbath should be observed on the seventh day of the week. She marries an Adventist preacher, James White, and they undertake an itinerant ministry preaching Seventh-day Adventism.

1848   The General Conference of the African Methodist Episcopal Church is petitioned to license women as itinerant preachers. The General Conference refuses, but AME women continue preaching anyway.

1848   The Spiritualist movement begins when the young Fox sisters claim to be able to communicate with ghosts by means of raps. Women take on roles as mediums, the first form of religious leadership widely available to American women.

1848   Elizabeth Cady Stanton and Lucretia Mott organize and hold the first conference on women's rights in a Wesleyan Methodist Church in Seneca Falls, New York. They adopt a "Declaration of Sentiments" on women's rights modeled after the Declaration of Independence. One of its resolutions calls "for the overthrow of the monopoly of the pulpit" held by men. The Seneca Falls conference initiates the "first wave" of feminism in America and the long struggle for women's suffrage.

1850s   Women as Spiritualist trance speakers address public audiences, something improper for women to do when conscious.

1852   The senior bishop of the African Methodist Episcopal Church requests the General Conference to incorporate independent preaching women into its structures officially. The AME General Conference refuses.

1852   Anne Ayres founds an Episcopal deaconess organization known as the Community of the Holy Communion in New York City.

1853   Antoinette Brown (later Blackwell), age twenty-eight, is ordained on 15 September by a Congregationalist church in South Butler, New York.

1853   Wesleyan Methodist minister Luther Lee publishes the sermon he preached at the ordination of Antoinette Brown, "Women's Right to Preach the Gospel."

1855   Ellen and James White settle in Battle Creek, Michigan, and begin to organize the Seventh-day Adventist Church.

1859   Phoebe Palmer's book, *Promise of the Father*, asserting women's right to preach is published.

1859   Catherine Booth publishes her pamphlet, *Female Ministry: Woman's Right to Preach the Gospel*.

1860   *The Free Methodist Church is founded.*

1860   The Universalist Theological School at St. Lawrence University reluctantly admits Olympia Brown as a student.

1860   The interdenominational Woman's Union Missionary Society is founded.

1861–1865   The Civil War is fought.

1861   *The Woman's Union Missionary Society has one foreign missionary*
              in the field (Burma).

1862   Mary Baker Glover (later Eddy) begins studying mind-cure with
             Phineas P. Quimby in Portland, Maine.

1863   *The Emancipation Proclamation goes into effect on 1 January.*

1863   The Seventh-day Adventist Church is formally organized.
             Ellen G. White is regarded as the church's prophet, and in this
             year she has the first of her visions on proper healthful living.

1863   Olympia Brown is ordained minister by the St. Lawrence
             Association of Universalists in Malone, New York.

1863   Augusta Chapin is ordained minister by Universalists.

1864   The African Methodist Episcopal Church General Conference
             states that AME women cannot preach and cannot hold any
             AME office.

1865   The Thirteenth Amendment to the Constitution abolishes
             slavery.

1865   Catherine and William Booth found a mission in London that
             leads to the eventual founding of the Salvation Army.

1866   Mary Baker Glover (later Eddy), age forty-five, is injured by a
             fall on ice in Massachusetts. She subsequently heals herself by
             discovering the truth of Christian healing, which she would
             term Christian Science, while reading the New Testament. She
             begins her teaching and healing ministry.

1866   Universalists ordain Phebe Ann Hanaford.

1867   Melissa Timmons (later Terrill) is ordained at the Christian
             Ebenezer Church in Clark County, Ohio. She receives credentials
             of good standing from the local Christian Conference that
             nevertheless asserts, "we do not approve of the ordination of
             women to the Eldership of the church, as a general rule."

1868   The Unitarian seminary in Meadville, Pennsylvania, admits its
             first woman student.

1868   The Woman's Board of Missions is founded by
            Congregationalist women.

1868   The position of "stewardess" is created by the African
            Methodist Episcopal Church. The stewardess assists the
            ordained pastor's ministry to AME women. A congregation
            should have three to nine stewardesses, and these can be men if
            qualified women are lacking.

1869   Elizabeth Cady Stanton and Susan B. Anthony, a Quaker, found
            the National Woman's Suffrage Association. Lucy Stone, a
            Quaker, Julia Ward Howe, a Unitarian, and others organize the
            American Woman's Suffrage Association.

1869   The Woman's Foreign Missionary Society is founded by
            Methodist Episcopal women

1869   Margaret Newton Van Cott, an itinerant preacher, becomes the
            first woman to be licensed to preach by the Methodist Episcopal
            Church.

1870   Woman's Foreign Missionary Societies are founded by the
            Presbyterian Church, U.S.A.

1870   Protestant institutions begin to be founded to train single
            women as deaconesses to serve as missionaries in foreign lands
            or in American inner cities to newly arrived immigrants.

1870   Amanda Berry Smith of the African Methodist Episcopal Church
            begins her preaching ministry as a traveling evangelist, which
            will take her to England, India, and Liberia.

1871   Unitarians ordain Celia Burleigh in Connecticut and Mary
            Graves in Massachusetts.

1873   The Woman's Baptist Foreign Missionary Society is founded by
            American (northern) Baptist women.

1874   The Women's Parent Mite Missionary Society is founded by
            African Methodist Episcopal women.

1874   The Woman's Christian Temperance Union is founded.

1875   The Woman's Board of Foreign Missions is founded by
            Reformed Church in America women.

1875   Rabbi Isaac Mayer Wise founds Hebrew Union College (Reform)
            in Cincinnati and encourages women to attend.

1875   Mary Baker Eddy publishes *Science and Health, with Key to the
            Scriptures*.

1875   In New York City, Helena P. Blavatsky and Henry Steel Olcott
            found the Theosophical Society.

1877   Helena P. Blavatsky publishes her first major work, *Isis Unveiled*,
            which presents a monistic Theosophical cosmology based on
            Neoplatonism, the Cabala, and certain Indian texts, and which
            stimulates widespread interest in occultism.

1877   The Woman's American Baptist Home Missionary Society is
            founded.

1878   The Woman's Executive Committee for Home Missions is
            founded by Presbyterian women.

1878   The Woman's Missionary Society is founded by Methodist
            Episcopal Church, South women.

1878   William and Catherine Booth found the Salvation Army in
            London to assist and evangelize the poor.

1878   Susan B. Anthony has an amendment introduced to Congress
            that states, "The right of citizens of the United States to vote
            shall not be abridged by the United States on account of sex."

1879   The Woman's Missionary Society is founded by Evangelical
            Lutheran Church women.

1879   A Salvation Army ministry is established in Philadelphia by Amos
            and Annie Shirley and their daughter, Eliza Shirley, from England.

1879–1898   Frances Willard, Methodist, as president of the Woman's
            Christian Temperance Union (WCTU), the largest women's
            organization of its day, works for the extension of women's
            influence and activities to the public sphere by gaining higher
            education, entering the professions, working for social purity,
            and gaining suffrage.

1880   Frances Willard, in her first speech as president of the Woman's
            Christian Temperance Union, advocates for woman suffrage.

1880   The Methodist Episcopal Church refuses to ordain Anna Howard
        Shaw and Anna Oliver. Anna Howard Shaw is subsequently the
        first woman ordained in the Methodist Protestant Church. Later,
        Shaw shifts her ministry to the cause of woman suffrage.

1880   The preaching licenses of Margaret Newton Van Cott and other
        women are revoked by the Methodist Episcopal Church because
        of increasing pressure from women for ordination.

1880   The Congregationalist Women's Home Missionary Association is
        founded.

1881   The Woman's American Baptist Home Mission Society founds
        in Chicago the Woman's Baptist Missionary School, the first of
        many schools to educate women missionaries.

1881   James White dies, and Ellen G. White becomes even more
        important as the prophet of the Seventh-day Adventist Church.
        She subsequently becomes an international evangelist and
        medical missionary, working in Europe in 1885–1887, and
        Australia and New Zealand in 1891–1900. On six continents, she
        encourages the building of thirty-three Seventh-day Adventist
        sanitariums that utilize natural remedies.

1883   Frances Willard publishes *Woman in the Pulpit*.

1884   The African Methodist Episcopal Church licenses women to
        preach as evangelists. Bishop Turner is reprimanded for
        ordaining Sarah Hughes of North Carolina.

1884   The Woman's Home Missionary Society is founded by
        Methodist Episcopal women.

1885   The Chicago Training School is founded by Lucy Rider Meyer as
        the first Methodist Episcopal institution for the training of
        deaconesses.

1885   The first deaconess is consecrated by laying on of hands in the
        Episcopal Church.

1885   Emma Curtis Hopkins, editor of the *Christian Science Journal*,
        breaks with Mary Baker Eddy in Boston, moves to Chicago, and
        founds her own seminary. Her pupils subsequently become the
        founders of various New Thought denominations, and Hopkins
        becomes known as the "Mother of New Thought."

1886   *The Jewish Theological Seminary is founded to train rabbis in Conservative Judaism.*

1886   Myrtle and Charles Fillmore attend a lecture in Kansas City given by a student of Emma Curtis Hopkins. Myrtle Fillmore subsequently heals herself of tuberculosis by focusing on an affirmation gleaned from the lecture, "I am a child of God, and therefore I do not inherit sickness."

1886–1894 Traveling Pentecost Bands, founded by Vivian Dake of the Free Methodist Church, operate in Pennsylvania and the Midwest. In 1892 two-thirds of these approximately 125 evangelists are women.

1888   Helena P. Blavatsky publishes her magnum opus, *The Secret Doctrine*, in which the Theosophical cosmology draws more heavily on Indian thought and teaches the doctrine of reincarnation. Subsequent publications of the Theosophical Society popularize the idea of reincarnation in the West.

1888   Emma Curtis Hopkins restructures her Emma Curtis Hopkins School of Christian Science in Chicago to form the Christian Science (New Thought) Theological Seminary.

1888   The Woman's Missionary Union (WMU) is formed by Southern Baptist Convention women.

1888   Deaconesses, single women living in community and doing volunteer social work, teaching, and nursing, are licensed by the Methodist Episcopal church.

1888   Clara Celesta Hale Babcock in Ohio is the first woman ordained by the Disciples of Christ (Christian Church).

1888   The African Methodist Episcopal Church General Conference reaffirms the ban against women's ordination.

1888–1892 Rev. Anna Howard Shaw serves as superintendent of the Franchise (Suffrage) Department of the Woman's Christian Temperance Union (WCTU).

1889   Charles and Myrtle Fillmore begin to publish *Modern Thought*. The work of Charles and Myrtle Fillmore eventually results in the founding of the most successful New Thought denomination, Unity, that is eventually headquartered at Unity Village outside Kansas City.

1889   Emma Curtis Hopkins in Chicago ordains 20 women and 2 men,
            graduates of her Christian Science (New Thought) Seminary, on
            10 January, thus becoming the first woman to exercise the
            powers of the office of bishop in modern times.

1889   *There are 4 Congregationalist women who are ordained ministers.*

1889   Dr. George P. Hays, Presbyterian minister, publishes *May Women
            Speak?*, which argues that Pauline texts commanding women's
            silence are relevant only to the specific situation of Paul's day,
            and that women can be ordained ministers.

1889   Ella Niswonger is the first woman ordained in the United
            Brethren Church.

1889   The Episcopal Church formally authorizes the order of
            deaconesses, who are considered laywomen although they are
            ordained by laying on of hands.

1889   German Evangelists in St. Louis found the Evangelical
            Deaconess Society, which subsequently establishes 13 additional
            deaconess institutions and trains over 500 deaconesses within a
            period of about thirty years.

1890   *Mississippi adopts a plan to disenfranchise black men by requiring
            literacy tests and poll taxes that is subsequently emulated by other
            southern states. Violence against African Americans, including
            lynchings, reinforces the disenfranchisement of black men. At this
            point, no women have the right to vote in U.S. elections.*

1890   The General Assembly of the United Presbyterian Church notes
            the outstanding work, particularly in raising funds, of the
            Women's Board of Home Missions and the Women's Board of
            Foreign Missions.

1890   Christian women organize the Woman's Board for Home
            Missions.

1890   The National American Woman's Suffrage Association is formed
            by the merger of the National Woman's Suffrage Association
            and the American Woman's Suffrage Association.

1891   Alma White's mentor, the Methodist minister W. B. Godbey,
            publishes *Woman Preacher.*

1891   Charles and Myrtle Fillmore are ordained by Emma Curtis Hopkins, and they begin to publish *Unity*.

1891   Bylaws of Mary Baker Eddy's Church of Christ, Scientist, provide for one male and one female reader in public worship. Christian Science practitioners engage in an egalitarian healing ministry, in which they seek to empower their clients to heal themselves.

1891–1892   There are at least 88 Church of God traveling women evangelists, many working in teams or "companies."

1893   The Woman's Ministerial Conference is founded by Julia Ward Howe and displays an album containing photographs of women preachers and ministers at the Columbian Exposition in Chicago. The membership of the Woman's Ministerial Conference is predominantly Unitarian and Universalist, with some Methodists and Baptists. Its annual meetings are held in Boston.

1893   Universalist minister Rev. Augusta Chapin, as chair of the Women's Committee, addresses the opening session of the World's Parliament of Religions at the Columbian Exposition in Chicago. Other Christian women to address the Parliament include: Rev. Olympia Brown (Universalist minister); Julia Ward Howe; Fannie Barrier Williams, the only African-American woman to address the Parliament; and Frances E. Willard, president of the Woman's Christian Temperance Union. Rev. Antoinette Brown Blackwell's address on "Women and the Pulpit" is read by Rev. Augusta Chapin. Susan B. Anthony reads the paper by Elizabeth Cady Stanton. Three additional ordained Unitarian women to address the Parliament are Ida Hultin, Marion Murdock, and Celia Parker Wooley. One other woman, ordained by a nondenominational group but with close ties to Unitarianism, Anna Garlin Spencer, delivers an address. They address how religions subordinate women, and prescribe practical measures to raise women's status. Fannie Barrier Williams speaks on "Religion's Duty to the Negro." The only Asian woman to address the Parliament is a Christian from Bombay, Jeanne Sorabji.

1893   Two Jewish women, Josephine Lazarus and Henrietta Szold, address the World's Parliament of Religions. The Congress of Jewish Women, organized by Hannah G. Solomon, is held in conjunction with the Parliament. Crowds attend lectures of

Henrietta Szold, Josephine Lazarus, and Ray Frank. The Congress of Jewish Women continues after the Parliament as the National Council of Jewish Women (Reform), the first national Jewish women's organization, with Hannah G. Solomon as president.

1893   On the recommendation of Rev. Augusta Chapin as chair of the Woman's Committee of the World's Congress Auxiliary, members of the Theosophical Society make presentations at the Theosophical Congress, held in conjunction with the World's Parliament of Religions. Women speaking on Theosophy include Annie Besant, F. Henrietta Müller, and Isabel Cooper-Oakley.

1893   Mary Baker Eddy's speech is read at the World's Parliament of Religions by a male student, Judge Septimus Hanna, to the agitation of mainline clergymen. Eddy is angered when her speech is published in newspapers and attributed to Hanna. The rewritten paper, subsequently published in the Barrows collection of Parliament speeches, exalts the spiritual nature of woman.

1893   Emma Curtis Hopkins's students in the Hopkins Metaphysical Association form the Columbian Congress of Christian Scientists (New Thought) to interact with the women's organizations affiliated with the Queen Isabella Association of the Columbian Exposition in Chicago.

1893   Myrtle Fillmore begins to publish *Wee Wisdom*, the earliest and longest-running children's magazine.

1893   Alma White (Methodist) begins to preach Holiness revivals throughout Colorado and the surrounding states.

1894   H. Emilie Cady's first lesson is published in *Unity*. These lessons become Unity's first and most popular book, *Lessons in Truth*.

1894   Mary Lee Cagle begins her ministry after the death of her minister husband, ultimately founding eighteen New Testament Church of Christ congregations in Tennessee, Alabama, Arizona, and Texas.

1894   Edith Hill is the first woman ordained by American Baptists.

1895   Mary Baker Eddy publishes the *Church Manual of the First Church of Christ, Scientist, in Boston, Massachusetts*, which vests primary decision-making power of the church in herself.

1895   *The National Baptist Convention is formed by African-American*
        Baptist churches.

1896   *The U.S. Supreme Court declares the Civil Rights Act of 1875*
        prohibiting racial discrimination in public places unconstitutional,
        thus sanctioning "Jim Crow" segregation of African Americans.

1896   *The Salvation Army has over 1,000 women officers in the United*
        States out of a total of 1,854 officers, or at least 53.9 percent.

1896   A second African Methodist Episcopal women's missionary
        society is organized by southern women, the Woman's Home
        and Foreign Missionary Society (WHFMS).

1898   *Woman's Bible* is published, consisting of commentary by
        Elizabeth Cady Stanton and other women on biblical passages
        relating to women. Stanton stresses the ways the Bible is used to
        oppress women.

1899   *There are 49 Congregationalist women who are ordained ministers.*

1900   Nannie H. Burroughs, age twenty-one, addresses the National
        Baptist Convention meeting in Richmond, Virginia, on "How
        the Sisters Are Hindered from Helping," which prompts the
        formation of the Woman's Convention, Auxiliary to the
        National Baptist Convention.

1901   Alma White, evangelist in the Wesleyan/Holiness movement,
        founds a religious association, Pentecostal Union, that
        subsequently becomes the Pillar of Fire Church.

1902   Florence Amanda Fensham, a Congregationalist foreign
        missionary, earns a bachelor of divinity degree at the Chicago
        Theological Seminary.

1903   Charles and Myrtle Fillmore found the Unity School of
        Christianity, which subsequently grows into the most successful
        of the New Thought denominations.

1904   Evangeline Booth, daughter of Catherine and William Booth, is
        appointed by her father to be commander of the Salvation Army
        in the United States.

1904   Social reformer Bertha Pappenheim founds the Judischer
        Frauenbund, the German Jewish Women's Organization,

to lobby the Jewish community for women's full religious rights.

1904–1915   Rev. Anna Howard Shaw serves as president of the National American Woman's Suffrage Association.

1906   The first Unity ministers are ordained, four women and three men.

1906   *The National Baptist Convention's membership is 2,354,789 or 61.4 percent of African-American church members.*

1906   The Methodist Episcopal Church gives women lay rights.

1906   The Methodist Episcopal Church South places women's missionary societies under its Board of Missions.

1906   The Universalist Beuchtel College in Akron, Ohio, appoints a man to the Chloe Pierce Chair endowed by Universalist women to insure the presence of at least one woman on the faculty.

1907   The Woman's Missionary Union Training School is established in Louisville, Kentucky, by Southern Baptist women.

1908   National Baptist churches adopt Nannie H. Burroughs's idea of an annual Woman's Day to promote sisterhood and to raise funds for the Woman's Convention.

1908   *In the Church of the Nazarene, clergywomen constitute 20 percent of its ministers.*

1909   *The Woman's Union Missionary Society has 4,610 single women missionaries in the field, with over 2 million supporters who provide more than $4 million.*

1909   The Congregational Training School for Women is founded in Chicago by Florence Amanda Fensham to provide graduate theological education to women. Its graduates go on foreign missions, perform social work in American cities, and serve as salaried pastoral assistants.

1909   Nannie H. Burroughs of the National Baptist Convention founds the National Trade and Professional School for Women and Girls in Washington, D.C.

1910   Ellen G. White, after breaking with Dr. John Kellogg of Battle
            Creek, founds the College of Medical Evangelists in Loma
            Linda, California.

1910   *There are 89 Congregationalist women who are ordained ministers.*

1910   *The Woman's Union Missionary Society supports 2,100 schools, 75
            hospitals, 78 dispensaries, and many other helping institutions in
            foreign lands.*

1910   The Congregational Woman's League of Church Assistants is
            founded by Florence Amanda Fensham.

1910   Helen Barrett Montgomery, president of the Woman's American
            Baptist Foreign Mission Society and of the National Federation
            of Women's Boards of Foreign Missions, publishes *Western
            Women in Eastern Lands*, on the work of women missionaries for
            women in foreign lands. In this book Montgomery expresses her
            belief that the Christian Gospel promotes equality and
            democracy, and will ultimately bring an end to class
            distinctions, including the "caste of sex."

1911   Hadassah, the Women's Zionist Organization of America, is
            founded by Henrietta Szold (Conservative) to bring improved
            health care to Palestine.

1911   Alice Paul, a Hicksite Quaker, revitalizes the woman suffrage
            movement in the United States with her confrontational tactics,
            outdoor meetings, marches, demonstrations, and petitions for
            passage of the Susan B. Anthony amendment.

1915   Aimee Semple McPherson preaches and heals at Pentecostal
            revivals in Canada, commencing an itinerant ministry that
            includes much travel in the United States.

1915   The United Presbyterian Church approves the ordination of
            women as deacons.

1916   Alice Paul and her coworkers form the National Woman's Party.

1918   Alma White is consecrated bishop by William Godbey (a
            minister separated from the Methodist Episcopal Church) and
            thus becomes the first American woman bishop. She
            subsequently directs the founding of educational institutions,

including Alma White College in New Jersey by the Pillar of Fire Church.

1919   *There are 300 Congregationalist women who are church assistants.*

1919   *There are 67 Congregationalist women who are ordained ministers, out of a total of 5,695 Congregationalist ministers (.01 percent): 18 of these women pastor very small churches, 14 are copastors with their husbands, 14 are religious educators or pastoral assistants, and 21 are employed outside the denomination.*

1919   The American Association of Women Preachers is founded.

1919   The Church of England's Archbishop of Canterbury's Commission to Reconsider the Office of Deacons reports that there is no reason not to ordain women, but that the time is not right.

1920   *The Nineteenth Amendment to the Constitution is passed, granting American women the right to vote.*

1920   *There are 109 Congregationalist women who are ordained ministers.*

1920   Hartford Theological Seminary (Congregationalist) admits women without requiring them to state that they do not expect to enter the ministry.

1920   The Methodist Episcopal Church approves the licensing of women as preachers but does not give them Conference membership, which would entail commitment of the denomination to place them with congregations.

1920   The Lambeth Conference of the Anglican communion decides that ordination of a deaconess "confers on her Holy Orders" and makes her a member of the clergy.

1920   Mother Leafy Anderson moves from Chicago to New Orleans and founds the first African-American Spiritual church there. The Spiritual religion as practiced in New Orleans becomes a syncretic blend of elements drawn from Roman Catholicism, African-American Protestantism including Holiness and Pentecostalism, nineteenth-century Spiritualism, and African-based religions such as Voodoo. Spiritual churches in New Orleans offer ordination to women leaders as evangelists, ministers, bishops, and even archbishops.

1921   The American Association of Women Preachers begins to
        publish the *Woman's Pulpit* as its journal.

1921   Alma White publishes her pamphlet *Woman's Ministry*

1921   The issue of ordaining a woman rabbi is first raised by
        Martha Neumark, a student at the Hebrew Union College
        (Reform) and daughter of an HUC professor. The HUC
        faculty and the Central Conference of American Rabbis
        conclude that there is no reason not to ordain women, but
        the HUC Board of Governors maintains the policy of
        ordaining only men as rabbis.

1921   Helen Barrett Montgomery is elected president of the American
        (Northern) Baptist Convention.

1922   The first *bat mitzvah* in the United States takes place for Judith
        Kaplan, daughter of Rabbi Mordecai Kaplan, who subsequently
        becomes the inspirer of Reconstructionism.

1923   The National Woman's Party (NWP) introduces into Congress
        the Equal Rights Amendment. Alma White's Pillar of Fire is the
        only denomination to support the ERA at this time. White
        begins publishing a periodical, *Woman's Chains*.

1923   The United Presbyterian Church absorbs the Women's Board of
        Home Missions and the Women's Board of Foreign Missions. At
        this time, women's missionary training schools are closed. The
        UPC General Council appoints Katherine Bennett and Margaret
        Hodge to study "the causes of unrest among women" in the
        United Presbyterian Church.

1923   Aimee Semple McPherson's Angelus Temple (capacity 5,000) is
        opened in Los Angeles, with a Prayer Tower for constant prayer
        and LIFE (Lighthouse of International Foursquare Evangelism)
        Bible College.

1924   Aimee Semple McPherson begins the first radio station, KFSG,
        owned by a church.

1924   The Methodist Episcopal Church begins ordaining women as
        local preachers but does not give them full membership in the
        General Conference. This means that the General Conference has
        no obligation to place them as pastors in churches.

1925   *Women constitute 32 percent of the pastors for the Church of God (Anderson), making 1925 women pastors' peak year in this denomination.*

1925   The Congregationalist Women's Home Missionary Federation is absorbed into the denominational missionary organization.

1927   *There are 100 Congregationalist ordained women.*

1927   Aimee Semple McPherson founds a Pentecostal denomination, the International Church of the Foursquare Gospel.

1927   Three Congregationalist women's missionary associations are absorbed into the denomination's American Board of Commissioners for Foreign Missions.

1927   The Hodge-Bennett report to the United Presbyterian Church recommends that Presbyterian women be allowed to "take their place wherever and however their abilities and the needs of the church may call."

1928   Alma White's Pillar of Fire begins operating a radio station out of Denver. With a second radio station in 1931 in New Jersey, the Pillar of Fire may be the first American denomination to operate a network of radio stations.

1929   Ethlene Boone Cox gives the Woman's Missionary Union report to the Southern Baptist Convention, probably the first time a woman is allowed to speak at the Southern Baptist Convention.

1930   The United Presbyterian Church permits women to be ordained as elders, meaning that women can serve in governing bodies as lay members. Women still may not be ordained as ministers.

1930   *Women constitute 2.2 percent of all clergy in the United States.[2]*

1930   *There are 131 Congregationalist women who are ordained ministers out of a total of 5,609 ministers, or 2.2. percent.*

1930   *There are 45 ordained women who are ministers of the Christian Church, out of a total of 917 ministers, or 4.9 percent.*

1930   The Lambeth Conference of the Anglican communion revokes its decision that ordination of deaconesses confers Holy Orders.

1931   *Congregationalist and Christian connection churches merge.*

1934–1950   Evangeline Booth is general of the Salvation Army.

1935   The Church of England's Archbishop's Commission to Study
            the Ministry of Women reports that the time is still not right to
            ordain women as priests.

1938   The Lutheran Church of Norway approves the ordination of
            women.

1938   Tehilla Lichtenstein is the first woman (nonordained) to serve
            her congregation as rabbi after the death of her husband,
            Rabbi Morris Lichtenstein. Tehilla Lichtenstein serves as
            leader of the Society for Jewish Science from 1938 until her
            death in 1973.

1940   *Women constitute 2.3 percent of all clergy in the United States.[3]*

1940   *There are 184 Congregational Christian ordained women, who
            constitute 3.1 percent of the total Congregational Christian clergy.*

1944   Due to the shortage of Anglican priests in China, the Anglican
            bishop of Hong Kong, the Rt. Rev. R. O. Hall, ordains a Chinese
            woman deacon, Li Tim-Oi (1907–1993), to the Anglican
            priesthood. The Rev. Li Tim-Oi ministers in Macao.

1944   The northern and southern AME women's missionary
            organizations merge. A resolution on the ordination of women
            is narrowly defeated at the AME General Conference.

1944   At Aimee Semple McPherson's death, her International Church
            of the Foursquare Gospel has an international membership of
            22,000, with 400 congregations in the United States and 200
            foreign missions.

1946   The first proposal to the Episcopal General Convention that
            women be eligible to serve as lay delegates is rejected.

1946   At Alma White's death, her eldest son becomes bishop of the
            Pillar of Fire Church with a membership of about 4,000.

1946   Kathryn Kuhlman experiences baptism of the Holy Spirit and
            begins her thirty-two-year itinerant Pentecostal healing and
            preaching ministry, attracting many thousands to her meetings.

1948   The African Methodist Episcopal Church General Conference approves the ordination of women as ministers.

1948   The Evangelical and Reformed Church ordains a woman as minister, Beatrice M. Weaver, the first woman to earn a B.D. degree from Lancaster Theological Seminary.

1948   The Lambeth Conference (Anglican) denies Bishop Hall's request to be allowed to ordain other women to the Anglican priesthood in China. The license of the Rev. Li Tim-Oi to minister as an Anglican priest is rescinded.

1950   *Women constitute 4.1 percent of all clergy in the United States.*[4]

1950   *Women constitute less than 30 percent of Americans with bachelor's degrees.*[5]

1951–1954   Paula Ackerman (nonordained) in Meridian, Mississippi, serves as rabbi to a congregation after the death of her husband, Rabbi William Ackerman.

1952   *Fourteen percent of leadership positions in Southern Baptist agencies and institutional structures are held by women.*

1953   The Presbytery of Rochester requests the United Presbyterian Church General Assembly to approve the ordination of women as ministers.

1953   The president of the Woman's Missionary Union is included as a member of the Executive Committee of the Southern Baptist Convention.

1955   Northern Baptist women's foreign and home missions societies are absorbed into the American Baptist Home Mission and the American Baptist Foreign Mission Society.

1956   Women ministers gain full ordination and Conference membership in the Methodist Episcopal Church.

1956   The United Presbyterian Church approves the ordination of women as ministers.

1957   *A new denomination, the United Church of Christ, is created by the merger of the Evangelical and Reformed Church with the Congregationalist Christians.*

1960   *Women constitute 2.3 percent of all clergy in the United States.*[6]

1960   *Women constitute 35 percent of Americans with bachelor's degrees.*[7]

1961   *Unitarians and Universalists merge to form one denomination.*

1961   The Lutheran Church of Norway ordains Ingrid Bjerkaas as its first woman minister.

1961   The ordination of women is approved by the Lutheran Church in Sweden.

1961   Fr. Elwood C. Voss in Pueblo, Colorado, initiates the founding of the Theresians of the United States, a women's organization consisting primarily of Roman Catholic laywomen including Sisters. Theresian women pursue the aims of spiritual growth, ongoing education, loving community, religious vocation, and ministry.

1962   The first three women are ordained in the Lutheran Church of Sweden.

1963   Marie Mathis is elected vice president of the Southern Baptist Convention.

1963   Betty Friedan publishes *The Feminine Mystique*, thus stimulating the "second wave" of feminism in America.

1963–1965   The Second Vatican Council meets to update Roman Catholicism in order to make it relevant in the modern world. To the proceedings of about 3,000 men 22 women are admitted as auditors. Subsequent to Vatican II, women begin to be admitted to Roman Catholic theological schools.

1964   The Presbyterian Church U.S. approves the ordination of women as deacons, elders, and ministers.

1964   The Unitarian-Universalist General Assembly resolves to recruit able candidates, men and women, for ministry; develop equal salary structures; and make financial assistance for theological school available to women as well as men.

1964   Anne Jordheim, after meeting numerous Lutheran women ministers in Europe, publishes an article entitled "Should Women Be Allowed to Occupy the Pulpit or Not?" in the American Lutheran Church's *Lutheran Standard*. The following

month, the Lutheran Church of America's *The Lutheran*
publishes a reader's question about the LCA's position on
women. Both the ALC and the LCA begin to note the actions of
other Protestant denominations to ordain women.

1964   Addie Davis is the first woman ordained by Southern Baptists,
        but no church in the Southern Baptist Convention will hire her
        to be its pastor. She subsequently is hired by a Baptist church in
        New England.

1964   *The Civil Rights Act prohibits discrimination according to race or sex.*
        Due to the separation of church and state, this law cannot be enforced
        in religious institutions by the United States government. But the
        passage of the Civil Rights Act promotes a greater social expectation of
        equality.

1965   The Second Vatican Council mandates that Roman Catholic
        women and men in vowed religious orders revise the
        constitutions of their institutes in order to update their rules and
        practices and renew the vowed religious life. Women's orders
        begin the shift to democratic forms of self-government but find
        difficulty in having their new constitutions approved by the
        Vatican.

1965   Episcopal bishop James Pike administers the holy order to a
        deaconess, making her a deacon, the Rev. Mrs. Phyliss Edwards,
        and puts her in charge of a parish.

1965   Lutheran Church-Missouri Synod approves women's suffrage in
        congregations as long as it does not contradict God's "created
        order" of women's subordination to men. The LC-MS stresses
        that it does not permit women to preach, teach, or exercise
        authority over men.

1966   *There are 181,000 Roman Catholic Sisters in the United States.*

1966   *The Association of Unity Churches (AUC) is formed as an*
        organization of ordained Unity ministers. The founding Board of
        Trustees is composed of nine men and one woman.

1967   The Sisters' Survey, a sociological survey instrument, is sent to
        157,000 American Sisters, thus prompting many Sisters seriously
        to consider appropriating and implementing the Vatican II
        agenda of the "special option for the poor."

1967   A commission reports to the Episcopal General Convention that there are no reasons not to ordain women to all orders of ministry. The General Convention appoints another commission to study the issue further and report in 1970.

1968   *The Methodist Church and the Evangelical United Brethren merge to form the United Methodist Church.*

1968   A report to the Lutheran Church in America convention states that there are no "biblical or theological reasons for denying ordination to women." The faculty of the American Lutheran Church's Luther Theological Seminary issue a statement that there is no "valid reason" why qualified women should not be ordained to the ministry.

1968   The Anglican Lambeth Conference states that women may be ordained deacons if the local province (national church) approves. The provinces of Hong Kong, New Zealand, Canada, and Kenya begin ordaining women as deacons and declare that deaconesses are members of the ordained diaconate.

1968   *The Reconstructionist Rabbinical College is founded in Philadelphia based on the ideals of Rabbi Mordecai Kaplan, a strong advocate of the equality of all persons.*

1968   Pope Paul VI issues the encyclical *"Humanae vitae,"* reaffirming the Roman Catholic prohibition on artificial contraception. Many Catholic married couples use contraception anyway, and numerous Catholics (married, single, priests, Sisters, Brothers, and bishops) do not find the logic of *"Humanae vitae"* compelling.

1968   Mary Daly publishes her book *The Church and the Second Sex,* which sparks the beginning of the feminist theological enterprise and its unmasking and critiquing of patriarchal theology.

1969   The Lutheran Church-Missouri Synod (LC-MS) convention officially gives women the right to vote and hold office in congregations but reiterates that women cannot hold pastoral office or exercise authority over men.

1969   The American Lutheran Church Women requests a study of the issue of ordination of women.

1969–1972 Cynthia Wedel (Episcopal) serves as the first woman president of the National Council of the Churches of Christ in the USA (NCC).

1970   *Women constitute 2.9 percent of all clergy in the United States.*[8]

1970   The Lutheran Church in America's Lutheran Church Women
            (LCW) calls for the ordination of women.

1970   The Lutheran Church of America and the American Lutheran
            Church both approve the ordination of women.

1970   A commission recommends to the Episcopal General
            Convention that women be ordained to all ministerial orders,
            but this recommendation is rejected. The General Convention at
            this time approves the ordination of women as deacons. The
            Episcopal General Convention approves the admission of
            women as lay delegates.

1970   The Anglican Consultative Council (consisting of clergy, bishops,
            and laity of all provinces) narrowly approves a measure that
            bishops may ordain women as priests if they have the
            permission of their province (national church).

1970   The Rev. Li Tim-Oi's ordination (1944) to the Anglican
            priesthood is officially recognized, and her license to minister as
            an Anglican priest is restored.

1971   Responding to continued shortage of male priests, the bishop of
            Hong Kong, the Rt. Rev. Gilbert Baker, ordains two women
            deacons as priests, the Rev. Jane Hwang and the Rev. Joyce
            Bennett.

1971   The Episcopal Women's Caucus is formed to work for equality
            of women in the Episcopal Church, including ordination of
            women as priests.

1971   The United Church of Christ appoints a Task Force on Women
            in Church and Society to study women's position within UCC
            institutional structures and to make recommendations to
            eliminate sexism in church and society.

1971   The Lutheran Church-Missouri Synod requests that the
            American Lutheran Church retract its decision to ordain women.
            The ALC in response rejects "order of creation" theology that
            subordinates women to men.

1971–1972   *Women constitute 8.5 percent of United Church of Christ seminary
            students.*

1972   *Women constitute 45 percent of Americans with bachelor's degrees.*[9]

1972   Sally Priesand is the first woman rabbi ordained in the United
            States by a Jewish theological seminary, Reform Judaism's
            Hebrew Union College in Cincinnati, Ohio.

1972   The American Lutheran Church establishes the Task Force on
            Women in Church and Society. The American Lutheran Church
            convention resolves to place more women in leadership
            positions, use more inclusive language, encourage women to
            theological leadership, and include more women at the next
            (1974) convention of the denomination.

1972   The Lutheran Church in America convention creates a
            Consulting Committee on Women in Church and Society
            (CCWCS) to survey participation and attitudes of LCA women,
            develop guidelines for inclusive language in published
            materials, develop strategies to increase proportionate
            representation of women in LCA decision-making bodies, and
            work with similar committees in other Lutheran denominations.

1972   Druecillar Fordham is the first woman pastor and the first black
            ordained woman in the Southern Baptist Convention.

1973   The Episcopal General Convention narrowly rejects a resolution
            to ordain women as priests and bishops. Those opposing such a
            measure argue that it will create schism.

1973   The first Jewish feminist conference convenes in New York City.

1973   Emma Richards is the first woman ordained in the Mennonite
            Church in North America.

1974–1984   Claire Randall (Presbyterian) serves as the first woman general
            secretary of the National Council of the Churches of Christ in
            the USA (NCC).

1974   The Leadership Conference of Women Religious (heads of Roman
            Catholic women's orders in America) adopts a resolution that all
            ministries in the Church should be open to women and men as the
            Spirit calls them, and women should have active participation in
            all decision-making bodies in the Roman Catholic Church.

1974   Three retired or resigned Episcopal bishops ordain 11 qualified
            white women deacons to the Episcopal priesthood in the

African-American Church of the Advocate in Philadelphia on
29 July. These ordinations are quickly termed by the Episcopal
Church as "irregular" and not valid.

1974   The Church of God (Anderson) resolves to make efforts to
promote women's opportunities for church leadership.

1974   Sandy Eisenberg Sasso is the first woman ordained by the
Reconstructionist Rabbinical College.

1974   *The number of women attending North American seminaries that
belong to the Association of Theological Schools of the United States
and Canada (ATS) is 5,255, constituting 14.3 percent of
seminarians.*[10]

1974   *The Unitarian-Universalist Women's Federation publishes a report
showing that of the more than 750 U-U clergy, fewer than 40 are
women and that only 5 of these have pulpits, and they are underpaid.*

1974   The Ministerial Sisterhood Unitarian-Universalist (MSUU) is
founded. Subsequently, affirmative action workshops are given
to congregations, and feminist educational materials are
distributed.

1974   *All We're Meant to Be: A Biblical Approach to Women's Liberation*
by Letha Scanzoni and Nancy Hardesty is published.

1974–1975   *Women constitute 21 percent of United Church of Christ seminary
students.*

1975   A retired Episcopal bishop "irregularly" ordains four more
qualified white women as Episcopal priests in the African-
American Church of St. Stephen and the Incarnation in
Washington, D.C. on 7 September.

1975   The United Church of Christ implements an Affirmative Action
Plan for women and minorities in UCC structures.

1975   The first Women's Ordination Conference (primarily Roman
Catholic) meets in Detroit and calls for a renewed (reformed)
and democratic priestly ministry, resulting in the national
organization called the Women's Ordination Conference.

1976   *The Unitarian-Universalist seminary student body consists of 57
women and 93 men.*

1976   The Episcopal General Convention approves the ordination of
            women to the priesthood and the episcopate. The fifteen
            "irregularly" ordained women priests are subsequently
            admitted to regular standing.

1976   In response to the debate in the Anglican communion over the
            ordination of women, Pope Paul VI directs the Congregation for
            the Doctrine of the Faith to produce a document spelling out the
            teachings of the Roman Catholic Church on the matter. The
            result is the "Declaration on the Question of the Admission of
            Women to the Ministerial Priesthood" ("*Inter Insigniores*"). It
            states that the Roman Catholic Church has to remain true to
            Jesus Christ's intent that women not be admitted to the
            ordained ministerial priesthood. It further argues that since the
            priest celebrating the Mass represents Christ in a nuptial relation
            to his bride, the Church, the priest must resemble Christ by
            being male. This reasoning is roundly rejected by feminist
            Roman Catholic women and men.

1976   Mrs. Carl Bates is the second woman elected to be vice
            president of the Southern Baptist Convention.

1976   *The Association of Evangelical Lutheran Churches (AELC) breaks
            with the Lutheran Church-Missouri Synod over proper interpretation
            of the Bible. The AELC approves the ordination of women as
            ministers.*

1977   *There are 10,470 women ordained to full ministry in the United
            States, constituting 4 percent of American clergy.[11]*

1977   *There are 157 clergywomen in the American Baptist Convention.
            There are 18 clergywomen in the American Lutheran Church,
            constituting .3 percent of the entire ALC clergy. There are 388
            clergywomen in the Christian Church (Disciples), constituting 5.7
            percent of the clergy. There are 94 clergywomen in the Episcopal
            Church, constituting .8 percent of Episcopal clergy. There are 55
            clergywomen in the Lutheran Church in America, constituting .7
            percent of LCA clergy. There are 75 clergywomen in the Presbyterian
            Church, U.S., constituting 1.4 percent of the clergy. There are 400
            United Church of Christ clergywomen, constituting 4.1 percent of
            UCC clergy. There are 319 clergywomen in the United Methodist
            Church, constituting .8 percent of the clergy. There are 295
            clergywomen in the United Presbyterian Church, USA, constituting
            2.1 percent of clergy.[12]*

1977   *The number of ordained clergywomen in the United States is estimated to be 4 percent of American clergy; 32.2 percent of women clergy are found in the Pentecostal family of churches; 30.4 percent are found in denominations such as the Salvation Army, Volunteers of America, and American Rescue Workers, and 17.7 percent are found in ten major denominations.[13]*

1977   *The four largest Holiness denominations report 4,119 women clergy: the Salvation Army, 3,037; the Church of the Nazarene, 426; the Church of God (Anderson), 272; and the Wesleyan Church, 384.[14]*

1977   Janith Otte becomes the first woman ordained by the Association of Evangelical Lutheran Churches.

1977   The Unitarian-Universalist General Assembly resolves to eliminate sexist assumptions and language by Unitarian-Universalist Association administrative officers and staff. The Women and Religion Committee is established.

1977   The first "regular" Episcopal ordinations of women priests take place. The Episcopal Church downplays the earlier ordinations of women. Women ordained at this time are praised for being patient.

1978   *The Association of Evangelical Lutheran Churches calls for union with the American Lutheran Church and the Lutheran Church in America.*

1979   *Women attending North American seminaries associated with ATS (Association of Theological Schools of the United States and Canada) number 10,204, constituting 21.1 percent of seminarians.[15]*

1979   *Unitarian-Universalist seminary students consist of 97 women and 92 men.*

1979   Teresa Kane, as president of the Leadership Conference of Women Religious, on 7 October welcomes Pope John Paul II to the United States and challenges him to give women access to all ministries of the Roman Catholic Church. When Pope John Paul II subsequently was asked what he thought of Teresa Kane's speech, he replied that he had not been able to hear it.

1979   The Jewish Theological Seminary (Conservative) Faculty Senate tables the issue of admitting women for rabbinical training as "provoking unprecedented divisions. . . . The bitter divergence of opinion threatens to inflict irreparable damage."

1979   Two books are published that mark the movement of feminist
            wicca (witchcraft) into the public sphere: Starhawk, *The Spiral
            Dance: A Rebirth of the Ancient Religion of the Great Goddess*
            (Harper & Row); and Margot Adler, *Drawing Down the Moon*
            (Viking).

1979   The United Church of Christ creates the Coordinating Center for
            Women in Church and Society, and the First National Meeting
            of UCC Women is held.

1979   The Black Ministers Conference of Baltimore and Vicinity
            (Baptist) admits women preachers.

1980   *Women constitute 4.2 percent of all clergy in the United States.*[16]

1980   *Women constitute 9 percent of United Church of Christ ordained clergy.*

1980   *Nearly one-fourth of students in mainline Protestant denominational
            seminaries are women. Women constitute 45 percent of UCC seminary
            students.*[17]

1980   The General Assembly of the Church of the Nazarene adopts a
            resolution affirming the historic right of women to be elected
            and appointed to positions of leadership.

1980   *A sociological survey by Edward C. Lehman, Jr., finds that only 1 to 4
            percent of Presbyterian laypeople would choose a woman minister to
            pastor their church over a male minister.*

1980   Marjorie Matthews is elected the first mainline Protestant
            woman bishop by the United Methodists.

1980   The Lutheran Church in America publishes *Emerging Roles of
            Women and Men in Church and Society* and *English Language
            Guidelines for Using Inclusive Liturgical Language in the Lutheran
            Church in America.*

1980   Sonia Johnson, a Mormon woman working for the passage of
            the Equal Rights Amendment, is excommunicated by the
            Church of Jesus Christ of Latter-day Saints.

1981   Christine Burton Gregory is elected first vice president of the
            Southern Baptist Convention. As of 1993 no woman has been
            elected to national office in the Southern Baptist Convention
            since Gregory.

1981   *The Unitarian-Universalist Association creates a new ordained position, minister of religious education, to replace the earlier certified director of religious education. Qualifications to be minister of religious education may be earned through independent study rather than attending seminary.*

1983   Roman Catholic women hold a conference in Chicago entitled "From Generation to Generation: Woman Church Speaks." This is an important beginning for the Women-Church movement.

1983   Canon 517.2 in the revised Roman Catholic Code of Canon Law states that due to the shortage of priests, a bishop may appoint a layperson or deacon (under the supervision of a priest) to provide "pastoral care" to a parish.

1983   The United Church of Christ ordained minister Carol Joyce Brun is elected the denomination's secretary, the second highest UCC staff position.

1983   The United Church of Christ advises its congregations not to discriminate against homosexual candidates for the ministry.

1983   A joint conference of American Lutheran Church and Lutheran Church in America women in Omaha, Nebraska, on "The Future of Women in the New Lutheran Church," calls for quotas for representation of women on decision-making bodies and for a self-supporting women's organization in the new Lutheran denomination.

1983   *The Presbyterian Church in the United States (PCUS) merges with the United Presbyterian Church in United States of America (UPCUSA) to form the Presbyterian Church (U.S.A.).*

1983   The Jewish Theological Seminary (Conservative) Faculty Senate votes to admit women for rabbinical training.

1984   Conservative Judaism's Jewish Theological Seminary admits 18 women into its rabbinical program.

1984   The Network for United Church of Christ Clergywomen is formed. It subsequently disbands in 1990.

1984   The Reconstructionist Rabbinical College faculty vote to admit gay and lesbian students.

1984   The Southern Baptist Convention passes a resolution stating that women and men are equal in dignity, but that God in the order of creation established the authority of men over women, so that women are prohibited from ordained ministry and should focus their concerns on the home.

1984   *Thirteen percent of leadership positions in Southern Baptist agencies and institutional structures are held by women.*

1984   Judith Craig and Leontine T. C. Kelly are elected bishops in the United Methodist Church.

1984   Roman Catholic laypeople and 24 Sisters sign an ad in the *New York Times* on 7 October stating that "A Diversity of Opinions Regarding Abortion Exists Among Committed Catholics." The Vatican subsequently pressures the Sisters to sign documents retracting this statement and stating that they abide by the Roman Catholic Church's position on this issue, or be expelled from their religious communities. There is much negotiation. Twenty-two Sisters sign compromise statements, some of which do not retract the Sisters' original stand, but the Vatican interprets these documents as retractions. Barbara Ferraro and Pat Hussey, two Sisters of Notre Dame, do not sign and in 1988 voluntarily leave their order.

1984   The *Inclusive Language Lectionary* prepared by a committee of 6 male and 6 female scholars appointed by the National Council of Churches of Christ in the U.S.A. is published, containing translations of biblical texts utilizing inclusive language for God, Jesus, and humans.

1984   A service is held in Westminster Abbey to celebrate Rev. Li Tim-Oi's ordination to the Anglican priesthood in 1944 in China.

1985   *There is a 20 percent decline in Roman Catholic diocesan priests in America since 1966, with an additional 20 percent decline expected by 2005. The expected increase of American Catholic laity from 1966 to 2005 is 65 percent. The 1985 ratio of Roman Catholic laity to priests is 1,418:1. The predicted ratio for 2005 is 2,193:1.*[18]

1985   *American Baptists have 199 clergywomen, who constitute 3 percent of a total 6,600 clergy.*[19]

1985   Amy Eilberg is ordained as the first Conservative woman rabbi.

1986   *There are 1,524 ordained clergywomen in the Presbyterian Church (U.S.A.), a 310 percent increase over the previous ten years.*

1986   *The United Church of Christ has 1,460 clergywomen, who constitute 14 percent of the total of 10,085 clergy.[20]*

1986   *In the United States, there are about 20,730 women ordained to full ministry, constituting 7.9 percent of American clergy. This is an increase of 98 percent in the number of ordained clergywomen since 1977. The major increases in clergywomen during this time were in the Assemblies of God (+2,146) and in the ten major denominations affiliated with the National Council of Churches (+5,686).[21]*

1986   *The four Holiness denominations report 4,105 women clergy: the Salvation Army, 3,220; the Church of the Nazarene, 355; the Church of God (Anderson), 275; and the Wesleyan Church, 255.[22]*

1987   Roman Catholic women hold a conference in Cincinnati entitled "Women Church: Claiming Our Power."

1987   The United Church of Christ Coordinating Center for Women in Church and Society is set up to support women's ministries.

1987   The Church of England admits women to the diaconate.

1987   The American Lutheran Church (ALC), the Lutheran Church in America (LCA), and the Association of Evangelical Lutheran Churches (AELC) merge to form the Evangelical Lutheran Church in America (ELCA). An ordained woman is considered for national bishop (president) of the ELCA, but a man is elected. Christine Grumm is elected as vice president of ELCA, making her chair of the ELCA's Church Council. The new ELCA establishes the Commission for Women to monitor hiring practices and to advocate for women, and establishes an independently incorporated women's organization, Women of the Evangelical Lutheran Church in America (WELCA). The ELCA sets quotas for churchwide assemblies: 60 percent laypeople, half being women; and 10 percent persons of color or persons whose first language is not English.

1987   Connie Fillmore, great-granddaughter of Charles and Myrtle Fillmore, becomes president of Unity School of Christianity, which coordinates Unity's prayer ministry, publications, and education.

1987   *Christian Churches (Disciples of Christ) have 744 clergywomen,*
              constituting 12 percent of 6,124 total clergy.[23]

1987   *The Episcopal Church has 1,167 clergywomen, constituting 9 percent*
              of 13,000 total clergy.[24]

1987   *The Presbyterian Church, USA, has 1,421 clergywomen, constituting*
              7 percent of 19,450 total clergy.[25]

1987   *Southern Baptists have 350 clergywomen, constituting .5 percent of*
              60,000 total clergy.[26]

1987   *There are 101 Reform women rabbis, constituting 7 percent of 1,450*
              Reform rabbis.[27]

1987   *The United Methodist Church has 3,444 clergywomen, constituting*
              about 9 percent of 39,136 total clergy. At United Methodist
              seminaries, women are almost 41 percent of M.Div. candidates.[28]

1987   *The Theresians are now an international association of women, with*
              83 groups in the United States, Canada, the Philippines, Hong Kong,
              England, Ghana, Kenya, and Thailand, and a membership of about
              2,500. Membership in the Theresians is open to all women.[29]

1988   Susan Morrison and Sharon Christopher are elected bishops in
              the United Methodist Church.

1988   The Jewish Women's Studies Project is begun by students and
              faculty at the Reconstructionist Rabbinical College to promote
              Women's Studies at that institution.

1988   The first draft of American Roman Catholic bishops' pastoral
              letter on women in church and society, "Partners in the Mystery
              of Redemption," is widely read and critiqued by Roman
              Catholic women and men after being published in March.
              Despite its many feminist features (declaring that "sexism is a
              sin"), the document is roundly rejected by feminists for not
              going far enough.

1988   In October, Pope John Paul II issues "On the Dignity and
              Vocation of Women" (*"Mulieris Dignitatum"*), a very
              conservative document that affirms the equal human dignity of
              women but sees women's vocation only in terms of virginity or
              motherhood.

1988–1989   Patricia McClurg (Presbyterian) serves as president of the
            National Council of the Churches of Christ in the USA (NCC).

1989   The African-American Episcopal woman priest Barbara C.
            Harris is consecrated suffragan (assistant) bishop of
            Massachusetts in the Episcopal Church on 11 February. She is
            the first woman bishop within the Anglican communion. On
            this occasion, the Rt. Rev. Harris concelebrates the eucharist
            with Rev. Li (age eighty).

1989   Church of God (Anderson) women clergy hold their first
            consultation.

1989   Wesleyan Women in Ministry hold their first conference.

1989   *A Presbyterian survey finds that only 2 percent of church members
            and elders would choose a female minister over a male, and over 50
            percent of church members said they preferred a male minister.*

1989   *There are 49 women pastoring Church of the Nazarene congregations
            in the United States, constituting less than 1 percent of the 5,129
            Nazarene congregations.*

1989   *Unitarian-Universalist seminary students consist of 233 women and
            136 men.*

1989   The New Revised Standard Version of the Bible is published,
            with Romans 16 correctly translated to refer to Junia and her
            probable husband Andronicus as being "prominent among the
            apostles." For centuries male translators had changed the name
            to Junias, indicating that this apostle was a man. This biblical
            statement that can be interpreted as saying that Junia was an
            apostle contradicts the Roman Catholic Church's argument that
            women cannot be priests because all of the apostles were men.

1989   Rev. Charlotte Ann Nichols is the first African-American woman
            appointed district superintendent in the United Methodist
            Church.

1989   Church of God women begin publishing *Women in Ministry and
            Mission.*

early   *There are about 99,000 Roman Catholic Sisters in the United States,*
1990s   *only 1 percent under thirty years old and 28 percent over eighty.*

early   *One-quarter of the 1,200 Unitarian-Universalist clergy are*
1990s   *women.*

1990   Rev. Mary Brown Oliver is the second African-American woman
            appointed district superintendent in the United Methodist
            Church. There are a total of 52 women district superintendents
            out of 450 in the United States.

1990   *One-quarter of Unitarian-Universalist ordained clergy are women.*
            U-U clergywomen still serve primarily in the smallest congregations of
            less than one hundred members.

1990   *Women constitute 18 percent of United Church of Christ ordained*
            clergy. A study of UCC clergywomen finds that there was a 100
            percent increase in ordained women in the previous ten years; only 13
            percent of UCC senior or solo pastors are women; women constitute
            52 percent of the UCC associate pastors or ordained Christian
            Education staff; 25 percent of the UCC clergy serving non-UCC
            churches are women; 38 percent of clergy in counseling or health care
            ministries are women; 29 percent of UCC clergy serving as chaplains
            or missionaries are women; 16 percent of UCC clergy serving in
            denominational work are women; and 25 percent of UCC clergy who
            are unclassified or on leave are women.

1990   *There are 2,257 ordained clergywomen in the Presbyterian Church*
            (U.S.A.).

1990   *There are 1,198 ordained clergywomen in the Evangelical Lutheran*
            Church in America, constituting 6.9 percent of the 17,253 ELCA
            clergy; 883 or 74 percent of ELCA clergywomen serve as assistants,
            associates, and solo pastors. In the ELCA, 96 clergywomen (8 percent)
            work for synods, hold chaplaincies, or teach in seminaries; 35
            clergywomen (2.9 percent) serve churchwide agencies; 34 (2.8 percent)
            are Asian, African American, Hispanic, or Native American. Fifty-
            four percent of ELCA clergywomen have been ordained during the
            previous five years, whereas only 7.6 percent of the ELCA clergymen
            were ordained during that time. ELCA clergywomen serve in one-third
            of all part-time ELCA positions.[30]

1990   *A survey by the Central Conference of American Rabbis (Reform)*
            shows that 57 out of 153 Reform women rabbis work full-time in
            congregations that belong to the Union of American Hebrew
            Congregations: 16 are assistant rabbis, 10 are associate rabbis, and 31
            are solo rabbis. There are only 37 Reform women rabbis with the

requisite experience making them eligible to become senior rabbi of a congregation of more than 900 members. Three years earlier, there were only 7 women rabbis who were so eligible. As of 1990, no woman rabbi has become senior rabbi of such a large congregation. Only 3 women rabbis head congregations of 300–600 members, while 90 women rabbis have the qualifications to do so.

1990   *There are 241 Roman Catholic parishes in the United States headed by nonpriests (Sisters, Brothers, laymen, and laywomen are all considered laity because all laity are nonordained; only men may be deacons, and they are ordained): 152 by Sisters (63 percent), 44 by deacons (18 percent), 27 by laity, of whom only 1 is a man (11 percent), 13 by Brothers (5 percent), 5 by teams (2 percent). Of the priestless parishes, 74 percent of them are pastored by women. These people are called "pastor" by their parishioners, but they have been given a variety of job titles by the Catholic hierarchy, the most common being "parish administrator."[31]*

1990   The Lutheran Church-Missouri Synod holds a one-day conference to defend its ban on the ordination of women on the basis of "the order of creation" in Genesis that sanctions the "headship" of men and the subordination of women.

1990   The second draft of American Roman Catholic bishops' pastoral letter on women, "One in Christ Jesus," is not adopted by the National Conference of Catholic Bishops.

1990   Rev. Penelope Ann Bansall Jamieson is elected Anglican bishop in New Zealand, the second woman bishop in the Anglican Communion.

1990   The Central Conference of American Rabbis (Reform) votes to admit openly and sexually active gay men and lesbians to the rabbinate. Earlier, Reconstructionism, Unitarian-Universalists, and the United Church of Christ began ordaining lesbians and gay men.

1990   Rev. M. Susan Peterson of the Evangelical Lutheran Church in America in installed as senior pastor of the 2,000-member Gloria Dei Lutheran Church in St. Paul, Minnesota. She is the third ELCA clergywoman to be called as a senior pastor, and Gloria Dei is the largest ELCA congregation headed by a woman minister. Rev. Peterson formerly served as associate pastor to Gloria Dei.

| 1990 | *Women numbering 17,501 are enrolled in North American seminaries belonging to ATS (Association of Theological Schools of the United States and Canada), constituting 29.7 percent of the seminarians.*[32] |

1990   *The General Conference of the Seventh-day Adventist Church votes to uphold the prohibition against ordaining women. About 60 percent of the 6 million Seventh-day Adventists are women, but only about 2 percent of the church leaders are women.*[33]

1991   Bernice King, daughter of Martin Luther King, Jr., is ordained a Baptist minister.

1991   Pamela Chinnis is elected the first women to head the Episcopal Church's House of Deputies.

1991   Kathy Magnus is elected the second vice president of the Evangelical Lutheran Church in America.

1991   Joan Campbell (Disciples) becomes the general secretary of the National Council of the Churches of Christ in the USA (NCC).

1991   *There are 168 women rabbis ordained by the Hebrew Union College (Reform); 40 percent were ordained during the previous five years; 80 percent were ordained during the previous ten years. Women rabbis constitute about 10 percent of Reform rabbis.*

1991   *Since 1920 there have been at least 175 Spiritual congregations in New Orleans, and at least 60 percent led by women ministers. As of 1991, about half of the 50 Spiritual churches in New Orleans are led by ordained women and their ordained women assistants. Churches led by women are small, often being prayer rooms in women's homes. The two national associations of Spiritual churches headquartered in New Orleans are led by men, and one will not consecrate women as bishops.*[34]

1991   In November, Bishop Kenneth Untener, Saginaw, Michigan, becomes the first U.S. Roman Catholic bishop publicly to call for ordination of women.

1992   The Presbyterian Church (U.S.A.) adds to its Constitution a Brief Statement of Faith that the Holy Spirit "calls women and men to all ministries of the church."

1992   *Ordained women constitute 12.5 percent of the Presbyterian Church (U.S.A.) clergy, more than doubling the 6 percent that clergywomen*

*constituted of the total pool in 1983. A survey of 1,665 clergywomen
by the Research Services for the Presbyterian Church (U.S.A.) reveals
that 9 percent of these clergywomen serve multiple congregations, 20
percent serve in nonparish clergy positions such as campus minister, 9
percent are unemployed, 31 percent are employed part-time, 14 percent
searched for five or more years to receive their first calls to ministerial
positions, and 37 percent have been subjected to sexual harassment.
Around 40 percent of these Presbyterian clergywomen have considered
leaving the ministry, or have already left. The nature of this sample
excludes most of the Presbyterian Church (U.S.A.) clergywomen who
have already left the ministry.[35]*

1992   Out of the 34 provinces (national churches) of the Anglican
            Communion 14 ordain women to the priesthood.

1992   Maria Jepsen is elected bishop of Hamburg by the North Elbian
            Lutheran Church in Germany, becoming the first Lutheran
            woman bishop.

1992   Rabbi Susan Grossman is elected as the first woman to serve on
            the Committee on Jewish Law and Standards of Conservative
            Judaism's Rabbinical Assembly.

1992   The LaCrosse Area Synod elects Rev. April Ulring Larson the
            first woman bishop of the Evangelical Lutheran Church in
            America on 12 June.

*1992   Women numbering 1,438 are ELCA pastors, constituting almost 9
            percent of all ELCA pastors (17,367). More than 60 ELCA women are
            pastors of congregations of 1,000 or more.[36]*

1992   Three women—Ann B. Sherer, Sharon Z. Rader, and Mary Ann
            Swenson—are consecrated bishops in the United Methodist
            Church, bringing the total number of women bishops
            consecrated in the United Methodist Church to 8.

1992   Bishop George A. Stallings, Jr., founder of the African American
            Catholic Congregation (1989), ordains a deacon and former Oblate
            Sister of Providence, Rose Marie Vernell, as Catholic priest in
            Washington, D.C. Rev. Vernell presides at her first Mass on 22
            September 1993 in Philadelphia, stating, "This will be the first day
            that a woman will celebrate a Mass in the history of the world."

1992   A few days before the National Conference of Catholic Bishops'
            meeting described below, on 11 November, the General Synod

of the Church of England votes to approve the ordination of
women as priests. This decision cannot be implemented until
there is approval from Parliament and the monarch.

1992   At the annual meeting of the National Conference of Catholic
            Bishops on 18 November, the fourth and most conservative draft
            of their pastoral letter on women is not adopted: 137 bishops
            vote for the pastoral, 110 against. A two-thirds majority, or 190
            votes, is needed to approve the document as a pastoral letter.
            Earlier, in the 25 September 1992 issue of *Commonweal*, P. Francis
            Murphy, auxiliary bishop in Baltimore, criticized the pastoral
            letter. Even earlier, in an August issue of *America*, Michael H.
            Kenny, bishop of Juneau, Alaska, published a criticism of the
            third draft, in which he cited the inadequacy of using the
            nuptial analogy to prohibit women from being ordained to the
            priesthood. The defeat of the final draft of the American
            bishops' pastoral letter on women is seen as a victory by
            Catholic feminists, who regard the letter as inherently flawed,
            and by conservative Catholic women, who think that the
            American bishops have no business writing a pastoral letter on
            women when the pope has already done so (1988).

1992   A few days after the NCCB meeting described above, in
            November, the third woman is consecrated bishop in the
            Anglican Communion. Jane Hart Holmes Dixon is made
            suffragan bishop of the Episcopal Diocese of Washington, D.C.;
            female and male priests and female and male bishops
            participate in her ordination. The participating bishops include
            Bishop Barbara Harris of Boston and Bishop Penelope A. B.
            Jamieson of Dunedin, New Zealand.

1992   *A survey by the National Pastoral Life Center in New York City finds
            that there are about 20,000 nonordained paid parish leaders serving in
            about half of the 19,000 Roman Catholic parishes in the United States;
            85 percent of these are women and 15 percent men; 60 percent are lay,
            and of these 45 percent are laywomen and 40 percent are Sisters. Forty
            percent of these Sisters are over age sixty, and only 6 percent of the lay
            leaders are over sixty.*

1992   *A Gallup survey find that 67 percent of Roman Catholics in the
            United States agree that "It would be a good thing if women were
            allowed to be ordained as priests." Of this 67 percent, 37 percent
            "strongly agree" with this statement and 30 percent "somewhat
            agree."*[37]

1992   *Unity, the largest New Thought denomination, has 602 churches and
            166 study groups. More than 400,000 people receive the
            denomination's monthly magazine,* Unity, *and over 2.5 million people
            annually contact its prayer ministry, Silent Unity. Of 545 Unity
            ministers, 287 (52.6 percent) are women.*[38]

1992   *The percentage of women ministers in the Church of God (Anderson)
            is 15 percent.*

1992   A newsletter, *New Horizons,* for Church of the Nazarene
            clergywomen is begun.

1992–1993   *Women constitute 61 percent of United Church of Christ seminary
            students pursuing the M.Div.*

1993   *Women constitute 9 percent of Christian Churches (Disciples of
            Christ) pastors, serving mainly in associate and small solo positions,
            and earning about $5,000 less than men of comparable experience.*[39]

1993   *There are 1,796 ordained women in the United Church of Christ, or
            17.7 percent of a total of 10,142 UCC clergy.*

1993   *The United Methodist Church has 6 active women bishops. Of 2 other
            women bishops, one—Bishop Matthews—has passed away and one has
            retired.*

1993   *Ordained clergywomen constitute approximately 10–12 percent of all
            Protestant ministers in the United States.*

1993   *National Baptists have 311 women serving as pastors of churches: 91
            as pastors, 220 as associate pastors, with 110 of these women ordained.*

1993   The third Women-Church conference, entitled "Women-Church:
            Weavers of Change," is held in April in Albuquerque, New
            Mexico. African-American women express a desire to confer on
            African-American women and the church without white women
            present. Native-American women say that they resent white
            feminists appropriating elements of Native-American
            spirituality.

1993   Donella M. Clemens becomes the first woman elected moderator
            (2-year term) of the Mennonite Church in North America,
            consisting of 114,000 members and 1,165 congregations in the
            United States and Canada.

1993   Elizabeth A. Johnson, a Roman Catholic Sister and associate
              professor of theology at Fordham University, wins the
              University of Louisville Grawemeyer Award in Religion
              ($150,000) for her book *She Who Is: The Mystery of God in
              Feminist Theological Discourse* (Crossroad, 1992). Dr. Johnson was
              the first woman to earn a Ph.D. in the department of theology at
              Catholic University and was later the first woman to obtain
              tenure in that same department.

1993   *The Hebrew Union College-Jewish Institute of Religion (Reform) has
              ordained a total of 205 women rabbis by June. Of the 224 students
              currently enrolled in the Hebrew Union College, 101 are women,
              constituting 45 percent of the student body.*[40]

1993   On 1 November, Mary Adelia MacLeod is the first woman to be
              consecrated diocesan bishop (of Vermont) in the Episcopal
              Church. Bishop Jane Dixon and Bishop Barbara C. Harris
              participate in the service, with Bishop Harris preaching the
              sermon.

1993   "Re-Imagining," an international conference dedicated to the
              expression of feminist theology, in support of the World Council
              of Churches Ecumenical Decade for Women and the Churches in
              Solidarity with Women, meets 4–7 November in Minneapolis.
              Attendance includes 1,743 women and 83 men from 49 states
              and 27 countries, and participants are encouraged to re-imagine
              traditional Christian doctrines. The attendance at the
              Re-Imagining conference includes 30 American Baptists, 16
              Baptists, 266 Roman Catholics, 100 members of the Evangelical
              Lutheran Church in America, 142 Lutherans, 51 Episcopalians,
              386 Methodists, 404 Presbyterians, 145 members of the United
              Church of Christ, 15 Unitarian Universalists, 82 members of
              United Church, Canada, 2 members of the Church of God, 18
              Disciples of Christ, 13 Mennonites, and 6 Quakers. Two-thirds of
              those attending are lay, and one-third are clergy.
                    Subsequently, conservatives in the United Methodist Church,
              the Presbyterian Church (U.S.A.), American Baptist Churches,
              USA, and the Evangelical Lutheran Church in America condemn
              the conference and its participants for taking re-imagining into
              the realm of heresy. Re-Imagining speakers begin to have
              denominational speaking engagements cancelled. Clergywomen
              associated with Re-Imagining begin to be rejected for
              consideration for ministerial positions.
                    Subsequently, the United Church of Christ issues a statement
              supporting the Re-Imagining conference. The conference

organizers work to continue the networking of women interested in re-imagining their religious traditions via a newsletter.[41]

1993   *Conservative Judaism has ordained a total of 52 women rabbis between 1985 and 1993. Of the total of 20 graduates who were ordained in 1993, 11 were women (55 percent).*

1993   *There are 49 women graduates of the Reconstructionist Rabbinical College out of a total of 140 graduates (35 percent). Seventeen women have been ordained in the past five years, and 32 women were ordained in the prior years.*[42]

1993   *There are about 1,000 ordained women in the Southern Baptist Convention.*[43]

1993   Rev. Diane Miller becomes the Unitarian-Universalist director of ministry.

1993   The North American Council for Muslim Women (NACMW) holds its first convention in Oakland, California, attracting over 300 women. Sharifa Alkhateeb is its president.

1993   Five Mormons are excommunicated by the Church of Jesus Christ of Latter-day Saints. Maxine Hanks had earlier edited *Women and Authority: Re-emerging Mormon Feminism* (Signature Books, 1992). Michael Quinn contributed a chapter to this volume entitled "Mormon Women Have Had the Priesthood Since 1843." Lavina Fielding Anderson contributed "The Grammar of Inequity." The president of the Mormon Women's Forum, Lynn Kanavel Whitesides, is "disfellowshipped," meaning that she cannot receive sacraments.

1994   Jeannette Flynn becomes executive director of church service in the Church of God (Anderson), becoming the first woman to direct an agency in that denomination.

1994   The first 32 women are ordained priests in the Church of England in March. By the following summer, there are nearly 1,000 women priests in the Church of England.

1994   The United Methodist General Commission on Christian Unity and Inter-religious Concerns reports in April that after its study of the Re-Imagining conference, "we find no reason for disciplinary

action as demanded by United Methodists for Faith and Freedom."
Instead, the commission recommends increased dialogue.

1994   The Wesleyan/Holiness Women Clergy Conference meets in
              April at Glorieta, New Mexico. The more than 377 attending
              include clergywomen in the Church of God (Anderson), the
              Church of the Nazarene, the Free Methodist Church, the
              Wesleyan Church, and Evangelical Friends, International, and
              the Salvation Army.[44]

1994   Official Vatican permission is given in April for Roman Catholic
              girls to be altar servers. Although this was already the practice
              in some parishes (according to the views of the priest), the
              Vatican up until this time had not approved "altar girls." The
              (American) National Council of Catholic Bishops quickly
              expresses endorsement of altar girls. Subsequently in 1994, the
              dioceses of Arlington, Virginia, and Lincoln, Nebraska, continue
              to permit only boys to be altar servers.

1994   Dashing the exhilaration of Roman Catholic feminists
              celebrating the papal approval of Roman Catholic altar girls and
              the ordination of women priests in the Church of England, Pope
              John Paul II issues an apostolic letter, "*Ordinatio Sacerdotalis*," to
              Roman Catholic bishops on 22 May stating, "I declare that the
              church has no authority whatsoever to confer ordination on
              women and that this judgment is to be definitively held by all
              the church's faithful."
                  Subsequently, it is revealed that American bishops had
              earlier persuaded the pope not to use the word *irreformable* in
              the apostolic letter to refer to this teaching, in order to avoid the
              implication that this is an infallible pronouncement. Instead,
              Pope John Paul II writes that this teaching is to "be definitively
              held" by Catholics, enabling some bishops to understand the
              apostolic letter as not being infallible, and leaving the door open
              for future change.
                  Roman Catholic feminist women and men promptly reject
              the pope's statement and declare that they will continue to
              speak out in opposition to the pope. Conservative Roman
              Catholics applaud the pope's apostolic letter for closing the
              debate on the ordination of women.

1994   Priests for Equality, "an international Roman Catholic
              movement of 4,000 priests, deacons, brothers and bishops," in
              June rejects the "definitive" nature of Pope John Paul II's most
              recent statement prohibiting the ordination of women in the

Roman Catholic Church. A press release issued by Rev. Joseph A. Dearborn and Priests for Equality states that "we apologize to our sisters, mothers, religious women, co-workers, friends and relatives, as well as all women of faith, for the insensitivity of our pope. And we renew our determination to work that much harder for the full participation of women in the church and society."

1994   The English translation of the new universal *Catechism of the Catholic Church* is published in June after a two-year delay, during which the gender-inclusive language of earlier drafts was changed to sexist language. "Man" or "men" is used to refer to humanity.

1994   A meeting of 111 Roman Catholic cardinals (out of 139) in Rome in June condemns feminist influence on the United Nations International Conference on Population and Development to meet in Cairo in September 1994. They condemn the preliminary draft of a UN statement on population, because it does not rule out abortion and it endorses artificial contraception.

1994   The Presbyterian Church (U.S.A.) at its General Conference meeting in Wichita, Kansas, in June approves an ambiguous resolution about the 1993 Re-Imagining conference that acknowledges "the use of imagination as part of our theological enterprise."

1994   Laura Geller becomes in July the senior rabbi of Temple Emanuel, an 850-member Reform congregation in Beverly Hills, California.

1994   The Women's Ordination Conference works in July to stimulate expression of opposition to Pope John Paul II's apostolic letter reaffirming the prohibition of women's ordination. Along with other strategies, the WOC encourages Roman Catholic feminists to write to bishops that they reject the papal statement and to enclose a photo of themselves, their daughters, nieces, grandchildren, and their families.

1994   Distribution begins in August of a sociological study by Miriam Therese Winter, Adair Lummis, and Allison Stokes, published as *Defecting in Place: Women Claiming Responsibility for Their Own Spiritual Lives* (Crossroad, 1994), of the relationship American Christian feminist women have to their denominations. The sample includes some feminist women who have left their denominations, but the majority of this sample are "defecting in place," adopting the feminist spirituality worldview while remaining in their traditional denominations. Many worship in feminist spirituality groups while continuing to participate and even exercise leadership in their denominations. Not surprising is the high level of participation in feminist spirituality groups of Roman Catholic Sisters and laywomen. More surprising is the revelation of Protestant women's participation in feminist spirituality groups, including ordained clergywomen. The voices of mainline Protestant laywomen and clergywomen revealed in the study often sound just as alienated from their patriarchal religious institutions and liturgies as the voices of the Roman Catholic women. But these mainline Protestant women and Roman Catholic women remain in their denominations in the hope of helping to effect transformation of the ministries, polities, theologies, and liturgies of their religious institutions. The nature of this sample precluded many of the post-Christian women who have left their denominations, although some of their voices are included as well.

1994   American Roman Catholics publish a letter addressed to Pope John Paul II in the *New York Times* in September stating that they disagree with his opposition to artificial contraception and that they oppose his trying to derail the attempts of the United Nations International Conference on Population and Development meeting in Cairo this month to address the world population crisis. The letter states, *"we say to you simply: on the issue of contraception, you are wrong."*

1994   Roman Catholic bishops meet in Rome in October in the Synod on the Consecrated Life and Its Role in the Church and the World. Fifty-one religious and consecrated women are allowed to attend the synod as observers, and eight are appointed experts. These women religious are permitted to speak at the synod sessions but they do not have voting rights. The National Coalition of American Nuns protests that nuns and Sisters have no voting representation in the synod which is discussing and making decisions about their religious lives in community. A small demonstration by women unfurling banners in Saint Peter's Square expressing opinions of the National Coalition of American Nuns is quickly removed by Italian police. The three banners read, "We shall not be silenced," "Women Want to Be a Part—Not Apart," and "They Are Meeting About Us—Without Us."

1994   On 10 October Bishop Ernest Kombo (Society of Jesus) from the Congo, Africa, addresses the Synod on the Consecrated Life and Its Role in the Church and the World, which includes Pope John Paul II, in Rome. Bishop Kombo states that "women should have access to the highest posts of the church hierarchy and they should be named cardinals." John Paul II responds with silence.

1994   On 25 October, the Vatican's Congregation for the Doctrine of the Faith overturns the U.S. Roman Catholic bishops' adoption of the New Revised Standard Version of the Bible (NRSV) for use in liturgy and catechetical instruction. The NRSV had been approved by the U.S. bishops in 1990 and this decision had been approved by the Vatican's Congregation for Divine Worship and the Sacraments. The reason given for rejecting the NRSV is its gender-inclusive language. This action of a Vatican congregation overruling the decision of national bishops and of another Vatican congregation is unprecedented.

1994   The Women's Ordination Conference publishes a signed ad in the 4 November issue of the *National Catholic Reporter* calling for dialogue with the pope on the issue of ordaining women.

1994   The National Conference of Catholic Bishops (NCCB) adopts a short statement, "Strengthening the Bonds of Peace," in November in response to Pope John Paul II's *"Ordinatio Sacerdotalis."* The bishops' statement rejects "authoritarian conduct" and sexism, pledges to guard against sexism "in church teaching and practice," resolves to continue honest dialogue with Catholic women, and expresses gratitude for leadership women already exercise in parish, diocesan, and educational contexts in the U.S. Roman Catholic Church. The American Catholic bishops call for further exploration of forms of leadership that women can exercise alternative to ordained leadership. The bishops affirm the need for the use of gender-inclusive language to make Catholicism relevant to North Americans.

1994   *The U.S. Roman Catholic bishops' statement, "Strengthening the Bonds of Peace," cites a 1992 study that reveals that 85 percent of nonordained ministerial positions in U.S. Catholic parishes are filled by women. To train lay Catholics for ministry, there are 50 graduate programs in U.S. Catholic colleges and universities affiliated with the Association of Graduate Programs in Ministry (AGPIM).*[45]

1994–1995   *Women are 64.7 percent of the United Church of Christ seminarians*
              who are pursuing a master of divinity degree.

1995   *American Baptists have 831 ordained women, but 1,398 women are*
              serving in American Baptist ministry positions. Southern Baptists
              have 1,130 ordained women with 60 serving as pastors and 90 as
              associate pastors. There are 225 ordained women in the National
              Baptist Convention USA, Inc.

1995   The Thirty-fourth General Congregation of the Society of Jesus
              (an international congress representing all Jesuits) meeting in
              Rome produces a statement entitled "Jesuits and the Situation
              of Women in Church and Civil Society." This document calls for
              individual Jesuits and their institutions "to align themselves in
              solidarity with women," for example, through "genuine
              involvement of women in consultation and decision-making in
              our Jesuit ministries." At this general congregation, Jesuits from
              Asia, Africa, and Latin America, for the first time, outnumber
              Jesuits from Europe, United States, and Canada.

1995   Sr. Carmel McEnroy, RSM, tenured associate professor of
              systematic theology at Saint Meinrad's Seminary in Indiana, is
              fired in May for signing the 1994 Women's Ordination
              Conference ad that appeared in the *National Catholic Reporter*
              asking the pope to dialogue with women on the issue of
              women's ordination. The firing was due to a recommendation
              made by a National Conference of Catholic Bishops team
              evaluating the seminary. In June the Catholic Theological Society
              of America issues a statement that Dr. Carmel McEnroy is a
              Catholic theologian in good standing and protests her firing
              without due procedure.

1995   Andrea De Groot-Nesdahl is elected bishop of the South Dakota
              Synod of the Evangelical Lutheran Church in America in June,
              making her the second woman bishop in the ELCA.

1995   Pope John Paul II issues a "Letter to Women" on 10 July
              expressing solidarity with women at the upcoming United
              Nations Fourth World Conference on Women in Beijing. The
              pope thanks women "for all that they represent in the life of
              humanity," acknowledges women for their contributions, notes
              the unjust discrimination against women, condemns violence
              against women, praises women who choose to give birth to
              children conceived by rape, expresses admiration for women
              who courageously work for women's rights, affirms the equal

human dignity of women, and reaffirms that God gives men and women different roles in the Church. The pope apologizes to women for the role the Church has played in the oppression of women.

1995   In July 1995 the organization called Women in Ministry of the Southern Baptist Convention disassociates itself from the Southern Baptist Convention because of lack of SBC sanction of ordained women and changes its name to Baptist Women in Ministry.

1995   In August at the Churchwide Assembly in Minneapolis of the Evangelical Lutheran Church in America, Bishop April Ulring Larson comes in second in the election for Churchwide Bishop. Bishop Larson appears to be a viable contender in the next election for ELCA Churchwide Bishop in 2001.

1995   The United Nations Fourth World Conference on Women meets in September in Beijing and adopts a "Platform of Action" to promote women's human rights and equality in family and society and condemning violence against women. Women of many religions attend the conference (more than 5,000 delegates from 185 countries) and the parallel conference organized by non-governmental organizations affiliated with the United Nations (about 20,000 attend). U.S. First Lady Hillary Rodham Clinton speaks for women's human rights, democracy, and free speech. Prime minister of Pakistan, Benazir Bhutto, condemns female infanticide. The Vatican delegation is headed by Mary Ann Glendon, a Harvard law professor; this is the first time a woman heads a Vatican delegation. Women all over the world network with participants in the Beijing conferences and each other via news broadcasts and the Internet.

1995   Catholics Speak Out publishes an ad entitled "We Ask for Bread—Will We Be Given Stones? (Matt. 7:9)" in the 8 October issue of the *Baltimore Sun*; the ad coincides with the visit of Pope John Paul II and asks for a dialogue with the pope on including women and married men in the ordained priesthood.

1995   On 18 October the Canon Law Society of America adopts a report concluding that women have been ordained permanent deacons in the Roman Catholic Church in the past and that therefore it is possible that women can be ordained permanent deacons in the future; all is needed is permission from the Apostolic See (the pope) followed by approval by the National Conference of Catholic Bishops.

1995   The Women's Ordination Conference celebrates its twentieth
                anniversary 10–12 November in Arlington, Virginia, with about
                1,000 participants. The keynote speakers, theologians Elisabeth
                Schüssler Fiorenza and Diana Hayes, declare that the WOC no
                longer seeks ordination for women in the patriarchal Roman
                Catholic Church but instead supports unordained ministry
                termed by Schüssler Fiorenza a "discipleship of equals."
                Women attending the conference immediately criticize this
                position as capitulating to the Roman Catholic hierarchy and
                charge the WOC with continuing the fight for women's
                ordination. At the conference there are additional tensions
                between women for whom devotion to Jesus Christ is primary
                and the women responsible for the conference liturgies lacking
                Christian content. Each conference talk is preceded by a chant to
                Sophia.

1995   On 18 November the Vatican Congregation for the Doctrine of
                the Faith makes public a *responsum* titled the "Inadmissibility of
                Women to the Ministerial Priesthood," dated 28 October and
                answering questions relating to Pope John Paul II's apostolic
                letter *"Ordinatio Sacerdotalis."* This *responsum*, which was
                approved by John Paul II, says that the position expressed in
                "Ordinatio Sacerdotalis" "has been set forth infallibly by the
                ordinary and universal magisterium" (in other words, the pope
                was exercising the ordinary teaching authority of the church and
                was not making a pronouncement *ex cathedra*). The *responsum*
                states that the prohibition on the ordination of women rests on
                "the written word of God" and the constant traditional practice
                of the Church. This view is to be "held always, everywhere and
                by all as belonging to the deposit of the faith." Cardinal Joseph
                Ratzinger's cover letter to the presidents of national bishops'
                conferences urges the bishops to make sure that the reception of
                the *responsum* is favorable so that contrary opinions are not
                articulated by theologians, pastors, and male and female
                religious.

                     Many Catholics immediately raise technical questions about
                infallibility and papal authority and point out that infallible
                pronouncements require wide consultation with bishops. Fr.
                Richard McBrien at the University of Notre Dame points out
                that in 1976 a Pontifical Biblical Commission convened by Pope
                Paul VI concluded that nothing in the Bible prohibits the
                ordination of women.

                     Neither *"Ordinatio Sacerdotalis"* nor the *responsum* base the
                prohibition of women's ordination on the nuptial analogy;
                instead they cite the word of God as recorded in the Bible and

the constant practice of the Church in fidelity to Christ's intent
that only men be ordained. The pope's view is that the
prohibition of women's ordination in no way diminishes the
human dignity of women which is equal to that of men.

1996   Marcia Falk's *The Book of Blessings*, a Jewish feminist prayerbook
utilizing inclusive language, is published by HarperSanFrancisco.
The prayers are written in English and Hebrew. The prayers
include a beautiful version of the "Sh'ma: Personal Declaration
of Faith" to be recited at bedtime and a "Blessing the Beloved"
dialogue for Shabbat evening at home.

NOTES

1. Henry Warner Bowden, *Dictionary of American Religious Biography* (Westport, Conn.: Greenwood Press, 1977); Elizabeth Clark and Herbert Richardson, eds., *Women and Religion: A Feminist Sourcebook of Christian Thought*
(New York: Harper and Row, 1977); Rosemary Ruether and Eleanor
McLaughlin, eds., *Women of Spirit: Female Leadership in the Jewish and Christian Traditions* (New York: Simon and Schuster, 1979); Jackson W. Carroll,
Barbara Hargrove, Adair T. Lummis, *Women of the Cloth: A New Opportu-
nity for the Churches* (San Francisco: Harper and Row, 1981); Rosemary Rad-
ford Ruether and Rosemary Skinner Keller, eds., *Women and Religion in
America: A Documentary History*, volume 1, *The Nineteenth Century*, and vol-
ume 3, *1900–1968* (San Francisco: Harper and Row, 1981, 1986); Margaret
Hope Bacon, *Mothers of Feminism: The Story of Quaker Women in America*
(San Francisco: Harper and Row, 1986); Barbara J. MacHaffie, *HerStory:
Women in Christian Tradition* (Philadelphia: Fortress Press, 1986); J. Gordon
Melton, *Biographical Dictionary of American Cult and Sect Leaders* (New York:
Garland, 1986); Elwood C. Voss and Patricia Mullen, *The Theresian Story:
Women in Support of Women* (Scottsdale, Ariz.: Theresians Publications,
1986); Annie Lally Milhaven, ed., *The Inside Stories: 13 Valiant Women Chal-
lenging the Church* (Mystic, Conn.: Twenty-Third Publications, 1987); Ruth
A. Tucker and Walter Liefeld, *Daughters of the Church: Women and Ministry
from New Testament Times to the Present* (Grand Rapids, Mich.: Zondervan,
1987); Marie Anne Mayeski, *Women: Models of Liberation* (Kansas City, Mo.:
Sheed and Ward, 1988); Gracia Grindal, "Getting Women Ordained," in
Called and Ordained: Lutheran Perspectives on the Office of Ministry, ed. Todd
Nichol and Marc Kolden (Minneapolis: Fortress Press, 1990), 161–79; Paula
D. Nesbitt, "Feminization of American Clergy: Occupational Life Chances
in the Ordained Ministry," Ph.D. dissertation, Harvard University, 1990;
John R. Hinnells, ed., *Who's Who of World Religions* (New York: Simon and
Schuster, 1991); J. Gordon Melton, *The Churches Speak On: Women's Ordina-*

tion, Gary L. Ward, contributing ed. (Detroit: Gale Research, 1991); Ann E. Feldman, "The Hesitant and the Embracing: Mary Baker Eddy and Hannah G. Solomon at the 1893 Parliament of Religions," paper presented at the American Academy of Religion, November 1991, in Kansas City, Missouri; Rosemary Skinner Keller, "A Down-to-Earth Heavenly Vision: Prophesying Daughters at the World's Parliament of Religions," paper presented at the American Academy of Religion, November 1991, in Kansas City, Missouri; Maxine Hanks, "Introduction," in *Women and Authority: Re-emerging Mormon Feminism*, ed. Maxine Hanks (Salt Lake City: Signature Books, 1992); Barbara J. MacHaffie, ed., *Readings in HerStory: Women in the Christian Tradition* (Minneapolis: Fortress Press, 1992); Ronald L. Numbers, *Prophetess of Health: Ellen G. White and the Origins of Seventh-day Adventist Health Reform* (Knoxville: University of Tennessee Press, 1992); Evelyn Brooks Higginbotham, *Righteous Discontent: The Women's Movement in the Black Baptist Church, 1880–1920* (Cambridge, Mass.: Harvard University Press, 1993); Paula D. Nesbitt, "Dual Ordination Tracks: Differential Benefits and Costs of Men and Women Clergy," *Sociology of Religion* 54/1 (1993): 13–30; Ruth A. Wallace, "The Social Construction of a New Leadership Role: Catholic Women Pastors," *Sociology of Religion* 54/1 (1993): 31–42; Susie Cunningham Stanley, *Feminist Pillar of Fire: The Life of Alma White* (Cleveland: Pilgrim Press, 1993); Catherine Wessinger, ed., *Women's Leadership in Marginal Religions: Explorations Outside the Mainstream* (Urbana: University of Illinois Press, 1993); Rita J. Simon, Angela J. Scanlon, and Pamela S. Nadell, "Rabbis and Ministers: Women of the Book and Cloth," *Sociology of Religion* 54/1 (1993): 115–222; *Daughters of Sarah* 19/3 (Summer 1993), issue entitled "Two Heads Are Better Than One: Reflecting on Womanist Concerns"; "Nun Wins $150,000 Book Award," *New Women, New Church* 16 (May–October 1993): 19; Catherine Walsh, "Bang the Drum—Not: Women-Church in the Desert," *Commonweal* (4 June 1993): 6–7; Kenneth Untener, " 'Humanae Vitae': What Has It Done to Us?," *Commonweal* 120 (18 June 1993): 12–14; Dirk Johnson, "Growing Mormon Church Faces Dissent by Women and Scholars," *New York Times*, 2 October 1993; "Mennonites Elect Clemens First Woman Moderator," *The Woman's Pulpit* (October–December 1993): 6; Letter to Catherine Wessinger from Carolyn D. Blevins dated 6 December 1993; Alice Medcof, "Threads of Many Colors: A Sermon on the First Anniversary of the Death of the Rev. Dr. Li Tim-Oi, 26 February 1993," *The Woman's Pulpit* (January–March 1994): 2–3; "Women Bishops Increasing Worldwide," *The Woman's Pulpit* (April–June 1994): 5; The Steering Committee, "RE-Imagining: Post-Conference Reflections," newsletter dated May 1994, available from Re-imagining, 122 W. Franklin Ave., Room 4A, Minneapolis, Minn. 55404-2470; Robin T. Edwards, "Some Welcome Letter as 'Unchangeable Forever,' " *National Catholic Reporter* 30 (17 June 1994): 11; Tom Fox, "Bishops Pull Pope Back from Brink," *National Catholic Reporter* 30 (17 June 1994): 3; Dawn Gibeau, "New Catechism Designed for Bishops, Educators: 816-

page Book Full of Male Nouns, Pronouns," *National Catholic Reporter* 30 (17 June 1994): 14–15; Peter Hebbletwaite, "New Cathechism Is Safe, Patristic, Predictable," *National Catholic Reporter* 30 (17 June 1994): 16; "Someday Church Will Ordain Women Priests," editorial, *National Catholic Reporter* 30 (17 June 1994): 28; Dorothy Vidulich, "U.N. Conference May Attract 20,000 Women to China in 1995," *National Catholic Reporter* 30 (17 June 1994): 19; Avery Dulles, Regina Plunkett Dowling, Catherine Mowry La Cugna, Fleming Rutledge, Robert P. George, and Sara Maitland, "Women's Ordination: Six Responses," *Commonweal* 121 (15 July 1994): 10–13; "Kombo from Congo Makes Plea for Women Cardinals," *National Catholic Reporter* 30 (21 October 1994): 10; Tom Roberts, "Vatican Rescinds Inclusive-language Approval," *National Catholic Reporter* 30 (4 November 1994): 8–9; "Women's Banners Blow Briefly in Vatican's St. Peter's Square," *National Catholic Reporter* 30 (4 November 1994): 7; David Crumm, "Bishops at Odds on Women," *New Orleans Times-Picayune*, 17 November 1994, B:8; U.S. Roman Catholic Bishops, "Strengthening the Bonds of Peace," *Origins* 24 (1 December 1994): 417, 419–22; Charles W. Hall, "Virginia Diocese Bars Girls from Altar," *New Orleans Times-Picayune*, 14 December 1994, A:16; Letter to Catherine Wessinger from Peggy L. Shriver, Professional Church Leadership, National Council of the Churches of Christ in the USA, dated 5 January 1995; William D. Montalbano, "Jesuits Will Seek Justice for Poor Women," *New Orleans Times-Picayune*, 23 March 1995, A:33; Thirty-fourth General Congregation of the Society of Jesus, "Jesuits and the Situation of Women in Church and Civil Society," *Origins* 24 (13 April 1995): 740–42; Catholic Theological Society of America, "On Sister McEnroy's Dismissal," *Origins* 25 (13 July 1995): 127–28; Pope John Paul II, "Letter to Women," *Origins* 25 (27 July 1995): 138–43; Marcia Falk, "A Foretaste of the Prayer Book to Come," *Lilith* 20 (Fall 1995): 19–21. Canon Law Society of America Ad Hoc Committee, "Canonical Implications: Ordaining Women to the Permanent Diaconate," *Origins* 25 (2 November 1995): 344–52; Letter to Catherine Wessinger from Carolyn D. Blevins dated 29 November 1995; Congregation for the Doctrine of the Faith, "Inadmissibility of Women to Ministerial Priesthood," *Origins* 25 (30 November 1995): 401, 403; Cardinal Joseph Ratzinger, "Cover Letter to Bishops' Conference Presidents," *Origins* 25 (30 November 1995): 403; Fr. Gus DiNoia, "Statement on Doctrinal Congregation's Action," *Origins* 25 (30 November 1995): 406–9; Pamela Schaeffer, "WOC Gathers to Promote Women's Ordination Amid Conflicting Visions, Goals," *National Catholic Reporter* 32 (1 December 1995): 9–11; Letter to Catherine Wessinger from Gracia Grindal dated 3 December 1995; Pamela Schaeffer, "Assessing Ambiguous Infallibility Factor," *National Catholic Reporter* 32 (8 December 1995): 36; Joan Chittister, "Ratzinger Raised Bigger Issues Than Ordination," *National Catholic Reporter* 32 (8 December 1995): 7.

2. Carroll, et al., 4.
3. Carroll, et al., 4.

4. Carroll, et al., 4.
5. Carroll, et al., 9.
6. Carroll, et al., 4.
7. Carroll, et al., 9.
8. Carroll, et al., 4.
9. Carroll, et al., 9.
10. "In N.A. Nearly 1 in 3 Seminarians is Female," *The Woman's Pulpit* (January–March 1992): 7.
11. "Women Clergy in US Almost Double in Decade," *The Woman's Pulpit* (July–September 1989): 2.
12. Carroll, et al., 7
13. Constant H. Jacquet, Jr., *Women Ministers in 1986 and 1977: A Ten Year Review* (New York: Office of Research and Evaluation, National Council of Churches, 1988), 3.
14. Jacquet, 4.
15. "In N.A. Nearly 1 in 3 Seminarians is Female."
16. Carroll, et al., 4
17. Carroll, et al., 7.
18. Ruth A. Wallace, "The Social Construction of a New Leadership Role: Catholic Women Pastors," *Sociology of Religion* 54/1 (1993): 33–34, citing work by Schoenherr and Young.
19. "Clergywomen in the U.S.A.," *The Woman's Pulpit* (July–September 1988): 5. Statistics compiled by Jeannette Stokes of Resource Center for Women and Ministry of the South.
20. Ibid.
21. "Women Clergy in US Almost Double in Decade"; and Jacquet, 3, 12–13.
22. Jacquet, 4.
23. "Clergywomen in the U.S.A."
24. Ibid.
25. Ibid.
26. Ibid.
27. Ibid.
28. "Support for Women Clergy Grows in UM Churches," *The Woman's Pulpit* (October–December 1988): 5.
29. "Theresians of the United States—Fact Sheet" (March 1987), available from Theresians of the United States, 2577 N. Chelton Road, Suite 207, Colorado Springs, Colorado 80909.
30. "Women Clergy 6.9% of ELCA Roster," *The Woman's Pulpit* (October–December 1990): 5.
31. Wallace, 31.
32. "In N.A. Nearly 1 in 3 Seminarians is Female."
33. "Adventist Women Challenge Ban on Women as Clergy," *The Woman's Pulpit* (April–June 1991): 3.
34. David Estes, "Ritual Validations of Clergywomen's Authority in the African American Spiritual Churches in New Orleans," in *Women's Leadership*

in Marginal Religions, ed. Catherine Wessinger (Urbana: University of Illinois Press, 1993), 150–51.

35. "Presbyterians Survey Rostered Clergywomen," *The Woman's Pulpit* (April–June 1994): 6.

36. "5 U.S. Clergywomen Elected Bishops," *The Woman's Pulpit* (October–December 1992): 8.

37. Bill Bole, "Polls: Catholics Would Like to See Women Priests," *National Catholic Reporter* 30 (17 June 1994): 7.

38. Dell deChant, "Myrtle Fillmore and Her Daughters: An Observation and Analysis of the Role of Women in Unity," in *Women's Leadership in Marginal Religions,* ed. Catherine Wessinger (Urbana: University of Illinois Press, 1993), 102.

39. "Disciples Study Advances of Women in Ministry," *The Woman's Pulpit* (July–September 1993): 7.

40. Letter to Catherine Wessinger from Rabbi Janet R. Marder, associate director, Union of American Hebrew Congregations, Los Angeles, CA, dated 10 November 1993.

41. The Steering Committee, "RE-Imagining: Post-Conference Reflections," newsletter dated May 1994; "U.S. Conference 'Re-Imagines' Faith," *The Woman's Pulpit* (April–June 1994): 3.

42. Letter to Catherine Wessinger from Rebecca Alpert dated 24 November 1993.

43. Letter to Catherine Wessinger from Carolyn D. Blevins dated 6 December 1993.

44. Stan Ingersoll, "Holiness Women: Recovering a Tradition," *Christian Century* 111 (29 June–6 July 1994): 632.

45. Rev. Philip J. Murnion, *New Parish Ministers* (New York: National Pastoral Life Center, 1992), 27, cited in U.S. Roman Catholic Bishops, "Strengthening the Bonds of Peace," *Origins* 24 (1 December 1994), 419, 422; H. Richard McCord, "New Research Looks at Preparing Laity for Ministry," *Gifts* 3 (1994): 1.

Notes on Contributors

INTRODUCTION

Catherine Wessinger, associate professor of history of religions and women's studies, Loyola University, New Orleans, earned her Ph.D. in the history of religions from the University of Iowa in 1985. She has published *Annie Besant and Progressive Messianism* (Edwin Mellen Press, 1988), and she is editor of *Women's Leadership in Marginal Religions: Explorations Outside the Mainstream* (University of Illinois Press, 1993). She is currently writing a textbook on women in religions and cultures.

PROTESTANT WOMEN

Presbyterians

Rebecca Prichard is assistant dean and assistant professor of historical theology at Christian Theological Seminary in Indianapolis, Indiana. She is a minister member of the Presbytery of Whitewater Valley. Formerly she was associate presbyter with the San Francisco Presbytery, and her duties included pastoral care of clergywomen. She has taught at Pacific School of Religion and San Francisco Theological Seminary. She is an ordained Presbyterian minister and has her Ph.D. in theology from the Graduate Theological Union. Her current research focuses on women in the Reformation era.

United Church of Christ

Barbara Brown Zikmund is president and professor of American religious history at Hartford Seminary. She earned her doctorate in American church history at the Divinity School and Graduate School of Duke University. She was ordained to ministry in the United Church of Christ in 1964. She is presently the general editor of a forthcoming seven-volume collection of documents on the *Living Theological Heritage of the United Church of Christ*. She has served on UCC committees concerned with ministry, as an officer of the International Association of Women Ministers, as president of the Association of Theological Schools in the U.S. and Canada, as president of the American Society of Church History, and as a commissioner for the World Council of Churches Programme on Theological Education. Her numerous publications include: "The Struggle for the Right to Preach," in *Women and Religion in America*, vol. 1 (Harper and Row, 1981); "Winning Ordination for Women in the Mainstream Protestant Churches," in *Women and Religion in America*, vol. 3 (Harper and Row, 1985); "Women in Ministry Face the '80s," *The Christian Century* (3–10 February 1982); and "Women as Preachers: Adding New Dimensions to Worship," *Journal of Women and Religion* (Summer 1984). She is editor of and contributor to *Hidden Histories in the United Church of Christ*, 2 vols. (United Church Press, 1984, 1987).

Unitarian-Universalists

Cynthia Grant Tucker is professor of English at the University of Memphis. She has written *Kate Freeman Clark: A Painter Rediscovered* (University Press of Mississippi, 1981); *A Woman's Ministry: Mary Collson's Search for Reform as a Unitarian Minister, A Hull House Social Worker, and A Christian Science Practitioner* (Temple University Press, 1984), reissued in paperback as *Healer in Harm's Way: Mary Collson, a Clergywoman in Christian Science* (University of Tennessee Press, 1994); and *Prophetic Sisterhood: Liberal Women Ministers of the Frontier, 1880–1930* (Beacon, 1990), paperback ed. (Indiana University Press, 1994). She is the recipient of the 1989 Feminist Theology Award from the Unitarian-Universalist Women's Federation. She earned her Ph.D. in comparative literature at the University of Iowa in 1967.

Methodists

Rosemary Skinner Keller is academic dean, vice president of academic affairs, and professor of religion and American culture at Garrett-Evangelical Theological Seminary. She is also a member of the graduate faculty at Northwestern University, Evanston, Illinois. Her publications include *Patriotism and the Female Sex: Abigail Adams and the American Revolution* (Carlson, 1994) and *Georgia Harkness: For Such a Time as This* (Abingdon, 1992). She is the editor of *Spirituality and Social Responsiblity: Vocational Vision of Women in the United Methodist Tradition* (Abingdon: 1994), and co-editor with Rosemary Radford Ruether of *In Our Own Voices: Four Centuries of American Women's Religious Writings* (HarperCollins, 1995) and the three-volume *Women and Religion in America: A Documentary History* (Harper and Row, 1981, 1983, 1986).

African Methodist Episcopal Church

Jualynne E. Dodson is associate professor of religious studies at the University of Colorado, Boulder, and the Center for Studies in Ethnicity and Race in the Americas. She is co-author of "Something Within: Social Change and Collective Endurance in the Sacred World of Black Christian Women," in *Women and Religion in America*, edited by Ruether and Keller, and the author of the "Introduction" to Amanda Smith, *An Autobiography: The Story of the Lord's Dealings with Mrs. Amanda Smith the Colored Evangelist* (Oxford University Press, 1988). Her article "Class Consciousness and Resistance: Southern Women of the AME Church" is forthcoming in *A Liberated Past*, edited by Dennis C. Dickerson. She earned her Ph.D. in sociology at the University of California, Berkeley.

Weslyan/Holiness Churches

Susie C. Stanley, professor of historical theology at Messiah College, Grantham, Pennsylvania, was coordinator of women in ministry and mission for the Church of God (Anderson) from 1989 to 1992 and helped to plan a Church of God publication, *Called to Minister, Empowered to Service* (Warner Press, 1989), in which she has a chapter entitled "Women Evangelists at the Turn of the Century." She has also published "Empowered Foremothers: Wesleyan/Holiness Women Speak to Today's Christian Feminists," *Wesleyan Theological Journal* (1989), "Phoebe Palmer and the Ministry of Women," *Journal for Case Teaching* (1989), and *Feminist Pillar of Fire: The Life of Alma White* (Pilgrim, 1993). She chairs the Wesleyan/Holiness Women Clergy Conference. She received her Ph.D. in American religion and culture from the Iliff School of Theology and the University of Denver.

Baptists

Carolyn DeArmond Blevins is associate professor of religion at Carson-Newman College. She earned her M.A. at Southern Baptist Theological Seminary in Louisville, Kentucky, and she is an ordained Southern Baptist deacon. She has published "Patterns of Ministry Among Southern Baptist Women," *Baptist History and Heritage* (July 1987); "Women in Baptist History," *Review and Expositor* (Winter 1986); "Ordination of Women: Wrong or Right?," *The Theological Educator* (Spring 1988). She is the author of *Annotated Bibliography of Women in Church History* (Mercer University Press, 1995).

Lutherans

Gracia Grindal is professor of rhetoric at Luther Seminary in St. Paul, Minnesota. She has published numerous articles on Lutheranism, including: "Getting Women Ordained," in *Called and Ordained: Lutheran Perspectives on the Ministry* (Augsburg, 1990); "Luther's Theology as a Resource for Feminists," *dialog* (Winter 1985); "Inclusive Language in Hymns: A Reappraisal," *Currents in Theology and Mission* (June 1989); and "Inclusive Language," in *The Concise Encyclopedia of Preaching* (Westminster/John Knox Press, 1993). She earned her M.A. at Luther Northwestern Theological Seminary.

Episcopalians

Suzanne Radley Hiatt, John Seely Stone Professor of pastoral theology at Episcopal Divinity School, is one of the eleven women "irregularly" ordained as Episcopal priests in 1974. She earned her M.Div. at Episcopal Theological School and M.S.W. at Boston University. She served on the 1970 World Council of Churches Consultation on Ordination of Women, and was consultant to the Movement for the Ordination of Women, Church of England (1979), Church of the Province of Kenya (1982), and Anglican Church of Australia (1989). In addition to numerous articles, she is co-author of *Women Priests: Yes or No* (Seabury, 1973).

ROMAN CATHOLIC WOMEN

American Roman Catholic Sisters

Marie Augusta Neal, a Sister of Notre Dame de Namur, is professor emerita of sociology for research and teaching at Emmanuel College in Boston. She has published numerous sociological studies of Catholicism and Catholic Sisters, including "Catholicism in America," in *Religion in America*, edited by McLaughlin and Bellah (Houghton Mifflin, 1968); "Religious Communities in a Changing World," in *The New Nuns*, edited by Muckenhirn (New American Library, 1968); "Women in Ordained Ministry," in *Women in Ministry* (National Association for Women Religious, 1972); "Models for Future Priesthood," in *Women and Catholic Priesthood* (Paulist, 1976); "Pathology of the Men's Church," in *Religion of the Eighties* (Seabury, 1980); *From Nuns to Sisters: An Expanding Vocation* (Twenty-Third Publications, 1990); and "Democratic Process in the Experience of American Catholic Women Religious," in *A Democratic Catholic Church*, edited by Ruether (Crossroad, 1992). She earned her Ph.D. in sociology at Harvard.

American Roman Catholic Laywomen

Virginia Sullivan Finn is associate dean of students and coordinator/ faculty for Supervised Practicum in Spiritual Direction at Weston School of Theology. She is past president of the National Association for Lay Ministry (1988–90). She is a retreat director of the Ignation eight-day and thirty-day retreats. She was adviser to the National Conference of Catholic Bishops' Committee on the Laity. She has published *Pilgrim in the Parish* (Paulist, 1985) and *Pilgrims in the World: A Lay Spirituality* (Paulist, 1990), and she has contributed chapters to *Celibate Loving* (Paulist), and *Unfinished Agenda* (Paulist), which is about Vatican II. She earned her M.Ed. at the University of Massachusetts-Amhert, her M.Div. at Weston School of Theology, and has taken Advanced Training in Spiritual Direction at the Center for Religious Development in Cambridge, Massachusetts.

JEWISH WOMEN

Reform Judaism

Janet R. Marder is associate director of the Union of American Hebrew Congregations, Pacific Southwest Council. She earned her B.A. at the University of California, Santa Cruz. She was ordained rabbi in 1979 by Hebrew Union College-Jewish Institute of Religion. "How Women Are Changing the Rabbinate" was published in *Reform Judaism* (Summer 1991).

Reconstructionism

Rebecca Alpert graduated from the Reconstructionist Rabbinical College in 1976 and was the dean of students there from 1978 to 1988. She continues as adjunct faculty at the Reconstructionist Rabbinical College to this date, while serving as the codirector of the Women's Studies Program at Temple University. She has written numerous articles on women for Reconstructionist journals and on Reconstructionism for a variety of books on Judaism, including "The Making of American Rabbis," *Encyclopedia Judaica Yearbook (1983–85)*.

Goldie Milgram, a former executive director of the Jewish Federation of Cumberland County, New Jersey, graduated from the Reconstructionist Rabbinical College in 1993 and served as founding chairperson of its Jewish Women's Studies Project. She is the spiritual leader of Reconstructionist congregation Temple Beth El of Hammonton, New Jersey.

Conservative Judaism

Sydell Ruth Schulman is associate dean of the Graduate School of Applied and Professional Psychology at Rutgers, the State University of New Jersey. She earned her Ed.D. at the Rutgers Graduate School of Education. Her dissertation, "Ordination and Empowerment" (1992), was on Conservative women rabbis.

The Challenge of Feminism to Judaism

Sue Levi Elwell is rabbinic director of Ma'yan: The Jewish Women's Project of the Jewish Community Center of the Upper West Side of New York City. The founding director of the American Jewish Congress Feminist Center in Los Angeles, she has taught at the University of Cincinnati, UCLA, and the Academy for Jewish Religion. She is editor of *The Jewish Women's Studies Guide* (University Press of America and Biblio Press, 1987), and co-author of *Jewish Women: A Mini-Course for Jewish Schools* (Alternatives in Religious Education, 1986). She received rabbinic ordination from the Hebrew Union College-Jewish Institute of Religion and a doctorate from Indiana University. She has served congregations in Ohio, Alabama, California, and New Jersey.

Index